A STEP TO THE RIGHT

The Life & Times
───── *of* ─────
Alexander Downer

TONY PARKINSON

Published in 2025 by Connor Court Publishing Pty Ltd.

Copyright © Tony Parkinson

ALL RIGHTS RESERVED. This book contains material protected under International and Federal Copyright Laws and Treaties. Any unauthorised reprint or use of this material is prohibited. No part of this book may be reproduced or transmitted in any form or by any means, electronic or mechanical, including photocopying, recording, or by any information storage and retrieval system without express written permission from the publisher.

Connor Court Publishing Pty Ltd.
PO Box 7257
Redland Bay QLD 4165
sales@connorcourt.com
www.connorcourt.com

ISBN: Paperback, 9781923568105,
    Hardback. 9781923568099

Cover Design by Ian James

Cover image: Downer addresses Parliament on the sixth anniversary of the September 11 attacks (Kym Smith, Newspix).

Printed in Australia.

Contents

Foreword—*John Howard*	v
Prologue	1
1. On the Grid	10
2. The Near North	21
3. Hands across the Ocean	47
4. In Their Footsteps	61
5. The Long, Hard Road to Power	80
6. Setting the Course	102
7. *Tampa* and Turnback	122
8. A Dagger to the Heart	127
9. The Aftershocks of War	142
10. Japan and the Arc of Generations	174
11. The Forbidding City	181
12. Trade Offs	187
13. Head for the Hills	201
14. Neighbourhood Watch	209
15. The Nuclear Age	234
16. The Final Stanza	252
17. What Next?	265
18. The One That Got Away	278
19. Ancient Hatreds	284
20. Back to Britain	300
21. Permafrost	310
22. The Axis of Upheaval	318
23. The Lightning Bolt	335
24. The Art of Statesmanship	353
Acknowledgements	363
Bibliography	365
Index	369

Foreword

John Howard

It is a real honour to provide this Foreword to a biography of the person I regard as Australia's best Foreign Affairs Minister.

Although Alexander Downer held that position for longer than any other, that is not the only reason I hold him in such high regard. He brought intelligence, skill and tact to the role. In every way he was a safe pair of hands.

I relied on him and trusted his judgment on many of the delicate foreign policy decisions faced by him and me and our colleagues over the almost 12 years he was the Minister for Foreign Affairs.

Tony Parkinson has written with style and elegance. He provides deep insights into the many foreign policy challenges the Howard Government faced.

In particular, his narrative of the decisive intervention in East Timor, as well as Australia joining the United States in the military operation in Iraq, provides full context for these and other decisive events. Parkinson's treatment of the difficulties faced after the successful military operation to overthrow Saddam Hussein are particularly valuable. The comments he cites from the former CIA Chief, General David Petraeus, are not only relevant but revealing. It underlines the errors made after Saddam was ousted.

Although Alexander Downer and I did not agree on everything, we shared a similar world view based on strong alliances with powerful friends such as the United States as well as building close bilateral relationships with our regional neighbours. We also valued our historic links with the United Kingdom and those other Commonwealth members with whom we had much in common.

Alexander Downer's career since his role in government ceased in November 2007 is a case study in how to conduct oneself in that context. He remained active in the foreign affairs arena, drawing on personal relationships he had established in government.

He was a close friend and colleague. Our association has continued and deepened since we both left active politics.

This book is a great read.

Alexander Downer portrait (Peter Bennett/Newspix)

Prologue

> Death closes all: but something 'ere the end,
> Some work of noble note, may yet be done...
> Come, my friends,
> 'Tis not too late to seek a newer world.
>
> *Ulysses* — **Alfred Lord Tennyson**

Alexander Downer's 11-year odyssey at the helm of Australia's foreign policy came at a time of great dynamism — and gathering dangers. When the Howard Government was elected to power in 1996, the starburst of optimism that had initially accompanied the end of the Cold War was beginning to flicker and fade. As Australians confronted a new set of strategic challenges in the world around them, Downer's impact would be serious, substantial ... and, often, controversial.

This book, a study of the life and times of Australia's longest-serving foreign affairs minister, offers the opportunity for a considered assessment of Downer's uniquely well-informed perspectives on many of the big issues that remain front and centre in our world today.

Few are better positioned to provide first-person insights into the people and events — the politics, personalities and principles — that can tell us why things in our world happened the way they did, and why things are happening the way they are now.

Downer's accounts of meetings with key decision-makers provide vivid detail on some of the landmark moments defining the early 21st century: the September 11 terror attacks and their aftermath; a resurgent, more assertive China; fragmentation of politics in Western democracies; Russian aggression in Europe; wars in Afghanistan and Iraq, and the many failed attempts to broker peace in the Middle East.

This biography brings to light a series of unreported or underreported conversations between Downer and people in power in Australia and overseas. It provides a view from the inside on how the world of diplomacy works —and where and when it has faltered — that many readers will not have seen or heard before.

Downer, now in his seventies, is unconvinced there is much of an audience for an account of his life and career. Several times, in interviews for this book, he wonders whether anyone really cares any more about what he did, or why he did it: "To be honest, I don't know that people are that interested, to be brutal about it."

But with the 30th anniversary of the election of the Howard Government approaching in March, 2026, it is surely worth reflecting on the approach this highly successful government brought to its work: the priorities it set, the values it sought to instil, and the influence it had not only on the lives of a generation of Australians — but also the impact of that government on events in our neighbourhood, as well as far from Australia's shores. Here, in particular, there can be no more authoritative source than Alexander Downer. It helps that he is a talented storyteller.

He shares his recollections of interaction with some of the world's most feared regimes: exchanges with the inner circle of Russia's Vladimir Putin; involvement in the decades-long efforts to stabilise the Middle East; his engagement with Communist leaders in China and North Korea. The book also explores Downer's personal connections to a series of American Presidents and a vast network of powerbrokers in the world's leading democracy, the United States.

Downer has witnessed global diplomacy at its rawest. Over the journey, he concedes that some of his most respected friends and contemporaries have made some very bad calls.

He was unimpressed with the level of US commitment to enforce peace after East Timor's independence vote in 1999. He calls out the Pentagon for critical errors in administering Iraq after the removal of Saddam Hussein's regime. He thinks the West failed by not more fulsomely supporting green shoots of liberal reform — especially among women — in Iran in 2009. And he will never forgive the political Left for turning climate change into an emotive, millenarian slogan rather than a practical policy challenge to be worked through like any other — requiring policy-makers to search for a sensible, proportionate balance between competing needs, interests and priorities.

In his reflections, Downer is quite prepared to subject his own decisions to critical review. He admits to occasions when he has misread people in power and geopolitical trends.

Putin's Russia is a case in point. Downer was far from alone in not anticipating the reversal to Soviet-style autocracy — or, as many would call it, tyranny. Almost nobody in the Western capitals read Putin well, proof that none of us are flawless in judgment. When difficult, complicated appraisals have to be made, there will sometimes be mistakes. It is a fact of life that there are sometimes no good answers.

For that reason, this book cannot be a vanilla monologue. It will include the views of some of Downer's chorus of critics. Politics, by its nature, is a swirl of competing interests vying for ascendancy. In a robust, noisy democracy such as Australia, there have been — and will always be — people with strong, passionately-held opinions about where Downer got it wrong.

That counter-narrative will get a hearing. It is important to understand when, where and why he was seen by detractors to have failed.

Downer would expect no less. He has always been up for the contest of ideas. During a series of interviews for this book, Downer volunteered some free advice: "You should talk to people who don't like me, too. They won't be hard to find."

Yet there has to come a time when we look past the carping and criticism and focus on the substance and achievements.

For Downer, like most senior political leaders, achieving success in the upper stratosphere of public life involved extraordinary personal motivation and, sometimes, considerable personal sacrifice. It is often too quickly overlooked that, in a highly competitive, adversarial democracy, it requires significant risk-taking to make the judgments — then prosecute the arguments — to achieve enduring policy outcomes.

Intense scrutiny of policy-makers is one of the inherent strengths of a democratic system. A free and robust media is critical to holding to account elected office-bearers. But columnists, commentators and opinion leaders at newspapers and in the electronic media are not without responsibilities. To their audience. To their society. Nor are they omniscient. They need to bring some humility, and a sense of balance, to the judgments they make. The same goes for biographers.

Anyone can be an expert in hindsight. But what would these commentators do if faced with the same excruciating choices that leading figures in government must sometimes address — as an example, the life-and-death decisions around deploying troops or police to dangerous places? Would they be prepared to carry that responsibility, to put their reputations on the line, knowing that serious mistakes could cost lives and leave their credibility shredded?

Who among us would enjoy their friends and family having to endure the misery of watching a loved one being pilloried and ridiculed for a poor decision made in good faith? As elected politicians know only too well, they go into politics as volunteers — their families are conscripts.

This is arduous enough at those times when the traditional media hunts as a pack. How much more gruelling has it become in the age of social media, when politicians can come under assault from armies of keyboard warriors descending on them like a plague of locusts?

More than a century ago, Teddy Roosevelt did his best to capture this equation. The early 20th century US President spoke and wrote in the idiom of his day, an unusual mix of Homeric romanticism and raw-boned American straight-talking:

> It is not the critic who counts, nor the man who points out how the strong man stumbles or where the doers of deeds could have done better. The credit belongs to the man who is actually in the arena; whose face is marred with dust and sweat; who strives valiantly; who errs and may fall again and again, because there is no effort without error or shortcoming... who does if he fails, at least fails while daring greatly, so that his place shall never be with those cold or timid souls who know neither victory nor defeat.

Boiled down, as Roosevelt intimated, the judgments of history are about success or failure; the good or the bad. All chroniclers of their times, like most of today's journalists, face the same bleak calculus: the fact is that trauma, tragedy, cruelty, misfortune and failure tend often to be far more newsworthy than progress, happiness, contentment or success. Another US President Bill Clinton summarised succinctly the commercial reality: "Negative stuff sells more."

The same goes for political history. But that shouldn't deny the opportunity to focus on landmark achievements.

Alexander Downer came from a strong family tradition of public duty.

He believed in a vision of nation-building. He also believed in the power of reason, ultimately, to prevail over passion or prejudice.

In his dealings with the world, Downer would grapple with a plethora of difficult, demanding and confronting policy choices — of a magnitude that might keep most of us awake at night. His philosophy was simple: know your facts, then front up and deal with it. This has made his life both consequential and controversial.

Some of his critics would seek to cast Downer as a crusty, stuffed-shirt conservative. These lazy stereotypes are common enough in public life. They are part of the pantomime of politics. Were these same critics to explore a little deeper, though, they might find Alexander Downer to be a man of classical liberal instincts.

The same politician who could be ruthless and uncompromising in the bearpit of Australian politics, could, in private, reveal himself as a bit of a fun-lover. Those who worked closely with Downer know him to be gregarious, amiable... and, yes, compassionate. Especially when the lives of everyday people are threatened by forces beyond their control.

Like most people living busy, demanding lives, Downer would often seek solace in the company of family, friends and colleagues —now and then he would be up until well past midnight, swapping yarns over a bottle or two of red and a cigar. Then he would rise for his early-morning calls and briefings, with barely a sign of wear-and-tear.

Downer loves laughter — perhaps a little too much, given an off-colour joke he delivered unscripted at a Liberal Party function in 1994 became a contributing factor to denying him any chance of becoming prime minister. Despite that experience, his mischievous sense of humour could never entirely be locked away.

As one of his media advisers was once heard to complain: "It can be difficult to get the smile off his face, and the twinkle out of his eye."

This endearing characteristic would sometimes come to the surface in unexpected places. At high-octane meetings with world leaders, Downer had a habit of breaking the tension, lightening the mood, by injecting some *bonhomie* into these conversations.

In 1996, long before the advent of the smart phone and social media, an image of a youthful Alexander Downer went viral across Australia.

As the up-and-coming political leader posed for a camera in full suit and tie, he grinned as he lifted his trouser to the knee to reveal a fishnet stocking and a faux leopard-skin stiletto.

It was a publicity stunt performed with good intentions — to promote ticket sales for a *Rocky Horror Show* charity night in his hometown,

Adelaide. Yet the national media would never tire of resurrecting the image. It became a plaything for a generation of cartoonists... and rich fodder for his opponents in the Australian Labor Party.

Downer's political opponents targeted him as someone they needed to tear down quickly. Labor's Paul Keating, ever the bare-knuckle political brawler, sought to pigeonhole Downer as "the idiot son of the aristocracy". He led attempts to ridicule Downer as a fop, a dilettante, or, as one Press Gallery wit would have it, a character who might have leapt from the pages of Evelyn Waugh's *Brideshead Revisited*.

Undaunted, Downer stayed around for the fight. He would prove his opponents wrong. He developed the steely demeanour essential to the practice of hard-edged, adversarial politics. He learned quickly to get onto the front foot, to turn defence into attack. He learned not to sulk about insults thrown his way. He also learned an invaluable communications skill — the power of plain speaking.

Downer became a political warrior unafraid to tackle difficult issues head-on. Like the time he went live on CNN to scold his American allies for refusing to commit ground troops to restore stability in East Timor. Or when he hauled in a Chinese envoy to explain in polite if abrupt language why a diplomatic tit-for-tat was a road to nowhere for both nations. Or when he shouldered the task of explaining to an apprehensive nation why troops should be sent into the badlands of Afghanistan or the slaughterhouse that was Saddam Hussein's Iraq.

Or when he fronted up to one of Australia's most successful prime ministers to tell him many senior colleagues thought his time was up.

Downer became an accomplished statesman, sure-footed on the global stage. Across his career, he became a resolute driver of policy change in Australia — and beyond.

At its crux, Downer believed the processes of globalisation and free trade from the 1970s onwards had delivered massive net benefits to many societies across the world. More people had been lifted out of extreme poverty than at any time in human history.

This book explores the role Downer played in building Australia's relations with like-minded nations to secure "peace and plenty" in East Asia and the Pacific. Nowhere did he work harder than in Australia's own neighbourhood, leading dramatic interventions to end conflict and bloodshed in East Timor, the Solomon Islands and Bougainville.

His activism in the design and development of new architecture to help sustain a power balance across the vast and dynamic region known today as the Indo-Pacific is where his contribution may have its most lasting impact. Like his painstaking efforts across several years to bring to life the Trilateral Security Dialogue with Japan and the US.

This would prove a foundation stone for much of what has followed — the Quad, bringing India into the arrangements; AUKUS, reintroducing Britain into the Pacific security framework; and, more recently, the notion of extending a version of AUKUS-lite to include security partners like South Korea, Canada and the Phillipines.

Some would caricature Downer as an ideological warrior — a "right-wing death beast". Others have called him a Neo-Conservative Realist.

Certainly, he has strong views about what is right and what is wrong. Just as he has strong views about what policy approaches have proved most effective in advancing Australia's national interests.

Yet his is a worldview tempered by experience, and more nuanced than many might think. In an imperfect world, the search for sound, commonsense solutions is forever colliding with emotion, slogans, dogma — the interplay of fear, hatred, prejudice, greed and, sometimes, blood-curdling ruthlessness.

The startling foreign policy gambits in the first months of the second Trump presidency in the US were proof of how quickly long-held assumptions about geo-politics could seemingly unravel. You can be a conviction politician yet still have to acknowledge that you must often grapple with realpolitik to get the best result you can.

Early in his career, Downer workshopped his foreign policy approach with people like Michael L'Estrange and Greg Hunt, both of whom would go on to substantial careers in government and diplomacy. The formula they used to describe it was "enlightened realism." In Downer's view, there must never be an abandonment of the principles underpinning freedom, democracy and human rights. These Western Enlightenment values — open societies, a free and uninhibited exchange of ideas, fair and open elections, equality under the law— must constantly be reaffirmed, supported, defended.

Yet Downer is forensic and unsentimental in his analysis. He is, unapologetically, a rationalist. He is an admirer of the United States, lauding the great postwar achievements of the superpower. *Pax*

Americana. But, like all trusted friends, Downer is prepared to call out strategic failures, even epic miscalculations, by Australia's closest ally.

He speaks, regretfully, of poor decisions by recent White House administrations that have diminished America's stature as the leading global power — at the very time strength of leadership was needed. In his judgment, one undeniable explanation for uncertainty and instability in today's world has been a gradual weakening over the past two decades of American — and Western — power and resolve.

He sees this as creating the conditions for significant geo-strategic risk to the democratic order globally. He acknowledges that a comparison between the 1930s and the 2020s is something that is up for debate.

Downer is far from alone in his view that the 2020s presented a set of formidable challenges to the Western democratic model: the brutal war of aggression by Russia against Ukraine; Iran's sponsorship of assaults on Israel's sovereignty by its proxies, Hamas and Hezbollah; and China's bellicose threats to annex Taiwan and the South China Sea.

He is acutely aware that these authoritarian regimes form a nexus, or what he describes as a "loose alliance". They are in contact with each other about how to achieve strategic goals. In the US intelligence community, it is described these days as The Axis of Upheaval.

He believes the worst possible response in this dangerous climate is for the Western powers to react weakly or meekly. Just as the pleas of Neville Chamberlain for "peace in our time" went unheeded by Hitler's Germany and the other Axis powers in the 1930s, so he worries that Western political leaders might again be misreading today's aggressors. In his view, the leaders of democracies have no real choice but to stand up more resolutely to the threats and challenges. Calls for de-escalation and ceasefires are no longer the safest option. Not when those creating chaos and disruption have come to calculate that, on the basis of what they have seen in some of the anaemic Western responses, there is no serious risk for them in escalation.

Downer worries about the political pressure from Western capitals, including Washington, for countries like Israel and Ukraine to step back from conflicts they did not seek or initiate — to sue for peace. In his view, the US and its allies should be making the demands for peace not of their friends — but of their adversaries. Deterrence only works when all sides understand the unacceptable risks of escalation.

While not a pessimist by nature, much less a doomsayer, Downer is not one to sugarcoat awkward or confronting realities. There are difficult choices ahead for middle power democracies like Australia. Whether it be the Middle East, Eastern Europe, the South China Sea or Taiwan Straits, there will be moments when Australia and other Western allies will face the invidious question: when and how must we intervene to stop subversion and disruption of the rules-based global order?

Downer's advice is not to panic. And certainly not to appease or fawn to those who would seem to threaten most. His approach is phlegmatic, unflustered yet unrelenting — hold fast to the core values of freedom-loving societies and, with other like-minded nations, act resolutely to discourage those undermining stability and security.

Across his career, Downer brought a formidable intellect and relentless work ethic to his job. During his years as foreign minister, and his activism across the years that followed, he would play a leading role in how Australia positioned itself in the world — and in forging the nation's future. This book seeks to tell that story.

1

On the Grid

It took 12 frustrating years on the Opposition benches in the federal Parliament in Canberra before Alexander Downer would have his chance to steer Australia's relations with the rest of the world. It was far longer than he would have wanted stuck in the slow-lane of politics.

Downer is a bloke with a passion for fast cars. Colloquially, he is what is known as a "revhead". Behind the wheel, he has clocked 250kmh on a practice circuit, taking off at tearaway speeds in a Lamborghini, a Brabham racing car and — an old favourite — the Holden SSV V8. By any measure, this is high-velocity, 'pedal to the metal' stuff.

If Downer's love of motorsport tells us anything about his underlying instincts, it is probably the tendency to go full speed ahead for the destination he has set for himself, hurtling and weaving through whatever thrills or spills may come his way.

It is not his only hobby. He enjoys golf and tennis, too. He likes a contest. And he likes to win. By nature, Downer is fiercely competitive.

Across four decades in public life, Downer has provoked unusually strong reactions. In his early days, he was denounced as too flippant and frivolous. In later years, some critics complained he was too imperious and unyielding — Lord Downer, they called him.

Too often, politics is reduced to caricature. What all the barbs and insults thrown at Downer may reveal most is that, from the beginning, he stamped himself as a distinctive brand. Temperamentally, he would never be a bland, cardboard cutout of a politician.

People who actually meet Downer might find that he can bounce easily from conservative and cerebral to effusive and exuberant.

A flinty glare can transform into a smirk, then a grin — sometimes, a chuckle. Like most humans, he reveals himself through a mix of light and shade. But, beneath it all, Downer is an individual with strong core beliefs. In all his years in politics, and beyond, he has demonstrated an inexhaustible appetite for making the case, forcefully, for how Australia should best position itself in a rapidly-changing world.

For his admirers, Downer would become a champion of conviction politics, ready to risk unpopularity rather than shirk the tough decisions. As Australia's longest-serving Foreign Affairs Minister, Downer established a formidable footprint in policy-making and politics, founded on sturdy liberal democratic principles. Australia's intervention in East Timor in 1999 was just one among many examples of the big national security challenges he would tackle head-on.

Downer entered politics in Canberra in 1984, at the age of 33. For an ambitious Liberal Party MP in Australia, these were to be among the leanest of times — the 'wilderness years' as they were commonly known. Facing a modernising Labor Government, with formidable leaders in Bob Hawke and then Paul Keating, the Liberals spent more than a decade out of office: chronically divided, and poorly resourced.

That extended stretch in Opposition, with several tyre blowouts along the way, would be turned ultimately to Downer's advantage. It would provide important lessons on the values of patience, persistence and staying-power. It would also allow him more time to build his knowledge base in what had been a lengthy apprenticeship in the practice of politics — and in the study of how the world worked.

The long wait ended in March, 1996, when the Liberal and National parties in Australia defeated the incumbent Keating Labor Government in a landslide election victory. The new Prime Minister, John Howard, rewarded Downer's loyalty and commitment by appointing him to one of the great offices of state — as Minister for Foreign Affairs.

Alongside Treasurer Peter Costello, these three would come to represent the unshakeable pillars of leadership for the Coalition across more than a decade in power. By 2007, all remained in the same jobs for which they had been sworn in back in 1996.

In an interview for this book, John Howard notes that this is a unique phenomenon in Australia's political history:

> It is the only time since Federation that the same people have been Prime Minister, Foreign Minister and Treasurer — arguably the three most important positions in government — for such a long period of time. It was a

major contributor to stability. Downer was outstanding as foreign minister. He was in every way a safe pair of hands."

The Howard Government's longevity in office was not gifted to them — it wasn't there just for the asking, or the taking. Howard, Costello and Downer and their team had to prosecute the argument, across four successive election victories, that they brought to the job a policy and management approach, at home and in the wider world, that would deliver the results most Australians — at heart, a practical and pragmatic people — wanted or favoured.

Key to this was the challenge of creating the right economic conditions to lift confidence and generate wealth. By the 1990s, the Liberal-Nationals Coalition had renovated its philosophical approach, adopting broadly the neo-liberal economic model known to some as the Washington Consensus.

The Howard Government achieved a string of budget surpluses, cut public debt and moved to deregulate the labour market, privatise state-owned enterprises and encourage a lift in private sector investment. Several of these reforms had been tough, politically. But the pay-off to the economy was greater productivity and a strong export performance. The pay-off for Australian households was a 'golden era' of rising living standards.

That first successful election campaign was not dominated by national security issues. Far from it. All of that would come in later years.

The 1996 election was fought and won almost exclusively on bread-and-butter economic debates, accompanied by an underlying weariness in the electorate after 13 years of Labor in power. Howard captured the mood astutely by declaring that Labor had delivered only "five minutes of economic sunshine."

Approaching polling day, neither John Howard nor Alexander Downer had sought to unfurl an extensive agenda for their approach to international relations. Foreign policy was not the main arena for the political contest — although Labor Prime Minister Paul Keating would do his best to make an issue of it. During the campaign, with his defeat ever more likely, Keating would assert baldly that the major Asian powers would want nothing to do with a Howard Government. It was a shrill political scare, aimed at unnerving undecided voters.

But it was built on a narrative Keating had worked hard to manufacture, based on the singular foreign policy theme Howard and Downer neither liked nor accepted — and would never adopt.

It was Keating's stated opinion — and the prevailing wisdom among much of the foreign policy establishment in Canberra through the early post-Cold War years — that Australia would be better positioned strategically if it peeled away gently from its traditional allegiances and friendships with countries like the United States and Britain and redirected its energies to a wholesale realignment with the economies, societies and cultures of its neighbours in Asia.

Only a year earlier, Downer's predecessor as Minister for Foreign Affairs, the erudite Labor lawyer, Gareth Evans, had flown home from a regional conference in Brunei with a new accessory in his toolkit.

He had unveiled a map redefining Australia's place in the world at the centre of a new configuration, the East Asian Hemisphere. Drawn up by Australian officials, the map was intended to send a message about what Evans saw as the geostrategic realities facing modern Australians.

"The East Asian Hemisphere is where we live," Evans said. "This is where we have to find our security. This is where we can best guarantee our prosperity. This is where not only our neighbours are, but our closest friends."

As Howard saw it, this was an argument built on a false dichotomy. As he would maintain consistently for the next decade and beyond, Australia should not have to choose between its history and geography.

Downer, too, dismissed Labor's vision of "enmeshing" in Asia. Of course the region was critical, strategically. But he had problems with the idea of Australians retreating to a quiet corner, in the hope they might remain untroubled and unnoticed — a small target — by confining diplomatic interest and influence to their own neighbourhood.

An avid and energetic internationalist, Downer argued history had demonstrated — and the future would demand — that Australia must be active globally. As Minister for Foreign Affairs, Downer would say: "In the modern age, no distance is great, no nation is isolated. There is no major international challenge that does not have a global dimension... I firmly believe that Australia's interests are global in scope and if Australia is to be secure and prosperous, we must work globally."

Australians had learned the hard way in the 20th century that no nation, however far-flung, could cocoon itself from threats to freedom.

Neither isolationism nor narrow regionalism offered a buffer against the great global challenges.

Once that was understood, Australia had little choice but to engage at every level to advance and protect its interests. In the 1996 election campaign, Downer ran on the message — "Asia first, not Asia only."

The 45-year-old from the Adelaide Hills came into the foreign minister's role on the back of the hard slog of Opposition politics and through earlier careers as a diplomat and as a bank economist.

This policy breadth was noted early by the likes of Bill Farmer — Downer's first boss at the Department of Foreign Affairs and Trade and, at various times, Australia's envoy to Malaysia, PNG and Indonesia, as well as Secretary of the Immigration Department. "Downer could speak on industrial relations, on the economy, on almost anything," says Farmer. "That's quite unusual for a foreign minister. He spoke to the whole agenda."

Years later, in a column for his home town newspaper, *The Advertiser*, Downer reflected on how his background had informed his understanding of real-world diplomacy and of how foreign and trade policy intertwined with domestic political imperatives:

> A good foreign minister has to have a strong understanding of political and economic history. Foreign policy problems are, after all, political problems and political problems are a function of public opinion and the interaction between leaders and the led.
>
> It's one thing to talk glibly about the need to strengthen our ties with Asia. The question is, how do you do it? That requires knowing the background to how the region is structured, the weft and weave of the relationships throughout the region... Just rocking up as an Australian politician saying you care about Asia, but without any understanding of how it has evolved and how it works, won't get you far. It's the same everywhere... you need a

The three pillars: John Howard, Peter Costello and Alexander Downer served in the top three jobs over almost twelve years in government
(Ray Strange/Newspix)

Speed merchant: Downer in full kit for a celebrity car race
(Brett Hartwig/Newspix)

foreign minister who 'knows stuff' and has thought about these issues over a long period of time.

In November, 1996, not yet nine months into the job, Downer set out the government's main foreign policy priorities in a speech titled, *Australia's Place In the World*.

He designated a vast region stretching from the Pacific, through East Asia, and across to the Indian sub-continent as "the vital sphere of our economic and strategic interests". It was home to the world's six largest armies (China, the US, Russia, India, North Korea and South Korea) and, after the Middle East and the former Soviet Union, the world's three most volatile flashpoints — the Taiwan Straits, the Korean Peninsula and Kashmir. A prosperous and peaceful future for this region was key to the "continued prosperity of all Australians."

Safeguarding security and stability in the Indo-Pacific meant having to work constantly to discourage any attempts at military adventurism. As Downer saw it, a strong and active American presence in the region had been — and would remain — fundamental.

For Downer, the most effective means of protecting Australia's interests in the region, as well as driving solutions to global problems, was to leverage off the nation's strengths, and to work hard on shared goals with its key international partners — not only the US but also the likes of Japan, Indonesia and, increasingly, India. Entering the 2000s, if not so much today, the "peaceful rise" of China was regarded as very much part of that mix.

Whether it was the threat of terrorism, the proliferation of weapons of mass destruction, or the need to advance the global free trade agenda, Australia dedicated itself to strong, principled action. In all these areas, the Howard Government would look to build with its partners the critical mass necessary for an effective international approach.

Nurturing strong and enduring relationships in Asia would be foremost among the challenges. Part of the job would be to reassure Australia's neighbours that the attitudes of Australians towards Asia had shed all remnants of the chauvinistic mindset Australia's political class had exhibited during the first half of the 20th century.

In that same speech in November, 1996, Downer found himself having to deal with an ugly relic of Australia's past, brought back from the dead by incendiary comments by the maverick MP, Pauline Hanson.

In her maiden speech to the federal Parliament in September, 1996, Hanson, who would later form her own One Nation Party, had voiced strident objections to Australia's immigration policies — in particular, to immigration from Asia. The controversy generated nasty headlines in the neighbourhood. The Department of Foreign Affairs and Trade began sending bundles of cables to ministers chronicling the media reaction across Asia. The DFAT Secretary at the time, Philip Flood, had warned the reaction in parts of the region "was strongly adverse."

Did the region still need to be convinced, 30 years after the demise of the White Australia Policy, that this new Australian Government had no time for the divisive race-based posturing of Hansonism? John Howard, as Prime Minister, would come under intense scrutiny for how he handled the controversy. His view was that it was best to deny oxygen to Hanson's crusade. "A full-frontal attack by the Prime Minister would only have elevated it," he would tell the ABC.

But this approach would be viewed by Howard's political opponents, media commentators, some of his most senior officials — and quite a few in his own party — as a long way short of the response required. Almost universally, this was judged in the context of Howard's own history on the issue.

Almost a decade earlier, as Opposition Leader, Howard himself had complained about the risks of too great an influx of immigrants. Although in far more moderate terms than Hanson's "swamped by Asians" rhetoric, Howard, too, had called for a reduction in the Asian component of the immigration intake. In August, 1988, he argued the pace of Asian immigration "has probably been a little too great" and should be "slowed down a little" to preserve social cohesion.

The headlines spiralled into a frenzy. As a political defence against accusations of discrimination, Howard sought refuge in the remarks of Labor's Bob Hawke in 1977, before he became Prime Minister. At that time, Hawke led the Australian trade union movement. Raising fears about boatloads of refugees from Indochina arriving in Darwin, he stated bluntly: "Any sovereign country has the right to determine how it will exercise its compassion and how it will increase its population."

Across his career, Hawke seemed to have unique licence — a special dispensation — from voters. In contrast, Howard would pay a price for ventilating his concerns. His comments may well have reflected the fears of a significant cohort of Australians. Nonetheless, in 1996, as Prime Minister, the issue would yet again rise up against him.

Downer, as the incoming foreign minister, soon found out there was less controversy in the capitals of Asia about this issue than the Howard Government's domestic critics were making out.

One leader who came to the defence of Australia during the Hanson controversy was Malaysian Prime Minister, Mahathir Mohamed. After a meeting with Downer in Kuala Lumpur, Dr Mahathir said it had never been his personal experience that Australians were anti-Asian.

Not always a friend of Australia — and renowned for his public spats with Paul Keating — Mahathir stated publicly that while he didn't like at all what Hanson was saying, he did not believe her views on Asian migration were typical of Australians.

For his part, Downer sought to smother the issue before the story gathered serious momentum beyond Australia's shores:

> I want to reiterate in the clearest possible terms this Government's commitment to a non-discriminatory immigration policy. In fact, when visiting Malaysia, in my first visit to the region since this issue became prominent in the media, I made this point abundantly clear. I repeated this point during my recent visit to India…
>
> I stated then and re-state again today that the Government completely rejects any notion that the immigration policy should have any reference to race. I personally find and the Government finds any such notion to be repugnant. Australians in general regard such sentiments as repugnant. We reject them in their entirety. Australia has a proud record for welcoming migrants from all around the world. We will not let that achievement be threatened in any way.

Downer's comments were reported extensively and prominently across the news media. Howard himself had yet to repudiate Hanson's comments. This created an obvious, unflattering contrast.

"Howard rang me in a fury after watching the Channel Nine News," Downer recalls. "We sometimes disagreed. But we didn't often disagree vehemently." As Downer would reveal many years later in the

ABC documentary, *The Howard Years*, it was the first and only time he can remember being rebuked by the PM:

> I think I'm right in saying that, in my 12 years as Foreign Affairs Minister, it was the only time he had rung me to chastise me. He said, 'Well, it's only going to leave me out there. The media's going to say, 'Look, Downer has done the right thing, why doesn't Howard?'

Downer was not happy either. The maul of negative publicity around Hanson's comments had made infinitely more difficult his job of persuading Australians of the reality of Australia's good relationships across Asia. It also became a messy backdrop to Downer's mission of reassuring the nation-states of Asia that Australia under the Howard Government would prove itself a valuable and committed partner.

Over succeeding years, Downer would set out an ambitious gameplan to demonstrate Australia's relevance to the future of the region.

"We have abiding economic, security and other interests in Asia," he would explain. "These interests reach across both the Indian and the Pacific Oceans, and from New Zealand to India, to North Asia. Japan, Korea and China remain vitally important, as do the emerging giant of India and the region of South East Asia.

"Our efforts to maximise the benefits of all these relationships will include developing people-to-people links, exploiting our advantages in education and training and nurturing our own cultural diversity."

Then came the over-arching strategic goal:

> In pursuing relations with Asia, we must continue to find the right balance and interplay between Australia's engagement with Asia and our broader international relations. This is not about choosing between regions… it is about maximising our strengths.
>
> Indeed, we have shaped our foreign policy so that the various strands are mutually reinforcing. Just as our strong relationships outside the Asia-Pacific enhance our standing in the region, so do our strong regional links improve our international standing.

From 1996, Downer would get to work on his plan of action. As foreign minister, he would soon be flying as many air miles as some commercial pilots — with a clear policy direction in mind.

He felt he had the authority, while never complete autonomy, to command much of Australia's foreign policy and strategic approach.

He believed he had the confidence of the PM to make many of the everyday judgment calls. As he told *The Howard Years*: "John Howard felt more comfortable at home, dealing with domestic issues than international issues in his early days. That's only natural…"

One of the things that impressed Howard about Downer was his courage to speak his mind openly — in crisp, and sometimes blunt and abrasive, language. As Foreign Affairs Minister, he was not afraid to dispense with the polite, sometimes prissy, protocols of diplomacy.

"He could always tell you what he thought of people and why, and that's a very good quality in a foreign minister," says Howard. "The job tends to be rather robotically associated with tact and diplomacy. Downer knew when to be tactful and diplomatic — but when the circumstances required, he was anything but…"

One of Downer's trademarks as foreign minister was a battered bright yellow suitcase that was shuffled on and off luggage carousels on every continent, bar Antarctica. This suitcase became totemic when the ABC filmed a two-part documentary on Downer for *Australian Story*.

To some, the notion of flying in and out of world capitals might seem a glamorous jet-setting lifestyle: a high-altitude cocktail circuit. In fact, when your home base is Australia, the schedules can be gruelling.

On overseas visits, Downer would be accompanied almost always and almost everywhere by staffers carrying highly-secure briefcases. Downer would use the opportunity of long-haul flights to work his way assiduously through his in-tray. Volume after volume of official documents and briefing notes — millions of words a year — would be scrutinised and absorbed under a cabin reading light. Officials might be called on at any moment to answer queries or provide extra detail.

Then, when the aircraft landed, the working day would begin. There would be no allowance for jet lag. It would be wall-to-wall meetings with senior ministers of the host country, official lunches and dinners, speeches, press conferences.

Across almost 12 years, half of all of his flights would be into Asia.

2

THE NEAR NORTH

As Australia's Foreign Affairs Minister, Alexander Downer would visit Indonesia more than any other country.

Jakarta — Indonesia's bustling, gritty, bursting-at-the-seams capital — would be his first stop on his first overseas trip after being sworn in as minister in 1996. He would return to the country another 27 times.

His final trip as foreign minister to Australia's largest and nearest south-east Asian neighbour, in March, 2007, would end in tragedy and heartbreak, with the horrifying crash-landing of a Garuda Airlines passenger jet at Yogyakarta Airport.

Five Australians would die in the accident. These included four colleagues and friends of Downer from the Australian Embassy in Jakarta: public affairs officer, Liz O'Neill; aid director, Allison Sudrajat; and two police officers, Commander Brice Steele and federal agent, Mark Scott. Also lost in the accident was a talented young Australian foreign correspondent, Morgan Mellish, of *The Australian Financial Review*, who had joined the travelling party during Downer's visit.

Downer would arrive in Yogyakarta to find the molten aircraft wreck lying in a paddy field. He would summon senior diplomats and police chiefs to a meeting to review plans to locate missing Australians, assist the injured and confirm any deaths. He would go to the local hospital to visit Cynthia Banham, a foreign affairs writer for the *Sydney Morning Herald* who had suffered awful injuries and burns in the crash.

Standing at Banham's bedside, he demanded of nursing staff that they provide the barely-conscious reporter with more effective painkillers. Not convinced they would oblige, DFAT set up an emergency evacuation flight for Banham to a specialist burns unit at a hospital in Perth. "We'll get you home, mate," she was promised.

Later that day, with his old friend, the Australian Ambassador, Bill Farmer, Downer would go to the homes of the diplomats and police. Their deaths were not yet confirmed but he shared with their families the feelings of shock, grief and foreboding. "He was very shaken," says Farmer. Downer would later describe the experience as his worst moment, personally — "by a big margin" — in all his years in the job.

Seventeen Indonesians also died in the plane crash. Indonesia's president, Susilo Bambang Yudhoyono, would send Howard and Downer a personal note expressing his sadness at the loss of life, and eulogising the Australian embassy officials who died. He paid tribute to Liz O'Neill as "a warm, kind person who smiles at everybody" and to Allison Sudrajat as a "dedicated and creative AusAid officer… we will forever appreciate her compassion and good work…"

At that time, the two nations would come together poignantly, in a moment of shared grief and mourning.

It was not always thus. Of Australia's most important bilateral relationships, there have been none more complex and, at times perplexing, than the dialogue with Indonesia.

Across the decade of the Howard Government, there would be great gains in building trust and affinity between two nations with very different histories and cultures.

But, along the way, Downer had to navigate through desperate moments of disharmony and convulsion. These included the crushing effects on Indonesia of the 1997-98 Asian Financial Crisis; then came a difficult political transition for Indonesia as it emerged from decades under a military autocracy led by the ageing general, President Suharto, to become the world's largest Muslim-majority democracy.

Later, there would be horrifying terrorist attacks on Australians and others by Java-based extremists in Bali and Jakarta, followed by the devastating impact of the Indian Ocean tsunami on the Indonesian province of Aceh in 2004.

And, of course, the watershed moment, and, for the Howard Government, perhaps the most invidious of all foreign policy choices: Australia's dramatic military intervention in East Timor.

The management of these challenges would become defining for the Howard Government — in positioning Australia more strongly as a constructive, capable and reliable partner in the region.

So, just as Jakarta would be the first port-of-call for Downer as Australia's Minister for Foreign Affairs, so it makes sense for it to be the first step in exploring the mindset and trajectory of foreign policy under his stewardship.

It is the story of how the Howard Government worked to reset relations with modern, democratic Indonesia.

Greg Hunt, who would later serve as a Cabinet Minister under three Liberal Prime Ministers, was Downer's senior ministerial adviser on that first trip to Jakarta. Philip Flood, the head of the Department of Foreign Affairs and Trade, and one of his deputies, John Dauth, an experienced East Asia hand, would also join them.

Hunt says any notion that the incoming Australian Government would get a frosty welcome in Asia was very quickly dispelled:

> I've been on trips and in meetings where people are just going through the motions, This wasn't like that at all. It was a full-court press to engage the new Australian Government.
>
> It was not just cordial. The Indonesians were very focussed. They went out of their way to be extremely professional.
>
> Suharto was still the President, of course. He was highly engaged at our meeting. Ali Alatas was still the Foreign Minister, and he spent an enormous amount of time with Alexander. He invested very seriously in the visit. As for us, we set about making concrete plans — on trade and investment, on security, and on educational support for some of Indonesia's outer islands. We didn't arrive empty-handed. John Dauth and Ambassador John McCarthy knew the relationship very well.
>
> The philosophy was that if you could trade and engage with Indonesia, then they would become more integrated and more aligned strategically with the US orbit than the Chinese orbit. The journos who were with us wrote afterwards that it was absolutely clear that this government could deal with Asia, and that Asia would deal with this government. That was the political takeout. The strategic takeout was that we had a solid base and a solid working relationship with Indonesia. After China, this was one of the big tests for Alexander.

The vexed issue of East Timor was barely raised at those first meetings. "But this was 1996," says Hunt. "At that time, there wasn't really talk of independence. More about greater autonomy and freedom."

John Howard, whose first visit overseas as Prime Minister was also to Jakarta, agrees:

> Ali Alatas came out to the airport to greet me and to talk about my call on Suharto. We both agreed we had better steer clear of East Timor to the extent that was possible. At that time, it was a bipartisan position in Australia that, when it came to East Timor, you did everything you could not to upset Jakarta. People will say different things now but that was the reality.

The Keating Government had taken to new levels this deference to the political sensitivities of Suharto's Indonesia. In December, 1995, Australia signed a security treaty with Indonesia — almost as if to overlook, if not erase, ongoing controversy over the fate of East Timor.

Howard remembers taking a call in his car from Labor foreign minister, Gareth Evans, to brief him on the deal. "He was literally breathless — 'We've done it, we've done it' he said.

"And I said, 'What have you done?' And he said, 'This magnificent, epoch-making agreement'. And I said, 'What's it gunna do?' And he said, 'It's going to guarantee security and stability'.

"I think they — sort of believed it."

That treaty, signed in the Keating Government's last months in office, would become a poster child for Labor's claims that a Coalition Government could never match the strategic framework Labor had built with Australia's most important regional neighbours.

Howard, as the new Prime Minister, was dismissive of Keating's taunts that his Government would struggle to find friends in Asia. Howard had met Suharto three times previously: in 1982, as deputy Liberal leader; again, as Opposition Leader during the mid-1980s; and, yet again, as Opposition Leader in the 1990s. "Suharto was fine… he would always make time to see me. He was friendly, charming," he says.

But there were undeniable challenges at the heart of the relationship with Indonesia. The interests of Australia and Indonesia did not always coalesce. They were close geographically. Culturally and politically, however, they could sometimes seem worlds apart.

Flying into East Timor (Department of Defence Images)

Through the later Opposition years, and peaking by 1998, Downer became more and more persuaded of the need for Australia and Indonesia to get the relationship onto a more solid footing; especially when it came to what Alatas had described as "the pebble in the shoe" — Indonesia's controversial suzerainty over East Timor.

Downer remembers discussing the dilemma with his senior officials:

> I was saying how the status quo was unsustainable. Every time there was an incident in East Timor with the Indonesian military it put pressure on our bilateral relations with Indonesia.
>
> The media in Australia would go feral, always taking the side of the East Timorese. Maybe that was fair enough. But all of this pointed to the need for there to be a change to the status quo.

Ultimately, this would lead to a crunch moment for the Howard Government. Nothing before or since would test the relationship with Indonesia like the seismic impact of Australia's decision in 1999 to lead a United Nations-endorsed military force to support the decision of the people of East Timor to secede. Not for the first time, the two neighbours would face a plausible risk of open confrontation.

The deployment of Australian troops to East Timor to end the bloodbath that followed the micro-state's vote to declare independence from Indonesia would be among the most momentous decisions taken by an Australian Government in the postwar era.

The risks were massive. So, as it turned out, would be the rewards.

Today, Downer would say the intervention in East Timor ultimately helped to inject far greater stability into Australia's often difficult relations with Indonesia, by removing a persistent source of friction. "It hasn't been perfect and there have been jolts along the way," he reflects. "But, today, the relationship is fantastic."

Downer was far from the first Australian foreign minister to have to deal with prickliness in the dialogue with the Republic of Indonesia. Over the decades of diplomatic engagement between Indonesia and Australia, gaps in values and strategic priorities would erupt episodically into bouts of ill-will and turbulence.

In the immediate postwar era, ties between Jakarta and Canberra could not have been more promising. Australia was a strong and vocal advocate of Indonesia's aspirations to independence.

Despite a determined British and Dutch campaign to resist the dismantling of colonial rule, the Chifley Labor Government would play a leading role in the negotiations that led to the birth in 1949 of the Republic of Indonesia.

As the map of postcolonial Asia was redrawn, the two peoples had every reason to get along. The countries share the world's longest maritime borders between close neighbours. Christmas Island, one of Australia's external territories, lies only 500km from Jakarta. Further to the east, only Papua New Guinea is closer to Australia.

Inevitably, however, the two nations would at times bump up against each other, bringing into a harsh light their differences. Public disagreements would expose an uneasiness — sometimes a clear divergence in priorities, if not values.

One flashpoint had been Indonesia's confrontation with the newly-emerging confederation of Malaysia from 1963 to 1966 over sovereign rights to the island of Borneo. Australian troops engaged intermittently in armed skirmishes with Indonesian militia to defend East Malaysia's Sabah and Sarawak provinces. In effect, it was an undeclared conflict.

Then, in 1969, came Indonesia's incorporation of the western half of New Guinea as its easternmost province. Once called "Netherlands New Guinea" — or West Irian, as Jakarta would have it — the province shared very similar Melanesian demographics to PNG itself.

A bizarre legacy of the patchwork of colonial rule in the region was that the western half of the island fell under Dutch control from 1828 while the eastern half was split under German and British control.

For much of the 20th century, as the European colonising powers receded, PNG was administered by Australia, mandated by the League of Nations and later the UN. While PNG became independent in 1975, the postwar history of Western Papua was to be far murkier.

From 1949, the new Republic of Indonesia took the view that it was the rightful successor state to all of the Dutch colonial possessions in the Indonesian archipelago — and all of the trading ports of the former Dutch East India Company. Grudgingly, the Netherlands ceded authority over almost all of its former territories to Indonesia.

The one exception was West Papua. In 1962, Indonesia sought to change the facts on the ground, by landing paratroopers on the island. Fearing war, the UN sought to broker a transitional agreement.

In August, 1962, the so-called New York Agreement required the Dutch to cede control over West Papua to a UN trusteeship — pending a vote in West Papua at some future date to decide whether it would integrate with Indonesia or seek independence in its own right.

Under the terms of the Agreement, Indonesia would assume administrative control of West Papua in 1963. Whatever the concerns of the Dutch, Australia — or the West Papuans themselves — this concession was driven predominantly by President John F. Kennedy's strong desire that Indonesia resist seduction by the Soviets and remain at the very least a neutral in the Cold War conflict.

Within West Papua, separatist stirrings would soon emerge, embodied in the *Organisasi Papua Merdeka* — or Free Papua Movement.

A UN peacekeeping force was initially deployed to ensure a ceasefire was upheld. Australia sent a contingent of Royal Australian Air Force crew and a medical team, partly to help quell a cholera outbreak.

The plebiscite to determine West Papua's future was held in 1969. By this time, General Suharto had come to power in Jakarta. The so-called *Act of Free Choice* was supervised by the Indonesian military.

The vote was conducted village by village through a show of hands. Far from all villages were actually consulted. There have been claims then and since of violence and intimidation to rig the vote in support of integration with Indonesia.

Six years later, Australia would again be cast in the role of queasy bystander to an act of territorial expansionism by its neighbour.

In December, 1975, Suharto's Indonesia invaded and annexed the former Portuguese colony of East Timor, lying about 1000km southwest of West Papua across the Banda Sea. Whether this invasion happened with or without a 'green light' from the Whitlam Government became a lingering controversy in Australia.

What was never in doubt was the profound impact on relations between Australia and Indonesia. The deaths of five Australian journalists reporting from the war front in East Timor — and the suspicion, long denied by Jakarta, that these men were shot by Indonesian troops — would leave an indelible imprint on the consciousness of many Australians.

Yet, for a quarter of a century, Australian Governments would acquiesce to the 'realpolitik' of Indonesia rule.

There were two reasons for this: one, that Australia wanted to do nothing that would jeopardise relations with a large, influential and strategically important south-east Asian neighbour; secondly, it did not particularly want to sow instability on Australia's immediate northern approaches by encouraging the emergence of a weak, vulnerable micro-state — aid-dependent, and unable to fend for itself.

Through the 1990s, the chorus of international condemnation of Indonesia's conduct in East Timor began to intensify. The November, 1991, massacre by Indonesian troops of 250 pro-independence demonstrators at the Santa Cruz cemetery in Dili proved totemic in creating an image of a people suffering murderous, heavy-handed repression by an authoritarian Indonesia.

Through all of this, Australia was depicted as a meek onlooker as state-sponsored violence happened on its doorstep.

Greg Hunt recalls discussions within senior Coalition ranks that last year in Opposition — exploratory at first — about whether and for how much longer Australian Governments could credibly maintain an unquestioning stance on Indonesian sovereignty over East Timor.

The 800,000 citizens of East Timor — or what Jakarta called the "27th Province" of the Republic of Indonesia — occupied the eastern half of an island that lay closer to Melanesia than to Java or Sumatra. They were mostly Roman Catholics. Many spoke Portuguese or Tetum. In the world's largest Muslim-majority nation, they were an odd fit within the Republic of Indonesia — culturally and demographically.

"Keating rejected the idea of independence completely," says Hunt. "We were always more circumspect. Not based on ideology. Based on principle. We talked a lot about Timor in '95 and '96.

"Personally, I think both Alexander and John Howard held the view that it was actually a place with a separate identity. There was a strategic framework and purpose to their thinking."

Towards the end of 1997, the volatility and disruption caused by the Asian Financial Crisis would dramatically shift the axis of strategic thinking in both Canberra and Jakarta. The value of the Indonesian rupiah collapsed. Indonesia found itself on the brink of tumult.

The International Monetary Fund and World Bank were prepared to come to the rescue with a support package but only if Suharto would agree to implement a blitzkrieg of economic reforms.

In January, 1998, IMF chief, Michel Camdessus, flew to Jakarta. He insisted that Suharto sign up for the IMF emergency bailout in front of the nation's TV cameras. It was a humiliating moment for a leader who had ruled virtually unchallenged for more than a quarter of a century.

One of the austerity measures imposed, reluctantly, by the Suharto Government was to remove government subsidies on petrol and electricity. Everyday Indonesians were hit hard. As Indonesia faced an increased threat of instability, Australia and other East Asian neighbours feared the consequences of social and political unrest.

Downer was in Jakarta a week after the Camdessus visit. There were already protests in the streets. He met with Suharto, who looked and sounded increasingly frail. Downer pledged that Australia would provide financial support to help keep the Indonesian economy afloat.

In March, 1998, he flew to Washington to personally confront Camdessus, and the US Treasury's deputy secretary, Larry Somers.

"The austerity measures they had forced on the Indonesian Government — and the Indonesian people — were really, really tough," Downer recalls. "I told them these conditions were just too brutal ...

withdrawing all these cost-of-living subsidies and so on. All it's going to do is create a revolution in Indonesia. 'We don't want that'. .

"And Larry Somers said, 'Well, they need a revolution. They need to get rid of Suharto'."

Downer admits to being alarmed by this hardline response: "It's not that I would particularly defend Suharto and his regime. He was an old man who had overstayed his time as president.

"But I said in reply, 'We live right next door to Indonesia so a revolution there would be very bad news for us'.

"Anyway, Camdessus agreed to adjust the program. The crisis still brought Suharto down. But there wasn't some great revolution …"

Howard recalls giving an address at Harvard in 2008, discussing Australia's active support for Indonesia at that moment of crisis a decade earlier. Larry Somers was in the audience: "He said to me, 'You people buggered that up.' He obviously opposed any relaxation (of the IMF's austerity measures)… but he didn't have to deal with the Indonesians. I mean, we had the largest Muslim country in the world on our doorstep …"

Under the pressures of the economic crisis, it was all but inevitable that Suharto's New Order regime would crumble. In May, 1998, he stepped down. The days of one-man rule were over.

This would set in train a rapid evolution in the politics of Australia's giant neighbour to the north. As political debate opened up, powerful voices seeking a more vibrant participatory democracy were coming to the fore. They included the near-blind cleric, Abdurrahman Wahid (known to most as Gus Dur), the leader of the National Awakening Party; and Megawati Sukarnoputri, the leader of the Democratic Party of Struggle, and the daughter of Indonesia's first president.

Meanwhile, Australia and Japan would pour billions into financing loans to help Indonesia through the worst of the financial crisis. Similar help was extended to Thailand and South Korea.

"Peter Costello was a big part of it," says Downer. "Between the two us, we did that. We were the only country to provide support to all three Asian countries through the IMF.

"We also put aid into Indonesia for democratic transition. This would not have been critical though. The critical factor was the Asian Financial Crisis… and Habibie."

B.J. Habibie would succeed Suharto as interim President, pending national elections. Looking back, Downer is full of praise for Habibie's role in the reinvention of his country:

> Eccentric as he may have seemed as a person, he was extremely clever. And his instincts were very good. He had trained in Germany as an aircraft engineer. I think that experience of living in Germany had exposed him to Western concepts of democratic legitimacy and so on. As the vice-president to Suharto, he may have seemed an improbable person to do this .... but he really was the midwife of Indonesian democracy.

With the emergence of a new, more liberal political outlook in Indonesia, the fall of President Suharto raised hopes internationally that a new president might revisit the fate of East Timor. After assuming the presidency, Habibie signalled he was ready to consider a plan for "special autonomy" in East Timor.

Back in Canberra, Downer and his senior Department of Foreign Affairs and Trade officials began workshopping a new approach that might help defuse East Timor as a difficult and disruptive issue internationally for both Indonesia and Australia. This was to become a signature moment — for Downer, for Howard, and for Australian foreign policy.

The head of the South-East Asia desk at DFAT at the time was a former Ambassador to Iran, with a background in intelligence, Nick Warner. He had also worked closely with Downer as head of the public affairs branch of DFAT — effectively, the public voice of the organisation.

Warner recalls a meeting at Downer's ministerial office in June, 1998. It was attended by a handful of Australia's top East Asia officials, including Dr Ashton Calvert, Flood's successor as DFAT Secretary. Calvert was a former Ambassador to Tokyo. He had also worked as an international adviser to Labor Prime Minister, Paul Keating.

The changing dynamics of Australia's relationship with Indonesia, and the future of East Timor, were discussed in depth: "This was the first articulation, as far as I can recall, of Downer looking for a new policy approach," Warner recalls. "He said, 'We have to do what we can to end the bloodshed'."

Testing the appetite for a new dialogue with Indonesia, Downer called publicly for the release from the Cipinang prison in East Jakarta of the leader seen as the living embodiment of East Timorese resistance, Jose Alexander (Xanana) Gusmao.

In the meantime, Warner and other DFAT officials began engaging more directly and intensively with the various factions in East Timor — the Fretilin resistance movement, the pro-Indonesian integrationists, and the East Timor diaspora in Australia and elsewhere overseas. They met with 29 leading figures from East Timor — 11 on the island itself, and another 18 living abroad.

The thinking at the time was that the only means of avoiding further chaos and conflict was to get the warring factions in East Timor to sit down with each other and agree a position on whether and how autonomy for the province might be made to work.

In July, Downer met Ali Alatas in Jakarta. He put to him the idea of bringing together the key figures in East Timor for a consultation on ways of ending the conflict: in effect, to run a survey of East Timor's factions to see whether there was any appetite for what DFAT offficials called "wide-ranging autonomy".

"Well, you're doing it anyway," said Alatas. The Indonesians were sceptical, if not grumpy, about Australia's proactive involvement. Yet, paradoxically, the Australians took heart from the response of Alatas. "It wasn't a no," says Warner.

Back in Canberra, Downer and DFAT's activism on the issue began to raise eyebrows within the Department of Prime Minister & Cabinet. There remained an underlying concern about the unpredictability of this approach — and the dangers of upsetting Indonesia.

Over the weeks to come, there would be high-level discussions between Australian officials and leading figures in the East Timor resistance — notably, José Ramos-Horta and Mari Alkatiri.

"All that was remarkably positive," says Warner.

However, the unequivocal response from these leaders was that an offer of "wide-ranging autonomy" would never be enough. At the very least, they were seeking a commitment from Jakarta that, ultimately, it would offer East Timor an opportunity to vote for full independence.

This became the catalyst for a quantum shift in Australian policy.

At a meeting in December, 1998, Howard, Downer and other senior ministers canvassed a new set of options for dealing with the East Timor conundrum. They had before them a letter crafted by Ashton Calvert and Nick Warner, among others, at Foreign Affairs and Trade.

It suggested Indonesia propose a two-step solution to help douse international agitation. Cast as friendly advice, it suggested Indonesia make an immediate offer to the people of East Timor of greater freedom and autonomy within Indonesia — with the promise of a choice, further down the track, should they wish to proceed to an act of self-determination — or, in other words, a vote to stay or go. It carried the flavour of the Matignon Accords in New Caledonia.

Howard sent this letter to Habibie on December 19, 1998.

By now, there was extreme apprehension among some in DFAT, as well as some of the Prime Minister's key advisers. For its part, the Department of Defence felt it had been "blindsided". But Downer had asked for a bold initiative, and Calvert and Warner had delivered.

"I think Ashton Calvert was a bit ahead of his department on this" Howard says. "He wasn't in thrall to what I might call the 'Dick Woolcott school' — the prevailing view in government that, whatever you do in foreign policy, try not to upset Jakarta."

Says Warner: "Ashton is the unsung hero of East Timor as far as I'm concerned. Ashton was very straight-up, very determined."

It is important to understand that, at this time, nobody in Canberra's foreign policy, defence and security establishment — Howard and Downer included— were advocating, in the first instance, any outcome other than East Timor remaining, at least for the meantime, as part of Indonesia.

Howard's letter was not advancing an act of self-determination as a policy for the here and the now. Nor, more to the point, was he suggesting a now-or-never proposition. Rather, he was proposing a sensible, manageable circuit-breaker. A similar transitional model had been adopted in New Caledonia.

Even so, Downer and Howard both knew they were on the verge of a radical policy realignment for Australia.

Howard had told senior Cabinet colleagues this was "a very important moment" for Australian foreign policy. Later, he and Downer met privately, where Downer reinforced Howard's assessment. "This is big... really big," he told the PM.

In the letter, Howard told Habibie:

> Your offer of autonomy was a bold and clear-sighted step... to resolve an issue that has long caused Indonesia difficulties in the international community... it would be a real tragedy if the opening you have created is not taken advantage of and the situation worsens in East Timor.

Implicit in the letter was a blunt message: that this could be Indonesia's last chance to come up with a peaceable solution that might — just might — allow it to keep East Timor as part of Indonesia. That could only happen by involving the people of East Timor directly in the negotiations. Legitimacy could only come by consent.

Everyone involved knew there were significant risks inherent in the plan. "But it was the right thing to do," says Howard. "We had moved on. Certainly, as things turned out, it was the right thing to do."

Howard saw Habibie a week after sending the letter. Habibie would tell the ABC a decade later that he felt Howard had forced his hand. Howard is far from convinced of that: "Habibie had no romantic attachment to East Timor. It was not a big issue for him."

Certainly, that appears to have been reflected in Habibie's response when he received the official correspondence from Howard. Habibie clearly felt Indonesia had to deal with the issue decisively. Once and for all. "Why not independence?" he scrawled in a note.

Habibie took the Howard proposal to a full meeting of his Cabinet on January 27, 1999. Almost nobody predicted what was to come next.

A day after the Cabinet meeting, Habibie confirmed a dramatic policy switch by Indonesia — Jakarta would agree to conduct a "popular consultation" among the people of East Timor to determine their political status. They could either remain in the Indonesian Republic with an unspecified degree of autonomy — or they could accept the responsibility and risk of cutting themselves adrift as a stand-alone country. It was to become a blunt, binary choice: autonomy or independence. Take it or leave it.

Behind the scenes, in both Jakarta and Canberra, there was to be anguished debate about where exactly all this was heading, and the ramifications for stability and security in the neighbourhood.

Some in Jakarta took the Howard letter as an insult. Did Australia think Indonesia had something to learn from the Matignon Accords between France and separatists in New Caledonia? Was this an implicit moral lecture on the failings of "colonial rule" by Indonesia in East Timor?

Important figures in Indonesia's military leadership opposed trenchantly any surrender of control of East Timor. There were even said to be whispers of a coup in the making.

But Habibie made known he wanted the problem resolved: finally, conclusively, one way or another. Why, he asked, should Indonesia continue to subsidise East Timor if an offer of autonomy served only to intensify demands for full independence? This was not a policy headache he intended to handball to an elected successor.

"Why do we have this problem when we have a mountain of other problems?" Habibie would complain. "Do we get any oil? No. Do we get gold? No. All we get is rocks. If the East Timorese are ungrateful after what we have done for them, why should we hang on?"

There has been much speculation since on whether this was an act of brinksmanship— had Habibie calculated, wrongly, that the people of East Timor, like regional neighbours, had come to accept the realpolitik of Indonesian sovereignty? Whether or not this was so, Habibie had thrown open the door.

Events were moving far more quickly than anyone in Australia had anticipated. As Craig Stockings documents in *Born of Fire and Ash*, the official history of Australia's peacekeeping operations in East Timor, Habibie's shock announcement "triggered surprise in Jakarta, furrowed brows in Washington (and) caused tremors in Canberra."

Warner sums up the dynamic:

> That was not the response we expected. The reason we changed policy on East Timor was to do the right thing —as Downer had said, we had to do something to end the bloodshed. We headed down a difficult, but sensible, path. Then we got caught up in a fast-moving process we couldn't control.

In February, 1999, the authorities released Gusmao from prison — although he was kept under house arrest in Jakarta. Downer was the first foreign leader to visit Gusmao after his release.

Gusmao was dressed in a new suit and tie. Kirsty Sword (soon to become Gusmao's Australian wife and East Timor's inaugural First Lady) was his interpreter. Access to Gusmao had been a courtesy extended previously to very few, the likes of South African president Nelson Mandela, and US Secretary of State, Madeleine Albright.

In his meeting with Downer, the East Timorese leader was softly-spoken but supportive of attempts to achieve "reconciliation" in East Timor. Like everyone else, Gusmao was worried about the alternative scenario: renewed conflict between the resistance forces and the pro-integrationists (and, potentially, the Indonesian military).

Downer took him through the approach Australia was proposing, and explained the critical importance of East Timor's factions agreeing a political accommodation among themselves. Yet hopes of the competing East Timorese factions finding a workable compromise they could all support would soon prove forlorn.

These were becoming incredibly tense days in Australia's near-neighbourhood. Through 1999, there would be repeat episodes of violence in East Timor.

Pro-Indonesia militia leaders had warned of "winds of fire" if the East Timorese voted for independence. They had also warned of potential attacks on any Australian media and diplomats they deemed to be "interfering " in the internal affairs of Indonesia.

In those early months of 1999, there had been active discussions in Canberra about how to respond if the security situation in East Timor spiralled out of control. Nobody was ready to talk peace enforcement as such. Defence and security officials were hoping fervently that an intervention like that would not be necessary.

Australian officials had begun preparatory discussions with the UN on how to ensure the integrity of the process for determining East Timor's future status. Jakarta's proposal for a "popular consultation" was acceptable neither to the East Timorese, or their supporters internationally. Everyone remembered what had happened in West Papua. There had to be a formal ballot, independently supervised.

But what would be the potential security risks that might accompany such a vote? The Howard Government remained reluctant to canvas publicly the idea of inserting into East Timor a multinational security force to prevent violence: they did not want to embolden the pro-independence forces politically by encouraging a belief that, whatever course they chose, UN peacekeepers would automatically come to their rescue.

Behind the scenes, however, preparations were underway in Canberra to cover the contingencies of the worst-case scenario. Defence Minister John Moore put on notice one of the Army's combined arms combat brigades, the 1RAR in Darwin, that it should begin planning for a potential deployment to East Timor.

In March, Downer went to Portugal to see Prime Minister Antonio Gutteres (who would become UN Secretary-General in 2017). On the flight to Europe, Downer and Warner discussed whether a multilateral peace monitoring group, like that assembled by Australia and New Zealand in Bougainville, might be an option.

That same month, the UN sent one of its most senior diplomats to Canberra. "They were starting to get worried," says Warner. "We were all talking about whether this would go smoothly, whether it would go wrong, or whether it would go catastrophically wrong — all of those conversations."

In April, pro-Indonesia militia stormed a church in the East Timorese town of Liqica. At least 25 parishioners were shot or hacked to death. Some reports put the death toll much higher.

By this time, Australian intelligence officials were convinced that senior figures in the Indonesian military were not only aware of the involvement of some of their own soldiers in these atrocities — but that they were actively working to sabotage Habibie's referendum strategy.

In June, Warner gave testimony before a Senate Committee. He revealed some of the detail of the Australian Government's suspicions about what was happening on the ground in East Timor, and the role of the Indonesian military, the *Tentara Nasional Indonesia*: "There is evidence available that TNI has been actively involved in supporting and encouraging pro-integration militias in East Timor, including through the supply of arms..." Senior defence official, Hugh White, had provided similar testimony to Senate Estimates the previous day.

With rising fears that elements within Indonesia's Kopassus special forces were arming and training militia in East Timor, the Howard Government sent to Defence Headquarters in Jakarta its deputy defence chief, Air Vice Marshal Doug Riding, to flag these concerns directly with Indonesia's military command.

"In our opinion, the most significant threats to a genuinely free ballot come from the pro-integration militias supported by TNI," Riding told them. "This is very seriously damaging the credibility of the Indonesian Government and TNI. It is our assessment that TNI and pro-integration militias have intimidated the East Timor population as part of a campaign to maximise the chances of an 'autonomy' result."

It was a clear 'cut the crap' message, delivered in plain language. Yet nothing much resulted. Whatever Australia's intelligence relating to complicity on the part of some units of Kopassus, it remained only circumstantial evidence. There was no 'smoking gun.' In response, General Wiranto, Indonesia's defence chief, seemed either unable, or unwilling, to rein in these nefarious operations.

In that same month, Downer approved a proposal to provide UN Secretary-General, Kofi Annan, with a 'lightly sanitised' version of the intelligence brief on the machinations behind the chaos and violence in East Timor.

By now, almost everyone at the UN seemed to think it would be preferable if peacekeepers — "blue helmets" — were deployed at the earliest opportunity to prevent a bloodbath. And almost everyone, including the United States, seemed to think it was Australia's responsibility to take the lead.

The neighbouring ASEAN countries felt constrained by the regional grouping's commitment to "non-interference" in the affairs of an influential member state like Indonesia.

For its part, the US was making clear it felt the onus was on sub-regional powers to sort this out among themselves. Nobody wanted a direct showdown with Indonesia.

Stanley Roth, the head of the East Asia and Pacific desk at the US State Department, had been a prominent advocate of establishing an international military presence in East Timor ahead of the vote. But he did not have the support of the Pentagon — and, most critically of all, there was no agreement from Indonesia to allow foreign forces to land.

At one point, it was understood Habibie had told a colleague Indonesia would view any insertion of external forces into East Timor as an infringement of its sovereignty — in effect, a declaration of war.

Despite the risks, Downer made the call that Australia should support the ballot going ahead. It was a once-in-a-generation opportunity.

Howard had full confidence in Downer's capacity to navigate through the hazards:

> It was a difficult issue, and Downer understood it. He had worked out how to do it internationally.
>
> I give him a lot of credit for pointing me in the right direction and guiding it through. Downer knew his stuff when it came to Asian countries... completely contrary to the common perception that he was just interested in the gossip of Whitehall and Washington.

The vote was called for August 30, 1999 — before security plans were finally agreed. Four days later, the result was announced. It could not have been more emphatic — the East Timorese decided, by a 78.5 per cent majority, to stand alone rather than accept an offer of autonomy.

The response was savage and immediate. Pro-integration militia, supported in the shadows by elements of the Indonesian military, ran amok. It was an orchestrated campaign of terror.

The violence cost at least 1000 lives, and reduced to rubble East Timor's infrastructure: homes, schools, water supply, electricity. As images of carnage and destruction were beamed across the world, other nations looked to the UN — and Australia — to put a stop to it.

In Canberra, Howard and Downer were under extreme pressure to intervene. Yet the Australian Government could never be sure of the costs, the consequences, the potential level of casualties, involved in deploying troops to East Timor.

The Howard Government was now facing the very circumstances its diplomacy with Indonesia since June, 1998, had sought so desperately to avoid. The worst fears were in danger of becoming the reality. East Timor was in flames and the Indonesian military were complicit in some of the violence. Australia could be a bystander no longer.

Nick Warner describes the equation:

> The policy changes we made — and there were mis-steps along the way — accelerated developments in Jakarta and East Timor, and changes in approach and attitude

> in Jakarta. That, and the deteriorating situation in East Timor, changed policy approaches in Australia. It's not as if we said — day one, we want an independent East Timor. We didn't want that. We expected East Timor to remain part of Indonesia. But it all shifted and changed over that 18 months…

Howard and Downer sought a commitment from the US for its active, unambiguous support. Downer was not impressed by the response: "We always had to drag the Americans to the table on East Timor."

It was not that Downer was not getting along well with the Clinton Administration. But there was significant skirmishing between Washington and Canberra about the level of US engagement in the region — conspicuously, the limited resources President Bill Clinton was prepared to commit to an East Timor intervention.

As Downer explains it:

> We wanted them to come in and provide some support for us in East Timor. We wanted them to send troops. We didn't need a lot of troops. We just wanted an American presence — boots on the ground. Initially, they refused to provide any support.

The motivation behind Australia's request was self-evident. It was important everyone in the region — in particular, elements in the Indonesian military — be left in no doubt that any hostility towards troops deployed under the UN banner would be met with an overwhelming response.

Australia did not get a sympathetic hearing in Washington.

The scars of the Vietnam years had created deep unease in the US about "wars in far-off Asian jungles." And the Clinton Administration had several major foreign challenges competing for attention.

First, the stubborn defiance by Saddam Hussein's regime of a series of UN Security Council resolutions demanding Iraq allow UN weapons inspectors full unhindered access to the country. Towards the end of 1998, President Clinton had ordered a three-day bombing campaign of key military and strategic sites in Baghdad.

Soon after, in March and April, 1999, the US had led an intensive

NATO bombing campaign to force a retreat by Serbian militia from "ethnic cleansing" atrocities in Kosovo.

Then, in July, 1999, Clinton had to intervene personally to persuade Pakistan's then prime minister, Nawaz Sharif, to pull back troops from Kashmir, averting any risk of a nuclear confrontation with India.

Such was the 'bed of nails' for the world's sole superpower.

Howard had phoned Bill Clinton directly, seeking his support on East Timor. "He said to me, 'John, we can't put any boots on the ground'."

"You what?" Howard responded indignantly.

"I pointed out to him that we were the first country to plant a flag in the ground in Vietnam, with the Menzies commitment of an infantry battalion in 1965. We had gone out on a limb in Vietnam.

"Clinton said, 'John, you've got to understand that we took out an enormous peace dividend after the end of the Cold War. We ran our forces down'. He said, 'I can provide other help'.

"And he was as good as his word on that. He sensed when people were genuinely unhappy. And I was unhappy. I had given him the impression — which I wanted to give —that we felt let down."

Alexander Downer was not in a mood to forgive.

He recounts a terse phone conversation he had with Clinton's national security adviser, Sandy Berger, who was insistent the US need not be involved militarily in East Timor.

Berger chose a homily to reinforce his message: "Look — if I hear that my daughter's room at her college is in a mess, I don't go all the way to Boston to tidy it up."

In other words, the Australian Government should accept responsibility for dealing with this challenge in its own backyard without having to call on American forces to back them up.

This infuriated Downer. He left the ministerial wing of Parliament House and marched straight up to the TV studios in the Press Gallery. "I went on CNN and said we were very disappointed. We had always been there for the Americans in their times of need…"

Bill Clinton's Secretary of State, Madeleine Albright, was in Hanoi when the Downer interview was broadcast by CNN:

No sooner had I got back from the Press Gallery and gone down to the Cabinet room, I had a message that Madeleine wanted to speak to me.

I spoke to her straight away. She had been sitting up in bed watching the interview on TV. She was really upset. She told me she was doing all she could to persuade the President that they should provide some support, and that it didn't help her cause by going out on the airwaves and saying what I had said publicly.

I liked Madeleine. To her endless credit, I think she was always in favour of providing help to us. They did end up providing some logistical support... but they didn't offer up boots on the ground.

The Americans were happy to provide Australia with additional horsepower for the UN operation — just not the combat troops, from day one, that Downer had wanted. An amphibious assault ship, the USS *Belleau Wood*, was soon to be stationed offshore in the Timor Sea. Carrying 1000 troops, it was to serve as a "strategic reserve" should peacekeepers come up against significant armed opposition.

In Canberra, American technicians were installing at Defence headquarters at Russell Hill the latest state-of-the-art battlefield surveillance technology providing real-time intelligence on any movements by troublemakers in East Timor.

And the unparalleled political clout of the US President would come into play on the critical issue of persuading Indonesia to allow the INTERFET peacekeepers, led by Australia, into East Timor.

Howard had set as a strict condition of Australian involvement that the Indonesian President must give a green light to any UN deployment. Without the consent of Indonesia to allow peacekeepers to land, any intervention risked disaster. Australian wanted a UN Security Council Resolution endorsing the military deployment, and that was unlikely without Jakarta's explicit approval.

The Americans were acutely aware of the dangers of attempting to proceed without the shield of legitimacy provided by a Security Council go-ahead. The then US ambassador to the UN, Richard Holbrooke, had warned Australia's ambassador in Washington, Andrew Peacock, that in the absence of a strong UN mandate, pro-Indonesian militia in

East Timor might assume they had carte blanche to wreak havoc: "You could have another Srebrenica..."

In that first hectic week of September, Howard and Downer had flown to Auckland for an APEC Summit. Clinton was expected to arrive in the next 24 hours. Howard and Downer managed to get him on the phone from Honolulu, where Air Force One was being refuelled.

"Clinton had to persuade Habibie to let in the UN peacekeeping force," says Downer. "That all required some effort."

Howard says Clinton dispatched to Jakarta his Defence Secretary, Bill Cohen, a straight-shooting Republican, to put the hard word on the Indonesians. "In the end, Alatas agreed," Howard says. "He was very reluctant, Alatas. I don't think Habibie, personally, was worried about it but he had to go along with those around him. So it was Alatas, albeit reluctantly, who gave it their blessing."

When UN Secretary-General Kofi Annan called Howard to confirm the intervention would be UN-sanctioned, Australia insisted on one non-negotiable condition: if Australian forces were to make up the biggest contingent in the UN operation, then Australia must lead it.

On September 20, 1999, the Australian troops, making up the bulk of the UN-authorised INTERFET force, landed in Dili, commanded by Major General Peter Cosgrove. It was the single biggest commitment of Australian forces overseas in 30 years — the most significant military operation since Vietnam.

Anyone with an appreciation of the history of relations between Australia and Suharto's Indonesia knew this to be a truly radical repositioning. It need only be measured against the declaration by Howard's predecessor, Paul Keating, that he would never put the Australia-Indonesia relationship in 'hock' over East Timor.

Yet here was the Howard Government, led by a prime minister the 'progressive left' so loved to hate, taking up the risks of alienating Indonesia for the cause of East Timor's freedom.

In the end, the Australian-led peacekeeping forces were able to put a stop to the violence quickly and restore stability on the island. Initially, Australia sent 5500 troops to East Timor, peaking at 6500 in the first two years. There were also 1600 Thai soldiers and 1200 Kiwis. The British sent 260 British Army Gurkhas and HMS *Glasgow*. Over the duration of the mission, there were 10,000 troops from 20 nations.

Japan, constrained from deploying troops overseas by its peacetime Constitution, provided funding of $US100 million to support the operation. The UN would send in one of its most distinguished diplomats, the late Sergio Vieira de Mello, to head up the transitional administration towards full independence in 2002.

Australia's commitment represented a crucial — probably decisive — intervention in support of East Timor's long and traumatic quest for nationhood. Howard and Downer would receive much praise at the UN, and effusive expressions of gratitude from East Timor's leadership.

A quarter of a century later, Greg Hunt considers it one of the great foreign policy achievements by any Australian Government.

"Ultimately, a peaceful resolution would not have happened without Howard and Downer," he says. "And it was done without causing irreparable damage to Australia's relationship with Indonesia.

"It was how to find a pathway to independence without permanently destroying relations with Indonesia. It was all about patience. Then history opened up very quickly. Howard and Downer were intellectually prepared when the opportunity arose... although we thought it may have taken a lot longer than it did."

Australia's role in East Timor was welcomed at UN headquarters in New York as one of the most proactive, principled commitments ever by a regional power to help procure and protect the sovereignty of one of the world's newest, most vulnerable nation-states.

Howard credits his Foreign Affairs Minister as one of the architects of that success:

> I regard the intervention in East Timor as not only the right and noble thing to have done. It was also extremely well executed. And Downer played a major role in that.

The mood in Indonesia, for a few years to come, would remain .... sullen. Mending fences between the two neighbours would be a critical work-in-progress for Downer throughout his years as foreign minister.

There was much trauma to come.

It began in 2000 when fishing boats from Indonesia carrying unauthorised would-be migrants from the Middle East, Afghanistan and Sri Lanka suddenly began arriving in large numbers in Australia's territorial waters. In 2002, terror attacks on Australian targets began —

first in Bali, followed by two more in Jakarta. Then, in 2004, came the terrifying impact of the Indian Ocean tsunami on the people of Aceh.

Through all of this disruption and destruction, Downer and his department harnessed the support of the Australian Defence Forces, the Australian Federal Police, the Immigration Department and other agencies to step up engagement with their Indonesian counterparts. Later chapters will detail how the relationship began to blossom.

One early sign of a potential thaw in relations with Jakarta came with the visit to Australia in 2001 by Gus Dur — the first Indonesian President to make a state visit to Australia in 25 years. The visit was the Indonesian President's idea. The Howard Government was more than happy to welcome him. As President, Gus Dur was focussed on the possibilities of a new chapter in relations between the two nations.

Veteran foreign policy specialist, Bruce Grant, in an article for *The Age*, wrote of Gus Dur's approach:

> He liked to ride on Melbourne's trams. He described the excitement of being among ordinary Australians, watching them get on and off, what they were wearing, how they related to each while strap-hanging... he was almost blind (I never knew the exact degree) but his sense of occasion was tangible. He was the first of Indonesia's presidents to confront the Australian public on its own terms — open, democratic, humanist, humorous.

Australia's relations with the newborn East Timor would also flourish ... for a while. In 2002 and 2006, Downer took SOS calls from Prime Minister José Ramos-Horta pleading for Australian military assistance to quell uprisings by renegade forces on the island. Twice, the Howard Government would send in troops to restore law and order.

However, soon after the Howard Government departed office, Downer's erstwhile friends in Dili would begin making accusations against the Australian Government.

The headline grievance could be boiled down to claims that the Howard Government, as part of Timor Sea negotiations, had been seeking to grab the giant's share of revenue from oil and gas assets in the Timor Gap — and that it had sought the upper hand in negotiations through electronic eavesdropping on senior East Timorese negotiators at their offices in Dili. The allegations would leave Downer with a bitter aftertaste. This, too, will be explored in further detail in later chapters.

As for the relationship with Washington, the fact no US troops were deployed on the ground in East Timor proved an awkward moment for Clinton and Albright, for Howard and Downer — and for the alliance.

It had not been the only awkward moment. In July, 1999, when Howard made his second trip as PM to Washington to meet Clinton, the President had set the tone by announcing new tariffs on Australian lamb exports just as Howard was due to land. A protocol mix-up then left the prime minister sitting in a parked car in pouring rain outside the White House for 20 minutes before he was shuffled inside for a meeting that lasted less than an hour.

The commentary that followed — let alone the images beamed back to Australia — were not helpful.

With the next US President, there would be fewer shades of grey.

3

Hands across the Ocean

"There is only one thing worse than fighting with allies and that is fighting without them."

Winston Churchill

Alexander Downer was the first member of the Howard Government to shake hands with George W. Bush. In the late 1990s, on the advice of his old boss, Andrew Peacock — by then Australia's Ambassador to the US — Downer paid a visit to Texas to make a call on the Republican governor of the state. Peacock had told him George W. was a better than even-money chance to become the next US President.

Downer had been foreign minister for only two years. He and Bush established an immediate rapport. After their meeting, Bush would write Downer a letter saying he was "very impressed that your country would have a foreign minister who was so youthful and so bright".

That meeting would prove an important marker in the evolution of the alliance into the 21st century. Downer was eager to rekindle the relationship with the American superpower — both at the strategic level, and in building closer people-to-people contacts. As a keen student of alliance history, he knew that maintaining deep personal connections had been crucial to the durability of the relationship.

The ANZUS alliance was forged and strengthened through the shared sacrifice of two world wars, followed by wars against the encroachment of Communism in Korea and Vietnam. This was turbo-charged, militarily, during the War on Terror.

Australia is the only nation to have fought alongside the US in every major conflict in which the superpower has been involved in this century or the last.

Yet it was Downer's strong view that those who derided the Alliance as merely "Australia fighting someone else's wars" were adopting a shallow, one-dimensional perspective.

He says too many Australians underestimate grievously the depth, the breadth — the meaning and purpose — of the relationship. He rejects as "childish" a widely-held view that the key premise of the alliance is to provide a US security guarantee to Australia in the event of conflict.

On the 70th anniversary of ANZUS in 2021, Downer provided a hard-nosed 'realist' summary of his thoughts on the purpose and relevance of the alliance. Published by the US Studies Centre at Sydney University, it was written from the perspective of someone who had spent more than a decade immersed in the inner workings of the relationship, with first-hand experience of the costs and benefits:

> The ANZUS Treaty has much more fundamental meaning than a simple commitment to common defence. Indeed, academics and commentators frequently perceive ANZUS through the lens of a mechanism designed to defend Australia in the event of it being subjected to a military attack. Certainly, it would come in handy for Australia should that ever happen!
>
> For the Australian foreign minister, the defence minister and even the prime minister, ANZUS has a much more profound *raison d'etre*. In 1996 at the AUSMIN summit in Sydney – which was the first I attended as foreign minister – we signed the Sydney Declaration. For some reason, this has been largely forgotten but it was an attempt by the new Australian Government to articulate jointly with our American visitors what ANZUS meant to us *in practice*. That Sydney Declaration is as relevant today as it was 25 years ago.
>
> First and foremost, from Australia's perspective, the ANZUS Treaty is designed to anchor the United States in the security architecture of what today we call the Indo-Pacific region.
>
> The deeper and the more permanent the US engagement in the region, the less likely the region is to fracture and that the status quo be challenged, or even changed, by the use of force.
>
> Or, put another way, the US presence in the region helps to underwrite a regional balance of power. Take away that balance and the region would become deeply unstable.

The two key alliances that keep the United States anchored in our region are the alliance with Australia in the south and the alliance with Japan in the north. Although the United States has other allies in the region, these two alliances are the most substantial and enduring.

Secondly, the Alliance with the United States gives Australia access to the best of American military technology. This is frequently overlooked by critics of the Alliance. Although Australia is a rich country, its small population and its huge size present a number of challenges when structuring the defence force.

Australia has no choice but to depend on the very best technology for its security and the security of its region. Australia simply doesn't have the size or the capacity to develop that technology itself. The Alliance gives us that edge over other regional countries not in alliance with the United States.

Thirdly, the Alliance gives us access to American intelligence. This is a huge advantage for Australia. We have access to information which almost no other country in the region has — even Japan.

That gives our diplomacy a major advantage. The Americans also gain out of this relationship as Australian intelligence in its own neighbourhood is unequalled.

Finally, Australia's intimate Alliance, its access to American technology and intelligence and extensive bilateral diplomatic engagement, as well as economic links, enhances very substantially Australia's status in the region.

Given the United States' huge power both militarily and economically, relations with the United States matter to every nation in the Indo-Pacific. Neighbours know we have a closer relationship with the US military, the US intelligence community and many aspects of the US economy than any other nation in the region. That enhances Australia's soft power and status in the region.

In my nearly 12 years as foreign minister, I was very conscious regional neighbours knew that Australia, more than any other Indo-Pacific country, had the ear of Washington. There were many occasions in that period when we exercised that influence to guide successfully American policy on issues as wide-ranging as China, Indonesia and the Asian financial crisis.

Downer continues to argue that the benefits of the Alliance have been chronically under-valued in much of the debate within Australia:

> I must have attended more AUSMIN meetings than almost any other Australian. That doesn't mean much, of course, but I can speak from experience: very few other countries have the same access year after year to the US Secretary of State and Secretary of Defence, as well as people such as the National Security Adviser, the Chairman of the Joint Chiefs of Staff, and the head of the CIA. I came to know these people well, and in some cases they became my friends…
>
> It gives us an enormous advantage in terms of promoting our national interests given the huge power of the US.
>
> Some argue that a close relationship with the Americans limits our capacity to engage in our neighbourhood. I say, from experience, that the opposite is true. We gain huge prestige in the Indo-Pacific region from a particularly close relationship with the US.

To demonstrate how the Alliance had strengthened and broadened, it is worth remembering how and where it began.

While the alliance came into being formally in the early Cold War years it was constructed on the back of decades of the two Pacific nations lining up together to meet common dangers.

Shared values as liberal democracies, and similar worldviews as nation-states, were fundamental; so, too, the goodwill created by successive generations of leaders in both countries.

This dated back to the warm welcome extended by Prime Minister Alfred Deakin in 1907 for the visit to Australian port cities by Teddy Roosevelt's Great White Fleet. A decade later, the two Pacific nations would fight together on the battlefields of Europe. On America's Independence Day in 1918, Australian and US forces led the assault on one of the last, crucial German strongholds in the Somme, in the Battle of Le Hamel. This battle was noteworthy for the respect shown to General Sir John Monash by the American GIs who served under him.

A generation later, President John F. Kennedy would owe his life to an Australian who orchestrated his rescue during World War 2, after his patrol boat was sunk off the Solomon Islands by a Japanese destroyer.

Swimming from the shipwreck to a nearby island, the young Navy lieutenant came across two locals in a canoe. JFK gave them a crude SOS he had carved into a coconut shell. They took it to Reg Evans, an Australian coastwatcher hiding in the jungle atop a dormant volcano.

Evans made contact with the nearest US base. Kennedy made it home.

Long forgotten is that, in his last speech as President, on that fateful visit to Dallas, JFK would not only reference the alliance with Australia but would also speak excitedly about a new partnership on next-generation military technology. Almost exactly 60 years before AUKUS, the US and Australia were about to change the game in the Asia-Pacific.

"In the not too distant future, a new Fort Worth product ... the TFX, Tactical Fighter Experimental... will serve the forces of freedom and will be the number one airplane in the world today," Kennedy said.

"It will be the first operational aircraft ever produced that can literally spread its wings through the air... the Government of Australia, by purchasing $125 million of these TFX planes before they are off the drawing boards, has already testified to the merits of this plane..."

It worked out to be a good deal all round. The F-111, as it came to be known (dubbed the "Pig" by RAAF pilots and crew), would become the staple of Australia's air power for the next 40 years.

President Lyndon Baines Johnson also served in the Pacific, as a Navy reserve officer on bomber missions. He met the future Australian Prime Minister Harold Holt while stationed in Melbourne in 1942. LBJ had his own adventures on his tour-of-duty, including an emergency landing at the Winton air base in Queensland when his aircraft suffered a mechanical fault. President George HW Bush, a Navy fighter pilot during World War 2, had to be scooped from the Pacific by a submarine, after his plane was shot down.

An uncle of President Joe Biden wasn't so fortunate. He died when his aircraft was fired on over PNG during joint US-Australian operations to repel the Imperial Japanese Army's attempts to seize Port Moresby.

In 1942, the US involvement in the defence of Australia — from the Battle of the Coral Sea onward — was vital to withstanding the threat of a Japanese assault on northern Australia.

Likewise, Australian support in places like Bougainville, and in the grim contest over Guadalcanal in the Solomon Islands, was also important to the successful US campaign to reverse the conquests of the Imperial Japanese Army in the Pacific islands and East Asia.

None of this meant the relationship was without moments of tension. The formula has been described as something like this: "We are allies because we agree (but) we do not agree because we are allies."

Australian overtures to Washington for a formal strategic partnership between the Pacific nations were born out of desperate necessity.

It goes back to perhaps the bleakest and most fearful moment in Australia's history as a nation. With the Imperial Japanese Army surging south, Prime Minister John Curtin wrote a letter to *The Herald* in Melbourne on December 27, 1941, setting out in stark terms the challenges his people were facing. Famously, it included this plea to Washington: "Without any inhibitions of any kind, I make it quite clear that Australia looks to America, free of any pangs as to our traditional links or kinship to the United Kingdom."

Initially, President Franklin D. Roosevelt was not impressed. Australia seemed intent on insinuating itself into the key decision-making in the US about the prosecution of the war in the Pacific. Convinced it could no longer rely on British strategic support to defend itself, Australia was now cosying up to a new 'great and powerful friend'.

Ultimately, though, the US had little choice but to engage. Strategically, Australia offered the only credible option as a base from which the US could launch its prolonged and arduous struggle to reverse Imperial Japan's territorial expansion across East Asia and the Pacific.

Likewise, the immediate postwar push by Australia for a security pact with the US — the ANZUS Treaty — met strong resistance within the Truman Administration. Only North Korea's brazen aggression in June, 1950, in attempting a military takeover of the south of the country — at a time the Soviets were boycotting the UN Security Council and unable to veto a US-led intervention — forced Washington's hand.

The Menzies Government quickly committed to send forces in support of the US. Ending Australia and New Zealand's obstruction of a peace treaty with Japan was also key to shifting official sentiment in the US.

Yet Menzies went into the alliance with his eyes wide open. He believed that all nations, ultimately, would act to promote and protect their own interests. Australians could not expect to rely on the US — always, and in all circumstances — to come to their support in the face of an external threat. To make that assumption of the ANZUS Treaty was to build national security "on a foundation of jelly".

Australia had to be prepared to carry its weight by sharing the burden of alliance responsibilities. One key initiative was the hosting of joint communications and surveillance bases in outback Australia — at Pine Gap, Nurrungur and on the Exmouth Peninsula.

The Vietnam War years were defining for the US and Australia. Massive anti-war protests would re-cast politics in both countries. What is too often overlooked in retrospectives on the Vietnam years is the decade of breathing-space that the war afforded newly-independent nations of Singapore, Malaysia, Indonesia and Thailand in building resilience and resistance against Communist imperialism in south-east Asia.

In 1975, the US generated some resentment in Canberra with its blunt insistence that Australia should accept the realpolitik of the Cold War and not oppose or resist Indonesia's takeover of East Timor.

In 1976, the incoming Coalition Government in Australia signalled a degree of anxiety about the mutual security provisions under ANZUS. In his first major foreign policy statement, Prime Minister Malcolm Fraser spoke to the question of whether there could ever be such a thing as a security guarantee. Fraser said:

> In our relations with the United States, as in our relations with other great powers, our first responsibility is independently to assess our own interests. The United States will unquestionably do the same.

In 1985, the Hawke Government, to appease rising anger in Labor's left-wing faction, formally opposed the Reagan Administration's plans to test long-range MX missiles in the South Pacific.

And, as recounted in the previous chapter, Alexander Downer in 1999 had his own terse exchanges with the Clinton Administration about US support for the Australian-led intervention in East Timor.

Yet it would be in the earliest years of the 21st century that the biggest test of all would come — a dramatic step-up in the operating rhythms of Australia's alliance with the US.

Just one day after celebrations in Washington to mark the 50th anniversary of ANZUS, Al-Qaeda's mega-terror attacks on New York and Washington on September 11, 2001, would lead to the toughest, most traumatic, decisions taken over the decade of the Howard Government in the realm of foreign policy: decisions involving the life-or-death issues of deploying Australian troops to faraway wars.

The Howard Government's decision to join the US and Britain as original partners in what would become the "Coalition of the Willing" would become the most contentious, and the most challenging politically, of any during the government's 11 years in power

John Howard was in Washington for the ANZUS celebrations and met George W. Bush for the first time just one day before the 9/11 attacks. On the morning itself, the prime minister was working on official papers in his hotel when news of a passenger aircraft flying into New York's World Trade Centre came through.

Howard would then watch from his hotel window as columns of smoke began rising from the Pentagon building. By now, it was becoming clear this was an unprecedented assault on the American mainland. Almost 3000 people would die on that one morning.

Later that day, Howard spoke solemnly to the media:

> This is a very tragic day in the history of a great nation… the sense of horror I know is shared by all Australians here in Washington and I know will be shared by our fellow countrymen and women back home… We feel for our American friends. We will stand by them. We will help them. We will support actions they take to properly retaliate in relation to these acts of bastardry against their citizens and against what they stand for.

Downer was at home in Adelaide, late into the evening in Australia, when news came through of the emerging drama in New York. Downer was in his study watching *Lateline* on the ABC. Josh Frydenberg, then a senior adviser, phoned and spoke to Downer's wife, Nicky.

When Downer came to the phone, Frydenberg told him to turn over to CNN. Straight away. At first, as Downer listened to the commentary, and watched a plume of smoke seeping from the World Trade Centre towers, he thought this was just a story about a light aircraft accident. "It wasn't clear what had happened," says Downer.

But, as he and Nicky watched the live coverage, a second passenger aircraft struck. Then, the World Trade Centre towers began to topple. The full scale of the horror was unfolding before their eyes. "I knew then that this was one of the tragic events that changes the course of history ... which it was," Downer says. "That wasn't a brilliant insight on my part. That was a statement of the bleeding obvious..."

Downer was angry. "I couldn't help but think of all those people trapped in those buildings. It was horrific." Clearly, September 11 represented an attack on the US like no other.

In the immediate aftermath of the attacks, Howard was rushed to Andrews Air Base in Washington D.C., and put on board Air Force Two, the vice-president's aircraft, to get him safely back to Australia.

He was accompanied by the US Ambassador to Australia, Tom Schieffer — a close friend of Bush. During that flight, a call came through from Downer.

The Foreign Affairs Minister was anxious to speak to Howard. He had been giving a lot of thought to how Australia could respond meaningfully to demonstrate its support for its ally. To have this conversation with the PM, Downer had to step out from a meeting in the Adelaide Hills at the local council chambers at Mount Barker. He stood alone in a park as the connection was made.

"We had a long conversation," Howard recalls. "He said, 'Why don't we invoke ANZUS?' For the first time. It was Downer who first raised that with me. I agreed it was appropriate. I said, 'We might want to run it by the lawyers but it sounds pretty good to me'."

Article IV of the ANZUS Treaty, signed in 1951, commits both Australia and the US to come to the aid of each other to "meet the common danger". This would be the first time the Treaty provisions had been triggered in the history of the alliance.

"And so we did," says Howard. "And I went down the back of the plane where Tom Schieffer was, and he said, 'Gee, Prime Minister, that's pretty cool' or something to that effect. He was very touched by that."

As soon as Howard arrived back in Australia, the National Security Cabinet met, and approved what Howard and Downer put to them.

It may have been largely a symbolic gesture at the time but it would come to have direct and immediate real-world implications.

The US was always going to respond with elemental force to the al-Qaeda attack on its cities and people. Washington and its allies had little choice but to confront the security threat festering in the badlands of Afghanistan. As the War on Terror was unleashed, Australia would be there in support.

Says Howard:

> At a press conference on our Embassy grounds, before heading to Andrews Air Base, I said that we would give all appropriate support to America. I did that without any reference to Cabinet because I knew it was something everyone would agree with. And they did. I don't remember anyone complaining.

To some, this may have seemed a conflict occurring in a distant land, remote from Australia's direct interests. John Howard and Alexander Downer took a very different view. In successive fatwas, al-Qaeda's leader and chief financier, Osama bin Laden, had identified Australia as an enemy. Indeed, he had specified the Howard government's role in support of East Timor in 1999 as one of al-Qaeda's grievances.

According to this narrative, Australia had conspired to expropriate East Timor from "Muslim sovereignty". As the Bali bombings in 2002, and a terror attack on the Australian Embassy in Jakarta would later demonstrate, the radicals of al-Qaeda and their support networks of copycat terrorists in East Asia had declared Australians a target.

The Howard Government understood there could be no quarantining of the nation from the challenges and responsibilities of meeting this threat. Al-Qaeda bases in Afghanistan had to be destroyed, their Taliban protectors removed from power, and a global effort undertaken to confront the predatory, punitive and imperialistic ideology of the Islamist extremists.

Another point critics of the Howard Government's role in the 'global war on terror' seemed not always to grasp was that, although bin Laden and his followers celebrated loudly and grotesquely any successful strikes against Western interests, the real targets in their sights were the modernisers of the Muslim world — not just in the Arab heartlands, but also in South-East Asia.

A democratic Indonesia was becoming the very antithesis of all that al-Qaeda had come to represent. Similarly, countries such as Malaysia were eager players in global trade and investment, and active participants in the information revolution. These nations valued the importance of overseas education and other cross-cultural exchanges with the wider world. As such they posed a compelling counter-narrative to the medievalism of the Islamists — and their nostalgia for rule by Caliphate across the Muslim world.

For these reasons, the conflicts in Afghanistan, and later Iraq, would be pivotal to Australia's interests. The longer al-Qaeda and its ilk were able to survive and thrive in the heartlands of the Middle East and central Asia, the greater the threat to Australia's own region.

Once the extremists took the battle for hearts and minds to a new front, against mainstream Muslim leaders in South-East Asia — and that is exactly what they did — it was inevitable that the War on Terror would come to Australia's neighbourhood.

While Australia worked closely with the region to heighten co-operation in counter-terrorism and policing, the broader strategic imperative, in the view of the Howard Government, required that Australia support the US in confronting the threat directly at its source.

The deployments of US, Australian and NATO troops to Afghanistan in November, 2001, marked the beginning of a prolonged, gruelling struggle to rebuild, virtually from scratch, a country cursed by war, tribal and ethnic divisions, religious extremism, and dire poverty.

Over the next 20 years, Australia would send naval, air and land forces into battle in Afghanistan. Forty-one soldiers would die in the conflict. Many would suffer grievous wounds, both physically and mentally.

Two members of Australia's elite special forces would be awarded the Victoria Cross for gallantry. Some in the SAS would come home only to face accusations of war crimes. The war in Afghanistan would prove a tough and traumatic experience all round.

Visiting Australian forces in Afghanistan (Department of Defence Images)

In Oruzgan province, where Australian operations were centred, Australian forces would help build new schools, install infrastructure for fresh water supplies, and provide training in trades for the young.

Downer flew into Kabul in 2005 to visit Australian troops and meet local political leaders. It was a high-security operation, following only a day after a visit to Iraq. Both countries were still war zones. In Afghanistan, Hamid Karzai was the elected President, but the Taliban's insurgency persisted, and security in the capital remained fraught.

Downer was accompanied by a guard of SAS soldiers in plain clothes. They travelled to the city from a nearby air base in bulletproof Land Cruisers. One staffer in the convoy remembers the constant clicking of heavily-armed soldiers locking cartridges into assault rifles: "There were all sorts of baddies running around the place. Kabul was a mess."

Ultimately, despite almost two decades of investment, outside intervention could not deliver long-term peace, stability — or durable democratic processes — to Kabul or the provinces of Afghanistan.

While the last Australian combat troops were withdrawn in 2013, a rotation of Australian defence personnel would provide ongoing training and other support for another eight years.

Then, at the end of August, 2021, almost exactly 20 years after the 9/11 attacks on the US, the Biden Administration would order the hasty withdrawal of all US forces from Afghanistan. Biden sought to justify the decision by declaring it the end of "a forever war."

Twenty years is a long time for the US and other nations to invest in the effort to liberate Afghanistan. The political and financial costs — and, most painfully of all, the sacrifice of lives — were prohibitive.

Yet, for all the tragedy and trauma of the Afghanistan deployment, Downer considered Biden's decision a grave strategic error.

In his view, pulling out US forces, and effectively clearing the way for a return of the Taliban, sent entirely the wrong signal at precisely the wrong moment. It represented a demonstration to the world — allies and enemies alike — of a lack of resolve and willpower in Washington.

As Downer would reflect in the *Australian Financial Review* a week after the US withdrawal:

> It's said the Taliban used to say to the Americans: 'You've got the watches, we have the time'.
>
> I thought about that watching President Joe Biden's press conference … when he defiantly justified his decision to pull all American troops out of Afghanistan. It followed harrowing pictures of desperate Afghans clinging to a US Air Force C17 as it spirited the lucky few to a faraway airbase. Those scenes will be forever with us, along with the helicopter leaving the American embassy in Saigon on April 30, 1975.
>
> These were terrible events: moments of great humiliation and defeat for a great nation which has been the bastion of liberalism and freedom throughout modern history.
>
> Now there is an awful question hanging over America. Has it lost its unifying national values, which were the foundation

of its very existence, and has it lost its will to lead the world? I passionately hope not. But I fear they may have.

In a more pragmatic moment, Downer acknowledges that all wars must end either in victory or defeat, or through a negotiated ceasefire:

> It would have made sense to have a negotiated ceasefire with a power-sharing structure in place, which would obviously have to include the Taliban but also the democratic forces, My criticism (of the Biden Administration) is that they just cut and run. I don't think you should ever do that. If you decide to go into a war, you need to win it — you need to achieve your objectives.
>
> I don't think it would have mattered too much to the Americans and the West if the Taliban had been part of a power-sharing arrangement, even though the Taliban were a creation of the Pakistani intelligence services. My recollection, going back to 2021, is that the Taliban support was running at about 20 per cent (of the population). They had plenty of support so it wasn't unreasonable to expect them to be part of a power-sharing arrangement.

According to Downer, this would have been an outcome very different to the scenes of abject surrender that followed the sudden departure of US troops. Taliban militants stormed back into power with little resistance, re-establishing a repressive system of state control.

To Downer, this was repugnant. The fight to defend freedom and democracy is fundamental to his philosophy — intrinsic to his DNA.

In the darkest days of the 1940s, Downer's parents had been part of Australia's struggle during the Pacific War to defend its own freedoms from the threat of invasion. His father was lucky to survive that war.

That they and millions of others had put their lives on the line to protect Australia's democracy — and the rights of all Australians to live freely — had a profound impact on his thinking.

This serves as one explanation for the deep roots of Alexander Downer's commitment to the ethos of freedom.

4

In Their Footsteps

Alexander Downer's mother, Mary, served as a truck driver for the Australian Army during World War 2. She enlisted on the day of her 18th birthday in 1942. After learning how to manoeuvre a General Motors truck, she was posted from Adelaide to Perth to work for a searchlight battalion.

Her job in the early months of 1943 was as designated driver for one of the mobile searchlight units that would patrol up and down the coastline near the Western Australian capital, on the alert for any Japanese bomber squadrons headed south. Darwin had been bombed a year earlier. Singapore had fallen. The American fleet at Pearl Harbour had been all but destroyed. The fear across the port cities of Australia was that more attacks would come.

In an oral history interview recorded in 2014 for the University of South Australia, only months before she died in London, Lady Downer said she felt compelled to volunteer: "My brothers had all been in the Army so I thought the Army would be the one for me. I had to do something. I didn't think I could sit around and do nothing. My parents were sad. When I went interstate, my mother was very upset."

She was part of a group of young women recruits who were put on a train. They slept on the carriage floor. All they knew was that they were westward-bound. Mary Downer spent the next 18 months in slapdash barracks just south of the port of Fremantle.

Like the Downers, Mary had come from an old Adelaide family. Unlike the Downers, her family had almost nothing to do with politics. She didn't meet Alexander Downer's father, Alick, until 1946 — although her older brothers knew him. What she did know from their stories was that this young man was having a horrible war.

Alick Downer was an accomplished lawyer, graduating from Oxford with honours in law. He was called to the Bar at London's auspicious Inner Temple. But his trajectory to the top of the legal profession was interrupted by the global conflict engulfing Europe and the Pacific.

He enlisted as a gunner with the Australian infantry in 1940, and was sent to British headquarters in Singapore. When British defences collapsed in February, 1942, unable to halt the southward surge of the Imperial Japanese Army, Downer was captured and would spend almost four years as a prisoner of war in the brutality of Changi.

These were grim and gruelling times for the Downers, as they were for many millions of people. As Mary learned to crank up an old diesel generator to power a two-metre diameter searchlight she and her team hauled around Fremantle, Alick Downer had to survive on the brink of starvation at a disease-ridden prison camp in occupied Singapore — a camp from which 7,000 fellow Australians would never come home.

In that context, it is perhaps understandable Alexander Downer would grow weary of hearing himself described by political opponents as a child of privilege. In those war years, his parents did the hardest of yards. Whether from prominent families or not, the greatest privilege throughout those awful moments in human history was just to survive.

After Alick returned from Singapore, he met Mary at a cocktail party at the famously elegant "South" hotel in inner-city Adelaide in July, 1946. He was 15 years older than her. He didn't talk about his Changi experience. "I don't think many of them did really," Mary recalled in her interview with historian, Dr Kiera Lindsey, for the University of South Australia archives. Mary found Alick Downer handsome and charming. They married within a year. One of his fellow POWs at Changi, an Anglican priest, Aubrey Payne, officiated.

The marriage lasted 34 years, through to Alick's death in 1981.

They brought up their four children in comfortable, secure surroundings in Adelaide and, for a decade, London. Alexander Downer himself considers his biggest advantage in life as being the unconditional love of his parents for him and his three sisters.

His family connections also meant that, from a young age, he was immersed in the history, culture and ethos of the Liberal Party. Alongside John Howard, Alexander Downer by the 2020s was able to stake claim to being the only living Liberals to have met every leader of the party from Robert Menzies through to Sussan Ley.

"I met Menzies many times," he told his eldest daughter, Georgina, in an extended interview recorded for the Robert Menzies Institute, the library and museum at Melbourne University dedicated to the memory of Australia's longest-serving Prime Minister. "My father was one of his ministers and they had a very close friendship. As a relatively small child, I remember him coming to stay with us in the Adelaide Hills."

Downer can recall the cigar fumes billowing from his father's study whenever Menzies was at their home. Often, this coincided with the Adelaide Test. He remembers the echoes of that deep, sonorous voice that was a Menzies trademark: "He was a very kindly man. Much more of a people's person than you might imagine. He was a very grand figure, of course. Very friendly and personable … but also a bit intimidating. He was a master of words, and he had this great knowledge of the history of Western civilisation."

Occasionally, Downer would be taken to Canberra by his father during summer school holidays:

> As a child, I would go around to The Lodge and play cricket with Robert Menzies' nephew. The PM would come home for lunch and watch us play. I don't remember him ever bowling a ball at us but he was always fascinated by cricket.
>
> I can also remember him coming to see us in the UK, when my father was High Commissioner and Menzies had been appointed the Lord Warden of the Cinque Ports. We went down to Woolmer Castle and had lunch there with him and Dame Patti.

The interview with his daughter, part of her *Afternoon Light* podcast series, provides glimpses of an Alexander Downer not always seen or heard publicly. Georgina, a former diplomat and lawyer who became CEO of the Robert Menzies Institute, invites her father to reflect on the learnings of his early life: the politics of the times; the influence of his family history in shaping his outlook; the development of his own political values. She probes carefully, and sometimes very acutely.

It can be fascinating to hear a political leader interrogated by a son or daughter about their life. There is no time wasted on artifice or theatrics. Direct questions are answered candidly, unreservedly.

While the subject matter is serious, it can resemble the free-flowing chatter — a sharing of knowledge and swapping of opinions — that many parents and adult children might have around a kitchen table. In the podcast, Georgina encourages her dad to delve into his innermost understanding of how and why he came to be the person he is.

Alexander as a 10-year-old with his father (News Ltd/ Newspix)

Downer remembers the Menzies era as, essentially, a time of stability and certainty:

> That's how I perceived it, as a child. All seemed well with the world. There was that sense Bob Menzies knew what he was doing and that a lot could just be left to him... There was steady growth, rising home ownership, rising living standards, a steady immigration program and growing population. On the whole, an extraordinarily harmonious and increasingly prosperous society ...
>
> I don't think, in my lifetime, any Prime Minister has given the country a greater sense of stability and comfort.

But he admits also that society back then was less demanding of its political leadership: "I don't think people were anything like as questioning of the government as they are today. Nothing like as contentious as today. I think society was a good deal calmer."

In an interview for this book, Downer elaborates:

> The worst that's been said about the Menzies era by people like Paul Keating is that these were the Rip Van Winkle years. Our country just slept through it. Well, what was the country meant to have been doing? What would they wish it to have been? A country in turmoil, in vicious debate, in constant conflict. Well, it wasn't like that. It was a country of steady but extraordinary achievement... full employment throughout that entire period...
>
> There were many in the Labor Party who were quite enthusiastic about the idea of state intervention and state control. So it wasn't as if that wasn't part of the public agenda. But people were substantially less educated than they are today and, as a function of that, they may have been less questioning, more ready to accept the authority of a leader rather than challenging everything they did. The media was very different, and we didn't have social media, of course. We had newspapers and radio. And television.
>
> My parents wouldn't buy a television for many, many years — it wasn't until 1972 that we had a television in our house. My parents thought television would not be good for the children. I'm not sure that's turned out to be the case.

Downer makes clear he did not share all the political views of his parents. Downer the elder, while forward-looking on social reform, was an economic protectionist, who believed fervently in tariff walls to protect local industry. Downer the younger was an economic rationalist, who preferred to call himself a "Progressive Conservative."

"The notion of being a conservative sounds reactionary," he says in an interview for this book. "That all you want to do is conserve things as they are. I never thought that. Everything changes. We all know that.

"Society needs to adapt to changing needs, changing demands .. and to changing fashions… at our best, and this is a very hazardous undertaking, we need to try to anticipate changes that might occur in the future so that we are prepared for them.

"So, in that sense, I would be a progressive conservative. I don't believe at all in changing things for the sake of change. If something is working well, and is likely to continue to work well, then leave it alone. But always be ready to adapt to changing circumstances."

Downer is miffed that the word 'progressive' more recently has been occupied like a house squat by the political Left: "They used to call themselves socialists. When they discovered that wasn't popular with the punters… they co-opted the word 'progressive'. Which is a pity."

Downer has no doubt that his parents helped shaped his political values — but not in the sense of direct hand-me-downs or a slavish mimicry of their ideas. "I would have disagreed with my father on some things and not others. He was surprisingly liberal on social issues for his day. He understood people had different lifestyles and preferences. My mother was much the same. She used to quote that cliché, 'it takes all sorts to make the world'. You would never hear them denouncing categories of people on the basis of sexual preference, or race, or identity."

Downer says his family also instilled in him a sense of public duty: not the high-minded, haughty concept of *noblesse oblige* but something more prosaic — a basic sense of civic obligation. "Through my family, I grew up believing in the value of public service," he reflects.

"If you went into Parliament, and became a good MP, there was virtue in that because of what you could contribute to the community. I say that because, nowadays, people don't see becoming a politician or MP or a Cabinet minister as particularly meritorious. The reputation of politics or politicians has declined. Not because (the standards) of politics or politicians have necessarily declined. But public attitudes and public expectations have changed so much. ..."

Downer says he was taught as a child that devoting yourself to making money was not, of itself, an admirable pursuit:

> It might be better to have money than not to have money, but, in my family, it was not seen as a definition of success. A nice thing to have but not a definition of great success. Service to the nation was the definition of great success.

Self-evidently, the Downers were never fire-breathing revolutionaries:

> It was a family that was happy with the way society was evolving — recognising, of course, that things change and that things sometimes need to change. Some people grow up with a sense of discontent with society, because of their family circumstances. Whereas I grew up thinking society worked pretty well, for all of its flaws....

So did Downer consider himself privileged? "Critics use the term 'privilege' because they tend to value money more than anything else," he says. "We had plenty of money but we were not super-rich. We could afford private schools and holidays. But I think the greatest privilege was loving parents. In that sense, I was very privileged.

"Both of our parents loved all four of us. And that gave us confidence as human beings. We grew up in a stable environment."

He believes this strong sense of security across his childhood years served as a springboard for his later achievements in public life.

Alexander Downer arrived in Canberra in 1984 as an elected federal parliamentarian for South Australia — as his father had done 35 years earlier, and his grandfather more than 80 years earlier.

Even as a junior Opposition backbencher, in his early thirties, Downer came to the Parliament with deeper knowledge and experience of international diplomacy and the politics of the Western alliance than all but a handful of members of the Hawke Labor Government.

After graduating from the University of Newcastle, in northern England, Downer would return to Australia in 1975 after more than a decade of living in Britain. But for one summer holiday in his teens, it was the first return to his homeland since 1964. "I was not all that familiar with my own country," he recalls.

His first job was as an economist with the international division of Westpac Bank in Sydney's Martin Place. This helped provide some policy breadth, giving him keen insights into the needs of business, and an understanding of the policy settings required to attract inward investment to Australian at a time when global capital was becoming increasingly footloose and tariff walls were beginning to topple. Then, he joined the Department of Foreign Affairs and Trade in Canberra.

Bill Farmer, a veteran diplomat — who would later serve as Australia's Ambassador or High Commissioner in Indonesia, Malaysia and PNG — was Downer's first boss at DFAT.

In 1976, he was in charge of training the Department's new intake of diplomatic cadets. He was impressed by Downer's talents: "He was very bright, full of ideas, and very direct and upfront. Not one to hide his light under a bushel."

But when Farmer compiled his assessment report at the end of that year, there would be one significant caveat amidst the praise. Farmer wrote: "Downer has the capacity to be the best diplomat of his generation — but he will need to control a tendency to bumptiousness."

Downer has a long memory. Almost 20 years later, he would arrive in Port Moresby as the shadow Minister for Foreign Affairs. Bill Farmer, by now Australia's High Commissioner in Papua New Guinea, was there to meet him at the airport. So were other senior colleagues from the High Commission.

Downer had apparently come with a prank in mind. He would deliver a display of 'bumptiousness' on steroids. He walked straight up to Farmer and unleashed an intemperate spray: "When I am foreign minister, you are finished, finished — finished!"

The DFAT staff looked sideways at each other. But Farmer knew Downer — and his offbeat sense of humour: "I said, 'Well, that's an amusing introduction — would you like to elaborate on that?"

Downer maintained his veneer of furious indignation: "I will never forget the things you wrote about me in my training years…"

Farmer knew Downer was joking but played along. "Well, I remember exactly what I said, and I would stick by that judgment…"

Downer continued the wind-up: "And that is why you're finished…"

Both broke into laughter.

In 1977, Downer's career in diplomacy began with a posting to the Australian mission to the European Union in Brussels.

In 1978, he married British broadcast journalist Nicola Robinson (Nicky), who he had met while at university.

During the Brussels posting, Alexander took leave briefly to return with Nicky to her family home in Chesterfield, England, where Nicky gave birth to their eldest child, Georgina.

At the outset of his DFAT career, Downer came under the tutelage of Jim Plimsoll (later Sir James Plimsoll), a legend of Australian diplomacy. Plimsoll would arrive as Ambassador to the European Union in Brussels during Downer's posting there.

Downer was a 26-year-old junior officer. But, soon enough, Plimsoll had earmarked him as an emerging talent and set about fast-tracking his real-world understanding of how dealings between nations worked.

"He was a great mentor to me," Downer says, in an interview for this book. "He had been Ambassador to Washington, Ambassador to Moscow, Ambassador to the UN. And I suppose I became something like a private secretary to him. I travelled around Europe with him.

"We would go to the European Parliament in Strasbourg, to meetings in Paris. He was a wonderful person. Fascinated by politics. He taught me all about what a good ambassador should be. He was a great networker and such a strong intellect. He had a massive knowledge base. And he was able to influence people who mattered to Australia."

This posting gave Downer access to the thinking of the major Western powers as they worked through the challenges of Cold War jostling with the Soviets. On this, he had the benefits of expert tuition — Plimsoll knew the contours of the Cold War as well as almost anyone.

"I think he is probably Australia's greatest-ever diplomat. Nobody comes close. He knew everybody," says Downer. "He knew Richard Nixon. He knew Leonid Brezhnev. He knew all these people, right back to Richard Casey as foreign minister."

One thing Downer owes to Plimsoll is his love of opera. Plimsoll gifted him a copy of Kobbe's *History of Opera*. Twice, Downer has sat through Wagner's four-opera 'ring cycle'. Once in Brisbane, once in Bayreuth. A true test of stamina and commitment for the opera buff.

With Plimsoll's guidance, Downer would spend his working days engaging with EU politicians and officials. He was also assigned a role of liaising with officials of the North Atlantic Treaty Organisation in Luxembourg and Rome.

"I was always very interested in politics," Downer says. "That was one of the things I enjoyed about Brussels — meeting all of the politicians and the Australian ministers as they came through."

In 1977, a young John Howard travelled to Europe on his first official duties overseas as a junior minister in the Fraser Government. He arrived in Brussels as the Minister for Special Trade Negotiations.

There, at a reception, he met an even younger diplomat "who had a lot of opinions". In an interview for this book, Howard remembers Downer bouncing around excitedly and enthusiastically — "almost a puppy-like quality," Howard laughs.

At the time, one of Downer's colleagues, Roger Pescott, was First Secretary at the mission in Brussels. He would go on to become a senior minister in the Kennett Liberal Government in Victoria.

"It was interesting, when you look back on it," says Downer. "John Howard came over and must have spent 15 minutes just chatting to Roger and me. As it turned out, we both became politicians. And John Howard and I ran into each other for the rest of our lives."

Downer returned to Australia in 1980. He worked in the OECD-EC economic policy division in Canberra. He found the bureaucracy and paper-shuffling far less exhilarating than his time with Plimsoll: "I had loved my job in Brussels. It was a fantastic job and I had a rails run."

At that time, he renewed acquaintances with Bill Farmer. Their wives, Elaine and Nicky, became close friends at their children's play group. Downer was beginning to acquaint himself with the reality that the joys of raising a young family would involve trade-offs, personal sacrifices — of having to compromise on things like his love of sporty cars.

"When I was in Brussels, as a diplomat, you were able to buy cars tax-free and bring them back to Australia at the end of your posting," he recalls. "I had this Porsche 924. It was metallic green.

"I loved this car. But it was a small car and not very practical when it came to children. So when (his second daughter) Olivia was born,

I had to trade in the Porsche. I was quite sad about that. We got this Volvo instead. I didn't much like the Volvo."

By now, Downer was also looking for new opportunities. His hankering for a career in politics began to crystallise.

Downer had been honing his skills. At university, he had been co-chair of the Politics Society and vice-chairman of Newcastle University's Conservative Association. He was on a debating team that ran second to Dublin's Trinity College in an inter-University debating competition. His partner in the debates was Mike Foley, the leader of the university's Labor Club. "I was a Tory, he was Labour. He was gay, I was straight. Mike and I got on really well, and we were a good team."

In 1980, Prime Minister Malcolm Fraser appointed a South Australian MP, John McLeay, as Consul-General to Los Angeles. This meant a by-election would be held for the federal seat of Boothby, in suburban Adelaide.

Against his father's advice, Downer nominated for pre-selection. He ran second in a field of 15 to Steele Hall, a former SA Premier who had returned to the Liberal Party after leading his own political movement.

Soon after, Downer's father fell gravely ill. Downer, Nicky and their children returned to Adelaide so they could be with the family.

He took a job in the economic development division of the South Australian Premier's Department. After Sir Alick's death, Downer became even more determined to pursue the family tradition and look for further opportunities to try his hand at politics.

A year later, he ran for pre-selection for the seat of Bragg in the South Australian Parliament — again, he came second. "That was a near-miss," he grins. "I'm not sure I would have enjoyed state politics."

Undeterred, he took a job as a political staffer working in the office of Prime Minister Malcolm Fraser.

After the defeat of the Fraser Government in 1983, Downer applied successfully for the role as executive director-designate of the Australian Chamber of Commerce and Industry, a leading peak industry group. He and Nicky moved their young family to Canberra.

It was a well-paid job. The family lived in comfort in the suburb of Deakin. "We had a nice house, two children, a dog. I've known Canberra all my life. We knew a lot of people. Had a lot of friends."

Downer was able to reinvest in his choice of car to get around the ring roads of the national capital — a classic V8 Jensen Interceptor: "We had a nice life there."

Then came an unexpected opening for another shot at politics.

The new Hawke Labor Government chose to legislate a significant increase in the number of seats in the federal Parliament. Two new seats would be created in South Australia: Makin and Mayo.

Mayo would encompass the town and villages of the Adelaide Hills, where Downer had spent most of his childhood. It overlapped with parts of his father's old electorate of Angas.

This time, Downer would win the support of local Liberals, and set himself on the path to his career in federal politics. In preparation for the 1984 election, he resigned from ACCI and took up a role as adviser to Andrew Peacock, then Leader of the Opposition.

Peacock lost that 1984 election to Hawke, despite achieving a 1.5 per cent swing against a first-term Labor Government. But, in Downer's electorate, the Liberal victory was emphatic. He was elected by a thumping two-party-preferred margin of 12.5 percent. He would be the first MP for Mayo — and would remain so for the next 24 years.

At only 33, Downer's was an impressive CV. Shrewder Labor judges might have been apprehensive about the intellectual heft someone like that might bring over time to the big policy debates.

So they went after him pre-emptively on what they saw as his greatest vulnerability — that he was, in their eyes, a blueblood. In the raucous, percussive bullring of Australian politics, Downer had to endure ceaseless mocking over his political pedigree. The taunts from Labor Prime Minister Paul Keating, one of the more pugnacious political street fighters, came thick and fast.

Downer's fellow South Australian, Labor Senator Chris Schacht, was another of his noisiest tormentors: "He is the last vestige of 18th century Australian aristocracy — he was brought up in the Adelaide Hills (on) 200 acres, deer running around ... his mother won the preselection for him."

While the notion of a class divide in Australia has never been as acute as in Britain or Europe, political opponents could not resist the temptation to portray Downer as a silver spooner: as someone who could not empathise with the strugglers in society; as someone out of touch with the preoccupations of everyday working families.

It was a tried and tested formula for the Labor Party. They had played the "class envy" card, more or less effectively, against most Liberal leaders. Keating had described Robert Menzies, no less, as a "dreadful fop", and a "vacuous dandy".

In the 1970s, it was Prime Minister, Malcolm Fraser, the son of a prominent farming family in Western Victoria, who was targeted. As Geoffrey Barker would write in *The Australian Financial Review*: "Malcolm Fraser was too easily caricatured as the towering born-to-rule Tory grazier with the granite face and the disdainful view of those who did not enjoy his social and economic privileges. In fact, Australia's 22nd prime minister was a paradoxical and complex politician…"

In the 1980s, the urbane Andrew Peacock would also be teased about his affluent, cosmopolitan lifestyle. Keating sought to mock the Liberal leader as "a painted, perfumed gigolo" — and would deliver the legendary political put-down: "Can a soufflé rise twice?"

Having worked for both Fraser and Peacock, Downer knew what was coming. In a society that assigns a high cultural value to the principle of egalitarianism, inheritance can be a burden as much as a blessing.

In rural Australia, there had been a lingering class divide rooted in 19th century struggles between wealthy squatters with sheep and cattle runs extending across vast stretches of the countryside — and new settlers seeking small plots of land they could call their own.

This manifested in resistance to, and resentment of, the social dominance of the gentry, the patricians — the landed elite.

This wasn't Downer's lineage. Yet it was true that he had come from a prominent family with a background of relative affluence.

Downer completed his early schooling at Geelong Grammar. As a teenager, while his father served as Australia's High Commissioner at the Court of St James, he boarded at the elite Radley College in the UK.

For his tertiary education, Downer studied politics and economics at the University of Newcastle.

The university boasted many notable Brits among its alumni,

including the renowned architect, Sir Terry Farrell, BBC war correspondent, Kate Adie, and the comedian Rowan Atkinson. But it was not especially known as an institution dominated by Britain's social elites.

Many years later, Downer would meet Atkinson at a speedway outside London. They were fellow "petrol-heads". Downer ranks Atkinson's *Blackadder* as his all-time favourite TV show: "I thanked him for all the joy he had given me."

The "born to purple" mantra hurled endlessly at Downer by Keating, among others, was a bit overblown — not to say hypocritical. After all, didn't Labor in Canberra boast its fair share of political dynasties?

Frontbenchers Kim Beazley and Simon Crean were both sons of prominent federal MPs, as was Lance Barnard, Whitlam's deputy PM. All had been talented and effective politicians. All had worked hard to make it to the top. So had Alexander Downer.

As veteran Press Gallery correspondent, Tony Wright, would later observe, Downer went on to prove himself a far more formidable force in Australian politics than his critics would ever have predicted. In a column in the *Sydney Morning Herald,* Wright wrote:

> His political foes saw Downer as splendid sport: a sort of throw-back to the foppish drones of Evelyn Waugh's *Brideshead Revisited,* minus the Catholicism (Downers are, of course, Anglican). In doing so, those who sought to lampoon him also underestimated him.

John Howard, a product of the state school system, agrees. He thinks the ridicule from the Labor side had a lot to do with Downer's clipped accent. "Look, he lived for 10 years in Britain," says the former Prime Minister. "He went to Radley College. His wife's British …"

As the Australian poet, Judith Beveridge, once wrote evocatively:

"A place will seep into the voice of any local…."

Howard always considered the taunting of Downer puerile: "I mean, he was called a toff, and this, that and the other."

Howard remembers being particularly incensed the day Keating made a remark about Downer's father, Alick. "I just exploded. 'Don't you know he was in Changi. As a prisoner of war?'

"I think Keating's great mentor, Tom Uren (a champion of NSW's

Labor Left, and also a former POW) would have been just as annoyed. The Downers were a hard-working, patriotic family, like millions of others. There was nothing silver-spooned about it. It's just an easy sledge."

Howard never met Alick Downer — "we were of a different political generation". But he has fond memories of Downer's mother, Mary:

> Not long after the 2004 election, Alexander became our longest-serving foreign minister. I invited him and Nicky, his mum and his four children to a dinner at Kirribilli House.
>
> We had a very pleasant night. Mary had some practised vulgarisms (from her army days). She was a real character. That's where he gets his slightly outrageous sense of humour.

Sir Alick Downer (National Library of Australia)

Sir John Downer, one of the fathers of Federation

In the Parliament, there was no point in Downer becoming indignant about attempts to ridicule his personal and political background. In any case, he was proud of his family's contribution to the history of South Australia and the nation: "Our family have been nation builders. We've helped to make this nation great. You can abuse us and criticise us and we'll take it … because nation-building is in our blood."

In this assertion, Downer had history on his side.

For the truth is, there can be no meaningful history of politics in Australia that does not include reference to the inter-generational contribution of the Downer family.

His family history was distinguished — albeit from modest beginnings.

The first Downer to arrive in Australia, Alexander's paternal great-grandfather, Henry, was a Navy tailor from Portsmouth.

He and his wife, Jane, raised a daughter and five sons in South Australia, after arriving in the infant colony in 1838. Henry would set up a grocery store on Adelaide's Hindley St.

Downer's maternal great-grandfather was the surveyor and explorer, William Christie Gosse. This, too, was hardly a line of work for the pampered or faint-hearted. Many adventurers had trudged off into the dizzying heat of Australia's parched interior, never to return.

In 1873, Gosse would lead an expedition on horses and camels seeking to map the lands between Alice Springs and Perth. During the journey, he became the first European to climb Uluru, the iconic sandstone monolith in the desert heart of Australia. Gosse would name it Ayer's Rock — controversially, as it would later turn out. He did this in the company of an Afghani camel-driver, Khamran, and an Indigenous boy they called Moses.

Ultimately, Gosse failed in his mission to get all the way to Perth. There was not enough food or water for the horses. They were falling ill after eating spinifex plants sprouting from the desert sand dunes. The expedition had to turn back to Charlotte Waters.

It was Downer's grandfather, Sir John Downer, who first brought distinction to the family name. In his day, John Downer was among Australia's pre-eminent lawyers and political leaders. He was a twice-elected colonial Premier of SA who became a central figure in the federation debates of the 1890s.

He would become one of the lead drafters of the nation's birth certificate, the Constitution of the new Commonwealth of Australia, and one of the nation's first senators. He was also an early champion of women's rights and opposed a racially-based immigration policy.

John Downer achieved this as a self-made man. Not unlike Menzies, his rise to prominence happened only because he was talented enough to win a scholarship that created a pathway to university and the law.

Downer never knew his grandfather. John Downer died in 1915, when Downer's father, Alick, was a small child:

> He didn't have any influence on me except through

my father. And given my father was only five when my grandfather died, he would have had limited influence on him. What I would say is that he was a nation-builder...

He invested a good deal of his time in the creation of a workable federation in Australia. He was one of the three drafters of the Constitution, a Constitution that has lasted incredibly well. It's a document that has been able to adapt to changing eras without radical upheaval. He also had a role in the irrigation of the Murray riverlands, and in securing property rights for married women. So he was clearly a very substantial figure...

Downer tells of how his grandfather left federal politics and returned from Melbourne to South Australia, disillusioned, after his friend, Sir Edmund Barton, was unable to deliver on a commitment to appoint Downer to the High Court bench. "Politics brings with it quite a lot of disappointment as well as exhilaration," Downer concedes.

Despite the lessons of John Downer's experience, Alick Downer would follow him into law and politics. On returning to Australia from the prisoner of war camp in Singapore, he entered Parliament in 1949.

Although pigeon-holed as a conservative Tory, Alick Downer became a critical player in the postwar reassessment of relations with Japan — and in the dismantling of the White Australia Policy, and its replacement by one of the world's most open immigration programs.

For all that, Alick Downer never sought to hide his connections to high society. He raised his family in the stately Arbury Park mansion in the Adelaide Hills, a property built loosely in the style of an English estate.

Sometimes, he would drive the streets of Adelaide in a Rolls-Royce.

When Alexander and his sisters questioned their father over whether this might raise a few eyebrows in the electorate, Alick Downer was untroubled: "Anyone who really cares what sort of car I drive is unlikely to be voting for me anyway."

As a twelve-year-old, in 1964, Alexander Downer was taken by his parents to the christening in London of the firstborn son of one of his father's close mates, a British aristocrat, Johnnie Althorp.

At the time, the Downer family were living at Stoke House, the residence of the Australian High Commissioner in Britain. Downer's father and Johnnie had both served in World War 2. They had become friends when Johnnie came from England to work in Adelaide in 1947.

Alick Downer was asked to be the baby's godfather. The godmother would be the baby's 'Aunt Lillibet'—otherwise known as Her Majesty, Queen Elizabeth II.

The service was held in the exquisite Henry VII chapel at Westminster Abbey. The child was christened Charles Edward Morris Spencer. He would become Viscount Althorp, later the 9th Earl Spencer — and, today, one of Britain's better known authors and podcasters.

Alexander Downer has only hazy memories of the pageantry of the occasion. He recalls it as an unusually hot summer's day for London.

During the hymns, he felt woozy, as if about to faint. One of the Queen's ladies-in-waiting came to his rescue, producing some smelling salts to clear his head.

But one thing Downer does remember from that day is that Charles Spencer's three-year-old sister, Diana, didn't make it to the service. She had hurt her hand in an accident at home.

Almost 34 years later, Alexander Downer, as the Australian Minister for Foreign Affairs, would return to Westminster Abbey — as the nation's official representative at the funeral of Diana, after her tragic death in Paris at the age of 36. More than two billion people worldwide would watch the televised coverage of the funeral service.

Downer had met Diana several times at official functions: not as Lady Di, as she was popularly known; but later, as Diana, Princess of Wales.

He doesn't pretend to have known her well.

But he remembers sitting in the surrounds of the Cabinet room in Canberra when the message came through from the Department of Foreign Affairs about funeral arrangements in London following the death of the princess.

The protocols issued by Buckingham Palace, via the British Foreign Office, were explicit: Commonwealth nations could send foreign ministers to the service — heads of government would not be invited.

Downer read the note to his colleagues. The Prime Minister seemed a touch disgruntled: "I'm not sure the Australian public will like that."

Downer didn't flinch: "I think they'll get over it."

5

THE LONG, HARD ROAD TO POWER

There is little scope for sentiment in the hard school of Australian politics. It is a world of swirling constellations of power, where allegiances between ambitious people can wax and wane. Lasting friendships can and do exist — but never absent the risk that rivalry or betrayal might transform an old friend into a new enemy.

As John Howard once said of the strategy of his Liberal colleagues in plotting the internal coup in 1989 that dumped him as leader in favour of Andrew Peacock: "You had to give them 10 out of 10 for guile."

Through their years in government, John Howard and Alexander Downer became as close as any on the non-Labor side of politics. Says Howard:

> Downer and I found our views were very similar. I was involved in a few ballots (as a leadership contender) and I always had the impression he cast a few ballots in my favour. We were good friends. He wasn't antagonistic to (Howard's fierce rival) Andrew Peacock or to anybody else. But we were good friends.
>
> I liked his sense of humour. It would get him into trouble. Terrible trouble. But he had a capacity to say what a lot of people were thinking and weren't game to say.

The story of Howard and Downer's relationship as political allies is well known to anyone with a passing interest in Australian political history.

Howard succeeded in his long struggle to become Prime Minister only after Downer agreed to step down as Opposition Leader in 1995, and bequeath the job to Howard in a bloodless transition.

Years later, Howard remained generous in declaring what that self-sacrifice said about Downer's character: "He behaved magnificently and he really did put the interests of the Liberal Party ahead of his own feelings. It's something I never forgot in the years that followed."

It wasn't the first time Downer had agreed to take a hit for the team. In 1987, after serving only one term in federal Parliament, Downer was approached about surrendering his South Australian seat of Mayo so the Liberals could recruit to their front bench — and, potentially, to the party leadership — a heavy hitter from outside the Parliament.

Ian McLachlan was thought to be one candidate who might provide that horsepower. The former head of the National Farmers' Federation had a lot of backing from corporate Australia, where Liberal support had been flagging. It was hoped that bringing him into the Parliament would help boost fund-raising for the next federal election campaign. "The Liberal Party was on the bones of its arse," Downer explains.

As it turned out, McLachlan knocked back the offer of Mayo. He would eventually contest successfully the rural seat of Barker in SA, and would later serve a term as a Defence Minister for the Howard Government before leaving politics altogether.

But the party's fortunes would not be turned around quickly. The Liberals were left in disarray after the disastrous collapse of Howard's first campaign for the prime ministership in the 1987 federal election. Coalition unity fractured in the midst of the bizarre and disruptive "Joh-for-PM" push — a campaign by then Queensland Premier, Joh Bjelke-Petersen, to storm into power in Canberra.

Downer was at that time a young, ambitious junior shadow minister, eager to make his mark. He had impressed Howard, as party leader. In 1988, Howard was planning to bring a Matter of Public Importance to the House of Representatives, attacking the Hawke Government over economic management. He invited Downer to speak in support.

This was a big deal for Downer. But there were complications — major complications — on the home front.

Nicky Downer was nearing the full term of her pregnancy with their third daughter, Henrietta (Hetty). On the Sunday evening, with Alexander packing his bags and preparing to fly from Adelaide to Canberra for the parliamentary sittings, Nicky confided, "I think the baby might be coming very soon."

The baby was not due for another week or more. But Nicky's instincts were telling her that the baby had its own schedule. "I have this feeling," she told her husband. Either Alexander wasn't convinced or he wasn't really listening. He was excited by the idea of taking part in an important economic debate in the Parliament.

Alexander reassured Nicky that they had at least a few days to go before the birth was likely. He boarded his flight to Canberra. It would prove a salutary lesson in balancing work priorities and family responsibilities — almost never an easy thing for federal MPs.

Not long after he touched down in Canberra, the late-night call came through from Kerry Minchin, the wife of another up-and-coming Liberal from SA, Senator Nick Minchin. She had been phoned by Nicky Downer and had taken her to hospital — the baby was on its way. Downer knew he had to get home in a hurry. But he could not get a flight until first thing the next morning. As it turned out, he ended up missing out on the MPI — and the birth of a daughter.

Today, Downer admits it was not an edifying moment. His eagerness to perform on the big stage — his ambition — had got the better of him. "The baby seems reasonably forgiving of me for that," he says.

Leading into the next election, in 1990, the Liberals under Andrew Peacock made up much of the ground they had lost to the Hawke Labor Government. The Coalition would win the two party preferred vote, and Labor would lose nine seats in Peacock's home state of Victoria. Having pushed Labor close in two elections, Peacock decided his race was run — he would resign the Liberal leadership in favour of a young economics professor, John Hewson.

Then, in 1993, Paul Keating's wrecking-ball tactics against the Liberals' ambitious *Fightback* manifesto for economic reform — particularly his unrelenting assault on a proposal for a 15 per cent broad-based goods-and-services tax — would restore a comfortable Labor majority.

"The launch of *Fightback* was initially applauded by the public," says Downer. "But it was then dissected quite effectively by the Labor Party and its fellow travellers — and poorly defended, I guess, by John Hewson. People like Peter Reith and John Howard and Peter Costello… we all made a huge effort to defend it … but over time, the public became anxious about it. So our position in the polls began to decline.

"We went into the 1993 election with a small lead but, during that campaign, things went from bad to worse. By the time the election arrived, we were not so surprised that we lost … but it was nevertheless a huge disappointment. For somebody like me who had gone into the Parliament in 1984, and having served in various shadow portfolios… to lose, yet again, was pretty depressing.

Downer hits the election trail in his first campaign for Mayo
(Private Collection)

The family portrait (L to R): Alexander, Georgina, Olivia, Edward, Henrietta, Nicky. Seated in front is Lady Mary Downer – known as 'Cuddles' among her grandchildren (Private Collection)

"Having said that, I think the policies of *Fightback* lived on. And much of *Fightback* would later be implemented by the Howard Government."

Keating hailed the 1993 result as a victory for Labor's "true believers". The underlying truth, however, was that his party had been in power for more than a decade. Keating's forcible removal of Bob Hawke as Prime Minister had caused much pain and heartache for the Labor faithful. But who among the Liberals could bring Keating down?

After the 1993 election defeat, Howard signalled to all that he felt far from finished as a political leader: "Hewson had been a mistake. He was embraced because he seemed to have everything going for him. We all went along with it. We wanted to win. Then he lost in '93."

Following the election debacle, Howard contested Hewson's leadership and lost. He concedes this was a leadership bid destined to prove futile: "The 'you can't go back to Howard' forces were still strong."

Although he survived as leader, Hewson struggled to regain authority after his humiliation at the hands of Keating— in what many had deemed "the unloseable election". Hewson sought quickly to rejuvenate his frontbench. He appointed Downer as Shadow Treasurer.

At that time, there were plenty who doubted Downer had the skills to make a success of this senior frontbench role. The media adviser he hired in 1993, Cheryl Cartwright, admits she was among those yet to be convinced he had what it would take. In fact, when they first met, Downer had asked her what the journalists in the Press Gallery thought of him. She did not mince words. "They think you're a f***wit. We have a lot of work to do," she replied bluntly.

"He was a little taken aback by that but it was true," Cartwright says. "He wasn't held in terribly high esteem in those days.

"When Downer became Shadow Treasurer, Laurie Oakes (the most famous and feared journalist in Canberra's Press Gallery) had written in his *Bulletin* column that it was a stupid choice."

But Cartwright would soon be persuaded of Downer's talents: "He was a very, very intelligent man, very enthusiastic and not afraid of hard work. He was actually very good at media. Just needed a little bit of a rounding out…"

She recalls a lunch they had with radio journalists in the Canberra

Press Gallery, including the prominent ABC radio reporter, Fran Kelly: "It was good for the journalists to know this was a fun guy, good brain. He cracked jokes right through lunch."

However, where Downer excelled, according to Cartwright, was in distilling commentary on complex economic data into sharp, succinct attack lines: "He is very articulate. He honed his phrases to deliver a 10 second grab, or a 30 second grab. He could do that as he was speaking. I was in awe of that. It was just brilliant that he could do that."

Downer soon began delivering bruising blows to the Keating Government's credibility on the key issue of economic management. The political world would begin to sit up and take notice.

In December, 1993, a Press Gallery columnist, Chris Wallace, writing for *The Australian Financial Review*, pointed to his growing stature. "Alexander Downer used to be everybody's favourite target for jolly jibes in Canberra. Federal politics' very own young fogey," she wrote. "The rich, pink-cheeked, wet behind-the-ears, establishment boy displaced in time from Menzies' Australia. But if the Federal Liberal Party had a most valuable player award at the end of each parliamentary year, Downer would deserve to win the 1993 gong pretty comfortably."

Before long, even Laurie Oakes began to shift in his thinking, warning in a column that he may well have got it wrong — and that it was a mistake for anybody in Canberra to underestimate Downer.

Alexander Downer's colleagues were also carefully appraising his performance. By this time, he was entering the conversation as a leader who might have the capacity to return his party to government.

Even some of the moderates were swinging in behind him, including sworn enemies of Downer in the South Australian Liberal Party — people like Christopher Pyne. In *The Australian* on the weekend of May 23-24, 1994, political correspondent, Mike Steketee, revealed a conversation that happened several months earlier between Pyne and Downer on a flight to Adelaide from Canberra. "Obviously, the leadership is going to be a problem," Pyne had confided. "Much as it gets on my quince, of all the candidates, it looks like you might be the one that the moderates end up voting for."

In March, 1994, after the sudden resignation of Labor frontbencher John Dawkins, the Keating Government would face a by-election for the Labor-held seat of Fremantle in Western Australia.

Unwisely, the struggling Hewson urged the voters of Fremantle to "send a message to Paul Keating". Far from answering this call, the voters elected former West Australian Labor premier Carmen Lawrence — with a significant swing to the ALP.

Downer's moment had come. Suddenly, his conversations with the Liberal moderates began transforming into hard-and-fast declarations of support. Cartwright remembers the WA backbencher, Judi Moylan, coming to the Downer office for a chat.

"She was the first to say to him that he should be the leader," Cartwright recalls. She says Downer emerged excitedly from the meeting with to report the news:. "Guess what? It's happening."

Over the next six weeks, Downer would engineer a challenge to Hewson's leadership, promising generational change. By May, he had brokered a unity ticket with another young and talented frontbencher, Peter Costello, as his deputy.

They hyped it as The Dream Team.

"Yes — I remember that well," says John Howard, smiling. He recalls how the emergence of Downer and Costello, as the new guard of the Liberals, was seen by many as ending once and for all Howard's ambitions to return to the leadership for another tilt at the prime ministership: "Everybody just assumed it was all over — except me."

Only the previous year, Downer had told Howard he was happy enough with the job of shadow Treasurer and had no plans for a run at the leadership. But, as the prize was dangled before him, Downer was clearly mindful of what another long-standing political ally, the former SA Premier, John Olsen, had once told him: "If the opportunity occurs, you grab it with both hands and run like hell. It is no good waiting for the right time because the right time might never come."

Downer's ascension to the leadership on May 23 came rapidly, unexpectedly. As Phillip Hudson reported in the *Herald Sun*, Downer, at only 42, was the youngest-ever federal Liberal leader. "I am born of the Liberal Party and I am a creature of the Liberal Party," Downer proclaimed. While his mother, Mary, was proud, she conceded she had not expected his elevation would come so soon.

Privately, though, Downer was acutely conscious of his relative lack of experience. Howard and others were not aware that Downer himself was seized by uncertainty about whether he was fully equipped for the top job in Opposition:

I had been travelling pretty well as shadow Treasurer, which is why I was in line to become leader. But I'll never forget the night before the ballot. I had booked on an early commercial flight the next morning to get to Canberra. As I'm getting into bed the night before, I remember saying to Nicky, 'I'm not sure I really want to win this ballot. I don't think I'm ready for this job'. I never thought I was mentally prepared for it. I hadn't thought through what I would do if I became the leader of the Liberal Party. Where I would like to take it? How would I set things up? It sort of just happened. Suddenly.

As I recall, the ballot was on a Monday. Me against Hewson. So when I won (by seven votes), I was a bit stunned by it all. If I'd had the time to think it through, I would have done things very differently…

Downer began his leadership in a business-like manner. He brought in one of the country's most experienced public servants, Ron Harvey, to run his office. They had worked together before. Harvey had been the principal private secretary in the office of Prime Minister Malcolm Fraser, where Downer was employed as a speechwriter.

Ironically, Harvey had only re-entered the political sphere at the urging of Liberal Party federal director, Andrew Robb, in an effort to rescue John Hewson after the 1993 election. Harvey had agreed despite knowing Hewson's leadership was probably terminal.

Downer persuaded Harvey to stay on. Together, they planned the post-*Fightback* rebuild. But they had no radical policy overhaul in mind.

"I came into the job as an economic rationalist," says Downer. "In that sense, I didn't really have a problem with much of *Fightback*. I didn't think we should just abandon all we had been arguing for in the last few years. Just tone down our zeal a bit. Take off the sharp edges. And we should concentrate on the weaknesses of the Labor Government…"

Initially, Downer's progress would be spectacular. One opinion poll only weeks after his arrival in the job had Downer leading Keating 54-31 as preferred prime minister, and the Coalition leading Labor 60-40 on the two-party preferred vote. These were the pre-conditions for a landslide victory at the next election … if all went to plan.

Howard acknowledges that Downer and Costello made a stunning impact in the early months: "He got off to a very good start... extraordinary," says Howard. "And I thought, 'This is good'. So I decided to stick around."

Veteran Liberal moderate, Fred Chaney, was among those impressed by Downer's early efforts to resurrect the party's fortunes. Chaney had retired from politics to return to WA in 1993. He flew back to Canberra a year later to deliver a public lecture at Parliament House. During that lecture, he credited Downer for assembling a formidable team: "He seems to me to have picked a group of people who will take the fight to the government, which is a pretty ferocious show."

Chaney was upbeat about Downer's leadership potential: "I am personally delighted they have chosen someone with Alexander's breadth of experience and background. He has much greater breadth of experience than most members of the House of Representatives ... I came to a personal view some time ago that he was the person of the next generation whom I would most like to see as Prime Minister."

But Chaney also had a warning for Downer. He predicted Labor would not stay on the back foot for long. Keating would come at Downer like a steam train: "We all know there is going to be the most ghastly abuse of Alexander Downer ... It is going to be a very unpleasant experience. I just thank God that Alexander has ... a very thick skin."

Optimism about the Downer and Costello unity ticket continued to percolate. Howard recalls getting some free advice when he checked into the Mater hospital (in Sydney) for a knee reconstruction.

"I thought I could ski as fast as my 18-year-old. I couldn't and still can't," he laughs. "Anyway, the anaesthetist had some advice to offer. 'I like the Dream Team,' he said. 'And you're sticking around, too. That's the wise thing to do'. I said, 'Yeah' and then went to sleep. He'd done his job... and shut me up'."

However, in the second half of 1994, Keating, as predicted, would apply the full blowtorch to Downer. He was forever on the lookout for fault-lines in the Coalition. And he applied a laser-like focus to any hints of disunity. He would find plenty of fuel to work with.

Initially, Downer was unperturbed. He felt the Coalition was strongly-positioned on the broad economic policy debates: "In many areas, our policy positions were well established and didn't require any adjustment." But unifying the Coalition would prove a bridge too far.

Downer was unable to contain or control Coalition splintering across a range of social, legal and cultural debates ignited by Keating: Indigenous land rights, equal rights for gays on the island state of Tasmania, and, of course, Keating's push for an Australian republic.

On all of these issues, the party room would divide into competing camps. As a result, Downer would soon find himself trudging through a quagmire of disunity and dissent.

For the Opposition Leader, the Dream Team would soon transform into a nightmare. Making it worse was that much of the damage was self-inflicted "I was not ready for the job," Downer admits candidly.

The downward spiral began when Downer went to a Liberal Party state council in Western Australia in July, 1994, and committed publicly, that, if elected, the Coalition would scrap the Keating Government's *Native Title Act*.

The 1993 legislation was the Labor Government's response to the High Court's *Mabo* judgment, which had ruled that Indigenous Mer communities in the Torres Strait islands had unextinguished rights to ownership of Murray Island because of a continuous connection with the land. The judgment set off a furious debate over the implications for other native title land claims across Australia.

Downer's announcement was greeted with wild applause among the Liberal Party's supporters in Perth. The *Native Title Act* had been opposed vociferously by the WA Premier, Richard Court, along with many large mining and pastoral companies in the West, fearful of the potential economic impact of a raft of native title claims in the state.

These issues would be played out over the next two decades, with all states, including WA, ultimately reaching agreements on native title claims over large areas of unoccupied Crown land across Australia.

But, in 1994, with the consequences for pastoral and mining leases uncertain, it became an incendiary political and legal stoush.

Downer's words in Perth had enthused the Liberal Party's political base in WA. The problem was he had another visit on his schedule in the coming days. This was a trip to Indigenous communities in outback central Australia: remote townships like Yuendemu and Utopia, where living conditions were among the worst in the country.

The abject poverty and derelict infrastructure in many of these communities was confronting. And news of Downer's comments in

Perth had travelled fast. There were angry voices — and angry placards — awaiting him at Yuendemu. They read: "What a Downer."

During his visit, the Opposition Leader sought to reassure Aboriginal communities that he was not rejecting the *Mabo* judgment. He told them he would not seek to turn the clock back on what they had achieved. Instead, he sought to turn the heat back on the Keating Government. "I do not think in Australia in the 1990s that it is acceptable that our indigenous people are treated in the way they are treated," he said in a radio interview. "I think it's a big moral issue that we need to address in this country — that our indigenous people live in such disadvantaged circumstances compared to other Australians."

On Labor's native title legislation, he sought to clarify his position. Arguing the legislation was unworkable in its existing form, he pointed to the fact that two states — South Australia and Western Australia — were mounting High Court challenges, and predicted the Keating Government would itself have to amend the Act. "Were that not to happen, I would repeal it if we had to and obviously replace it."

The Keating Government's legislation, though, had set another trap for the Coalition, foreshadowing a Land Fund to support Aboriginal communities unable or unlikely to succeed in a native title claim. Hewson, as leader, had opposed this fund. On his trip to the NT, Downer vacillated.

In media reporting, he was accused of making confusing, contradictory statements — of fudging and back-pedalling. Keating lambasted him as a "redneck" anyway.

In the space of just six weeks, from the end of July to mid-September, Downer's approval ratings plummeted to 34 per cent. After such dizzying peaks of support early in his leadership, this was a jarring collision with political reality.

Greg Hunt arrived in the Downer office at this very moment. A Yale graduate and former associate to the Chief Justice of the Federal Court, Hunt joined the Downer team on the recommendation of Andrew Peacock, among others.

"I remember Alexander having a chat with staff — and saying how these things happen," Hunt says. "He was very calm. But that drop in the *Newspoll* was massive… and, literally, on the day I arrived."

Like Downer, Hunt had also come from a family background in politics. His father, Alan, had been a long-serving Cabinet minister in the family's home state of Victoria. So Hunt knew all about the vicissitudes of political life; the pressure of the scrutiny. But to confront a Liberal Party meltdown on his first day on the job? Hunt smiles: "It was an early introduction to the ups and downs…"

Today, with the benefit of many years of experience, Downer says he would have handled the issues of Indigenous land rights differently:

> Not that the positions I took were particularly wrong, or that I regret them. But the way we got to them was incredibly clumsy. We were responding the whole time to the agenda set by Keating. I don't think all this was necessarily designed just to destabilise us. But it did.

While the Liberals had been generating some traction in the electorate with the party's new slogan, The Things That Matter, Downer would find it increasingly difficult to stay on-message. In August, there was another flare-up of divisions within the Liberal Party.

The Keating Government had flung another grenade into Coalition ranks by introducing legislation to over-ride Tasmania's 19th century-style prohibitions on gay rights. The debate created a significant split within the Coalition parties — on issues of conscience, on the one hand, and states' rights on the other.

Downer fought a campaign within his own party room to sway his colleagues to support the decriminalisation of homosexuality. As he would tell colleagues: "I was in favour of the government legislation over-ruling Tasmania's law … we're not in a position of telling people how to live their lives."

At that time, it was a stance that prompted threats from frontbenchers to resign in protest. None of them did. Yet the damage was done.

In the shadows, John Hewson and his supporters, still grating from his loss of the leadership, had a campaign of whispers underway, questioning Downer's leadership capacities. "They were just feral, and I didn't have the capacity to hold the show together," Downer says. He felt he could tolerate no longer the campaign to undermine him when, in his car before boarding a flight to Launceston, he heard an ABC radio report that could only have been sourced to a leak from a Shadow

Cabinet meeting. Convinced Hewson was the culprit, he sacked him from the frontbench.

The backlash would prove severe. Hewson would declare himself the conscience of the party. The Opposition looked hopelessly divided.

In Hunt's view, this signalled Keating's success with a clever, if cynical, tactic to stir tensions within the Coalition — aimed at delivering a succession of crippling blows to Downer's leadership: "It was a conscious attempt by Keating to use federal law to divide the Liberal Party. That was within his rights as PM to do that. It was unfortunate that people on both sides of our party — both the conservatives and the more moderate and libertarian strand — took the bait rather than looking for a common way through. There was no compromise given."

In Parliament, Keating taunted the Opposition Leader as an arch-conservative: "Mr Downer is as far removed from the needs of the modern Australian political system as it is possible to be."

By now, Downer was looking and sounding shell-shocked. Every second day, Keating was throwing haymakers at him in the Parliament. Everyone could smell blood. "You could feel it sliding," says Hunt.

In September, Downer went to Sydney for a NSW Liberal Party gathering, where he was to launch Coalition policies to address domestic violence. Nicky Downer was there to introduce him.

She did so, warmly, with some light-hearted mocking: "After that trip to the Northern Territory — you know the one — Alexander came back to the house a little dusty and mud-spattered, both literally and metaphorically. Needless to say, he hadn't really been pulling his weight around the house, so I asked him when he was going to do something about the washing. And he muttered something about national debt. I asked him about the gardening, and he whispered: 'Land Fund'. I asked him when it would be his turn to do the dishes and his eyes glazed over with the word 'Tasmania' dropping from his lips. In a fit of exasperation I said to him: 'Oh come on, Alexander, when are you going to concentrate on the things that matter?'"

The audience laughed and applauded. Downer then stepped forward to the podium, grinning sheepishly. "I have to congratulate you on that," he said in thanking his wife for her introduction. "And I think it probably renders anything I have to say tonight virtually redundant…"

Inexplicably, he then detoured into some mystifying word play: "So… from the things that matter … to the things that batter …"

It may have been intended as a joke, a pun. "I like jokes," Downer admits openly. Problem was, the subject matter he was about to address was nothing to laugh about. The awkward attempt at humour left his audience dumbfounded.

Hunt admits to collaborating with Nicky Downer about her words of introduction: "If I might say, it had some moments of humour which she carried off beautifully. She was so naturally funny. It seems Alexander then decided he would have a crack at something…"

Hunt wasn't in Sydney for the event and insists he still doesn't know why his boss chose to stray into the territory he did — or who, if anyone, had floated the idea with him. Nor did he investigate: "I still don't know — it was like (everyone was) running for the hills. Anyway, he said what he said. And that was really the *coup de grace*. As time wore on, I could see he was feeling the pressure and not enjoying it."

The public was unforgiving of Downer's plight. His opinion poll ratings slumped further still, and rumblings within the party soon went far beyond mere gossip. Now, Howard supporters were also agitating for a change of leadership. "I'm not knocking that," says Downer. "But if ever I had any clear air, they made sure it didn't last for long."

By now, as Hunt points out, Howard was not only back in the frame — he was "clearly, if unexpectedly, back in the ascendancy."

Discussions among party powerbrokers about whether or how Downer could survive in the leadership were occurring in the back channels.

Michael L'Estrange, Ron Harvey and Brian Loughnane, a future Liberal Party federal director, were key intermediaries for Downer.

Nick Minchin, a leading conservative from South Australia and friend of Downer, kept communications open with Howard. By mid-November, the front-page headline of *The Australian* would read: "Downer pleads for time in leadership fight".

With fires burning on several fronts, Downer sought desperately to dampen down divisions within the Coalition over another of Keating's political campaigns. "What was a big issue at that time — made a big issue by Paul Keating — was the republic," Downer recalls:

> It became a fashionable issue. It was one of those issues where the Liberal Party atomised, and that was hugely difficult to manage.

Keating made all these speeches denouncing the British monarchy as an institution. The journalists flocked to it as well. There was seemingly huge support for a republic ... and I thought, 'how are we going to manage this when the Liberal Party is so divided?'

So I came up with this idea of a Constitutional Convention, borrowing from my grandfather's experience. You would at least have some of the delegates elected, and the Convention could work out whether it wanted to develop a model for a republic, and that could be put to a vote if they could agree. Well, I didn't last much longer as leader but, eventually, in 1999, it came to pass that the Convention was held...

Greg Hunt's lawyerly advice was sought in developing the model. "It was criticised a lot at the time," Hunt concedes.

"But when Nick Minchin had a look at it in later years, in government, it was exactly the model he adopted. It had a natural logic and purpose to it. It involved the public directly in the process but it meant there were also guiding hands. We put that model on the table..."

By December, 1994, however, Downer was running out of time.

A *Newspoll* published early that month had Downer trailing Keating 24-53 as preferred Prime Minister. His attempts to forge compromise within the Coalition were proving futile. Internal critics leaked a story that Downer had announced the Constitutional Convention proposal without shadow Cabinet approval.

Keating's strategy of poking and prodding at tensions within the Coalition had become a powerful tool in his campaign to destroy Downer's leadership. In the last sitting day of Parliament for the year, Keating gave one last twist of the knife, pillorying the Opposition Leader as "the Christmas turkey — awaiting decapitation."

Downer readily concedes he was under the pump: "I didn't have the experience — or the better word here, probably, is the *authority*. When I became leader, although a majority of the party room voted for me, the minority who didn't fell into two categories: the pro-Howard people — and the Hewson people, who were unforgiving."

The question for Downer became how to avoid yet another catastrophe for the Liberal Party with yet another divisive leadership brawl. With the threat of a party room showdown by early February, Jeff Kennett, the Victorian Premier, offered Downer some advice.

He, too, had suffered career-challenging setbacks as an Opposition Leader before going on to become a colossus of Liberal Party politics: "Sometimes, it is better to survive … and return to fight another day."

Downer acknowledges he spoke to Kennett frequently at the time. He doesn't recall that specific advice but says it pretty much reflected his own view that he could not expect to remain as leader. "I am not a megalomaniac, right… I'm not mad like a lot of people who become political leaders. I could see what had happened to my relationship with the public. Forget the party. My poll ratings were poor."

As the weeks passed, it became clearer that the patience of the party was wearing thin. Howard had been approached by leading Liberals anxious to make changes at the top before Keating could call the next election, due by 1996. These included Victorian powerbroker, Michael Kroger. Howard was also visited by the father-and-son heavyweights from Western Australia, Charles and Richard Court.

Downer laughs as he thinks back to some of the unsolicited advice he received from colleagues at the time:

> I remember Ian McLachlan coming to see me at my electorate office in Stirling and saying to me that I should stand down as leader. And I just said, 'Thanks for coming to see me. I appreciate that'.
>
> I didn't think what he said, or what others like Andrew Peacock or Michael Kroger were saying, was all that germane. What was relevant was my relationship with the public.
>
> So here is the calculation I made: if I had thought I could beat Keating at the forthcoming election, I would have fought these people. But I didn't think I could win. And I figured that the only person that could win — although I wasn't sure that he would — was John Howard.
>
> The main game wasn't me. The main game was beating Keating. I thought the Keating Government was an abomination. Terrible.
>
> Sure, the Hawke Government did a lot of things, good and

bad, but the Keating Government did almost nothing good. I thought beating them was the main game.

To satisfy himself that his instincts were right on this, Downer called in Andrew Robb, federal director of the Liberal Party, and asked him to poll the issue. Did the Liberals under Downer have any chance of defeating Keating at an election?

Robb flew to Adelaide to brief Downer in person. The feedback was bad. Downer can't remember revealing anything directly to Robb at the time about his state of mind on the issue but he knew he had the proof he had sought. "I thought, 'I'm going to have to engineer a handover here to John Howard. I think I've blown this'."

On December 13, Downer joined Howard and Costello for after-dinner drinks at the Adelaide Club. His recollection of the conversation is that they discussed the plight of the party, and that Downer indicated to them that, unless there was some recovery in the party's polling over the Xmas-New Year holiday season, he would be forced to consider standing down from the leadership.

Says Downer: "Costello was in favour of that. There was no argument about it...."

At this point, Downer grins. Almost as an afterthought, he adds: "Howard was very much in favour of it... well, understandably."

At this meeting, Downer gave no commitment to Howard that he would hand over the leadership to him — partly because nobody could be sure that Howard could turn around the party's fortunes.

Downer would hold off on his decision in hope of a shift in the polls. But the die was cast. "Things started to go wrong and we all know what happened," says Howard. "Alexander was disappointed, of course — but I never felt that our basic friendship was damaged."

Over the Christmas break, the internal pressures for change became irresistible. "It became progressively clearer that it was almost unsustainable for Alexander," Hunt recalls.

Behind the scenes, this set in train the search for what Greg Hunt calls a "velvet transition" between Downer and Howard: "Alexander had a series of discussions with party grandees. Brian Loughnane played an important role and Nick Minchin was brokering a lot with Howard."

There was never any suggestion from either side that surrendering his leadership would be tantamount to the end of Downer's career. But what role would be befitting for a former leader? Costello was always going to keep the Treasury portfolio, whatever the outcome of the leadership issue.

Hunt remembers discussing with Downer his options. They agreed Foreign Affairs 'would be the natural fit'.

By this time, Howard was aware that supporters of his old rival, Andrew Peacock, were unlikely to stand in his way should he make another bid for the leadership.

Likewise, Howard also knew of some Liberal MPs like Amanda Vanstone and Eoin Cameron — people he describes as "sensible moderates" — who were ready for change. And he also knew the former Liberal Party President, Tony Staley, was "on manoeuvres".

It was time for Howard to make his move — to follow through on the discussion he had with Downer at the Adelaide Club.

A lot of Liberals were circling, eager to bring their influence to bear on the leadership jostling. Yet Howard rejects the notion that networks of deal-makers were having to mediate between he and Downer: "If I had something serious to say to Alexander, I'd do it directly."

In late January, 1995, Downer and Howard met for dinner at the Athenaeum Club in Melbourne. "I thought by then that he was toast," says Howard, in a blunt assessment of the political realities. It was time to bring to a close the discussions they had begun at the Adelaide Club a month or so earlier.

"What I said to him on that night was, 'Alexander, we have always been good friends, and this is difficult… but I think you have lost the bulk of the party'." Howard then reminded Downer of Howard's pledge that he would return to the Liberal leadership only if 'drafted' by the party — in other words, on the proviso Howard's colleagues were insistent on his comeback, and would re-elect him unopposed: "Alexander, I have always operated on the 'I'll only be drafted' principle but it's got to a point where the party wants it resolved. I think you're in trouble. If it's not resolved soon, I may have to reconsider my 'draft only' attitude."

The message was crystal-clear. Howard was warning there was a strong mood for change across the Liberal Party and, if necessary, he would have no choice but to challenge for the leadership.

For his part, Downer didn't need persuading or prodding. He had already made a pragmatic, clear-eyed choice. "We had a discussion about it, and I said, 'I think it might be better if I hand over to you'."

The outcome of a meeting of this magnitude was not going to stay private for very long. The following morning, the newspaper headlines revealed Howard would soon be making his return for a third time as Liberal leader — "Lazarus with a triple bypass", as Howard would famously describe it.

Downer had to address a Business Council breakfast in Melbourne that morning. He was chased by hordes of media as he entered and left the venue. "I remember it being a fairly dire experience," Downer recalls.

Downer found the headlines tough going. He knew the leaks had probably come from someone, somewhere within the Howard camp.

Yet he was philosophical:

> People in the party had been playing these games for years. The Liberal Party had being doing it for years. They were at it again. But, basically, I felt there might be a chance of winning with Howard. It was no certainty. I know we did end up winning but we had a been losing a lot of elections up until then. So we were not sure we could. And Keating was incredibly confident…
>
> It's all very well looking back on it now. But it was a risk at the time. Don't forget, there was a huge anti-Howard lobby within the Liberal Party.

Soon enough, Howard took a call from Liberal Party operative, Grahame Morris, an old friend who would later serve as Howard's chief-of-staff: "China — Alexander will see you tomorrow at 11am."

Downer's decision to resign and hand over to Howard had still to be navigated through the party room. But there is little room for sentimentality when a political party faces these choices. Both Howard and Downer understood that the over-riding calculus at times of leadership crisis is almost always this: "Who is more likely to lead the party to victory?"

Not everyone was convinced the "velvet transition" was the ideal solution. Says Downer:

> I remember Peter Reith being very unhappy about this because he thought, well, I had just handed it over to Howard and maybe he himself could have had a go.

I think not. We had tried out the new generation and it was time to go back to the old hands. That was basically my argument.

Howard had known six weeks earlier that events were heading favourably in his direction. Yet he still found himself admiring Downer's conduct and demeanour through those torrid weeks. As a political leader in his early 40s, he had seemed for a while to be on an unstoppable trajectory to the highest office in the land. Yet here he was agreeing to an orderly handover of the leadership:

> Alexander was keen to preserve the position of Greg Hunt, his close adviser, and he wanted to be foreign affairs spokesman:
>
> I was ready to agree to that and a lot more. But that's what he wanted. And I said, 'You will have it'.
>
> He didn't try to demand it or extort me in any way. But I think he had come to the conclusion his position was, to say the least, difficult. The best thing was to agree, and if it could be amicable, that would help.
>
> As good as I could, I committed to making him Foreign Minister and keeping Greg Hunt. He wanted to announce it in his own time and his own way. And he did that very well. He was extremely gracious.

Downer held his press conference to announce his resignation as Liberal Party leader on Australia Day, 1995. Greg Hunt says Downer's loyalty to the party at that time should never be under-estimated:

> Yes, there had been errors, which had been out-sized in terms of the political impact. But Alexander really believed in the party.
>
> There was a desire to put the party ahead of himself — coupled with the fact that the family was really not enjoying it. He could see there was a pathway. And he also really liked Howard. He respected him.

Less than a week later, Howard was elected unopposed as the new Liberal leader. His task was to bring down a Labor Prime Minister who had been the bane of the Liberals in Opposition. Howard took the view that Keating was "eminently beatable." It would be the Liberal Party's best chance of returning to office in more than a decade.

While Downer may have been distraught about the unravelling of his leadership of the party in only 250 days, he had also been hardened by the experience. And he wanted desperately to see the back of Keating.

Greg Hunt considers Downer's act of self-sacrifice a critical factor in laying the foundations for the success of the Howard Government:

> He was never once resentful. From the day we came back (after the change of leadership) he was incredibly focussed. And that was fundamental to the whole Howard Project.
>
> He didn't wring his hands and say, 'I wish I could have stayed and become prime minister'. He accepted it. Without that commitment from Alexander, the government would never have survived let alone thrived. As we know, if you had a former leader throwing rocks — who was unreconciled — that's enough to destabilise ... but not once did he rail against Howard.

Downer, on reflection, is brutally frank about his tumultuous months as Opposition Leader: "I hated the job. I just hated it."

Hunt noticed there was almost a sense of relief in Downer. Perhaps even an acceptance that the accommodation reached with Howard meant that things "may have aligned in the best possible way."

"The moment the pain lifted, he lifted," says Hunt. "He didn't look backwards. He might have said to himself, 'Well, I could have done this or that better'. But there wasn't that sense of anger or regret. Or vengeance. That is the most striking feature. Not how he lost the leadership — but how he reacted to the loss of the leadership."

On accepting his new role as foreign affairs spokesman, Downer and his office would make full use of their remaining time in Opposition by getting to work on detailed foreign policy plans.

According to Greg Hunt, they defined their operating principle as one of "enlightened realism" — that Australian foreign policy should reflect an understanding of the world as it was, not as people might want or imagine it to be. It was not to be an approach hostile to the United Nations, or to signal any retreat by Australia on its traditional commitment to humanitarian aid and support for developing nations.

Rather, it would be a policy informed by the Liberal Party's long-standing commitment to the Enlightenment values underlying modern democratic institutions. Crucial to the approach was an acceptance of the realities of how the world functioned — dealing with the facts, not the fantasy. The policy was called A Confident Australia

In the public arena, in an attempt to galvanise community support for the change of leadership, Downer was hard at work reminding everybody that he was fully invested in the changes at the top.

He went so far as to threaten publicly to "kneecap" anyone who sought to undermine Howard as the new leader.

Hunt believes Downer, having himself fallen prey to party disunity, committed in his own mind to become something akin to a praetorian guard, ready to crack down hard on anyone stoking internal dissent.

The Howard team remained highly disciplined throughout the 1996 election campaign, rarely if every nudged away from its relentless critique of economic management under Paul Keating.

It was pretty much Howard's last roll of the dice, politically and electorally, and he made it count. For his part, Downer would be instrumental in Howard taking a united team into the campaign.

In Hunt's view, the unwavering commitment of Downer to a Liberal victory in 1996, despite the high price he had paid personally, proved a major turning-point for the party:

> Without Alexander's fulsome backing through 1995, and leading into the 1996 election, you just couldn't have had the platform for success that Howard had. And that support continued across all four terms in office. That was a positive for the country.

The truth is, success in politics rarely happens without fighting through adversity. And, from 1994 into 1995, Downer had been put through the wringer. If he was able to survive that *annus horribilis* in his political career, he could probably survive just about anything.

He would soon be given every opportunity to redefine himself as one of the big beasts of Australian political life. Which was just as well. Ahead of him would be some serious tests of strength of character and resolve — not only in Australia but on the open plains of global politics, where many an apex predator roamed.

6

SETTING THE COURSE

From the time of their first meeting in 1997, Alexander Downer always made a point of visiting Henry Kissinger whenever he was in New York. He didn't care that the elder statesman — as a hard-core practitioner of global power politics — had as many detractors as admirers.

During the annual September sessions at United Nations headquarters, Downer would find time to make a detour to Kissinger's office at 351 Park Avenue. They would sit down and share thoughts on the pressing strategic challenges of the day. Sometimes, it would be dinner with the Kissingers at their art deco apartment tower, perched majestically on the banks of New York's East River.

Downer valued Kissinger's insights on history, strategy and statecraft.

As a university student, and later as a junior diplomat, Downer had studied Kissinger's writings on the early 19th century peace negotiations among the great powers of Europe at the Congress of Vienna; on America's wars in Indo-China: and on the nuclear arms reduction talks Kissinger led under President Richard Nixon during the Cold War. He was also acutely aware of Kissinger's involvement in some of the most ruthless and contentious foreign policy gambits in postwar history: among them, the US carpet bombing of Cambodia; various nefarious interventions in the politics of Latin America; and turning a blind eye to Indonesia's military takeover of East Timor.

But here was also the man who, as national security adviser to Nixon, had orchestrated the resumption of diplomatic ties between the American superpower and Communist China; the man who put an Egyptian President and an Israeli prime minister in the same room to engineer an historic peace treaty between two nations long at war; and a winner of the Nobel Peace Prize for brokering the Paris agreements that would finally secure a US exit from the nightmare in Vietnam.

The UN General Assembly sessions in New York each September

were high-intensity events. They provided the opportunity for the diplomatic equivalent of speed-dating — the chance for face-to-face encounters with senior ministers or heads-of-state from every country on the planet. Mostly, these meetings would be cordial, well-mannered — sometimes edgy — but they provided an invaluable opportunity to share insights with the leaders of nations you might never otherwise come across in the course of regional summits or bilateral visits.

Ambassadors and a retinue of diplomatic sherpas would work in a near-frenzy to align duelling diaries to make these meetings happen, with not a minute to be spared. Around the world in 80 hours.

Amid all of this, Downer would try to find the time to see Kissinger.

Downer admired Kissinger's intelligence and his mastery of the detail — and the context — in analysing big turning-points in history. He was impressed by his unparalleled network of connections in all of the major capitals of the world. He did not regard him necessarily as a hero or role model. But Kissinger had Downer's respect. When it came to raw politics on the global stage, the old guy knew his stuff.

Downer himself had spent most of his early adult years tutoring himself on the workings of international diplomacy, and particularly the politics of the Western alliance. After completing his university studies in economics and politics history, he had joined the Australian Department of Foreign Affairs. Downer had a ringside seat to observe how Washington and the leading Western European powers navigated their way through the final years of the Cold War confrontation with the Soviet Union. Kissinger, of course, had been a pivotal player through much of this.

Downer also had the advantage of learning at his father's knee some of the dynamics behind the American superpower's network of alliances globally, including with Australia.

As it happens, Sir Alick Downer, as Australia's High Commissioner to Britain, had been part of a high-level meeting in 1971 with the former British Prime Minister, Alec Douglas-Home, where they discussed Kissinger's diplomatic manoeuvrings to end the isolation of Mao Zedung's People's Republic of China.

All of this was an endless source of fascination for Downer as he built up his knowledge base of the behind-the-scenes workings of these critical relationships. It was Kissinger who would tell him many years later: "It is too late to learn about foreign policy once you have been appointed foreign minister ... you have to know stuff."

Coming to power after more than a decade out of office, the Howard Government would have very little time to find its feet. Domestically, the first shock to the system was the Port Arthur massacre in April, 1996, when a lone, crazed gunman shot dead 35 people — including a mother and her two young daughters — on the site of the historic former prison colony in southern Tasmania.

This was the worst modern-day massacre in Australia's history, and came only six weeks after the Howard Government had been sworn into power. The entire nation was shocked and appalled. Everyone knew there would have to be dramatic changes to the way governments policed the ownership and possession of firearms.

The result was a gun amnesty. This resulted in the destruction of many weapons in the community, and much stricter codes governing high-powered firearms. But the Coalition parties paid a price. While there was much kudos in the wider electorate for acting decisively, the National Party, in particular, suffered a backlash in the bush, with defections of its vote to ideological outriders like the One Nation Party. Downer himself would not be spared the wrath of One Nation voters.

In foreign policy, too, there was to be an early, unwelcome test for Downer of his diplomatic skills — and of his political nerve.

Three weeks after the March 2, 1996, federal election in Australia, the island of Taiwan was to hold its first truly democratic presidential election. China was bristling at the pro-independence rhetoric of the leading candidate, Lee Teng-hui. In a crude and hectoring warning, the People's Liberation Army spent weeks before voting day firing missiles into the Taiwan Straits, within 60km of Taiwan's coastline — the penalty for what it saw as Lee's attempts "to divide the motherland."

On March 8 — that is, three days before the Howard Government was formally sworn into office in Canberra — the Clinton Administration in Washington responded with a show of force. It sent two aircraft carrier battle groups into the Taiwan Strait to remind Beijing that the superpower would not stand idly by as China interfered in the democratic processes on the island.

As soon as he assumed formal responsibilities as Minister for Foreign Affairs, Downer spoke out in support of the US action, saying it "demonstrated (US) interest in participating in regional security in a very practical way." No other nation in the region came in behind him.

"Look, there wasn't doubt on the advice of Foreign Affairs — nor any doubt in the conversations with the Prime Minister's office. None of that should have been any surprise," says Hunt. "The statement was made, consciously, at the level of the Foreign Affairs Minister. And we expected blowback. But, equally, we were resolute that it was the right thing to do from an ethical position — but also absolutely critical that we did not show weakness at the first test.

"This was unsought and unwanted, but it was the first test — I mean, you can have all your plans but Alexander was always big on the idea that you can be judged on how you respond to events like this."

The response from Beijing was near-apoplectic. Seated just in front of Downer in the House of Representatives Chamber, Howard watched the pressure build on his foreign minister. "It was a very difficult start," he acknowledges. "That was a very testing year. But we got through it."

The detail of China's punitive response to Downer's first engagement on the vexed issue of Taiwan will be covered in a later chapter. But to say there was an immediate chill in relations is an understatement.

It didn't help that one of the spending cuts in a tough first Budget for the Howard Government was to deliver on an election pledge to wind back import assistance to some developing nations.

China was among the hardest hit. When Downer told Parliament there had been no formal complaints from his ministerial counterparts in Beijing, the Opposition was able to get its hands on a letter from a senior official in the trade section of the PRC's Ministry of Foreign Affairs, raising concerns about changes to the import financing facility.

Beijing became angrier still when Downer issued words of condemnation when China conducted the latest in its series of nuclear weapons tests. "China should heed the strength and legitimacy of international feeling on this important issue," he said. "It should desist immediately from all further testing (and) move away from the now out-dated Cold War logic of nuclear confrontation."

Greg Hunt reminds us that China, in 1996, was very different from today. "It was evolving — it hadn't yet reached the apogee of its free-market engagement with the rest of the world, let alone slipped back into a more autocratic leadership approach. But we always presumed it was going to continue to grow as a military and economic power — remember the dominant thesis at this stage was Francis Fukuyama's *End of History* rather than Samuel Huntington's *Clash of Civilisations*."

In contrast to the diplomatic freeze with China, however, Australia's relationship with Washington would soon step up significantly — in substance, tone and language — when the AUSMIN talks were held in July in Sydney. The result of this bilateral meeting between the most senior US and Australian decision-makers in foreign policy and defence was to become known as the Sydney Declaration.

At Downer's instigation, it proclaimed the ongoing relevance of the Alliance in the post Cold War world: "The Australia-United States relationship, having proved its value over five decades, will remain a cornerstone of Asia-Pacific security into the twenty-first century." It was a clear, unequivocal reinforcement of common intent.

For the next year and more, however, Downer would have to grapple with the awkward realities of balancing China and the US, two competing spheres of interests — and values.

In Downer's first year as Foreign Affairs Minister, the Keating narrative continued to resonate, almost as if a benchmark against which all of the Howard Government's diplomatic and strategic initiatives would be measured. Was Downer tilting towards Asia (by which most commentators meant China) — or was he betting the house on the alliance with the US? Reframing the debate to shift the focus in the media and foreign policy establishment away from that simplistic, binary code would be among his tougher challenges.

Significantly, Downer had declared in his first major policy speech as minister that "closer engagement with Asia" would be the Australian Government's highest foreign policy objective. In keeping with this, the Howard Government's first foreign policy White Paper listed the US as only one among Australia's four most important bilateral relationships — alongside Japan, Indonesia ... and China.

Given the flurry of activity so early in the new Government's first term, achieving a sense of equilibrium in this matrix would not be easy. For as much as China represented a trove of economic opportunity, it also posed complex strategic challenges. Not everybody on the

Coalition benches was mindful of the difficult dynamics at play. Some wondered aloud whether Downer was up to the job.

The disquiet peaked in November, 1996, after Downer provided his critics with another excuse to raise questions about his suitability for a senior leadership role in government. If Downer's preferred narrative was as a tough political warrior, this would soon be juxtaposed with a page three photo in Sydney's *Daily Telegraph* of the foreign minister posing for the camera with one leg adorned in a fishnet stocking and stiletto — in the style of the *Rocky Horror Show*'s Dr Frank-N-Furter.

Coming on the eve of an official state visit by the US President Bill Clinton, the publication of the photo created a minor uproar.

Labor's foreign affairs spokesman, Laurie Brereton, took up the chance to ridicule Downer, demanding that he have an opportunity to ask the Prime Minister in Parliament whether he was "'relaxed and comfortable about the Foreign Minister's foray into cross dressing".

Downer insists he has never really understood, then or since, what all the controversy was about. "I don't have a problem with it at all," he says. "I don't see why some people seem to think there was something terrible about it. It was just a publicity stunt for a charity.

"The Variety Club were holding this charity event. To help promote it, they ran a competition in the *Adelaide Advertiser* where readers had to guess whose leg it was. In my case, the photographer didn't just take the image of the leg and shoe. He took a photograph of all of me."

When the full-length photo was published, Downer was depicted in suit-and-tie, with a leg of his trousers rolled up to reveal the fishnet stocking and stiletto. The camera also captured Downer's impish grin.

Downer's opponents — "the Left" as he prefers to characterise them — seized on it immediately as a political vulnerability. "I don't know why they thought that, but they certainly piled it on me," Downer smiles. "I think it probably says more about them than me.

"It's interesting, isn't it? A lot of so-called progressives who criticised me over that photo are the same people who spend a lot of time talking about the importance of cultural diversity, and about their support for the arts and freedom of expression — as long as you happen to agree with them."

Over the years to come, newspaper cartoonists would deploy the fishnet stocking image incessantly. "It was never a worry to me," says

Downer's Rocky Horror Show promotion — the image that launched a thousand cartoons (Grant Nowell/Newspix)

Downer. "I quite liked the photo. It's not how I traditionally dress. I think 100 per cent of Australians know that. So it didn't cause me any concern. In the end, I doubt one person changed their vote for me or against me, one way or another, because of that photo."

Nonetheless, Labor supporters in the arts community seemed determined in their efforts to cement this image for all time in Australia's political folklore. Downer — fishnet stockings and all — would be parodied remorselessly in the musical comedy, *Keating!*, a popular stage show in the early 2000s. Downer seemed unperturbed. He went along to see the show for himself. As he would say later: "I enjoy satire as an art form and if you go into public life and if you have any degree of success, you have to expect that you will be satirised at some point. My overall take was that *Keating!* the musical was far better than Keating the prime minister."

The photo may have been a triviality yet not everybody in the Liberal Party was ready to shrug off doubts about Downer's political judgment. In an interview for this book, John Howard reveals that, towards the end of 1996, some in the Coalition actually came to him, imploring that he find someone to replace Downer.

"In his early times as Foreign Minister, he had a pretty rocky start," says Howard. "He had his critics, like we all did. Whenever anything went wrong, they would mutter, mutter, mutter. A few people said to me, 'Downer is too frivolous, we can't have him'. I said, 'No. We're sticking with him'. And I stuck with him. I thought he was very good."

Downer wasn't overly troubled by the scrutiny that came with the job.

First, he was comfortable he had the unwavering support of his prime minister. "A foreign minister has to have the full confidence of the prime minister — or the president in a presidential system," says Downer. "A prime minister has to feel she or he can leave the day-to-day running of foreign relations to someone utterly reliable."

Secondly, he backed his own experience and judgment, especially in his dealings with Asian leaders. "They didn't want a slanging-match with Australia over our history. Or our immigration policies. Many of these countries had their own issues on immigration and questions of race. They didn't want to dwell on the past. They wanted to focus on the present and the possibilities for the future."

Thirdly, Downer would surround himself with some serious intellectual horsepower. The incoming Howard Government appointed Philip Flood as Secretary of the Department of Foreign Affairs and Trade. They had axed Flood's predecessor, Michael Costello, along with six other department heads, within days of coming to office.

Flood had been working as the director of one of the nation's lead intelligence agencies, the Office of National Assessments. He came into DFAT's top job with almost 40 years' experience in government — an exemplar of Australia's foreign policy and security elite.

But while Flood had met John Howard many years before, he admitted to having had very little contact with the Minister he would serve. He recalled his one meeting with Downer had been at a dinner the previous May hosted by the New Zealand High Commission. Their discussion had been... lively.

As Flood recorded in his memoirs, *Dancing with Warriors*, Downer wasted no time in getting on the phone to congratulate him:

> While I was delighted, I was also a bit surprised that Downer had wanted me as Secretary, since he and I hardly knew each other, and not so long ago we had had a strong disagreement about Australian policy towards the European Union.

Downer, too, remembered the dinner. He reminded Flood they had disagreed on several other issues as well:

> You told me I was wrong about Indonesia, wrong about East Timor, and wrong about ASEAN. I decided then that, if we won, you were the man I wanted as Secretary. I want someone who will tell me when I am wrong. We should have a lot of fun together.

That conversation set the tone for a successful relationship. Downer wanted smart, strong-willed people around him. Flood's successors as DFAT Secretaries, Ashton Calvert and Michael L'Estrange, also met that definition as tough-minded foreign policy professionals.

Downer would work closely with many other senior DFAT officers who would help navigate foreign policy through its stormiest moments. These included Bill Farmer, Michael Thawley, Dennis Richardson, John McCarthy, Penny Wensley, John Dauth, Gillian Bird, Louise

Hand, Ric Smith and the two David Ritchies. David Irvine and Nick Warner were hardened professionals whose expertise Downer would call upon in the toughest emergency conditions.

None were shrinking violets. All would speak their minds. Sometimes, fur would fly. In their meetings, Downer could be deliberately provocative, inviting passionate arguments. He would put up unorthodox ideas he knew would prompt strong pushback.

This was not just to be a contrarian. It was strategic. There was a purpose. It was his way of testing opinions, teasing out nuance, exploring new ideas and different angles.

It could only ever work because it was underpinned by high levels of mutual respect and trust. "There is the assumption that public servants are mostly left-leaning," says Downer. "I don't know if the public servants who worked for me voted Labor or not. Probably they did. But I didn't have any real problems. I set out very clearly what I wanted to do, and they got on with it. They were very good."

Talented young men and women seconded to the Downer office by DFAT would in later years rise to some of Australia's most senior diplomatic postings: among them Angela Macdonald, Lucienne Manton, Patrick Suckling, Sandra Vegting, Kate Logan and Andrew Goledzinowski. The brave and brilliant Dave Windsor would serve as Charge d'Affaires in tough towns like Beirut and Kabul.

Downer's chiefs-of-staff, his closest and most senior advisers in the ministerial office, were almost always senior career diplomats, like Mike Smith, Bill Tweddell and Peter Woolcott.

One exception was Innes Willox, who came from a media and business background. Willox would serve later as Consul-General in Los Angeles, and would be appointed chief executive of one of Australia's leading peak industry bodies, the Australian Industry Group. Another was Chris Kenny, also from a media background. After leaving government, he would go on to become an influential and entertaining opinion leader and news anchor on *Sky News*.

Advisers including Brad Haynes, Amanda Hawkins, the late Andrew Park, Christian Bennett and Susan Borchers remained close friends of Downer long after he left office. Barbara Rayner was his faithful lieutenant in his private office. She, Pam Mayer and Kay McBride were with him for much of his entire journey in political life.

Downer set exacting standards, demanding intellectual rigour and strategic precision of himself and those who worked around him. He insisted on forensic examination of policy detail.

Says Philip Flood: "His sense of fun and frivolity sometimes misled others to underrate his acute intellect." Chris Kenny agrees: "Alexander's great fun and good to his staff. But he was the one very much in charge, as it should be."

Over the years, Downer's office alumni would include several people who would become prominent policy-makers in their own right.

Three of his senior advisers would later enter politics and rise to Cabinet rank in the Abbott, Turnbull and Morrison Governments. Josh Frydenberg would become the nation's Treasurer and deputy leader of the Liberal Party.

Greg Hunt would serve in senior Cabinet portfolios, including Environment and Health. Alan Tudge, too, would be elevated to Cabinet, as Minister for Education and Youth.

Josh Frydenberg, who, like Hunt, was a law graduate from Monash University, had completed his Masters in international politics at Oxford before joining the office of Attorney-General, Daryl Williams. He was also an elite tennis player, touring on the satellite circuit for a year. His biggest claim to fame at that time had been a victory against a doubles pair including future US Open finalist, Mark Phillipoussos.

He joined Downer's office in September, 1999, at the height of the East Timor crisis. Frydenberg became a close adviser and friend. Over the next few years, he would accompany Downer on many of his overseas trips. Sometimes, they would find an opportunity to sneak in a game of tennis between meetings. "I used to say that, as a doubles partner, Alexander made a very good foreign minister," Frydenberg laughs.

"He was a good mentor and leader. Not without his faults. He could have a temper. He could say things that were unnecessary. But he worked hard. And he was a person of conviction with strongly held beliefs. Not afraid to call it as it is.

"That would sometimes get him into trouble. Sometimes, he could be quick to comment without thinking through all of the repercussions. He made some mistakes but his record was strong."

Under the Howard Government, Frydenberg worked as a senior

adviser in the offices both of the Foreign Affairs Minister and the Prime Minister, an unusual vantage-point. Of the two men, he says: "Howard and Downer had a special relationship. There was mutual respect: an alignment of values and priorities and a high degree of trust."

Hunt, too, would remain a close confidant of the Foreign Minister. But not without occasional hiccups:

> In his first term, I went off to do a lecture at ANU. They had asked me to do a lecture on international law.
>
> We titled it, 'International Law in the Mind of the Minister'.
>
> At that time, there had been a bit of an issue running and Alexander had been in the headlines, right at the centre of a public debate. Anyway, this lecture was supposed to be Chatham House rules.
>
> I've realised ever since then that there is no such thing as Chatham House rules. That was a lesson.
>
> So, I began, 'I came here to speak about International Law in the Mind of the Minister before the Mind of the Minister became a national issue'. And that, of course, appeared in the *Canberra Times*.
>
> I was mortified. Even though I was his senior adviser, I still thought, 'This is not good'. I took it in to him to confess. He laughed it off. I always appreciated that. He had a great sense of perspective. That doesn't mean he didn't feel pressure or he didn't get grumpy. But he was able to show understanding.
>
> We debated a lot, we argued a lot. He respected people who would raise an argument with him...

Mostly, Downer tried not to sweat the small stuff — the distractions, the pinpricks, the trivia. Not always successfully.

Hunt recalls a commercial flight to Los Angeles where Downer and he were seated at the front of the aircraft on opposite sides of the aisle. There they encountered another passenger, who seemed keen to have a very spirited argument. "Behind us was some guy who was incredibly loud. He had been drinking," says Hunt:

> Alexander looked over at him a few times, as if to say,

'Settle down, mate'. He became more and more raucous. And then he bellowed, 'Isn't that the effing Foreign Minister of Australia?' I turned around and said, 'Yes it is. But out of respect for the other passengers could we quieten things down?' It was the middle of the night and a lot of people were trying to sleep.

But he got louder and louder. Eventually, Alexander turned to him and said, incredibly forcefully and with a finger to his mouth, 'Shush!'

And the guy screeches, 'Doesn't he know who I am?' And I said, 'Look, I apologise, but I don't know who you are'. And Alexander looked at me as if to say, 'You deal with it.' 'Oh, thanks a lot' I thought.

So this guy said, 'I'm Peter Fonda (the actor) and my brother in law is Ted Turner, who owns CNN, and I'm going to destroy your boss through CNN'. And I thought, 'This is a nightmare. I have an angry Alexander, and I have this guy who could do some damage'.

Fortuitously, Hunt had a draft of a speech Downer was to deliver to the UN. "Funny you should say that," Hunt told Fonda, "because I have this speech Alexander is just about to give where he is praising the role of CNN and Ted Turner during the Gulf War. Here is the section of the speech. We wouldn't want to take that out and say you were the cause of it'. Eventually, he went, 'Alright, I'll shut up' and left us alone.

"So we landed in LA and Alexander said, 'How did you turn that around?' I explained what had happened. And he said, 'Give me a look at that speech'. And he said, 'Throw out that bit. I'm not saying that'.

"So the speech had served its purpose — Peter Fonda had calmed down. But that part of the speech was never delivered."

Hunt says Downer was never under any illusions about the ruthless workings of power politics — at the UN, and in his dealings with allies or ideological rivals:

> He had the strategic context sorted in his own mind. Trade was important, obviously. In the geo-strategic equation, he recognised that the US Alliance was indispensable. And we did have constructive humanitarian duties...

But he was open-eyed about the shortcomings of the international system — the different arms of the UN and some of the areas of corruption or just obstruction. He had a philosophy about all of this. And, within that, he worked immensely hard. He was able to do the strategic, the granular and the diplomatic. Those were the core skills. He continued to grow ... and he never grew tired of it.

For all that, appraisals of Downer's performance as Foreign Affairs Minister were mixed. As the Howard Government approached the anniversary of its first-year in office, some in the media had no hesitation about delivering harsh judgments on how the government was faring in its prosecution of its foreign policy and strategic goals. Downer was on the wrong end of a lot of the commentary.

International affairs commentator for the *Sydney Morning Herald*, Peter Hartcher, a prominent and consistent critic, would later argue that Downer had been lucky to survive politically. Hartcher wrote that, "ordinarily a Prime Minister would have removed a minister with a first year as bad as Alexander Downer's as foreign minister."

Yet if there was one decision Alexander Downer had cause to regret more than any other in his first term as Australia's Minister for Foreign Affairs, it was nothing to do with policy towards the US, China, Japan, or Indonesia.

In hindsight, it would be the long-term repercussions of Australia's decision in July, 1998, to sign up to the Rome Statute to create the International Criminal Court. Almost 30 years later, the ICC would be weaponised against the state of Israel.

Downer is not known for blanket criticism of the institutions of the United Nations. He worked closely with UN leaders like Kofi Annan and Sergio Vieira de Mello to augment the birth of East Timor as an independent nation. In later years, he would take on the role of Special Adviser to UN Secretary-General, Ban Ki-moon, in attempting to mediate the long-running, sometimes violent — and stubbornly irreconcilable — divisions between Greek and Turkish traditions on the island of Cyprus. He acknowledges the UN's capacity and potential to do good works. But he is a pragmatic multilateralist. Just as he sees the UN's strengths, he also laments its failings.

The posturing and preening at the UN General Assembly — where dictators and demagogues would be greeted with standing ovations for vituperative speeches attacking the Western powers — was an endless source of aggravation.

But, for Downer, there was nothing more infuriating than the UN's punitive stance towards Israel, the lone democracy in the Middle East.

Decades earlier, in 1948, the UN had been fundamental to the creation of the Jewish state. In more recent years, through a weirdly monotonous ritual of UN General Assembly resolutions castigating Israel above all others, it began to look hell-bent on Israel's vilification.

This animosity peaked with the war in Gaza, ignited by the barbaric October 7 assault on southern Israel by Hamas operatives in 2023. It would serve to highlight what Israel and its friends have come to regard as blatant institutional bias at the UN against Israel's interests.

As they saw it, official UN condemnation of murder, rape and abduction of more than 1200 Israeli citizens by Hamas terrorists was relatively muted when compared to the howls of outrage that followed the inevitable Israeli reprisals against Hamas' networks in Gaza.

The controversy climaxed in the decision in 2024 by the UN's chief prosecutorial arm, the International Criminal Court, to indict Israel's Prime Minister, Binyamin Netanyahu, and Defence Minister, Yoav Gallant, for alleged war crimes.

Downer makes no attempt to hide his anger and frustration at the actions of the ICC in seeking to prosecute the elected leaders of Israel.

As he told Chris Kenny on *SKY News* in November, 2024, the abuse and misuse of the ICC's process had led him to regret ever signing up to the establishment of the judicial body:

> This decision represents the politicisation of the International Criminal Court and it leads me to a rather sad conclusion: the only courts we can rely on as Australians are our own courts... never again would I have gone down the path of getting involved in something like the International Criminal Court.

The concept of the ICC was born in the 1990s, shaped by global revulsion at atrocities committed during wars in the former Yugoslavia and in the brutal ethnic conflict in Rwanda. If dictators or warlords responsible for human rights abuses of their own or other people would never be prosecuted at home, the growing consensus was that this demanded a new approach — an international mechanism to ensure these crimes would not go unpunished.

Greg Hunt, while at Yale, had worked for the Special Rapporteur investigating war crimes in the former Yugoslavia. He was Downer's key adviser throughout the negotiations over the creation of the ICC.

"I had helped to write some of the grittiest, nastiest parts of the compilation of human rights abuses which then led on to the Select Tribunal on war crimes in the former Yugoslavia," he says. "So these issues were very live and very real."

Hunt reflects on a Human Rights Day speech in the first year of the Howard Government by then Australian human rights commissioner, Chris Sidoti, in which Australia had offered in-principle support for the concept of an International Criminal Court. Sidoti had said the special tribunal set up to investigate war crimes in the former Yugoslavia could become a template for something more enduring: "The Tribunal may well become what we have needed for a long time — a permanent international criminal court to try war crimes, crimes against humanity and gross human rights violations."

Hunt played a key role in steering the proposal through the Coalition:

> It wasn't necessarily all that controversial at the time. There were some who raised their eyebrows. I do remember recommending it to Alexander — absolutely, I own that — and he adopted it.
>
> Howard sort of said ok. Although he had reservations. And, of course, America was not signing on, even under Clinton. So that carried weight, particularly with the conservative wing.
>
> Anyway, as I recall, it was not really a major issue at that point. It brewed over a number of years.

Hunt would go with Downer to the Statute of Rome conference in July, 1998. Australia was at the table for the critical debates about the foundation principles for the creation of a new international legal body to investigate and prosecute war crimes.

Hunt remembers there being a lot of focus on "safeguards" to very carefully define the remit and powers of the Court. "Much of this seems to have been lost in the current debate," he says, pointedly.

By 2002, when it came to ratifying the Treaty, and actually bringing the Court into existence, the debate was to become more contentious, in Australia as elsewhere. By this time, Hunt was an elected MP. He combined forces with Josh Frydenberg, then a senior adviser in Downer's office, to gather support for ratification within the Coalition party room, and the Cabinet.

Josh Frydenberg, of the Jewish faith himself, threw his support behind his minister. "The government had committed to it. It was one of Alexander's key commitments," Frydenberg explains. "It would have made Downer's job difficult if he had been unable to see it through. That would've undercut him."

By this time, there was much greater scepticism within government about the risks and ramifications inherent in ratifying the ICC, including within the office of the Prime Minister.

The chief opponents included Cabinet minister, Tony Abbott and prominent backbencher, Bronwyn Bishop, along with several National Party MPs. "In the end, Howard backed his Foreign Affairs Minister," says Hunt. "I always thought that was a 'quid pro quo' for Alexander being faultlessly loyal to him. It doesn't mean they didn't have arguments or debates or grizzle about each other, now and then. But they backed each other in ..."

Yet that decision, in the longer term, would ricochet dramatically. For as long as the ICC has existed, there would be concerted efforts by supporters of the Palestinian cause to mobilise the ICC against one state actor more than any other — the government of Israel.

Across the first decade of the ICC, this campaign ran into insuperable legal hurdles. For one thing, the jurisdiction of the ICC was purportedly limited expressly to signatories to the Rome Statute. While Israel signed the Rome Statute in 2000, its legislature, the Knesset, had never ratified it. The US Congress adopted the same approach.

Forty other countries did not sign the treaty at all, including China, Ethiopia, India, Indonesia, Iraq, North Korea, Saudi Arabia and Turkey. Another three dozen signed the statute, but their legislatures did not ratify. Apart from the United States, these included Egypt, Iran, Russia, Sudan, Syria ... as well as Israel. So Israel was one among almost 80 countries that had not ceded to the jurisdiction of the Court.

As for the Palestinian Territories, the repeated failures to achieve a negotiated peace and agreed borders with Israel meant the citizens of the West Bank and Gaza could not have formal recognition as a state party under the remit of the ICC. As the law applied, this meant any allegations of war crimes or human rights abuses — on either side of the Israel/Palestinian divide — were effectively beyond the ICC's reach.

In 2009, the Palestinian National Authority sought to rewrite the rules.

It signed and submitted an *ad hoc* declaration, accepting ICC jurisdiction for "acts committed on the territory of Palestine since 1 July 2002." This was ruled invalid because the Rome Statute only permits "States" to make such a declaration.

In November, 2012, the UN General Assembly stepped up the pressure yet again, passing Resolution 67/19 which recognised Palestine as a "non-member state". But the new ICC Chief Prosecutor, Gambian lawyer Fatou Bensouda, again ruled that this decision did "not cure the legal invalidity of the 2009 declaration."

In July, 2014, the Palestinian National Authority renewed its efforts to bring its territories — and, by extension, Israel — within the purview of the ICC. This time, Bensouda yielded, despite Israel's strong protests that this was a travesty of international law. A year later, she recognised Palestine as a state party for the purposes of the ICC. Its prosecutors began working to assemble a human rights case against Israel to bring before the Court.

Once conflict erupted in Gaza — as a result of the October 7 attacks on Israel by Hamas — it was inevitable the ICC would swing into action.

In May, 2024, ICC Chief Prosecutor, Karim Ahmad Khan, announced indictments of Netanyahu and Gallant for crimes against humanity.

As if to feign even-handedness, he also cited the leader of the military wing of Hamas, Mohammed Deif (although Deif would never face prosecution given he is believed to have died in an Israeli bombing).

In doing so, Khan appeared to skate over an important foundational principle of the ICC — another legal barrier thought likely to prevent pro-Palestinian activists commandeering the ICC as their hunting-dog against the state of Israel. This was the rule of complementarity.

In short, this rule stipulated that the ICC would only be called into action when a state did not have its own independent judicial processes capable of prosecuting political or military leaders accused of crimes. Given the proven history of Israel's Supreme Court in trying political leaders who had breached the law, surely this would rule out any move by the ICC against Israel?

Yet, on November 21, a pre-trial chamber of the ICC, while war in Gaza was still raging, accepted Khan's pre-emptive strike against the leaders of Israel and ordered that the prosecution proceed. This created the opening for Netanyahu and Gallant to be arrested in any country that was a signatory to the ICC. Including Australia.

Hunt acknowledges the ICC had strayed far beyond the rules set for its establishment — and the intent of those who championed its creation:

> Today, everyone in the Liberal Party thinks (the indictment of Netanyahu and Gallant) is the wrong decision. But I still don't think it was the wrong decision at the time to sign up.
>
> There was almost an historic inevitability about it. And we were present at the table. To have stayed out of it would have created a position not unlike the refusal to ratify the Kyoto Protocol. It would have placed Australia in a very difficult position. I think it would have been harder to explain than Kyoto.
>
> Sadly, what has happened since is that there has been this whole movement towards prosecution along ideological lines. To be fair, some at the time warned of this. I accept that. I mean, the fact the ICC never indicted (Syria's) Bashar al-Assad. They haven't indicted anyone from Iran. Or Sudan and Somalia.
>
> The indictment of Netanyahu and Gallant was not a just process and certainly not a just outcome. It wasn't the court operating as a true and proper court.
>
> For Australia, the simple answer is to be very clear that we will not enforce this judgment because of profound concerns about the process, the justice, the intention of the prosecutor.

For his part, Downer is angered by what he sees as the betrayal by the ICC of the honourable ambitions that led to its founding. It was never intended for the Court to run political or ideological show trials of elected democratic leaders.

In his view, the only way to salvage the credibility of the Court would be to agree a series of reforms: "We should get together with like-minded countries and put forward amendments to the Charter. If those amendments are rejected, we should withdraw from it."

If nothing else, this would be to acknowledge that much has changed in the Middle East, and the wider world, since the ICC was first set up. Back then, the Oslo peace process was still very much alive. There was hope that Israeli and the Palestinians could resolve their differences. The optimism of the immediate post Cold War era still flickered.

That is not today's reality. In the succeeding decades, hopes for a broadly liberal global order would subside, with many governments across the world trampling the humanitarian rights of their people — in parts of Africa, the Middle East, Russia and its surrounds, and places like Afghanistan.

Distress and disruption for societies suffering under incompetent, corrupt, repressive rulers would proliferate.

The human costs continued to be intolerably high as people fled war zones and tyrannical governments in search of sanctuary — and, also, as a flood of 'economic refugees' left their homes and poured across the borders into Western nations in the hope of improved financial prospects and a better life for themselves and their children.

For the Howard Government, there were challenges aplenty to come, as a ragged armada of leaky boats began arriving in Australian waters.

7

Tampa and Turnbacks

The rule of the Taliban in Afghanistan was having a destabilising impact on Australia well before al-Qaeda's September 11 attacks on the US. From mid-1999, the exodus of thousands of Afghani citizens fleeing their homeland in hope of a peaceful, more prosperous life would contribute to a surge of would-be migrants arriving by boat — unannounced and unauthorised — in Australia's territorial waters.

Following World War 2, and the Soviet takeover of much of Eastern Europe, Australia had demonstrated a commitment matched by few other nations to resettling refugees driven from their homes by wars or hostile ideologies. Yet there would always be high levels of political and public discomfort in Australian communities whenever boatloads of people began arriving uninvited on the nation's shores.

Early in the 2000s, the spectacle of 8000 people a year descending on Australia, demanding to be treated as refugees, became an epic political, legal and humanitarian challenge for the Howard Government. This peaked with the so-called "Tampa Affair".

The response of the Howard Government generated much controversy, even hysteria — in Australia, and internationally. It would become a pivotal moment in the government's strategy to re-establish orderly processes around Australia's refugee intake. Downer and his colleagues saw their hardline response as critical to restoring public confidence in the integrity and stability of the nation's immigration program.

On August 26, 2001, a Norwegian freight ship, the *MV Tampa*, rescued 433 people from a disabled fishing vessel 140km from Christmas Island. These were mostly young Afghani men. When the captain of the ship, Arne Rinnan, began steering towards the nearest destination in Indonesia, the ferry port of Merak, a swarm of passengers came onto the bridge demanding the freighter turn back towards Australia.

The captain steered the ship around and set sail for Christmas Island.

When the Tampa attempted to enter Australian waters, there was a standoff. The captain was refused entry. The Howard Government was resolute: those on board the *Tampa* would not be landing in Australia.

The Norwegian Government was equally insistent. The captain had reported the *Tampa* was in distress. Under international maritime law, they argued, the ship had to be allowed entry into Australian waters.

Around 3am on August 27, Downer was phoned by the Norwegian Foreign Minister, Thorbjorn Ragland, at his home in Adelaide. His sleep disrupted, Downer was not happy about the call... or the conversation. His response was blunt: "I don't have to be very wide awake, Minister, to tell you that we are not going to allow them to land in Australia. The *Tampa* can take these people to Indonesia."

Downer was infuriated by the response from Oslo. The Foreign Minister told Downer, dismissively: "It doesn't really matter, in the end, what you think. The ship is going to land them in Australia."

"I said, 'Well, Minister, that is a bold thing to say — quite an aggressive thing to say. But I think I can give you an assurance that we won't allow them to land, and we can make sure that doesn't happen'."

Downer had already been involved in discussions with Howard and Defence Minister, Peter Reith:

> At the Cabinet meetings we had, Howard was insistent that these people would not come to Australia. There was some discussion about whether it was legally possible to stop the ship landing here. But Howard said, 'No they are not coming here'. He was absolutely insistent. He said to all the relevant ministers — Defence, Attorney-General, Immigration — 'It is your job to make sure this does not happen'. His resolve was impressive. It was that sort of determination that made him a standout.

Within 24 hours, Australian special forces landed on the ship, and took control. It was the first time a boat trying to enter Australia carrying asylum-seekers had been met with this type of force. The *Tampa* would never dock at Christmas Island.

Howard wanted an alternative solution. The Government would have to find somewhere else for the *Tampa* passengers to be landed.

Downer was able to deliver. He spoke to the president of the island state of Nauru, Rene Harris. The Pacific micro-state had only recently sought from Australia financial assistance to secure some much-needed energy supplies for the island community.

Downer had already committed Australia to help. Would Nauru now consider lending Australia a hand by providing some temporary accommodation for the *Tampa* boat people? Harris agreed.

So began the controversial Pacific Solution.

Like any nation-state, Australia has a sovereign right to determine who enters its territory. But the legal debate around this simple truth is complex and contentious. International treaty law requires that countries must not return refugees to other countries or territories where they might face persecution on account of race, religion, nationality, political opinion or membership of a party, or where they might face torture or cruel and degrading treatment or punishment.

In its response to the *Tampa* crisis, the Howard Government introduced a suite of new laws and regulations involving migration excision zones and offshore processing arrangements on Nauru, as well the maintenance of the mandatory detention laws introduced by the previous Labor Government for those unauthorised arrivals who were able to evade the defences and make it through to Australia. Critics called it a 'Fortress Australia' approach.

Christmas Island and other Australian territories in the Pacific would no longer come under the jurisdiction of Australian immigration law. The government also implemented a policy allowing the Royal Australian Navy and customs officials to turn back boats.

The Government made no secret of its intent: anybody attempting to make an unlawful landing by boat in Australia would be denied entry. They would instead be held in offshore detention centres, where their claims to refugee status would be processed.

Some of these policies caused an uproar in sections of the Australian community. Yet, like the decision to stop the *Tampa*, the policies had the support of a majority of Australians.

The Howard Government argued these policies did not contravene either the letter or the spirit of a humane, non-discriminatory immigration policy.

Indeed, Downer and others would insist the measures adopted were in support of the over-arching integrity of Australia's border control policies: first, by frustrating the criminal syndicates running 'people smuggling' rackets out of Java and other south-east Asian launch pads; second, by preventing tragic deaths at sea that were inevitable when people boarded cramped, leaky boats for ocean crossings — and, thirdly, by reassuring everyday Australians that asylum-seekers were not able *en masse* to poke holes in an orderly, well-functioning immigration system.

The *Tampa* episode also promoted a wholesale review by the Howard Government of how to deal with the curse of people-smuggling across the region — and, in particular, how to work in tandem with Indonesia.

Bill Farmer was Secretary of the Department of Immigration through much of this time. He was part of the diplomatic efforts to build greater co-operation with Jakarta:

> We agreed with the Indonesians to start the Bali process on irregular people movements. That was a very significant breakthrough. And we built on that with agreements with Indonesia to co-host new regional processes not only on people-smuggling, but also counter-terrorism and illegal fishing. It suited the Indonesians, too — Indonesia, as a democracy, could assert its leadership role in the region.

There was an immediate practical benefit for Indonesia that flowed from the Howard Government's tough stance on asylum-seekers. By Australia sending the unambiguous signal that it would not tolerate unauthorised boat arrivals on its shores, this in turn would discourage the flood of asylum-seekers to Java.

For his part, Alexander Downer couldn't be prouder of his government's record on immigration — and that of the Liberal Party from the time of its founding in 1947: "The Liberal Party, has been the great party of migration in Australia. Liberal governments have brought huge numbers of migrants to Australia during their terms in office… as part of that notion of building the nation."

Downer's father was, of course, a Minister for Immigration under Menzies. And he had set as his goal the creation of an immigration policy that would become the gold standard, globally.

This was the era of the 'New Australians'. Although this expression came to be regarded by some almost as a pejorative in its later life — it was, at the time, viewed as emblematic of the ambitions and aspirations of early postwar Australia to grow and prosper.

As Alexander Downer explains it: "It was this sense people had over the years: that modern Australia — not historic Australia, but modern Australia — was a new country. To build this new society here, you needed migrants. So the concept of advancing the nation couldn't happen without a successful immigration program."

But, as he is also keen to remind people, it was never about opening the floodgates:

> This had to be a very carefully thought-out and planned program. Random immigration is only going to lead to chaos.
>
> A well-constructed immigration program can prove to be incredibly successful ... and, of all the countries which have immigration policies, I think Australia has proved to be pretty much the most successful. Extraordinarily successful in — to use a phrase, 'deciding who comes to Australia, and the circumstances in which they come'. And I think we should stick with it. I don't think Australia, which is a huge continent, should abandon its ambition of continuing to build a great country ...

According to Downer, scrupulous planning had been vital to the success of Australia's immigration program through the postwar era. Governments had to maintain integrity and orderliness in the system to ensure continuing, widespread community acceptance and support. They could only do this by demonstrating the influx of new arrivals was administered in a methodical yet humane way.

The current vexed migration debates in many European countries, including Britain, illustrate the political risks — as well as the dangers to social cohesion — when a migration program is perceived as being out of control. Says Downer: "I think the public in Britain and Australia have the same attitude to immigration. In essence, they do. The people in the UK today are not against immigration. They never were... what they are against is uncontrolled, chaotic immigration. And I think Australians are the same."

8

A Dagger to the Heart

It was October 13, 2002 — nearing 4am on a Sunday. Chris Kenny, media adviser to Alexander Downer, was awakened from his sleep by his phone ringing at his Adelaide home. On the line was Ian Kemish, head of Consular at the Department of Foreign Affairs and Trade. He had called with ominous news from the Indonesian island of Bali.

"I'm not sure whether to call you or the chief of staff but you're in the same city as the Minister, so I have decided to call you," Kemish said. He then reported the news nobody wants to hear: "It looks like there's been an explosion in Bali. We don't know why or how. It is at a nightclub frequented by Australians. There could be casualties."

The details were vague. But Kenny knew this was serious enough for a senior DFAT official to rouse him from his sleep in the middle of the night. He thought about calling Downer immediately but realised he had too little concrete information to pass on. So he sat up by himself, checking whether there were any media reports that could shed more light on what had happened on the holiday island to Australia's north.

"Very soon after, I get another call from Kemish," says Kenny. "He explains that our consul-general in Bali has been down to the site, and what used to be the Sari Club is just a hole in the ground. And we knew there were likely to be a lot of Aussies there."

Kenny called Downer straight away: "Alexander. You need to know this. I will get dressed and come straight over."

Says Downer: "There was an assumption of Australian casualties … but the full horror of it didn't become clear until a few hours later."

These were to become some of the most intense and heart-wrenching days in modern Australia's history. The Bali bombings would be the single biggest terrorist attack on Australian citizens.

Eighty-eight Australian holidaymakers were among the 202 people who died in the car bomb attack on the Sari Club and the simultaneous suicide bombing of Paddy's Bar in the popular beach resort of Kuta.

It is important to understand the special significance of Bali to

Australians. For many young Australians, particularly, the short flight to the island destination is their first experience of overseas travel: tropical heat, glistening beaches, cultural immersion in idyllic towns like Ubud, and the popular bars and clubs offering a relaxed, no-frills nightlife of drinking, dancing and camaraderie.

The Bali bombing was an attempt to shatter that dream.

The perpetrators would later be revealed as adherents to an extreme Islamist sect, Jemaah Islamiyah, based on the main Indonesian island of Java. While suspected from the outset, this could not be confirmed publicly for days to come. All that Australians knew on that morning was that they had suffered a terrorist strike as cruel and inhumane as any since ... the September 11 attacks on America.

Kenny recalls the entire nation being in shock: "Alexander had to go out and explain this horror to the media. So that people in Australia had some understanding of what was going on."

As it happens, Downer already had a prior arrangement for an interview at his Adelaide Hills home that morning by Laurie Oakes on the *Sunday* program — on something completely unrelated. "I got there between 6 and 7," says Kenny. "My phone was in meltdown. His front yard at Bridgewater was over-run with 'live eyes' and TV trucks..."

By this time, Downer had been given primary responsibility to handle the crisis. DFAT would be the lead agency.

Help line numbers had been set up to assist people desperately trying to contact missing loved ones. The Australian Federal Police had been in contact with their counterparts in Jakarta.

By 10am on that Sunday, two RAAF Hercules aircraft were flying to the Balinese capital, Denpasar, with medical specialists on board. In the next day or two, another 10 emergency flights would land to ferry the wounded and the grieving back to Australia.

DFAT called a crisis meeting of all the key agencies involved in emergency health care, evacuation procedures, forensic sciences, counter-terrorism and policing. Hospitals in Darwin were put on notice to expect an influx of emergency cases.

Downer had spoken to the Australian Ambassador in Jakarta, Ric Smith. Indonesia had already declared the Bali bombing a terrorist crime. The Howard Government wanted to press the case for a full-spectrum joint investigation involving police and security officials from both nations. That afternoon, Prime Minister Howard made the same call, to the Indonesian President, Megawati Sukarnoputri.

"We immediately thought: Who did this, why did they do it, and how do we find out?" says Downer. "The short answer was that we obviously needed full co-operation with the Indonesians…"

This was a question of extreme sensitivity for the Indonesian Government. As Kenny explains: "They could easily have said, 'This has happened on our soil so leave it up to us'. Our focus was on getting a joint investigation happening so our people could assist in getting to the bottom of who was behind the bombings …."

Downer flew into Canberra the next morning for an emergency meeting of the National Security Committee of Cabinet. All the nation's defence, police and intelligence chiefs were in attendance.

Downer then flew into Bali late on that Monday night. Among those he took with him were the Minister for Justice, Chris Ellison, chief commissioner of the Australian Federal Police, Mick Keelty, the head of the Australian Security Intelligence Organisation, Dennis Richardson, and his ASIS counterpart, David Irvine.

Arriving at the site of the Bali bombings
(Choo Youn-Kong/ Getty Images)

Chris Kenny went along to handle the media crush.

"It's 23 years on and it still makes me weep," says Kenny. "It was terrible. Guys are coming up to me, saying, 'We're here on a surfing trip but we've lost our mate'. Parents saying, 'We can't find our kids'."

The immediate priorities were to identify the Australians killed, to provide pastoral care for families who had lost loved ones, to determine what had happened to those still missing, and to get the best medical assistance for the hundreds of people injured, burned and traumatised. This meant emergency flights to evacuate the most seriously wounded back to Australia.

But, always at the forefront, there was another pressing agenda — to identify and hunt down those responsible for the bombings.

On arrival in Denpasar, Downer went straight into meetings with the Bali police chief, Major-General I Made Pastika. On that Tuesday morning, the two Australian ministers laid wreaths at the bomb sites.

The scenes were horrific. But nothing could prepare the Australian delegation for what awaited them at the local Sanglah Hospital.

The medical infrastructure was rudimentary. Amid intense heat and humidity, the hospital only had the facilities to store six dead bodies in the refrigerated morgue.

On the night of the bombing, and the day that followed, ambulances and emergency workers brought the fatally wounded to the hospital's doors. The sheer scale of the carnage had overwhelmed the hospital's capacity to cope. They had no choice but to pile bodies on ice.

"It was non-stop …. and incredibly tough," says Kenny. "By mid-afternoon, we went back to the Consul-General's. Alexander was emotionally drained. He had showed no signs of this out there in front of people. He had held it together impressively. But he looked like a bloke who had the blood sucked out of him."

A meeting with Australian expats was organised for later that day, at the *Hard Rock Hotel* down on the beachfront.

"There were 200 or so people there, in boardshorts and what have you, all looking frantic," says Kenny. "Alexander spoke off the cuff, and asked people to tell us how we could help. They're coming up to him. He's holding their hands. They can't find their daughter. They can't find their mates. They're hugging him.

"Many of them might have been Labor voters… but he was there representing Australia, and promising to do everything we possibly could to help, and they were all just so grateful. It's difficult to explain the emotional intensity of it.

"I found it really hard to hold myself together. He was obviously in a much more difficult, high-stress position. You could easily have fallen into a blabbering mess. But he had the responsibility to work out what to do. He embraced people, listened to them, held it all together."

Reflecting on this, Downer speaks of that day as an unforgettably heart-wrenching experience: "It was very harrowing, incredibly emotional."

But he says he was reminded of a lesson from his mother: "Mate, it's not about you. It's about them. Don't think about your emotions. Think about them. These were people who had lost children. There were a lot of tears. I was there to help them. I was someone from Australia who had some power to help them."

That night, Downer flew to Jakarta. He went into meetings the next morning with Susilo Bambang Yudhoyono, at the time Indonesia's Co-Ordinating Minister for Security (who would later serve two terms as Indonesia's President). "We had a very successful meeting with their national security team," he says. "They agreed there would be full collaboration between all of our respective security agencies."

With Indonesian President, Susilo Bambang Yudhoyono and future Prime Minister, Malcolm Turnbull (Alan Pryke/ Newspix)

Downer regards this joint commitment, forged amid the gruesome tragedy of events in Bali, as among the most significant moments in his years in government. Nothing could ever be done to console the many families mourning the loss of loved ones. But ensuring the fanatics responsible for the murders were hunted down and prosecuted — and working closely with Indonesia to limit the dangers to other innocent lives — would at least provide some comfort that justice would prevail.

It served as a major inflection point in relations with Indonesia. "We had been through a tough time over East Timor," says Downer. "It hadn't been that long before. So here was the extraordinary thing — it was agreed there would be close co-operation with the AFP and ASIO and ASIS. A lot of countries might have resisted. We had a meeting with President Megawati, too, and she was all for collaboration. So we set up this joint operation — and it worked incredibly well."

These were the first steps in a dramatic reset of relations with Indonesia. But, in the immediate aftershock of the Bali bombings, the strategic significance of this was not a headline issue back in Australia.

Downer would return home to be confronted by a media frenzy over delays in identifying the victims of the Bali bombings. One Sydney radio host hammered Downer over the treatment of the family of a friend in the sporting world whose wife had been among the Australians killed. They knew this because they had identified her body in the morgue — she had a distinctive tattoo. Why was it taking so long to confirm this officially? This was heartless, incompetent. Why couldn't they bring her body home?

Chris Kenny remembers the interview: "Alexander stayed calm. He said it was very important that we get this right. We can't make any mistakes. We have to trust the experts." Weeks later, the AFP victim-identification team reported back on their findings from the morgue. Similar tattoo — but, as it turned out, it was, in fact, a different woman.

The hunt for the Bali bombers progressed rapidly. A week after the Bali attacks, Indonesian police in Java arrested Muslim cleric, Abu Bakar Bashir, the spiritual leader of Jemaah Islamiyah. Over the following months, more than 30 other JI militants suspected of involvement in the Bali attacks were arrested across South-East Asia.

One of the planners of the Bali terrorist operation, Imam Samudra, was arrested in November, 2002, and sentenced to death a year later.

He confessed his involvement in the attacks and claimed that it was his Muslim duty to fight infidels.

In December 2002 Ali Ghufron (also known as Mukhlas) was arrested in Java. He, too, confessed to involvement in the planning of the Bali bombings, and admitted to recruiting two of his brothers, Ali Imron and Amrozi bin Nurhasyim, to help assemble and transport the bombs used in the attacks. Mukhlas and bin Nurhasyim were sentenced to death, while Imron expressed remorse and was given a life sentence.

Two other men, Azahari Husin and Dulmatin, suspected of building and triggering the bombs, were killed during police raids.

The mastermind of the attacks, Riduan Isamuddin (known more commonly by his *nom-de-guerre* Hambali) was arrested in Thailand in August, 2003, in a joint operation by the CIA and Thai police. Hambali, the military leader of Jemaah Islamiyah, was a close associate of Osama Bin Laden and al-Qaeda's operational chief, Khalid Sheikh Mohammed. Hambali would be held for the next two decades as one of 14 "high-value detainees" at the US top-security prison, Guantanamo Bay.

Jemaah Islamiyah was founded in the late 1960s with the aim of promoting fundamentalist Islamic beliefs — predominantly in Indonesia but also Malaysia, Singapore, Thailand and the Philippines.

In the late 1990s, the organisation had become more radicalised, and was suspected of engaging in sporadic violence. It also established links with al-Qaeda and was known to have provided logistical support to Muslim militants in south east Asia.

However, it was only with the Bali bombings that JI announced itself as a perpetrator of terrorist attacks on Western targets.

In the Australian Parliament, Downer would be subjected to intense questioning over why JI and its militants had not been more firmly on the radar of Australian intelligence agencies before the Bali attack.

Seizing on the controversy at the time over intelligence failings in Iraq, Labor's then foreign affairs spokesman, Kevin Rudd, sought to pursue Downer on why the Government had not acted earlier to warn Australians of the risk of a terrorist attack in Bali.

Later, on the ABC's *Lateline* program, Downer would admit openly there were intelligence failures: " Of course there were, because we didn't have the information about the operation.

"There was an intelligence failure by us, by the Indonesians, by countries with enormous intelligence resources, above all the United States. We all failed in terms of picking up the intelligence."

But Downer defended his Department and the intelligence agencies against claims they been caught napping. "The travel advisory did warn of possible terrorist attacks, so it's not as though the department or the intelligence agencies were wrong," Downer said. "They just didn't identify Bali as a specific target ... obviously they should have done but they didn't have the information..."

JI's activities had been under surveillance. The Office of National Assessments had briefed Downer on its concerns about JI in July, 2002, four months before the Bali bombings.

But, as Downer would insist, the advice from the intelligence agencies had warned of potential attacks on civilian targets in Indonesia, Malaysia, Thailand and Singapore. While Bali had been listed as one among several notional targets, there had "no specific intelligence on a specific threat, at a specific time or place".

As the ONA would concede in a formal submission to a Senate inquiry: "Neither before the briefing nor later did ONA have intelligence identifying Bali as an actual target."

On this basis, Downer was advised not to update the travel warnings for Australians planning to holiday in Bali. Howard, as Prime Minister, would back Downer, saying: "You adjust travel advisories on the basis of specific information. There was no specific information."

As Australia and Indonesia worked with regional partners to scour all of south-east Asia in the hunt for JI operatives, the threat within Indonesia itself remained haunting.

On August 5, 2003, a suicide bomber detonated a car bomb outside the Marriott Hotel in Jakarta, killing 12 people and injuring 150. Police identified in the car bomb the same mixture of explosives as used in Bali. The 28-year-old bomber was soon identified as another JI recruit. This atrocity, like in Bali, had been a terror plot conceived by Hambali.

On August 7, 2003, *The Age* in Melbourne carried some analysis on the implications of this latest assault on Indonesia — another attempt to undermine the massive Muslim nation's efforts to embed a democratic culture:

Indonesia's police have performed beyond all expectations in their determination to round up the suspects in the Bali bombings. The rapid and resolute effort to track down the killers who caused so much damage to Indonesia's international profile appears to have worked wonders for the image of law-enforcement authorities among the Indonesian people. Given the sorry history of official corruption, this marks a significant step forward.

Sadly, however, the Jakarta bombing represents a reality check. The fact Islamic radicals were able to inflict grievous loss of life by bombing a major international hotel in Jakarta's business district confirms the unavoidable truth. Although Jemaah Islamiyah has been dealt a serious blow by international efforts to hunt down its operatives and shut off its financial and logistical support systems, this aggressive strain of religious fanaticism is far from defeated.

Indonesia has done well to detain more than 30 leading Islamic radicals, including the spiritual leader of JI, Abu Bakar Bashir. But this is a long way short of draining the swamp. Counter-terrorism experts have estimated that at least 500 South-East Asian Muslims trained with the jihadis in Afghanistan or the southern Philippines. Most are believed to be Indonesian nationals ...

What is at stake here is not just the survival of the new Indonesia, important though that is.

For every time the radical Islamists seek to undermine the stability of Indonesia, they are also striking a blow against the future security of this part of the world.

In September, 2004, the regional counter-terrorism efforts led by Indonesia and Australia would suffer another grievous setback. This time, Jemaah Islamiyah set out to deliver an audaciously terrifying message to the governments of both countries: this time, they would explode a one-tonne car bomb in the heart of the Indonesian capital — right outside the Australian Embassy in Jakarta.

Eleven people would die, with another 180 wounded, including an embassy security guard Anton Sujarwo, 23, and four Indonesian policemen on duty at the embassy. The other victims were civilians, including an embassy gardener, someone arriving at the embassy to apply for a visa and a passing pedestrian. The bomb also caused damage at the nearby Greek and Chinese embassies.

The bombing was carried out with the clear intent of intimidating decision-makers in Jakarta and Canberra. Both nations had elections scheduled for the coming weeks. A local Islamic website carried a message purportedly from Jemaah Islamiyah, claiming responsibility for the embassy bombing and warning of more to come.

"We advise Australians in Indonesia to leave this country or else we will transform it into a cemetery for them," the ghoulish message stated. "We advise the Australian government to withdraw its troops from Iraq. If our demand is not satisfied, we will deal them many painful blows. The lines of booby-trapped cars will have no end."

But if the planners of the attacks thought they might achieve their goals through terror and mayhem, the response from the two governments was not what they might have hoped for.

Far from submitting to fear, Indonesia and Australia redoubled their joint efforts to hunt down the sponsors and perpetrators of the attacks: more police, more resources, closer co-operation — and even greater dedication to rid the region of this menace.

For his part, Downer felt the Indonesian Government and its police authorities were adopting a sophisticated, carefully-calibrated strategy to isolate and identify the JI extremists while avoiding accusations of some sort of wider crackdown on those within Indonesia practising stricter, more conservative versions of the Islamic faith. To have done so would have risked alienating Indonesia's mainstream Muslims, potentially hindering the investigations. "I was very struck by how they handled the politics of this internally," says Downer.

He admits this sometimes caused him problems back in Australia. It could be awkward when senior Indonesian leaders made comments like, "Jemaah Islamiah is not an organisation — it is a set of ideas".

"People like Kevin Rudd would attack me," Downer recalls. "It was all my fault because I hadn't persuaded Yudhoyono of the true nature of Jemaah Islamiyah. Actually, it was nothing to do with that. It was Yudhoyono thinking about what his public messaging should be. He didn't want to make the situation any worse. He explained all that to me. Looking back, I think the Indonesians have done an excellent job."

Downer did his part to support the Yudhoyono narrative. In 2004, he sought to set out for Australians one of the key dynamics at work in meeting the challenge of terrorism in the region:

> We must guard against this war becoming something that it fundamentally is not – a clash between Islamic and Western civilisations.
>
> We must work with moderate Islamic leaders, particularly in our region, to defeat those who seek to extinguish human freedoms and are prepared to use horrific means to bring about their dark ends.

Downer as Foreign Affairs Minister identified the counter-terrorism initiatives with Indonesia as a crucial ingredient in Australia's broader policy response to the challenges of violent extremism: "Globally, we are a full participant in the war against terrorism, providing political will, logistical support and troops on the ground. We are also contributing to regional efforts to counter the spread of international terrorist networks. We are committed to using all the resources at our disposal — military, intelligence, law enforcement, and customs — to address this most insidious threat to security."

In 2005, Australia and Indonesia formalised the close liaison between security, police and intelligence agencies by establishing in the town of Semarang the Jakarta Centre for Law Enforcement Co-operation. This new facility would bring together specialists in counter-terrorism from across south-east Asia, and train new officers in investigation techniques. Australia provided a significant portion of the funding.

Over the subsequent years, JCLEC would train 44,000 law-enforcement officials from 94 countries. "You don't get credit for the things that go well — that's human nature," says Downer. "But Indonesia has handled well this challenge. I'm not saying they have not had terrorist attacks subsequently. They have. But it hasn't been an ongoing problem for them. They have kept it under control."

If collaborating on counter-terrorism had signalled a significant step-up in practical co-operation in meeting common threats, there was to be yet another event that would re-define dramatically the way the two countries had come to view each other.

The devastating tsunami that swept across the Indian Ocean

on December 26, 2004, all but obliterated the northern Indonesian province of Aceh. The tsunami would soon be counted among the deadliest natural disasters in human history.

That day began as a perfect dawn in the tropics, the Andaman Sea pristine and shimmering. Suddenly, not long after daybreak, the ground began to crack and heave.

A huge rupture had occurred in the fault line from the seabed down to a few kilometres beneath the floor of the Indian Ocean. The result was a magnitude nine earthquake, the fifth-largest since records began.

On the Earth's surface, the ocean foamed and raged. A massive column of water was surging west across the Indian Ocean at the speed of a passenger jet, bound for the Indian subcontinent and East Africa. Other tsunamis fanned out to the north and north-east, towards Burma, Thailand and Malaysia.

Over the next six hours, across 11 nations and two continents, coastal towns and villages would be swamped, tourist resorts wiped out, and sunbathers and fishermen alike swept out to sea. The world would be left to grieve more than 200,000 dead.

The Nicobar islands sat directly above the fault line, about 250 kilometres north of the earthquake's epicentre and about 150 km off the Indonesian coastline. A huge surge of water swept all before it in a 10-metre wave. Aceh's provincial capital, Banda Aceh, was hit at point-blank range. As many as 45,000 people died.

Back in Australia, people watched the images in horror. Within hours, the Howard Government had set in train its emergency relief effort, immediately dispatching four C-130 Hercules to fly rescue teams and medical aid into the region. Aid staff from Australian diplomatic posts in the region were dispatched to disaster areas to assess the impact. Staff from Canberra were sent to Indonesia, Thailand and Sri Lanka in support. More than 300 DFAT staff — half of whom returned voluntarily from holiday leave – were assigned specifically to the tsunami response. They worked around the clock.

It would become the largest peacetime operation Australia had ever launched overseas and its biggest disaster relief operation since Cyclone Tracy had struck Darwin 30 years earlier.

The Australian Government committed an initial $60 million in the first week for humanitarian assistance. But the scenes of destruction awaiting Australian aid teams in Aceh defied description.

Howard, Downer, Costello, and the entire Cabinet, knew Australia would need to step in — big time — to help Indonesia through this nightmare. On 5 January, 2005, the Australian Government announced a $1 billion aid package to Indonesia for recovery and reconstruction.

Later that same month, Downer and his officials attended a conference in Jakarta called by President Yudhoyono for international donors.

At the end of the conference, Downer was approached by Yudhoyono directly for a private conversation. He says it remains among the most touching memories of his time in office: "He came up to me, with tears in his eyes, and said, 'I will never forget Australia, and the generosity of Australia. I will never forget.' And he never did."

Only three months later, there was another natural disaster in Indonesia — an earthquake on the island of Nias. Again, Australia would send in rescue teams. This time, there would another tragic loss of life for Australia — the death of nine young Australian defence personnel when a Royal Australian Navy *Sea King* helicopter crashed while attempting to land humanitarian relief supplies on the island.

President Yudhoyono joined Prime Minister John Howard at a special memorial service in Sydney for the return of their bodies.

By the time Bill Farmer arrived in Jakarta as Ambassador to Indonesia later that year, bilateral relations were on a strong upwards trajectory.

Australian aid programs had been crucial in the reconstruction of Aceh. Australia was also committed to supporting the building of 2000 new high schools across Indonesia.

There were still occasion flare-ups, like in 2006, when the Howard Government granted temporary protection visas to 43 West Papuan asylum-seekers who landed in an outrigger canoe at Cape York.

But any lingering bitterness over East Timor had all but disappeared from the high-level agenda. That said, Farmer occasionally detected a degree of *schadenfreude* among military leaders in Jakarta whenever Australia had to send forces into East Timor to quell outbreaks of civil disorder: "Their attitude was — you wanted it, you've got it."

On November 13, 2006, Downer flew to the island of Lombok, to the east of Bali, for an historic meeting with his Indonesian counterpart, Dr Hassan Wirajuda. There they signed the Treaty of Lombok — restoring formal, wide-ranging security co-operation between the two countries after the abrogation by Indonesia of the Keating-Suharto security agreement during the East Timor crisis in 1999.

After seven tumultuous years, the Treaty of Lombok marked a new high-water mark in comity and co-operation between Canberra and Jakarta. It was only ever possible because of the commitment by Downer and Howard to creating a framework for more enduring, mutually beneficial ties with Australia's giant neighbour to the north.

Through all the many anxious days as Indonesia worked its way towards becoming a more open and truly democratic society, Australia was in the background, offering support where it could.

Critical, also, was the personal and passionate investment in a better relationship by President Yudhoyono.

"Yudhoyono was definitely ready to deal with the West, broadly defined," says Farmer. "He was our best hope, really."

Finally, it seemed, the difficult, despairing years of acrimony and distrust might be over.

In March, 2010, Yudhoyono addressed a joint sitting of Parliament in Canberra, the first Indonesian President to do so. In that speech, he cited the co-operation between the two nations in pursuit of the Bali bombers, and the outpouring of sympathy and support in Australia in response to the 2004 tsunami, as representing an "emotional turning point" in bilateral relations.

"Australia and Indonesia have a great future together," he said. "We are not just neighbours, we are not just friends. We are strategic partners. We are equal stakeholders in a common future, with much to gain if we get this relationship right, and much to lose if we get it wrong."

The facts attest to this reality. Indonesia and Australia are the only two countries that border both the Indian and Pacific Oceans; both are middle powers who support a rules-based international order; both are members of the G20 and APEC; in terms of economic size, as measured by gross domestic product, they are roughly similar in scale. But Indonesia has 10 times the population (the third largest democracy in the world), and Australia enjoys far greater per capita wealth.

If anyone thought the closer strategic alignment established during the Howard and Yudhoyono years would be looked back upon as some sort of historical anomaly, they had only to listen to Yudhoyono's successor, President Joko Widodo, when he gave his own speech to a joint sitting of the Australian Parliament almost exactly 10 years later.

He, too, mentioned how neither he, nor Indonesians generally, would forget how Australia came to Indonesia's aid after the 2004 tsunami. "Australia is Indonesia's closest friend," Jokowi said.

It is hard to imagine words that could signify a more dramatic transformation

Almost 20 years later, Downer looks back with pride on this reset of relations with Jakarta — as a signal achievement of all of his years in diplomacy. On this, there is no pretence to false modesty: "Quite honestly, I see the story of Indonesia under the Howard Government as one of the huge success stories of Australia's foreign policy."

9

THE AFTERSHOCKS OF WAR

Approaching 8pm in Washington on March 19, 2003, the clock was ticking towards the final seconds for the ultimatum issued by the US President, George W. Bush, to Saddam Hussein in Iraq.

For 12 years, Saddam's regime had played a cat-and-mouse game with UN weapons inspectors, obstructing and frustrating every effort to resolve the mystery of the status and whereabouts of Iraq's weapons of mass destruction programs. Bush would indulge this no longer.

Andy Card, the President's chief-of-staff, walked into the Oval Office the moment the deadline passed. Saddam and his sons had ignored the warnings. "All bets are off," Card said.

Over the coming hours, the US-led Coalition launched the first of what would become a week of cruise missile attacks targeting the vital organs of Saddam's regime. They called the strategy *Shock and Awe*.

Out in the far west of Iraq, a group of elite Australian special forces troops were already crossing the border from Jordan.

"The Aussies are in," Bush told his inner circle.

There was an immediate clash with Iraqi border guards. The first shots in the ground war were fired. The Australian troops then swept across the Western Desert surveilling scrub and sand dunes in search for Iraqi missile launchers.

"We actually got in there early, and immobilised some Scud missiles" says former Prime Minister John Howard, in an interview for this book. "What we did was of particular reassurance to the Israelis."

The objective was critical: to prevent a repeat of Saddam's missile attacks during the 1991 war on the cities of Israel and Saudi Arabia.

The threat that Iraq might deploy chemical or biological weapons remained very real in the minds of war planners. American infantry storming towards Baghdad were required to carry gas masks and to wear protective suits over uniforms to guard against chemical weapons. But another scenario they feared was this: Israel's response if chemical weapons were fired into its population centres.

"If you are fighting for the very survival of your country, as Israel is, you are going to fight like a Kilkenny cat," says Downer. "It would have been vicious. So it was a delicate balance to ensure this didn't become a West versus Arab World thing."

Having neutralised the missile threat, the Australian forces would go on to capture the al-Aqsa air base, and there discover 33 battle-ready MiG fighter jets hidden in the sands.

The war was over swiftly. Coalition ground forces took Baghdad within just over three weeks. There was relief in Canberra. Not one Australian soldier died on the battlefield.

"The Americans were brilliant militarily in overthrowing the regime," says Downer. "They did a spectacular job. It didn't take them very long even though the regime was prepared to fight. And so it came to pass that this appalling dictator was evicted from power."

Yet, back home, the battle was far from over. Politically. If Australia's commitment to the fight against the Taliban in Afghanistan had not been difficult enough, the Howard Government's decision to deploy armed forces to Iraq in support of the US-led campaign to remove Saddam Hussein's regime would prove far more contentious.

Howard and Downer had to stare down their many critics.

The taunt that President George W. Bush, and the prime ministers of Britain and Australia, lied to the world in order to justify the invasion continues to echo down the years. As does the accusation that the bungled aftermath of the war left the Iraqi people worse off than when the dictator ruled over them.

As John Howard would acknowledge in his reflections on the 10-year anniversary of war in Iraq, that decision to send forces into Iraq was "the most controversial foreign policy decision taken by my Government in the almost 12 years it held office."

In an interview for this book, the former PM elaborates:

> Well, Iraq was the most unpopular decision, and therefore among the most difficult. I never had any doubt we would end up wanting to back America. I kept the options open — just — that we might fall short of providing material assistance. But I always thought we would be there in the end. There was total support in the National Security Committee. Peter Costello was as hawkish as anybody. We

were all on the same page. Along with John Anderson (deputy PM and National Party leader). He was very good on foreign policy.... very strong.

Twenty years on, Alexander Downer doesn't seek to downplay the gravity of the decision to commit Australian troops to that war. Or the political and strategic implications for the US and its allies when the intervention in Iraq — whether through mismanagement, poor planning or strategic over-reach — fell short on delivering the hopes of everyday Iraqi people to live in peace and freedom:

> Look, these are tough decisions. There are obviously downsides to doing it. On the other hand, there are huge downsides to not doing it as well. What would the counter-narrative be if the Americans had decided to let Saddam Hussein continue to thumb his nose at the UN weapons inspectors?
>
> You can't prove the counter-factual. So these are all questions of judgment. But the counter-factual is quite scary.
>
> I mean, what were the most dangerous weapons — the easiest to hide and the hardest ever to find? Biological weapons capabilities. What might he have done? We can't really answer that question.
>
> What would have happened in the Palestinian-Israel situation if Saddam had remained? How much more complicated would it be if both Iran and Saddam's Iraq were throwing their weight behind Hamas and Hezbollah and Islamic Jihad? How would that have panned out?
>
> In all honesty, you can't know the answers to these questions. You can just make judgments about it.
>
> My basic view of it is that we did the right thing. Did the Americans do the right thing going into Iraq? I think they did.
>
> I also think the way they handled it subsequently was bad... the de-Ba'athification. All of that. We questioned that all the way through.

Twenty years on, he carefully weighs his conclusions about the successes and failures: "Iraq has settled down — sort of settled down.

ISIS is still active in Iraq. The Iranians are still firing up their militias, keeping them active there. I don't want to overstate what a glorious paradise Iraq must be. It is not. But you do have, today, a reasonably workable government. It is not a hostile government. And the country has some prospects…"

As this explanation demonstrates, Downer has never resiled from the fundamental principles involved in the decision to remove Saddam's regime from power — despite no subsequent proof that Iraq possessed weapons of mass destruction at the time of the 2003 invasion.

Nor has he backed away from his belief that Australia was justified in accompanying Bush's troops into Iraq. But was the Howard Government duped into committing Australian forces to that war? Downer would never cede to that narrative.

"When we judge historical events, we tend to do so out of context," he says. "Yet to understand decisions and to judge them, you have to understand the context."

For Downer, personally, the context goes back to 1995:

> When I was the shadow minister for foreign affairs I went to New York for the UN General Assembly. This was at the end of 1995 — four years after the first Gulf War. I was only half interested in the issue at the time but I knew obviously that nuclear weapons and other WMD had been a big problem with Saddam Hussein, and that a condition of the truce in 1991 had been that Saddam's regime declare and dispose under UN supervision all of its WMD capabilities and stockpiles.
>
> Richard Butler was our Ambassador to the UN. He introduced me to Rolf Ekeus, the Swedish diplomat and chairman of UNSCOM, the special commission charged with the responsibility of carrying out these weapons inspections in Iraq. And Ekeus was telling me how difficult it was… with all the obstruction they were facing.

This was Downer's introduction to the prolonged stand-off between Saddam and UNSCOM inspectors over his nuclear, biological and chemical weapons programs. It became a game of pea-and-thimble through the 1990s, with Iraq denying all activities — and only admitting to their existence once they were uncovered by inspectors.

The revelations included Iraq's production of many thousands of litres of botulinum toxin, anthrax and ricin. Inspections also revealed Iraq had continued its pursuit of long-range ballistic missiles programs. None of this was disputed.

The case against Iraq was mounting. The demands that his regime co-operate with inspectors became more and more insistent.

Across just over a decade, there would be a long succession of UN Security Council resolutions demanding that Saddam fully disclose and dismantle his regime's weapons programs, capabilities and stockpiles.

The Clinton Administration was as apprehensive as the subsequent Bush Administration about the dangers posed by Saddam's regime.

In 1997, Downer had an unexpected call from the US Secretary of State, Madeleine Albright. She wanted to talk about Richard Butler:

> Madeleine rang me at home. And Robin Cook, by then the British Foreign Secretary, also rang me. She said, 'I'm not really ringing you with very good news. We would like to have Richard Butler, your ambassador, as the head of UNSCOM. Would you release him?"
>
> It was the year after we were elected. As it happens, Howard and I basically wanted to get rid of Richard Butler. We thought he was a warrior for the Labor Party. And he was our ambassador to the UN in 1996 when we lost the vote to get onto the Security Council.
>
> We thought he may have been among the reasons we lost. So I acceded to her request — and Robin Cook's request. They thought I was doing them a favour. I thought they were doing me a favour.
>
> Anyway, every time I went to New York after that, I would have a confidential one-on-one meeting with Richard Butler.
>
> We would sit in the library at the UN and he would tell me how Saddam Hussein still had these weapons of mass destruction, how he was frustrating the weapons inspectors and how he was a lying bastard. Butler was convinced Saddam Hussein was concealing his weapons of mass destruction programs.

In 1998, Butler and the UN weapons inspectors withdrew from Iraq. Saddam's regime was persisting with its tactics of obstruction and obfuscation. The crisis was escalating.

From the beginning of that year, the Clinton Administration was under increasing pressure to deal decisively with Saddam's intransigence. Speculation about a potential military strike began to intensify.

In February, John Howard had spoken by phone to President Clinton. The Howard Government's National Security Committee would convene to begin contingency planning.

If war could not be averted, Australia would make an offer of support to its alliance partner in Washington. It would plan to send special forces personnel, two air-to-air refuelling aircraft, and medical and intelligence specialists.

In July, Downer met Albright at the ASEAN Regional Forum in Bangkok. She wanted a hard-and-fast commitment. "At the bilateral meeting I had with her, she said to me, 'If we do end up going to war with Saddam Hussein, I hope you will be with us'," Downer recalls.

"She said this quite forcefully.

"I was not surprised she would ask. But I remember saying 'I can't just give you an open answer on that.

"It would depend on the circumstances. Obviously, our Cabinet would have to make a decision'."

On December 16, 1998, the US, with support from Britain, began a four-day bombing campaign over Iraq.

More than 300 aircraft flew 600 bombing sorties, targeting Iraq's Defence Ministry, suspected weapons facilities, and the bases of Saddam's elite Republican Guard.

The Clinton Administration did not seek an explicit mandate from the UN Security Council for this use of force.

It argued Saddam's regime was openly and deliberately defying the will of the UN, and that the US was acting under the authority of previous Security Council resolutions. It is important to remember this was under Clinton's watch. Before George W. Bush. Before the 9/11 attacks.

The Australian Government was fully in support. As was the Labor

Opposition at the time, under the leadership of Kim Beazley, who accompanied Howard to an army base to farewell Australian forces.

Downer reflects wistfully on this contrast between the politics of 1998 and what happened five years later: "So why were they firing Tomahawk missiles into Baghdad, at the Defence Ministry and so on?

"Because they believed Iraq still had its WMD programs. They bombed Baghdad. But they left Saddam Hussein in power …"

By 2002, four years later, concern gripped the White House that if terrorists could achieve the most significant attack in almost 200 years on the continental United States, using box-cutters and civilian passenger aircraft, they would inflict far greater damage if they had access to weapons of mass destruction. There was intelligence at that time that al Qaeda was actively in the market seeking WMD.

"Yet still — in this new, febrile atmosphere —Saddam Hussein refused to co-operate with the UN," says Downer.

"That was madness on his part."

Through 2002, Downer sensed the Bush Administration was becoming increasingly determined to take strong action. While the US would persist with the diplomacy at the UN, the rising expectation was that military action would be necessary to force Saddam's Iraq to comply with its disarmament obligations.

In July, 2002, Downer was in Washington, where he met with Condi Rice, and US Defence Secretary, Donald Rumsfeld. "I concluded from my meetings that they were going to remove Saddam Hussein. I gave a press conference at the Willard Hotel where I said we had to be prepared for the possibility of there being a war in Iraq."

Those in Australia's security and intelligence circles knew momentum was building. As one official close to the discussions noted: "It was becoming serious. We in Australia needed to start talking about this."

On November 8, 2002, the UN Security Council passed unanimously Resolution 1441. It was seen widely as a last warning to Iraq.

Resolution 1441 found Iraq remained in "material breach" of 16 other Security Council resolutions dating right back to the war to evict Iraq from Kuwait, the neighbour it had invaded in 1990. It found Saddam's regime had blocked and stymied UN weapons inspectors in discharging their role in verifying the Security Council's demand for Iraq's destruction of its WMD and long-range missile programs.

Resolution 1441 demanded that Iraq supply within 30 days a full and accurate declaration of all aspects of its nuclear, chemical and biological weapons programs, ballistic missiles and other weapons delivery systems. This included the locations of all weapons plants and laboratories. It also required that Iraq allow inspectors unimpeded, unconditional and unrestricted access to any and all facilities, and provide the names of all personnel involved in its weapons programs.

Failing this, the Security Council would re-convene: "The Council has repeatedly warned Iraq that it will face serious consequences as a result of its continued violations of its obligations."

There was and remains a dispute over international law as it relates to Resolution 1441. Was it a Chapter VII declaration under the United Nations Charter — the trigger for enforcement, by military means if necessary, of the Security Council's rulings?

Pointedly, the UN Secretary-General at the time, Kofi Annan, described Resolution 1441 as a *"new opportunity"* for Iraq to comply.

The resolution itself put it more baldly, declaring it a *"final opportunity* (for Iraq) to comply with its disarmament obligations."

On December 19, weapons inspectors from the United Nations Monitoring, Verification and Inspection (UNMOVIC) and the International Atomic Energy Agency reported to the Security Council on Iraq's 12,200-page declaration in response to Resolution 1441.

They told the Security Council that Iraq had failed to answer many open questions. In some cases, they had information that directly contradicted Iraq's account. According to the United States, the evidence was plain to see: Saddam was not allowing inspectors to reveal to the world the truth about Iraq's weapons programs.

In a press conference that same day, Secretary of State Colin Powell would signal the Bush Administration's growing impatience:

> There is no question Iraq continues its pattern of non-co-operation, its pattern of deception, its pattern of dissembling, its pattern of lying.
>
> And if that is going to be the way they continue through the weeks ahead, we're not going to find a peaceful solution to this problem.

In the days leading into Christmas, the Howard Cabinet met in Sydney, followed by a dinner at Kirribilli House. "This was an annual tradition," says Downer. "We would do a review of the year but, more importantly, look at the challenges for the year ahead.

"So at the end of that year, 2002, we had a power point presentation of the latest polling. One of the issues in the polling was war in Iraq — if there was war in Iraq, and if we supported it, or contributed to it, was the public in favour of that or against. They seemed to be a bit against. Not violently against — but a bit against.

"And there was some discussion of that. Maybe we should go easy on this. Might prove to be unpopular. And Howard and I would say, 'But what is the meaning of an alliance (with the US) if you don't support each other in times of crisis, in times of war?'"

Downer reveals that, by this time, he and the Prime Minister had an informal understanding between them that, should it come to war, Australia would have to be there in support. They had moved beyond the "should we or shouldn't we?" phase.

Over the next few weeks, there would be further discussions within the National Security Committee of Cabinet. "The Cabinet were fine," says Downer. "So we discussed with Defence what we might be able to do."

Downer recalls the US requesting that Australia commit a battle contingent of 2000 troops to provide back-up for plans by the US Marines to surge forward to Baghdad.

The Howard Government would not agree to this.

Instead, Australia would consider a much smaller force of 500 elite troops from the Special Air Services — the fabled "phantoms of the jungle". Their skills would ultimately be assigned to a specialist task.

On 27 January, 2003, Chief UN Weapons Inspector Hans Blix addressed the UN Security Council, stating: "Iraq appears not to have come to a genuine acceptance — not even today — of the disarmament which was demanded of it and which it needs to carry out to win the confidence of the world and to live in peace."

Blix went on to state that the Iraqi regime had allegedly "misplaced" 1000 tonnes of VX nerve agent— one of the most lethal chemical substances ever weaponised. By mid-February, question marks about anthrax and long-range missiles also remained unresolved.

At this time, most of his allies believed Bush was still looking to convince Saddam Hussein to comply. But to do so persuasively meant having to position warships, aircraft and troops in the Middle East and its environs in readiness for a potential attack. There had to be a "credible threat of force." A final decision about whether to use force would be left to the last possible moment.

On February 23, 2003, Downer flew into Seoul for the inauguration of the new South Korean President, Roh Moo-hyun. He was to sit alongside US Secretary of State, Colin Powell, at the ceremony. They would also meet later at a hotel. Says Downer: "That was the last conversation we had before the war."

Powell, as always, was measured and restrained as he took Downer through the detail of the intelligence material on Iraq's weapons programs. They also discussed in detail whether the US would or should pursue another UN Security Council resolution against Iraq, and the politics of trying to achieve that outcome.

The US was facing an impasse with France and Russia, two of the five permanent members of the Security Council. Both had the power to veto any further action against Iraq.

They were becoming increasingly insistent that they would not pass another resolution affirming multiple breaches of Resolution 1441 by Saddam's regime. To have done so would have removed any uncertainty about a UN mandate for military action against Iraq.

Downer remembers acutely the flurry of events, the frenzied diplomacy, as war became ever more likely:

> The inspectors had been in Iraq — Hans Blix (the head of UNMOVIC) was there by then — and he was giving contradictory messages.
>
> In January, he had produced a report saying he thought Saddam Hussein did have WMD. Then, as the likelihood of war built up through February and March, Hans Blix started to get cold feet and he began saying he needed more time...
>
> We tried to help the Americans by contacting foreign ministers of other countries on the Security Council — Chile was one call I remember making. But we did not call France or Russia. That was for the Americans and the Brits

to deal with, to sort out ... to attempt to persuade them to abstain.

Despairing of the emerging stalemate at the UN, Downer's thoughts at his meeting with Colin Powell turned to how and when the US might launch an attack on Iraq. The US, Britain, Australia (and Poland) had all been planning the pre-positioning of their forces.

In the previous October, the US Congress had granted Bush authority to use military force. Come late February, war seemed all but inevitable. "There were practical issues to consider," Downer recalls. "The Americans had assembled all these forces for the invasion of Iraq. And you couldn't just leave these forces in the various places they were in the Middle East, waiting there indefinitely.

"The weather was also a factor. If war was to happen, it had to happen before the Iraqi summer, when the temperature can rise above 45 degrees. So the timeline was dictated as much as by the military exigencies..."

Australia had its own plans in place. "We had all our troops assembled. And our planes," says Downer. "We were ready to go."

But there was another critical conversation to be had. Based on the presumption the US would ultimately decide it had no choice but to invade, Downer questioned Powell on plans for the post-invasion phase. Had they thought enough about what happens if you get rid of a dictator like Saddam? How do you limit the risk of a power vacuum? How do you manage a country like Iraq, and keep it stable and secure?

Downer raised these issues in advance. Weeks after the US invasion, these questions would be put to the test. As events would later prove, the answers from the Pentagon would be dangerously ill-conceived.

By late February, any hope of an additional Security Council resolution was fast evaporating. "To be fair, the Americans thought it was a fruitless exercise, not worth doing," Downer reveals. "Whereas Tony Blair had needed this extra resolution — his backbench and a lot of people in the British Labour Party were really squeamish about it..."

On March 7, Blix delivered another report to the Security Council, complaining again of Iraq's refusal to co-operate fully, saying: "Iraq, with a highly developed administrative system, should be able to provide more documentary evidence about its proscribed weapons programmes. Only a few new such documents have come to light so far and been handed over since we began inspections."

At this point, the Bush Administration was insistent that Iraq remained, flagrantly, in material breach of UN Resolutions.

It asked that the Security Council convene immediately "to consider the situation and the need for full compliance with all relevant Council resolutions in order to secure international peace and security."

On March 10, before the meeting took place, the French president Jacques Chirac declared he would veto any resolution which would lead automatically to war. "Once France indicated it would veto, that was it," says Downer. "It was never put to a vote because it was clear the US and the British could never get the resolution through."

Chirac's role of obstruction was pivotal.

Back at the time of the 1991 war, France had been a willing contributor to the Coalition campaign to evict Iraq from Kuwait. But, come 2003, this was the France of Chirac, not of Francois Mitterrand.

Chirac had cultivated much closer ties to Saddam's Iraq than others in Europe. His personal contacts with Saddam traced back to the 1970s.

It was Chirac as a youthful Prime Minister who had gone to Baghdad personally to negotiate trade agreements with Iraq as well as the purchase by Iraq of a French nuclear reactor (subsequently destroyed by an Israeli airstrike in 1981). When Saddam visited Paris, he would be greeted by Chirac as "my personal friend".

After Iraq was subjected to international trade sanctions following its invasion of Kuwait, Chirac helped lobby Iraq for French firms to develop its oil fields. He would urge the other Western powers to ease the sanctions. By 2003, France was Iraq's chief trading partner.

Whether driven by mercantilist motives or not, Chirac's steadfast refusal to agree to authorise military intervention through another resolution (and the support for his stance by many other EU nations) created a damaging fault-line in the response of the NATO partners.

The failure of Bush and Chirac to reach agreement started a chain reaction that left the US and its allies exposed. It meant there could not be another Security Council resolution authorising the use of force.

This split within the Western alliance over whether military action was justified against Iraq would, in turn, lead to a widely-held perception globally that the US-led invasion of Iraq was illegitimate, if not illegal.

As the manoeuvrings over a new resolution at the UN limped inexorably towards a dead-end, Downer began to worry about the implications for the strength of the Western alliance. He feared the ramifications of a fracturing of unity. "I was thinking a lot about the solidarity of the alliance network," he recalls. "By the way, I feel I have been completely vindicated in this. You can't have an alliance where you pick and choose — an *a la carte* alliance.

"You are either all in it — or you are not in it. The Europeans want the Americans to underwrite their security in Europe, which you've now seen them do (in Ukraine). Yet when the Americans wanted help in another theatre, to shore up Western security elsewhere, it didn't politically suit some of the Europeans."

Downer welcomed positive support from Spain under Maria Aznar and Poland under Aleksander Kwasniewski. "But countries like Belgium and France — some European countries — went out of their way to criticise the Americans over going into Iraq and said they would have nothing to do with it. I thought that was a really bad idea."

According to Downer, the Howard Government did not see a legal requirement for a further resolution. On its advice, Resolution 1441 was sufficient in its own right to justify enforcement action. "We had legal advice to that effect through DFAT and the Attorney-General's Department. We were happy with the legal advice we had.

"Saddam Hussein had been in breach of 17 Security Council resolutions going back to the ceasefire in 1991 ... no question of that."

Arguably, Resolution 678 passed way back in 1990 still provided authorisation for the use of force, given Saddam's regime had not complied in full with its demands. It had never been rescinded.

Legal arguments were one thing. The political realities were something else again. "There was no persuading Chirac," Downer says.

The perception of division and disunity in the Western alliance empowered those seeking to stir internal unrest in the Middle East.

Later, this display of frailty or weakness would help fuel the Sunni-Shia conflict inside Iraq, and was a factor in the emergence and growth of radical Sunni groups, including Islamic State.

Downer found all this hard to stomach:

> Not only had Saddam failed to comply with enforceable demands of the UN Security Council but he had lost all legitimacy as a civilised leader of his country.
>
> He had tortured and murdered tens of thousands of his own citizens, he had waged a war on Iran which killed one million people and he had run a corrupt, kleptocratic, sectarian regime in Baghdad. He absolutely represented a threat to international peace and security.
>
> The Europeans could have just done what we did — we gave the Americans rhetorical and political support and we gave a minimal amount of military support. At that early stage.
>
> We used the SAS, we had some FA-18s, and logistics support. We had a ship there anyway, under the sanctions regime. That was it.
>
> The more I think about this, the more I think it was the right decision, absolutely the right thing to do.
>
> The alternative would have been domestically convenient, but folly in terms of our reliability as an ally of the Americans.

On March 17, Bush declared the negotiations over. The US President warned Saddam and his sons to flee Iraq within 48 hours — or face the consequences. In these frenzied days, Bush had called Howard from Air Force One to request support formally. A Cabinet meeting followed.

The final decision to commit Australian forces came just before the expiry of the ultimatum.

As the war in Iraq continued through towards the end of March, Downer visited the White House in person. He was sitting in the Roosevelt Room at a meeting with US Vice-President, Dick Cheney, and President Bush's national security adviser, Condoleezza Rice. George W. wandered across from the Oval Office to join them.

"One of the things we talked about was Iraq's propaganda," says Downer. At this time, spokesmen for Saddam's regime were still out on the airwaves, insisting — in the face of the fast-emerging reality — that the regime would survive the US-led invasion.

Downer said he could not understand why the US didn't just shut down their access to the media. It was a salient point: while the US-led military operation was succeeding at a spectacular pace, the battle for hearts and minds — in Iraq and elsewhere— was far from over.

On April 15, with Saddam's regime destroyed, the US had achieved its military objectives.

Two weeks later, President George W. Bush made his 'Mission Accomplished' speech aboard the aircraft carrier, the *USS Abraham Lincoln*: "Major combat operations in Iraq have ended. In the battle of Iraq, the United States and our allies have prevailed."

The speech was widely interpreted at the time as the President declaring the job done and dusted. But, in a very real sense, the Mission was only just beginning.

History overlooks that Bush actually acknowledged this in that same speech: "We have difficult work to do in Iraq. We are bringing order to parts of that country that remain dangerous. Our mission continues ... the War on Terror continues, yet it is not endless. We do not know the day of final victory, but we have seen the turning of the tide."

Over the years to come, Mission Accomplished would, for many, begin to look and sound like a hollow promise. Instead, Mission Creep would become the defining theme of the challenges in Iraq.

Just over three weeks later, on May 23, Downer flew into Iraq. Told by DFAT there was nowhere suitable to stay in Baghdad — none of the hotels were sufficiently secure — Downer said he would be more than happy to stay with the Australian forces.

The purpose of the visit was both symbolic and practical: to visit the Australian troops who had taken part in the successful invasion and to reopen the Australian diplomatic office in Baghdad in preparation, hopefully, for a new era for Iraq. Josh Frydenberg accompanied Downer on the trip: "Australia still had an embassy in Baghdad but we had withdrawn our ambassador years earlier, at the time of the Gulf War in 1991. The Australian Government continued to own the residence but we didn't stay there. We stayed in one of Saddam's palace complexes … on camp stretchers."

This was early in the post-invasion phase. Many Iraqis were still celebrating jubilantly their liberation from the dictator's rule.

But there were no illusions among Downer and his team about what they were heading into — Iraq remained very much a war zone.

The US military had secured the perimeters of the old city and the main government buildings. Militarily, there was no longer any strategic risk. But, after the rapid withdrawal of as many as half of its troops, the US no longer had the resources on the ground to prevent large-scale looting of government offices, museums, libraries.

"It was a shambles," says Downer.

Although it was not widely known at the time, mobs were conducting regular raids on Iraq's munitions stores, seizing guns and grenade launchers. The war was over. But who was in charge?

The flight into Baghdad from an air base in Jordan aboard a C-130 Hercules provided an early sample of what was in store. It was to be no joy ride. "We're all down the back of the Herc," says Chris Kenny, Downer's media adviser at the time. "As it's coming into land, they ask Alexander if he wants to take the 'jump seat' between the two pilots up the front. Great thing to do so, yeah, Alexander's happy to do that.

"The rest of us stayed down the back. And, as we're coming in — well, the Herc is pretty cumbersome — but, suddenly, it's throwing around this way, throwing around that way. We're wondering what is going on but there is no real alarm because we don't really know any different.

"But as we're getting off the plane, Alexander says, 'Shit! I'm sitting up there (with the headset on) and they suddenly shout, 'Missile Left' and they throw out the flares and the chaff'...."

Nobody in the ministerial team really knew at the time how very real the danger was — until, some 10 years later, a member of the RAAF flight crew went public with confirmation of the missile threat.

On the drive in a convoy into Baghdad, Downer sat in an armoured vehicle alongside Ambassador Neil Mules, along a stretch of road that would soon become infamous for attacks on Coalition forces — Route Irish. But these were early days. Iraqi kids could be seen clambering over US Abrams tanks parked at every second intersection, joking and laughing with young GIs. "It was Liberation Central" says Kenny.

Not much later — maybe a month or six weeks that same road would become a death trap. Along Route Irish, through to the barricaded Green Zone, Westerners would be shot at if they ventured out.

Accommodation in Baghdad on that first visit was at a palace complex built on a series of lakes or lagoons — known as the Water Palace. It was one of several palatial homes that belonged to Saddam Hussein.

Accompanied by Brigadier Maurie McNarn, the commander of Australian forces in Iraq, and his DFAT Iraq task force head, Bill Paterson, Downer visited the main presidential palace.

There, they found a crater about three floors deep. The invading US forces had sent a guided missile through its walls. Saddam was not in the building at the time it struck.

Downer and his advisers were then taken to a nearby mansion — three or four storeys tall with a large rooftop garden area. This was where some of the Australians troops were bunking. The minister was duly assigned his camp stretcher. At one side of the house, there was a helicopter landing area. Blackhawks flew in and out. Throughout that night, the sounds of gunfire could be heard in the distance.

During that first visit, Downer called by the Australian embassy residence. "There was a caretaker there," says Downer. "He had been there the whole time looking after the place. He had a little boy. We gave him a Socceroos jumper and a soccer ball, I remember ..."

At the residence, Downer organised a meeting with the leading Iraqi opposition leaders — those who had spearheaded the resistance against Saddam's ruthless regime. Several had returned from exile. Five had been appointed to the Iraq Governing Council. But they complained to Downer that they had no real or effective authority.

"These were all the key figures in Iraq," says Downer. "Not the Americans. Just the leading Iraqis. Some were from the diaspora. Ahmed Chalabi was among them.

"This meeting came only days after the UN Security Council had passed a Resolution which, in effect, had given the Americans — or the invading powers — temporary control of Iraq's civil administration.

"And these Iraqi guys, unanimously — and they would not have been into the idea of unanimity — said they thought this Resolution was a catastrophe. More power should have been handed to them.

"They should have been in charge of sorting out the transition to elections and democracy and the restructuring.

"I was really taken aback. We were not on the Security Council. The Americans were dealing with all of this ..."

Soon after, Downer went to another of Saddam's palaces for lunch with the head of the Coalition Provisional Authority, L. Paul Bremer III.

'Jerry' Bremer had been appointed by US Defence Secretary Donald Rumsfeld to take over the postwar administration of Iraq after General Jay Garner had managed the immediate post-conflict arrangements.

It was Bremer's role to oversee the Coalition's humanitarian and reconstruction programs and to engineer the transition to democratic elections for a new Iraqi Government.

"I had lunch with Bremer straight after my meeting with the Iraqis," he recalls, "and I told him I thought they had made a really powerful point. I was quite struck by it.

"Politically, it seemed to me to be much better for the Iraqis to run the show than having Americans trying to do that. Or the Brits. Or us, for that matter. We had a guy running the agriculture ministry for quite a while. But Bremer was completely dismissive. He was angry that I had raised it, and didn't wish to discuss it."

Apart from the failure to move more swiftly to Iraqi self-rule, two other issues troubled Downer. First, under the so-called de-Ba'athification program initiated by Rumsfeld and Bremer, a lot of officials and administrators with expertise in running the country had been forced out of their jobs. These were people from far outside Saddam's inner circle. Many were third or fourth tier bureaucrats. They had been members of the ruling Baathist party, because this was pretty much mandatory if you wanted to land government employment.

Under the edict from Bremer, many had been, in effect, thrown out onto the streets. The same went for many thousands of conscripts who had served as Iraq's regular infantry. They, too, were shown the door: unpaid, no job, back on the streets — and armed. They all knew the whereabouts of the Iraqi Army's ammunition dumps.

"They were conscripts, right?" says Downer. "They were mostly Shias. The officers were Sunnis. But the grunts were mainly Shias.

"So, suddenly, the army is disbanded and they have no way of earning any money. It would have been much cheaper to have kept paying them — much cheaper, much safer and much more sensible."

With US Secretary of State, Colin Powell (John Feder/ Newspix)

"There was no persuading Chirac" — with French President, Jacques Chirac (Francois Mori/Getty Images)

The Downer team fly into the Iraq war zone (Department of Defence Images)

Joint press conference with US Defense Secretary Donald Rumsfeld, deputy Secretary of State, Bob Zoelleck, and his South Australian colleague, Robert Hill (U.S. Department of Defense, Wikipedia Commons)

Over the months to come, Downer would be in regular contact with his British counterpart, Jack Straw, Foreign Secretary in the Blair Labour Government, discussing their mutual anxiety about the incendiary effects of decisions made by senior US officials in Iraq:

> I spoke to Jack several times about the performance of the Americans there. The Americans should have had more soldiers on the ground after the fall of Baghdad. They should have handed over power to an interim Iraqi government almost immediately. They should have been less zealous with the so-called de-Baathification process. They should have paid soldiers to stay in the Iraqi army.
>
> So I would never claim all went well with the invasion of Iraq. It didn't. The administration, particularly by Bremer, was … just appalling. And my dear friend Donald Rumsfeld — wonderful guy, but he got that part of it wrong. Badly wrong.

Downer's harsh assessment, then and since, is not hugely controversial, even in America. Henry Kissinger had warned Colin Powell that Bremer was a "control freak."

It is also a view shared by the likes of General David Petraeus, a senior US commander in Afghanistan who would go on to lead the US military in Iraq during the 2006-07 surge.

Petraeus has praised the job done by the US military and its allies in "taking down Saddam Hussein's regime … more rapidly than most people expected and with far fewer casualties. It was a tribute to the training and leadership of our forces." But, as recently as October, 2024, Petraeus conceded the US had been "wholly unprepared to consolidate the peace". In an interview with Rory Stewart and Alistair Campbell on *The Rest Is Politics* podcast, he went on to describe some of the strategic choices by the Coalition Provisional Authority as 'catastrophic'.

"They didn't consult any of us and we had been on the ground for months," Petraeus said. "We had already run an election in Mosul, where we had an interim provincial governor in place.

"We were rebuilding security forces and the police academy. It was going really well. We had 24-hour power up there, and everything else.

"And then he (Bremer) comes in and fires the entire Iraqi military, without telling them how they were supposed to feed their families. 'You're fired, you're on your own, Jack'. That was the really big mistake ... And, of course, they'd all had military training and they all took their weapons home. Bremer was told he would have a million enemies by the next morning ... it planted the seeds of insurgency."

Within the space of only 12 weeks, the street violence in the cities of Iraq began to metamorphose into organised resistance to the US-led occupation. This would have tragic consequences for Iraq — and for those seeking to help the people of Iraq.

On August 19, a suicide bomber rammed an explosives-filled cement mixer into UN headquarters in Baghdad, killing Sérgio Vieira de Mello, the UN special representative, and 22 staff members.

Downer was visibly distraught at a press conference soon after the attack. Having worked closely with Vieira de Mello in East Timor, he had been among those who urged the diplomat to overcome his initial reluctance and take on the role of bridge-builder between the US, the UN and the many rival factions in Iraq.

Verging on tears, Downer paid tribute to Vieira de Mello: "He was a good friend of Australia, a good friend of mine and the prime minister ... we will miss him very much."

In an interview a week later, with *The Australian Financial Review,* Downer made no effort to disguise his misgivings about the perilous and precarious nature of the job taken on by Vieira de Mello and others involved in postwar reconstruction: "He was making the best of things, as he always did... I have never had any illusions about the difficulties."

More carnage and horror was to come. In March, 2004, Al-Qaeda in Iraq would unleash a wave of suicide bombings, striking against Shiite Muslim holy sites in Baghdad and Karbala. The attacks killed hundreds.

In the Sunni city of Fallujah, four American contractors were slaughtered, burned, and hanged from a bridge, with a video of the atrocity shown around the world.

Then, in April, 2004, the world's media published photographic evidence of prisoner abuse inside the US-run Abu Ghraib prison. Seven soldiers would be convicted for torturing and humiliating detainees. It would prove a demoralising blow to the moral stature of the US campaign to rebuild and liberalise Iraq.

When Downer returned to Iraq in December, 2005, security demanded the visitors fly Blackhawk helicopters into town. They had to wait until sunset — daylight was too risky — and then fly low and fast over the desert and marshes.

Iraqis in 2005 were celebrating national elections — proudly displaying the purple-stained fingers that indicated they had exercised their right to vote. But the chaos and disorder unleashed by competing factions of armed militia continued to reign. In 2006, there were attacks by Sunni extremists on Shia mosques and holy sites.

Civil war beckoned, fuelled by Islamic State militants.

In the aftermath of the war, there was one issue — possibly beyond all others — that would continue to haunt the Bush Administration and also the Blair Government in the UK and the Howard Government in Australia. It went to the legitimacy of the original decision to remove Saddam from power: Where were these weapons of mass destruction he was said to be concealing? Where was the evidence to back up some of the critical calculations that led to war?

Downer and John Howard would face intense scrutiny as it became more apparent after the invasion that the WMD were nowhere to be found. More than 20 years on, Downer was still asking these same questions himself:

> In September, 2003, I was back at the UN General Assembly. Saddam had been well and truly thrown out by then — he was still in hiding. So I was at this reception at the National History Museum in New York for the heads of delegations.
>
> It was hosted by President Bush and Laura. I said hello to them, and we were milling around. I think John Bolton was there, as US Ambassador to the UN.
>
> Kofi Annan was there, too. He had been very opposed to the overthrow of the regime. I knew him pretty well by that stage — we had done the East Timor thing together, and he'd been to Canberra. So I knew him well, and we'd become quite friendly. Right up until when he died really I remained friendly with him… he was a lovely guy.
>
> Anyway, at this reception, he asked me about Richard Butler (who had been appointed to a minor vice-regal role

as Governor of Tasmania). He said, 'I just can't believe he became a state governor'.

I said, 'Well, it's not an elected position'.

He then said to me, 'If it hadn't been for Richard Butler, there would not have been an Iraq War'. It's obvious what he meant. That all these reports about defying the inspectors and hiding WMD in presidential palaces — Kofi Annan had concluded they were all wrong.

Downer remains unconvinced. "Well, they say there were no WMDs ... that's what they say. But, hang on ... the reason WMDs was an issue was not only that he'd had WMDs but that he had used them against his own people and against Iran. Chemical weapons.

"This argument that he was some sort of innocent ... I mean, the Left just get away with blue murder with these arguments."

But Downer admits he cannot explain the apparent intelligence failure: "I am not sure what the story is. It's hard to believe they couldn't find the weapons when the inspectors went in there after the war. Saddam clearly had these programs at some point — but they certainly didn't find stockpiles of shelves filled with chemical weapons."

While Downer has never resiled from his position that the removal of Saddam was fundamentally the right thing to do, nobody likes to be accused of being party to some sort of conspiracy or hoax.

In Australia, Downer had access to all of the information that had flowed across Western intelligence agencies. This analysis involved the informed judgments of intelligence experts, seasoned professionals — not mere purveyors of gossip:

> The Australian Secret Intelligence Service were pretty confident about the material they had given me. A ship had been intercepted carrying aluminium tubes to Iraq, and they concluded these aluminium tubes were to be used in centrifuge technology to enrich uranium. What else could they be used for? Maybe something to do with their Scud missile programs ... but not centrifuges, apparently.
>
> And the Germans — the BMD — were the ones who had all the intelligence and photos of these mobile biological weapons laboratories. We had looked at all of that.

Through 2004, as in the US and Britain, there would be a clamour of media demands for the Howard Government to come clean on whether it had exaggerated or doctored the claims it had made about intelligence on Saddam's WMD programs.

Infuriated, Downer would issue forceful denials: "The Government did not sex up intelligence or sex up the story in order to justify the overthrow of the regime of Saddam Hussein."

In 2004, a bipartisan parliamentary committee in Canberra found that while the government had been more moderate and measured than the US and British governments in framing the case for war, it had still exaggerated the threat posed by Iraq's weapons program.

The committee said the government had relied on flawed US and British intelligence in overstating the threat. But it cleared the government of pressuring intelligence agencies to 'juice up' their assessments of Iraq's capabilities.

At the time, Downer continued to emphasise that there were other factors involved in Australia's decision to go to war — primarily, the over-arching importance of supporting the US alliance network and, by extension, Australia's longer-term strategic interests.

He said it was the responsibility of government — not the intelligence agencies — to make a political judgment on what action to take. If Australia had not joined the US-led invasion (in effect, stepping back from the alliance) he believed this would have left the nation "very vulnerable" at a crucial time, given the continuing terror attacks by Islamist extremists in Australia's region and around the world.

"There is no question that was an issue," he said in response to the committee findings. "To have walked away from the Americans on an issue where we thought they were right anyway would have been a curious thing to do and would have weakened our alliance…"

On the recommendations of the parliamentary committee, Howard as Prime Minister agreed to order a new inquiry into Australia's intelligence agencies, headed by the former senior diplomat and intelligence expert, Philip Flood. His report was released in July 2004.

While chastising the Office of National Assessments and the Defence Intelligence Organisation for failing to "judge accurately the extent and nature of Iraq's WMD programs" Flood found they were more cautious in their assessments than their British and US counterparts.

For critics of the government, Flood would not deliver the bombshell they were seeking. He concluded there was "no evidence to suggest policy or political influence" on the agencies responsible for collating the intelligence. As the headline in *The Guardian* newspaper later that day stated: "Report clears Australian government on WMDs."

Across the years, Downer has continued to ask the questions many of us might want to ask of people who had innermost access at the time to the critical intelligence material.

In 2024, while at the Hoover Institution at Stanford University, Downer had a coffee with Paul Wolfowitz, who served as US Deputy Defence Secretary during those crucial months leading into the Iraq War.

"I said to him, 'What's the real story with these weapons of mass destruction?' He really just answered the question by saying we had all this intelligence coming from our agencies — there were differences of view about the certainty and uncertainty of it. That's what he said."

This was the conundrum at the heart of the debate about the reliability of Western intelligence on the state of Iraq's WMD programs.

Another theory is that the intelligence about WMD was indeed a hoax — yet a hoax perpetrated not by Western intelligence agencies but by Saddam Hussein himself.

Analysts like Kurt Volcker, the former US Permanent Representative to NATO, would later argue the reports from Western intelligence services (including Germany and France) that such a weapons program existed were based on false intelligence fed out through intermediaries by Saddam's regime.

According to this argument, Saddam's strategy was aimed at maintaining an image of strength domestically, in the region, and in the West. By failing to cooperate fully with the inspectors, he was seeking to preserve the myth of his invincibility. According to Volcker, the obvious problem, if this was so, is that it would be interpreted in the White House as Saddam hiding a genuine weapons program — rather than hiding the absence of such a program. If true, his own propaganda may have sowed the seeds of his demise.

The intricacies and ambiguities of this debate were perhaps captured most memorably by Wolfowitz's boss, Defence Secretary Rumsfeld, at a press briefing in February, 2002. When asked about intelligence gathering and assessment, Rumsfeld replied with a theorem that became known as The Rumsfeld Matrix: "Reports that say that something hasn't happened are always interesting to me, because as we know, there are known knowns; there are things we know we know. We also know there are known unknowns; that is to say we know there are some things we do not know. But there are also unknown unknowns— the ones we don't know we don't know. And if one looks through the history of our country and other free countries, it is the latter category that tends to be the difficult ones.".

Over the years, Downer has continued his conversation about the missing WMDs with senior figures involved in assembling the pre-war intelligence. One was Richard Dearlove, head of Britain's MI6 at the time of the war.

"I still see Richard from time to time," Downer says. "I once asked him straight up: you gave us all that intelligence showing there were weapons of mass destruction, and the Americans gave us this intelligence. So what's happened here — we turn up and there are no weapons of mass destruction?

"And he said he was almost certain they just got the material out of Iraq and into Syria before the invasion. And he said there were, you know, satellite photographs of trucks crossing the border and so on."

Downer's conclusion: "I think …. we just don't know."

So, all these years later, where does Downer believe most Australians have landed in their judgments about the war in Iraq?

He considers the question carefully. In reply, he seeks to separate the positioning of his political opponents at the time from those of everyday Australians.

"I think I know enough about the adversarial system of politics — and I'm in favour of it, don't get me wrong — but there's a point where you don't take terribly seriously the positions of the Opposition," he begins.

"Those positions are juxtaposed to those of the government and designed to attack the government on its weakest political point.

"And the public in Australia were apprehensive, hesitant, about going to war in Iraq. Once the war started, they were supportive. But, in the buildup to it, I think they were a bit against it…."

He acknowledges the very different reality today — that many more people now question the legitimacy of that decision to go to war.

A wholesale repudiation of the analysis of the Western intelligence agencies — as ill-founded, exaggerated or, in the eyes of some, simply a lie — has become the overwhelming narrative. There may have been more than one reason driving the decision to go to war. But the failure to verify the existence of WMD in Iraq — Exhibit A in the case for war — is the lynchpin for those who opposed military action.

"It seems to be the default position for everybody now ... that it was all a huge mistake," Downer says. "The received wisdom was against the Iraq War. It is still the received wisdom.

"I do think the way the Americans handled the administration of Iraq subsequently was a big mistake. With huge consequences for American policy ever since. But let's start exploring the counter-factual."

As Downer has often argued, the wars in both Afghanistan and Iraq were critical to Australia's alliances and to global security. You cannot have zealots flying hijacked aircraft into skyscrapers in Manhattan, killing almost 3000 civilians in the space of a few minutes, and not have the perpetrators hunted down. What sort of world would it be if those crimes went unpunished? And you cannot have a delinquent leader like Saddam defy no fewer than 17 UN Security Council resolutions and expect to maintain respect for a rules-based international system.

"How good would it have been for the Iraqis to have kept Saddam Hussein in power?" Downer asks. "Well, he would be dead by now — but his sons might still have been there. One of the consequences of the Iraq War — and there were many consequences flowing from it — was that it sent a clear message to the world that extreme cruelty coupled with bellicose threats won't be appeased.

"Another effect was the Arab Spring and the rising up of the public, starting in Tunisia and spreading to Egypt, Libya and finally Syria. It was contained in the Gulf.

"This sentiment was more than anything triggered by the overthrow of Saddam's brutal regime. I think that did create a sense in the Arab world — a feeling of liberation, if you like — from the rule of dictators."

This, too, though, has proved a complex debate. Ambitions and aspirations for liberty and freedom in the Middle East have bumped up against realities entrenched by history and culture.

Again, as Downer readily acknowledges, it was naive to imagine that what happened in Iraq or Afghanistan was going to spark some sort of geopolitical miracle: transforming the Middle East and North Africa in ways that would gift greater political freedoms to everyday people and encourage a whole-hearted embrace of liberal democratic values.

These are societies with ancient traditions, where tribal, ethnic and sectarian divides have been intrinsic to the political order.

As in Iraq and Afghanistan, the unanswered question almost always was about who exactly would be left to run the show. Who would have control of the finances? Who would have control of the guns? What people, and what agendas, would compete for ascendancy? Says Downer:

> I went to Egypt very soon after the overthrow of Mubarak (in 2011). I was working with the UN in Cyprus at that time.
>
> And I was in a UN car and I asked the security guard in the car whether she had gone to the demonstrations in Tahrir Square. And she said, 'Yes, I did'. So I said, 'How do you feel about Mubarak being overthrown?' and she said, 'It's fantastic'.
>
> And I asked, 'So, in practical terms, just in terms of your life, what will it mean to you?'. And she said, 'It means I will earn more money'. And I said, 'I don't know whether you will take anything I have to say seriously, and I don't blame you if you don't. But my guess it that it won't make much difference to you at all'.
>
> However, it would certainly make a difference if you were a political activist. If you were from the Muslim Brotherhood, it freed you up.
>
> Mubarak was no longer a great option — I admit that. But he did crack down on religious fanaticism. Then, the Egyptians got rid of Mubarak. Suddenly, he's gone. The only political organisation left standing was the Muslim Brotherhood. So who do we get in his place? The public go and elect Mohamed Morsi.

Morsi was, of course, a leader of the Muslim Brotherhood. He very quickly challenged the independence of the judicial authorities in Egypt, and began arresting journalists and sanctioning attacks on political demonstrators. "The Egyptians just had to throw him out," says Downer. "The guy was horrendous. So the upshot is that you tend to get people in charge who are antipathetic to Western interests."

Does he now dismiss the Arab Spring as a false dawn? Downer is philosophical on this point. Today, he sees a slow evolution by increments. He notes in particular the many free elections held in Iraq since the war. Yet he admits it is a journey for the wider region that is only just beginning: "Well, the Arab Spring turned to summer and, eventually, it went back to winter... there is a very long way to go."

An even more dispiriting scenario would play out in Afghanistan, despite a 20-year nation-building campaign by the US and its allies in Australia and Europe — costing $1 trillion and 10,000 lives — to help Afghanis create a more modern, more stable, less oppressive society.

"Of course, we've since surrendered to the Taliban," says Downer, barely hiding his disgust at the Biden Administration's hasty withdrawal of US forces in August, 2021, allowing the Taliban to storm back into power. "Who would have thought that would ever happen?"

Looking back on the politics surrounding these decisions, Downer is intrigued by an argument among some of his critics that military action in Afghanistan was more legitimate than war in Iraq — based on the premise that action by the US and allies to overthrow the Taliban in 2001 at least had the formal support of the UN Security Council.

"Well, that's obviously not what I think," he says. "But I'm familiar with the argument — that the Iraq War was seen by some as the 'bad war' and Afghanistan the 'good war'. However, if we subject this to a bit more analysis, we may find that Iraq has actually turned out better than Afghanistan. These days, Iraq is a more benign player in the volatile world of Middle Eastern politics. That's a big improvement on pre-2003 Iraq."

The other point Downer makes, insistently, is that Australia, throughout the mayhem, held true to its alliance obligations. On a visit to Washington in late 2006, Downer reassured Condoleezza Rice, by then the US secretary of state, that his government would not abandon the US in the face of its manifest challenges in Iraq, Afghanistan and the wider Middle East: "I don't think the Americans will find that Australians are weak, fair-weather friends."

For all his criticism of mistakes and failures by US officials in Iraq, Downer remained steadfast in support for the over-arching US strategy — if not always the way it was executed — right through until the Howard Government's fall from power in 2007.

In May, 2007, Downer and Rice held a joint press conference at the Reagan Library in California. Both reflected on the significance of the Alliance during one of its toughest and most testing phases.

Said Rice:

> Ours is an alliance not of governments but of peoples, one that reflects the deep bond of enduring ideals and shared history, colonial origins, democratic development, and shared political and cultural values. Most importantly, ours is an alliance that remains strong and unbending regardless of domestic political concerns in Washington or Canberra. Yes, we've had our differences, as any allies will, but we raise them freely and we address them openly as friends and we are stronger for it.

In response, Downer was equally resolute:

> Our alliance is built on strong historical foundations, but we don't take it for granted and this is an important point. If we did no more than the bare minimum, the United States and Australia would probably always be friends. But to

Joint press conference at the Reagan Library in 2007 with US Secretary of State, Condoleezza Rice (U.S. State Department /Wikipedia Commons)

achieve and maintain the level of trust, cooperation and warmth that now characterises the relationship requires a special degree of sincerity and effort. It involves standing by your ally not only when it is convenient but also when it is inconvenient.

There is little doubt the Howard Government paid a high price for this politically. In increasing numbers, Australians, like Americans, were wearying of the trauma of headlines from Iraq.

The emergence of Islamic State and the Sunni-Shia conflicts compounded fears and misgivings about whether this ever had been a war worth fighting.

Yet, in 2008, less than six months after leaving office, Downer remained unshakeable in his commitment to the fundamental, underlying principles. In a speech in Washington D.C., he said:

> In many ways, Australians and Americans are the most natural of allies.
>
> Our countries were settled by peoples fleeing persecution and discrimination and who sought the opportunity to achieve prosperity away from the class-based elitism of the old world. We grew to love a life of individual freedom and to place equal value on every person.
>
> We confronted and still confront three great adversaries over the last 100 years. We fought the bloody and heartless totalitarianism of fascism and we won. We fought the intolerance, cruelty and incompetence of communism and we won. And today we fight the fanaticism and ideological insanity of Islamic extremism — and we must win that fight as well.

Almost two decades on, however, there would be fresh questions raised about the sustainability and durability of Australia's alliance with the US in a more dynamic, and no less dangerous, world. What would the second iteration of Donald J. Trump as US president come to mean for global security and stability? And what would be the implications, in the coming years, for the meaning and relevance of the alliance, and Australia's almost century-long support for the values and priorities of American global leadership?

Downer's views on these issues will be explored in later chapters.

10

JAPAN AND THE ARC OF GENERATIONS

In January, 2005, Alexander Downer was in London, on his way to join John Howard at the World Economic Forum in Davos — the only time Howard as prime minister would attend the gathering of world political and business elites at the exclusive Swiss ski resort.

As he walked briskly through the midwinter streets of Knightsbridge, Downer took a phone call from his British counterpart, Foreign Secretary, Jack Straw. The British had a big ask of Downer.

Straw revealed the Dutch Government would be withdrawing from Iraq some of its troops that had been providing a shield of protection for Japanese engineers working on aid and reconstruction projects in Al-Muthanna province, in southern Iraq. Military operations in the province were under British command and control. The Japanese engineers represented a big symbolic commitment by the Government of Prime Minister Junichiro Koizumi to the Coalition campaign in Iraq.

It was Japan's first commitment since World War 2 of forces of any description to an overseas battlefield. It was a sensitive issue politically, given the constraints imposed by Article 9 of Japan's peacetime constitution, forbidding any deployment of its military beyond Japan's shores. Straw asked Downer directly: could Australia step in to help?

"I rang John Howard, and suggested it was something we might look to do," Downer recalls. "It would mean sending additional troops into Iraq… maybe another 500 troops, armoured vehicles. It might be a reasonably good idea in terms of strengthening relations with Japan.

"But look — we had sent in special forces and the RAAF to help the Americans in the initial invasion. It was not as if we wanted to get bogged down in Iraq. We wanted to get out.

"Howard wasn't sure. He said he would think it through. He said we should talk about it when we got back to Australia. He knew the public might not be excited about sending more troops back into Iraq."

Howard takes up the story: "I had said during the 2004 election campaign that we would not be making any new commitments to Iraq. I didn't apologise for what we had done but we had always made it clear to the Yanks and the Brits that we would contribute people at the sharp end ... but no more. When it was obvious the Dutch were pulling out — and it was equally obvious the Japanese would have to pull out if they didn't have the protection of somebody else — the Brits and Americans started making noises about us filling the gap. I remember Tom Schieffer coming to see me, and saying, 'John, I know it was the deal that you went in and out, but we have a problem here'."

Howard had to wrestle with this dilemma. The request from Australia's allies was about addressing a genuine need — justifiable on both strategic and humanitarian grounds. But, politically, it was much tougher. It ran headlong into an election pledge Howard had given personally to Australians.

"I had made this commitment — no more," Howard recalls. "So I started testing public opinion in different ways on what would the reaction be if we went in to help. The overwhelming response was, 'No problem, if it's to protect the Japanese'. That really impressed me.

I thought, 'Gee, we have come a long way'. That was a lesson to me in post World War 2 healing."

On their return to Australia, Howard and Downer discussed the issue with Cabinet colleagues. The Prime Minister was insistent on following a strict protocol — they could not consider the request unless the approach came directly from Japan. Senior ministers agreed.

Downer, as foreign minister, would have to deliver the message: "I was to tell the Japanese that if Prime Minister Koizumi rang Howard directly, he would look into it. So I communicated this to the Japanese. I can't say they were happy to hear this."

He arranged to speak directly by phone to Foreign Minister Taro Aso, himself a future Prime Minister of Japan.

The call from Aso came through at dinner time in Adelaide. Downer was attending a function hosted by his wife, Nicky, at the Queen Adelaide Club — "I was there as her handbag."

But this was not the best place to be. Downer was about to have a tough conversation with his Japanese counterpart about deploying more Australians to a war zone. It was of the utmost secrecy. And there were massive political sensitivities at both ends.

The Trilateral Security Dialogue — with US Secretary of State, Condoleezza Rice, and Japanese Foreign Minister, Taro Aso (Dean Marzolla/Newspix)

Downer hid himself in a cupboard to take the call:

> The foreign minister was very reluctant to have Koizumi phone Howard (but) I told him it was not politically feasible for Australia to volunteer more troops into Iraq to protect Japanese engineers if the request came from the British. It had to be a request from the Prime Minister of Japan. I remember the minister being very grumpy with me. Ultimately, though, he put the proposal to Koizumi, who said he was quite prepared to do this. So it all worked out well.

That agreement marked another significant step-up in confidence and trust between Australia and Japan entering the 21st century.

Governments in Japan had already noted Australia's extensive loans to the economies of East Asia during the 1997 Asian Financial Crisis.

They had admired the Howard Government's commitment in 1999 to despatch more than 5000 soldiers into East Timor to restore peace and stability after the ugly violence and upheaval in the small island nation that followed its vote to declare independence from Indonesia.

Now Japan and Australia were supporting US-led efforts to stabilise and rebuild a war-ravaged Iraq following the removal of the tyrant, Saddam Hussein. How far things had come since the dark days of World War 2.

Asked if there is one relationship with a country that best defines the contribution of the Downer family to Australia's more outward-looking foreign policy across the postwar era, many people might say it comes down to a simple choice of two — either the United States or Britain.

After all, Downer served in a government that joined the George W. Bush-led coalitions in contentious and gruelling conflicts in both Afghanistan and Iraq. As for Britain, both Alexander Downer and his father were long-serving Australian diplomatic representatives in London. Both placed high value on the legal, political and cultural traditions shared with Britain.

Yet, in fact, the answer to that question may well lie closer to home.

Among the most significant transformations in Australia's strategic thinking since 1945 has been the reinventing of relations with Japan.

The Downer family, across the arc of generations, was to prove pivotal in engineering that shift.

It began during World War 2, when Downer's father, Alick, was held by the Imperial Japanese Army as a prisoner-of-war at Changi. He had experienced all the brutality of war.

Almost half of the Australians taken captive in Singapore would die before the war's end. The suffering at that prison camp was something he would never forget. Could he ever bring himself to forgive?

In her oral history for the University of South Australia, Mary Downer referenced the psychological scars carried by her husband as a survivor of the depredations of Changi.

"He hated Singapore although he did go back there eventually," she said. "And it took him a long time to go to Japan. He became more understanding. But, having suffered under them for three-and-a-half years, it wasn't easy. He couldn't eat rice for years. They'd had 3900 consecutive meals of rice (in the prison camp). They kept count."

In September, 1951 — on the very day Alexander Downer was born — Australia signed the Treaty of San Francisco, the formal peace agreement with Japan. In Parliament, Alick Downer, crossed the floor to vote with Labor against the terms of the treaty.

Yet come 1957, the same Alick Downer, by now a minister in the Menzies Government, would be highly influential in galvanising support within government ranks for the approval and signing of an historic trade and commerce treaty between Australia and Japan. "If the Japanese can't trade, they will explode," he would say at the time.

Alexander himself would be instrumental in taking the relationship to the next level. Even as early as his first visit as Foreign Affairs Minister to Japan in 1996, Downer would discover that, with the advent of the Howard Government, there was a re-evaluation underway in Japan's foreign ministry, the *Gaimu-sho,* about Australia's role in the region.

"All sorts of factors came into that... but the increasing aggression of China and concerns in Tokyo about China's rising power was clearly part of it," Downer recalls.

In 2001, he began working to garner support for the proposal. He was surprised to find he would run into a brick wall.

"As Foreign Minister, I had this idea that the relationship with Japan was less than it should be," Downer recalls. "I had a meeting with Foreign Minister Yohei Kono. I said to him, 'You have a security agreement with the US, we have an alliance with the US — shouldn't we get together and meet at Foreign Minister level? You know... you, me, the US Secretary of State ... to discuss strategic issues in our part of the world? The Europeans have NATO. Wouldn't it make sense for the three of us to get together? It would seem very opportune right now."

Downer had discussed the concept previously with the US Deputy Secretary of State, Rich Armitage — a good friend of Australia. And Japan. Armitage had told Downer he thought it was worth exploring.

So Downer went into the conversation with Kono confident this was an idea with great potential. He was taken aback by the response from the Japanese Foreign Minister: one of diffidence — and not-so-diplomatic. "Australia is not to be compared to the United States," Kono replied, bluntly. "Why would we meet with a small country like Australia?"

At dinner that night, Downer mentioned his proposal to a top-ranking official from Japan's foreign affairs department. "He said it was a great idea and they would give it serious consideration. I didn't tell him his Foreign Minister had tried to put the kybosh on it."

Howard remembers Downer pressing the issue with senior Americans at every opportunity. "Alexander worked very hard on that. When Bush came to Australia in 2003, (Downer) had a bilateral with Condi Rice on that matter around the breakfast table at The Lodge."

Leveraging off the 2005 decision to provide military support for Japanese engineers, Downer stepped up his campaign to build more ballast into the security relationship with Japan.

So began the first embryonic moves to establish what would become the Trilateral Security Dialogue, an annual meeting of policy leaders from the US, Japan and Australia to discuss security and other challenges in the western Pacific. The first meeting was held in Australia in 2006. Downer would host Condoleezza Rice and Taro Aso.

It would mark another quantum shift in the relationship with Japan, potentially of considerable strategic significance in Asia and beyond.

A year later, the Trilateral Security Dialogue would serve as the foundations for a strategic grouping as or more significant — the Quad. This time, no less than the Japanese Prime Minister, Shinzo Abe, would take the lead, and India would agree to meet formally at heads-of-government level with the US, Japan and Australia, extending the strategic focus to include the Indian Ocean Rim.

From 1996, the four nations had been taking part in joint naval exercises known as Operation Malabar. With the emergence of the Quad, the grouping would step up its efforts to improve interoperability in air defences, anti-submarine strategies, military communications, logistics and supply.

Although this would anger China, always suspicious of any mechanism that might be interpreted as an attempt to contain or encircle Beijing's power, Downer thought it made sense for leading democracies to consult formally on security in the western Pacific. China denounced the grouping as "an Asian NATO."

In 2008, the new Rudd Government in Australia went cold on The Quad — perhaps fearing China's antagonism.

But, come 2017, with China behaving belligerently towards neighbours in the South China Sea, and Donald Trump in the White House, the Quad roared back into fashion.

At the 2017 ASEAN summit in Manila, the US, Japan, India and Australia agreed to restore the Quad at heads-of-government level.

In March, 2021 — in a statement headlined "The Spirit of the Quad" — the four nations described a shared vision "for a free and open Indo-Pacific," and a "rules-based maritime order in the East and South China seas." Comprising four long-standing democracies, with significant political and cultural leverage, and a combined GDP of almost $US40 trillion, it represented at the very least a powerful new dynamic in regional diplomacy. One that China could not simply ignore — even if it included "a small country like Australia."

That Japan and Australia were key to these arrangements was replete with symbolism. Building this new architecture had required turning around opinion in official circles in Japan on Australia's capacity to bring serious commitment and heft to the equation. "It wasn't just there for the asking," Downer says. "You had to demonstrate you could do things... that you could bring value to the region."

Twenty years after Alexander Downer set in train the idea of a closer partnership, Australia's ties with Japan were performing at something much nearer correct weight — not only strategically but at the people-to-people level.

Australia's beach resorts remained a favoured destination for young Japanese holidaymakers. Likewise, Japan's picturesque ski towns, the ancient beauty of Kyoto, and the buzz and vibrancy of Tokyo and Osaka had become highly popular with Australians looking to enjoy the charms of a winter Christmas in Japan.

For the Downer family, too, there would be increasingly deep connections to Japanese life and culture.

Alexander Downer's eldest daughter, Georgina, is fluent in Japanese. Like her father and grandfather, she has also worked in diplomacy. From 2010, she spent several years as second secretary at the Australian Embassy in Tokyo. Her first-born son, Henry Heath, was delivered at the Aiiku Hospital in the Japanese capital.

That 80-year arc describing the Downer family's relationship with Japan — from a prison camp in Changi to a maternity hospital in Tokyo — mirrors evocatively the progress in relations between two nations, two cultures. Alexander Downer admits to some pride and satisfaction in where Australia and Japan as societies have landed — as security and economic partners, and through mutual respect and friendship as people: "There is no doubt that perceptions have greatly changed."

11

THE FORBIDDING CITY

Back in 1996, the Howard Government experienced some of the toughest moments in Australia's relations with the People's Republic of China. In his first year as Australia's foreign affairs minister, Alexander Downer was in the thick of it.

As he took over the stewardship of Australia's foreign policy, Downer learned very quickly that the strategic outlook in East Asia was becoming more volatile. His first visit as Foreign Affairs Minister to Tokyo in 1996 had given him a strong sense of the emerging tensions, especially over the future of Taiwan.

But the series of upheavals that year in the relationship with China was something else again. Twenty years later, Downer's successors in Australia would have to go through much the same trial by fire — a refresher course on how precarious it can be dealing with an aggrieved, aggressive China.

Downer acknowledges that China under Xi Jinping became both more powerful and assertive than the nation he dealt with as Foreign Affairs Minister. But he rejects the idea that engagement with the PRC was ever a walk in the park. In his first year in office, he had direct experience of how difficult and disruptive its power elites could be.

At the 1996 election, Howard and Downer had repudiated Keating's attempt at a wholesale realignment of Australian strategic policy towards Asia and away from traditional allies like the US and Britain.

Not that they rejected the gravitational pull of the emerging powers of the region. But they believed Keating was over-egging it, ill-advisedly.

Moreover, they were angered by his claim a Coalition Government would be incapable of managing relations with governments in Asia.

Within weeks of coming to office, however, Downer, in particular, was feeling the full brunt of China's anger. Keating's provocative rhetoric may well have been ringing in his ears.

In those earliest days in office, the road to Beijing would be no

Hosted in Beijing by China's then Premier Wen Jiabao (John Feder/Newspix)

red-carpet ride. Coinciding with the Howard Government's election, the Republic of Taiwan was holding its first democratic presidential election. Chinese missiles began landing in the waters off Taiwan's coast. The US was appalled by China's attempt to intimidate the voters of Taiwan. Immediately, it sent two aircraft carriers to the region.

Both Howard and Downer issued statements supporting the US deployment, and urging China to show restraint. Australia was the only nation across Asia to voice support for the US action.

After Australia and US defence and foreign ministers held their annual (AUSMIN) talks in Sydney that year, China's *People's Daily* ran a terse editorial denouncing Japan and Australia, the northern and southern anchors of US alliances in the region, as being "the claws of a crab."

"They really put us to the test," Downer recalls. "When we supported the right of the Americans to sail through the Taiwan straits, they gave it to us. When I met the Dalai Lama, they gave it to us. Then, in our first Budget, we moved to wind back the Development Import Finance Facility programs in China (aid-related support to help developing countries win business contracts in Australia). They were really unhappy about that. They clamped down on us on just about everything. They were really hostile towards us."

Beijing cancelled all ministerial visits from Australia. And Chinese agencies stopped doing business with Australian companies.

Towards the end of 1996, Downer decided enough was enough.

He summoned the PRC ambassador at the time, Hua Junze, to his office at Parliament House in Canberra. Downer was determined to shift the atmospherics — to get Australia out of the deep freeze and restore a calm, sensible dialogue with Beijing.

"Ambassador, I just want to be frank with you in this conversation," Downer told him. "Let's work out ways to build a better relationship between Australia and China. All this stuff is leading us nowhere. There is no point to it. You can hold out as long as you like, you can refuse to meet with our ministers — for days, weeks or decades if you want — but it is not going to change anything.

"It is totally unproductive. It is just pointless."

Doubtless, the Ambassador's report on the meeting went straight back to Beijing. Perhaps the Chinese were also wearying of the diplomatic stand-off. They, too, had business to do in Australia, with Australians.

In early 1997, John Howard received an invitation to visit Beijing for a meeting with President Jiang Zemin. The ice had been broken. "That meeting didn't just happen," says Downer. "It goes back to that conversation with the Chinese Ambassador …"

After almost a year in the "sin bin", Australian ministers were back on speaking terms with the senior Chinese leadership. Discussions with Chinese officials became courteous, and mostly constructive. Growth in two-way trade surged. The complementarity of the two economies would open up unprecedented opportunities for both to prosper.

Over the next decade, there would be a more pragmatic dialogue. In Beijing, Hu Jintao was the president of a China making huge advances economically — its people aspiring to "grow rich before they grew old."

At that time, it seemed China was a lot easier for the rest of the world to work with than it is today. Downer capitalised on the moment.

The improving relationship meant the two countries would enter discussions on subjects that previously had been taboo — like China's human rights record.

In 1997, at Downer's instigation, China agreed to establish a formal Human Rights Dialogue with the Australian Government. This was a landmark development: the one-party Communist state would hear representations from Downer on Australia's concerns about its treatment of minorities like the Tibetans and Uighurs, and the jailing of political dissidents. How earnestly would China treat this dialogue?

There were a lot of sceptics. But Downer was determined to set in place a distinct, dedicated process to allow for these issues to be aired fully and forcefully with senior Chinese officials without necessarily dominating all other bilateral meetings between the nations. Realistically, what meaningful progress, if any, was it likely to achieve?

Downer's first priority was to get the ball rolling — a significant diplomatic task, in itself, given China's extreme wariness about any scrutiny on these issues. As a deputy secretary at DFAT, Bill Farmer was brought in to negotiate the parameters of the talks with Beijing.

When Farmer asked Downer what he hoped to get out of the first round of the Human Rights Dialogue, Downer's response was as pragmatic as it was succinct: "A second Human Rights Dialogue."

It took seven years of hard grind but by, 2003, Downer had restored Sino-Australia relations to a new high water mark — and found the elusive alchemy whereby Australia's relations with China and the US could strengthen and prosper simultaneously.

This was symbolised by an extraordinary two days of high diplomacy in the Australian capital: George W Bush one day, Hu Jintao the next.

The descent on Canberra of the two world leaders and their huge entourages posed an unprecedented logistical challenge for Australia's protocol officers, as they attempted to orchestrate the diplomatic equivalent of what old submariners call hot-bunking. But there were no complaints from within the Howard Government.

For Howard and Downer, having driven Australia's foreign policy agenda since 1996, this "double-header" of presidential visits from the US and China represented, symbolically, the sweetest symmetry.

Before 2003, only two foreign heads of state had addressed a joint sitting of the Australian Parliament: former US President George HW Bush in January 1992 and then US President Bill Clinton in 1996.

In more than 30 years of formal diplomatic relations with the People's Republic, only one Chinese head of state had previously journeyed to Australia. Now, the leaders of two of Australia's largest and most important international partners arrived within 24 hours of each other.

This was vindication for Downer and Howard. They had worked to roll back the notion of a strategic destiny exclusively in Asia.

The arrival of Bush and Hu on consecutive days demonstrated Australia could, and, should, work all of the global power centres at the same time. The images from that week in Canberra made for a powerful rebuttal of the idea that maintaining, even strengthening, ties to the US would risk isolating Australia among its Asian neighbours.

Both Bush and Hu would address special sittings of federal Parliament — the US President on the Thursday, China's president on the Friday.

"What better evidence can we present than Exhibit A — consecutive visits on consecutive days by the President of the United States and the President of the People's Republic of China," Downer told *The Age*, finding it hard not to gloat.

"It shows we're able to engage with Asia in a relaxed and unpretentious way and, at the same time, build the closest relationship Australia has had with the US since General MacArthur left our shores."

Within a year, Australia would sign a Free Trade Agreement with the US, the world's largest economy. It was not without controversy.

Even among allies, there are always winners and losers at either end of a Free Trade Agreement — and losers can include very prominent and powerful corporates and even more prominent and powerful industry lobbies. Like the farm sectors in the US and Australia.

Completing the FTA deal with the US involved high-level wrangling with the White House, the US Trade Department and the US Congress, leveraging the significant credits the Howard Government had banked for its support of the Bush Administration in the War on Terror.

Around that same time, Australian would also begin a long and laborious process of setting rules for the game in negotiating a trade and economic framework agreement with China, fast becoming the world's second largest economy.

This would serve as the precursor to the Free Trade Agreement Australia ultimately would finalise with China, and ratify under the Turnbull Government more than a decade later.

There were many obstacles to a Free Trade Agreement with a country that had been a command economy for much of the previous half century — an economy still dominated by state-owned enterprises linked intimately to the Chinese Communist Party.

In terms of the rules of global trade, could China ever really be identified as a "market economy" — the fundamental requirement for membership of the rules-setting body, the World Trade Organisation? These were considerations with which the US also struggled.

China felt Australia was always prone to allowing its strategic ties to the US to cross-infect its attitudes to trade. Beijing would confront Downer on this frequently:

> They used to say to me, 'This alliance you have with the Americans, this is Cold War diplomacy. We don't need these alliances any more. You should abandon this alliance'.
>
> And I would say to them, 'Look, I'll choose my friends, you choose your friends. You won't be choosing my friends for me, and I won't be choosing your friends for you.
>
> We have huge common interests, common history and common values with the Americans. We are always going to be together in a whole lot of different ways. That's how it is and you just need to understand that. You have your neighbourhood, your interests and countries you identify with, more or less.
>
> Your relationship with Russia is not my business. Or your relationships with Uzbekistan or Tajikistan. That's your business. Our relationship with America is our business'.

Yet, for all the geo-strategic tensions, there would remain at this time an underlying pragmatism in two-way commercial relations with China. In August, 2002, the Howard Government finalised a $25 billion deal to supply China with liquefied natural gas.

The gas deal was at that time Australia's single biggest export agreement. It was symbolic of how Australia's prosperity was rising partly on the back of its burgeoning economic ties with the Asian giant.

By the time the Howard Government left office, China was on the verge of becoming Australia's largest export market. But, as ever, the intertwining of trade and strategic interests would prove complex, with sometimes unforeseen consequences in the longer run.

12

TRADE OFFS

From the 1980s, governments in Australia finally came around to the view that a vibrant, open market economy was the best avenue to success in an increasingly competitive, globally-integrated, technology-led international economy. Wheat and wool exports — along with the discovery of gold — had underwritten prosperity in the colonial years. Entering the 21st century, global trade became Australia's lifeline.

Alexander Downer came into the role of Foreign Affairs Minister with a career history in diplomacy and economics — liberal, free-market economics. While he worked alongside senior National Party ministers in the trade portfolio, he always asserted — and was allowed — a lead role when it came to global trade policy. He pursued assiduously the opportunities to open new markets for Australian businesses.

It took Australia more than 200 years to achieve $100 billion in exports annually. From 1996 to 2006, largely encompassing the Howard Government's years in office, Australia's export earnings doubled to $207 billion. That spectacular growth curve, much of it in a low-inflation environment, goes a long way to explaining rising living standards. Iron ore, coal and natural gas exports, mainly to China and Japan, were a key factor in this. But that was only part of the story.

Attracting international students from Asia to Australia's top universities was another boom industry. So, too, wine and seafood — along with strong growth in Australia's more traditional exports of food and fibre. Australia's sustained economic success under the Howard Government owed much to efficient export industries, reliable transport, the free flow of capital, a strong and transparent banking system... and also some robust trade diplomacy.

The Howard Government's successes in achieving strong economic growth across more than a decade in office owed much to the fostering of a vibrant exports sector. But, along the way, there were repeat episodes where chasing business prospects in overseas markets created conflict and controversy — either within the internal politics of Australia or, as problematically, in trade tensions with other nations.

Straddling the intersection of domestic, economic, trade and security policy imperatives is one of the toughest asks of governments across the world. Like strategic policy, it is about balancing interests.

The various arms of policy-making cannot always work in perfect unison. Sometimes, inevitably, the legitimate profit-making ambitions of Australian businesses in the global economy can collide with — or even compromise — other domestic or foreign policy objectives.

Even with like-minded nations and societies, like the US and the European Union, the jostling for trade advantages can be brutal.

Ever since the 1960s, Australia had fought a long, frustrating campaign on behalf of its farm sector to combat the distorting effects of EU agricultural subsidies and import quotas on commodity markets. As Downer noted pointedly in 2004: "It is disturbing that high income countries, including those in the EU, spend nearly $1.8 billion per day on agricultural support and protection – a sum seven times greater than the amount they provide in development assistance, and twice the value of agricultural exports from all developing countries."

The Howard Government, like its predecessors, sought to eliminate these protectionist barriers through the Doha Round of global trade negotiations, and by forming tactical alliances with the Cairns Group, which included several leading Latin American countries, in defending and promoting Australia's agricultural trade policy interests.

And, long before the advent of Donald Trump tariff agenda, Australian lamb and beef producers, and steel exporters, had been slugged with punitive tariffs by the protectionist clique in the US Congress. Alexander Downer did not let this go unnoticed.

In 2004, he complained openly about the negative repercussions for Australian industry: "Our relationship with the United States is vital. But we must work to match the strong security relationship with a much better economic relationship. Too often, American decision-makers harm our trade."

In its third term, the Howard Government was able to deliver a Free Trade Agreement with the US, the world's largest economy. At the same time, the economic relationship with China was accelerating. But the policy (and political) challenges in achieving this were never straightforward. There were always trade-offs to be made.

Selling Australian wheat to Saddam Hussein's Iraq through the late 1990s was another prominent example where the money-making business of trade could create strategic and political problems.

In 2005-06, the Howard Government came under intense political pressure over allegations that the Australian Wheat Board had paid kickbacks to Saddam Hussein's regime to maintain Australia's lucrative wheat exports to the nation under the UN oil-for-food program.

From 1996 through to 2003, AWB had become the dominant supplier of wheat to Iraq, securing an average 65 per cent of all wheat sales into the market. By 2001, Iraq was Australia's largest customer for wheat.

In 2001–02, at the peak of the trade, Australia exported 2.2 million tonnes of wheat worth $800 million into Iraq, representing 82 per cent of Iraqi imports and 13.5 per cent of all Australian wheat exports.

However, by 2005, the UN itself was under investigation amid claims of massive corruption of the $64 billion oil-for-food program. Reports began to emerge from postwar Iraq of a vast range of individuals said to have been beneficiaries of oil sales contracts from Saddam's regime.

The allegations extended to bribes and kickbacks paid to Saddam and other senior Iraqi officials. This put the entire edifice of the UN's oil-for-food program in Iraq under microscopic scrutiny.

According to the AWB's main rivals in Canada and the US, there could be only one explanation for the extraordinary success of the Australian wheat trade in Iraq — that AWB had been involved in nefarious dealings with Saddam Hussein's regime.

The Canadian Wheat Board, which represented that nation's wheat growers, complained to the United Nations. The United Nations made inquiries of the Australian Government through Australia's UN mission in New York. Eventually, the Department of Foreign Affairs and Trade got the relevant contracts from AWB Limited and gave them to the UN. The UN said it was satisfied with the explanation it received.

But, by now, the controversy was up and running. The AWB was prominent in the headlines, globally.

In March, 2006, at the very time the Howard Government was meant to be celebrating 10 years in office, Howard, Downer and Trade Minister Mark Vaile would be called before a Royal Commission, presided over by former NSW Supreme Court judge, Terence Cole, to explain what, if anything, they knew about the AWB's dealings in Iraq.

Today, Downer is all but dismissive of the controversy: "Absolutely no prosecutions have come from it. Nobody on the Australian Wheat Board was taking bribes. The Australian Government wasn't even involved in it, as the Cole Royal Commission pointed out.

"I think Howard just over-reacted. I said that to his face at the time."

So did AWB — or for that matter, the Government — have no case to answer? Downer remains defiant. "I mean, it's just a mush of arguments that have come together. Most journos will take on the Labor Party's argument. Unless you can prove your innocence they basically condemn you as guilty. It's completely absurd."

Downer is calm and matter-of-fact as he gives his account of what happened:

> The Australian Wheat Board had a big market in Iraq. Oil-for-food comes in. They wanted to maintain their market so they said to the Iraqis, 'Can we keep this market?'
>
> The Iraqis needed to import wheat to feed their people. They said, 'We will import wheat from Australia on condition that you unload the wheat in Aqaba, and you have to use this Jordanian trucking company, Alia'. So the Wheat Board says, 'OK, that's fine' and they do use the trucking company.
>
> But Alia is partly owned by the Iraqi Government and they over-charged for the transport cost. They mark it up. They are a monopoly so they can easily do that.
>
> And the profits of this trucking company are shared between the Jordanian owners and the Iraqi Government. The Iraqi Government is able to make substantial profit out of this trucking company, because it is a monopoly and you can't sell wheat to Iraq unless you use that trucking company.
>
> I suppose everybody could have said, 'Well, we won't sell wheat to Iraq unless we are satisfied with the price of the trucking'. That seems improbable. So the wheat was sold to Iraq. And this is somehow a monumental case of corruption? I don't think so.

His one criticism of the Australian Wheat Board is that they misled people about their state of knowledge. They fully suspected the Iraqis were over-charging for the transport of the wheat yet chose not to disclose this. If nothing else, this had created the whiff of a cover-up. The AWB's rival wheat exporters in Canada and the US were quick to call for an international investigation.

Suddenly, the AWB — and, by extension, the Howard Government — found themselves at the centre of a scandal. Downer rejects to this day that there was ever substance to the allegations.

"Nobody was ever charged with doing anything illegal," Downer says. "It was basically just an opportunity for the Labor Party to attack the Howard government, and to play into the Iraq War narrative — which was playing quite well for Labor."

In November, 2006, with the report of the Cole Inquiry under his arm, John Howard went out publicly to declare that — as far he was concerned — the AWB scandal was dead and buried:

> We've had almost a year of forensic examination, we've had 76 days of sittings. We've had documents provided, we've had questions asked, we've had people examined on oath ...
>
> The case being alleged against the Government by the Opposition has not been established. Now you can't be more searching and transparent than that... If Cole had found evidence of wrongdoing, he would have asked for an extension of his terms of reference.
>
> Not only did he not ask for an extension of his terms of reference, but he also said that he found no evidence of knowledge by ministers, and he particularly examined the role of DFAT, and DFAT was not found wanting by the Commissioner.
>
> I don't think there's any doubt as to what Mr Cole has found. He found no illegality by the Government. He found there was no turning of the blind eye by DFAT. He did not find any evidence of the wrongdoing alleged by the members of the Opposition.
>
> He did not find any knowledge on my part or on the part of my ministers in relation to the activities of AWB or a communication of those activities. AWB has cast a shadow over Australia's reputation in international trade. That shadow has been removed.

Negotiations over the development of oil and gas resources in the Timor Sea became another issue where Australia's legitimate business interests bumped up against other political or strategic considerations.

Australia and East Timor are separated by only 650km of water. But in the seabed beneath that stretch of water lay valuable resources. The dispute over ownership and control of the oil and gas fields beneath the Timor Sea was to degenerate into an unseemly row.

Internationally, Australia — as the far bigger, wealthier nation — would be accused of bullying and worse over the splitting of revenue from the petrochemical riches straddling the maritime boundaries.

Most controversially of all, there would be accusations by East Timor that Australia had bugged the offices of its negotiators to give the Howard Government an unfair advantage during the haggling.

To this day, if there is one issue that gnaws at Alexander Downer above all others, it has been the conduct of East Timor's leaders during this dispute. "In my view, some have behaved contemptibly," he says.

In short, this became a debate about whether Australia unfairly pressured a tiny island nation — or whether, in fact, East Timor was running a cynical campaign to secure more than its fair share of oil and gas revenues by defaming and denigrating the neighbour that did more than any other nation to gift East Timor its independence.

In 1989, Labor Foreign Affairs Minister, Gareth Evan, negotiated a Timor Gap Treaty with his Indonesian counterpart, Ali Alatas. Under this agreement, Australia and Indonesia, which at that time claimed sovereignty over East Timor's seabed, created a Joint Development Area and agreed to split royalties 50-50 from the Bayu-Undan oil fields.

Ten years later, after the Australian-led INTERFET forces secured East Timor's independence, the Howard Government faced a quandary. It had settled its maritime boundaries with Indonesia and did not want to reopen those negotiations. But it would need to revisit with a new East Timorese Government a resource-sharing agreement on Bayu-Undan.

Downer says he went into the negotiations prepared to offer East Timor a deal which he regarded as exceedingly generous:

> When we entered into negotiations with the Timorese, I

said, 'We don't need the money as much as you. We're a rich country, you are a poorer country. But we do need the security of our maritime borders because we have maritime borders with Indonesia as well'.

I signed with Ali Alatas in 1997 what became known as the Treaty of Perth, which defined our maritime borders.

We had 1500 kilometres of maritime borders with Indonesia and I didn't want all of that to become unravelled, and lead to a deterioration in our relationship with Indonesia, when we had already solved that problem.

But the Treaty of Perth had still be ratified by the Indonesian Parliament. "I was worried that, as an act of revenge, they would unravel that and say, 'Well, if you're agreeing to something different with the Timorese, why not agree to something like that with us?'"

The negotiations with East Timor did not begin well. Nor end well.

Downer remembers a stormy meeting in his office in Parliament House in Canberra with the UN-appointed negotiator for East Timor, Peter Galbraith. The former American diplomat had been seconded by the UN to assist the interim government in East Timor ahead of the formal declaration of independence for the Democratic Republic of Timor-Leste in May, 2002. Downer says:

> I remember it like it was yesterday. I was rude to him because he was very aggressive. What he was doing was completely unacceptable. They were trying to rip us off.
>
> "So I say to Galbraith, 'I'm not interested in the money, I'm interested in the boundaries.' And he said, 'This Bayu-Undan should all be in East Timor. That's the international law.' And I said, 'Well, it is not, according to our lawyers'. And he said to me, 'What we will do then is take you to the International Court of Justice'. And I said, 'Well, given we have liberated East Timor, and led INTERFET, and spent billions of dollars helping to create this independent country, I think that would be a very hostile thing to do, and completely unnecessary.
>
> 'We should, between friends, be able to negotiate this. However, if you persist with this approach, I will withdraw from the jurisdiction of the court. I am not going to have

this litigated. I am going to have this negotiated'. And he said to me, 'You wouldn't dare do that'.

The next day I told the Department we were going to withdraw from the jurisdiction of the International Court of Justice when it came to delineating maritime boundaries. The media were all outraged, of course. But this left no choice but to negotiate.

So when it came to the final negotiations, which were also at Parliament House, Ramos-Horta was there. I wouldn't do a deal with Galbraith so I said I would talk to Ramos-Horta. In the end, he said he would do the deal.

There were many components to it but we were offering 80 per cent of the revenue to East Timor. He said he would do the deal if we offered them 90 per cent. And I said, 'OK, you can have 90 per cent of the revenue'. So they still get 90 per cent of the royalties from the JDA today ... although the revenue is running out all these years later.

East Timor received about $20 billion in revenues. At the outset, much of it was transferred by the East Timor Government to a sovereign fund, aimed at helping generate profits that would provide the island nation with longer-term financial security. Downer says that policy did not survive for long: "They've spent the lot on their recurrent Budget needs — it's mostly gone."

If the Bayu-Undan negotiations had been tough, worse was to come. On May 19, 2002, world dignitaries including UN Secretary-General, Kofi Annan, former US President, Bill Clinton, the new Indonesian President, Megawati Sukarnoputri, Portuguese Prime Minister, Jose Manuel Barroso, and Prime Minister John Howard all arrived in Dili to witness the birth of a new nation.

On the stroke of midnight of May 20, Kofi Annan formally handed over government to Xanana Gusmao.

Earlier that day, while not widely noticed, East Timor activists had organised a gathering in Dili's town market to protest the demarcation of Australian and East Timorese sovereignty in the Timor Sea. It was a dividing line that would lead to greater acrimony in years to come.

In the short term, East Timor needed Australia's ongoing support to maintain order in the fledgling nation. Come December, 2002, the dispute over oil and gas revenues would slip from prominence. Xanana Gusmao and Jose-Ramos Horta had far bigger problems to deal with. And they desperately needed Australia's help.

Downer recalls taking the SOS call from Ramos-Horta. On December 4, there had been riots in the heart of Dili. Two people had been killed. "The whole place started to fall apart again," says Downer. Australia agreed to provide military and police backup to quell the violence.

With stability restored, the two governments sat down the following year to discuss the sharing of resources from the other major Timor Sea energy field, Greater Sunrise. Here, Australia was in a strong bargaining position because, under the Timor Gap Treaty, 80 per cent of the gas fields lay within Australia's maritime territory.

But some in East Timor had other ideas. This time, Downer was negotiating with a new East Timorese prime minister, Mari Alkatiri, an avowed economic nationalist. Alkatiri wanted to rewrite the rules.

Says Downer: "Under the Treaty they had signed off on, 80 per cent of Greater Sunrise was in the Australian area.

"And they now say, 'That should be in the East Timorese area'. And I say, 'But you have signed off on this agreement'."

Facing another impasse, Downer agreed to reopen negotiations on the revenue split from Greater Sunrise.

"Ok, we'll give you more than 20 per cent," Downer told Alkatiri. "We go through a negotiation, and we gave them 50 per cent of revenue but we didn't move the maritime boundaries."

In 2006, there was more upheaval in Dili. A group of 580 government soldiers deserted their barracks on February 8. In April, these soldiers then rioted for five days on the streets of Dili. Five people died. In early May, a police officer was killed in another outbreak of political violence. Later that month, on May 25, government and rebel forces clashed openly. There were 21 deaths. Twenty thousand villagers on the outskirts of Dili fled their homes.

Xanana Gusmao was about to declare a state of emergency. Again, Downer took the panicked call from Dili. "Ramos-Horta rang me to say, 'Please, please can you send in troops?'

"And I said, 'You know I will have to ask John Howard and the whole National Security Cabinet — but, you know, probably we can'. And we did. And we pacified the place and got it back under control."

An Australian-led peacekeeping force, the *International Stabilisation Force* (ISF), was deployed in East Timor from May 25. The ISF consisted of 2000 Australian troops, with smaller contributions of troops and police from Malaysia, New Zealand and Portugal.

On June 3, Downer flew into Dili, to be escorted through the streets by the commander of the ISF, Brigadier Mick Slater. Makeshift tent cities had been set up as temporary accommodation for families rendered homeless by the violence and marauding.

The ISF had restored calm. Yet, at the government offices in the capital, shattered windows were still awaiting repair.

Downer was greeted by an ashen-faced Ramos-Horta, despairing that his dreams for his nation were under grave threat. Later, at the home of Xanana Gusmao, the president was visibly distressed as he told Downer of the violence and suffering endured by his people.

East Timor would need more help — much more help — from Australia, and others, to restore public confidence in the nation's viability.

Three months later, Downer flew back into Dili. This would be a very different meeting with Ramos-Horta. This time, Downer would be joined by Indonesia's Foreign Minister, Dr Hassan Wirajuda.

Jointly, the three governments discussed what they could do to improve East Timor's circumstances. Such a meeting would have been unthinkable in the Keating years.

This historic trilateral dialogue was early proof positive that Australia's intervention in East Timor would not poison indefinitely Australia's relations with Indonesia. And it offered the people of East Timor a greater degree of certainty about a more peaceful and stable future.

"I don't think they've had had any particular problems like that since 2006," says Downer. "We did all this — helped them to get their country going and, when it started to go off the rails, we put it back on the rails by sending in the ADF ... yet now all they do is attack us."

As oil and gas negotiations resumed, the mood and mindset in Dili shifted dramatically. Amid the political and security breakdown in May, 2006, Alkatiri and his policies as PM would come under attack.

Eventually, Gusmao would force him from power, and accuse Alkatiri of cutting a poor deal with energy giants like Woodside, Conoco Phillips and Shell — the Greater Sunrise consortium. The dispute over exploration and production rights in the Timor Sea was about to become more divisive still.

"So they had another argument with the consortium," Downer explains. "The East Timorese wouldn't agree to let Sunrise be developed if it meant the gas was landed in Darwin.

"The consortium wanted to land the gas in Darwin because it was cheaper. Secondly, they thought the sovereign risk was negligible compared to a high sovereign risk in East Timor. Well, the East Timorese never agreed ..."

The dispute would linger for many years to come..

Downer makes no attempt to hide his frustration: "If the Greater Sunrise project had been up-and-running 15 years ago ... they could

At the historic trilateral meeting in Dili with Indonesia's Foreign Minister, Dr Hasan Wirajuda, and East Timor's Prime Minister, Jose Ramos Horta
(Sarah Reid/Newspix

have had billions of dollars flowing into their economy. Instead, you have this crazy idea of the gas being landed in East Timor where they are proposing that the developers build a standalone petrochemical facility on a remote coastline…

"And then they started this fantasy about us spying on them… this allegation that we were spying on their Cabinet. It's just pathetic."

Downer is unyielding on this point. He cannot and will not comment on individual intelligence operations:

> Never will do. Until the day I die. That would be a betrayal of my country.
>
> But what I will say is this: we have intelligence services — ASIS and the Defence Signals Directorate — now called the Australian Signals Directorate. They collect intelligence, electronic and human intelligence, in one way or another from other countries.
>
> That's what they do. That's why they exist. If you think we should scrap our intelligence services … well, I would think that's an incredibly bad idea.
>
> Even today, people are still tweeting that I should be jailed for illegally spying on East Timor. Why? I introduced the Intelligence Services Act and put ASIS onto a legislative basis for the first time. Read the Act.

On this, John Howard is equally insistent: "As far as the activity of our intelligence agencies are concerned, I am confident that when I was Prime Minister they always behaved in accordance with the Australian national interest."

Downer seems almost hesitant about criticising Xanana Gusmao for his role in this political and commercial stand-off:

> Xanana is a poet, a great champion of independence for East Timor, and a brave one.
>
> But as a result of his very romantic plan to establish a whole petrochemical industry along the south coast of East Timor — and, after being told by Woodside and the other partners in the consortium that it was not economical to pipe it to East Timor, that it was much more economical to pipe it to Australia — Greater Sunrise has not been

developed. So, far from getting a petrochemical industry, he's got nothing. Absolutely nothing. And that's apparently our fault.

What rankles most with Downer is that the ill-will and discord over the oil and gas negotiations has tended to overshadow all that was achieved in winning East Timor's independence — and the commitment and sacrifice involved — by the Howard Government and the Australian Defence Forces, as much as anyone.

> They thanked us at the time, but there's no 'Avenue d' John Howard' in Dili or anything like that. I understand the domestic politics of this. I understand that they should not be lionising any of us at the expense of their own heroes: Xanana Gusmao, José Ramos-Horta, other warriors for their cause ... but they could at least be gracious towards us now, instead of just using us for political purposes.
>
> We did everything we could with them to set their country up. We poured in aid and we sent in soldiers. We went out of our way to help those people.
>
> But it didn't matter what we did — first, the Left in Australia condemned us for jeopardising the relationship with Indonesia; now we're condemned by the political Left in East Timor for not doing enough to help them.
>
> They were all smiles while we were in government. Then they began running this stuff about how we stole their oil. And spied on them. Honestly — I'm done with them. The Howard Government did more for the East Timorese than any foreign government has ever done. Yet they've treated us with complete contempt ever since.

Downer is aware some East Timor activists appear to want to plant the idea that, if Australia cannot deliver on East Timor's wishes, China will. Among the warnings — that China could end up "with an airbase on an unsinkable aircraft carrier just a stone's throw from our own northern coastlines."

Downer appears unfazed: "Have they had a look at China's economy recently? Do they think China has enough money to do other than solve its own problems. First of all, bringing in China would mean China would have to buy out Woodside and its consortium. That would be one important calculation, which East Timor seems unable to understand. Then China would have to build this processing plant. It's fanciful. Whatever people might say about China, they are not silly."

The East Timor dispute illustrates some of the challenges for governments in seeking to align foreign policy objectives with legitimate commercial interests. To what extent should altruism (or, for that matter, geo-strategic calculations) get a seat at the table when the negotiations involve billions of dollars of income for the country — affecting the livelihoods of many Australians?

As his general operating principle, Downer believes Australian Governments should never allow themselves to be seen as a 'soft touch'. Their job is to produce a sensible, equitable balance that seeks to serve the legitimate interests of both sides of an international negotiation. As he said way back in 2004: "We are not about trumpeting our own international good citizenry simply for the sake of it. That is a trap for the ideologues and the naïve. We are about good international citizenry where it can be shown to deliver tangible results — for our interests, and for those of other people."

13

HEAD FOR THE HILLS

As he travelled the world, living and working for long stretches outside of Australia, Alexander Downer would always look to return to the place he grew up. The Adelaide Hills met his definition of home.

"It's hard to explain this but every little road and every little township in the Adelaide Hills, I know them all," he once told a local newspaper. "I know so many of the people. I have so many memories. Most of my formative experiences were here."

The picturesque hilltops and valleys of the Adelaide Hills extend from the city's edge, into the world-famous wine district of the Barossa Valley and onward to the Fleurieu Peninsula and Southern Ocean. The Hills envelop a string of mountain communities — tiny towns like Cudlee Creek and Piccadilly — nestled among soaring eucalyptus forests, creeks and gullies, and spectacular flora reserves.

Today, the region is popular with tourists not only for its scenic delights but for its quality wines and gourmet food markets.

Downer and his sisters grew up on their parents' large property, Arbury Park, just outside the town of Bridgewater. They went to preschool at the Stirling Kindergarten, then on to state school in one of the local villages, Crafers, now pretty much an outer suburb of Adelaide. They always went to the butcher at Aldgate. Alexander and a sister played tennis for the local Bridgewater club. "We had an idyllic life — hot summers, chilly winters, beautiful gardens, a happy family."

Downer has painful memories of having to pack a suitcase at the age of 11 for the journey across the Victorian border to Geelong Grammar, where he would begin his secondary education as a boarder: "It wasn't that I didn't like Geelong Grammar. When I was there, it was quite good fun. But I was terribly homesick. It might surprise people to hear that — getting emotion out of me is a bit like blood from a stone."

As recounted in a previous chapter, when Alexander Downer set his sights on a career in politics, the Adelaide Hills was always his best option, and his preferred option, for building his political base.

The expansion of the federal Parliament for the 1984 election would create the new seat of Mayo, incorporating the Adelaide Hills, the Fleurieu Peninsula and Kangaroo Island. This was the ideal opening for Downer: "Well, that's the place I come from, right? It was where I was born and grew up. It is where our children grew up ...."

Downer held Mayo with comfortable majorities across his first five elections. Then, in 1998, his first election campaign as Australia's Foreign Affairs Minister, Downer, politically, had the scare of his life.

The Australian Democrats, a centrist party founded by a former Liberal Cabinet Minister, Don Chipp, had become a potent force. A previous leader, Janine Haines, a South Australian, had sought — unsuccessfully — to cross from the Senate to the House of Representatives in 1990. Yet the party continued to build effectively its profile as a moderate soft Left alternative to the major parties.

For the 1998 Mayo campaign, the Australian Democrats had nominated a former school teacher, John Schumann, to run against Downer. Schumann was prominent and popular — as lead singer and songwriter for the South Australian folk music band, Redgum.

He had composed and recorded a hugely successful song, *I Was Only Nineteen,* in tribute to Australian veterans of the Vietnam War. Through the 1980s, and beyond, it became something of a cultural anthem.

Schumann had another advantage going into the election.

Downer's strong words of condemnation as Foreign Affairs Minister of Pauline Hanson's anti-immigration rhetoric in 1996 would carry dire repercussions in Mayo. Likewise, his support for John Howard's gun law reforms. Hanson's supporters directed their preferences away from Downer. Schumann would be the unlikely beneficiary.

After a tense count, Downer scraped back in the seat with a 1.75 per cent majority — a margin of less than 3000 votes.

"It was a huge problem," Downer says of the One Nation backlash. "But I didn't lose. I got 45 per cent of the vote. John Schumann got 22 per cent of the vote, and got ahead of Labor. The One Nation vote was just over 7 per cent, which mainly came off my vote. He picked up most of their preferences, and those of Labor. That was really bad for me."

If there was a lesson from 1998 for Downer, it was the critical importance for a local member to fight for every last vote. To focus unceasingly on your electorate's needs. To listen intently to complaints or grievances. To make sure you stay in touch.

This was seldom easy or straightforward for an MP with the added responsibilities of a major portfolio requiring him to spend a lot of time in Canberra and overseas. But as political advisers like Josh Frydenberg would soon notice, Downer was fastidious about finding any opportunity to engage with his electorate: "The door knocking, the pub events, the regular appointments with locals at his electorate office, the school fetes — he worked incredibly hard."

In the 2001 subsequent election, Downer lifted his primary vote in Mayo by almost 6.5 percent, achieving a majority without having to go to preferences. Downer would eventually win nine elections straight in Mayo. He became the most powerful South Australian voice in the Howard Cabinet, and an high-energy advocate for his state and city.

Over the Howard years, no fewer than four other South Australian MPs would join Downer in the Cabinet. For a smaller state, the South Australians would consistently punch above their weight.

"We had Amanda Vanstone, Ian McLachlan, Nick Minchin and Robert Hill," says Downer. "We didn't have to fight to stay on the radar — we had huge weight."

Downer freely admits there was not a hint of hesitation among the SA ministers about using their collective power to influence major policy decisions that could boost economic development in their home state.

One such episode was their campaign to secure a major defence contract for the construction of three new Navy air-warfare destroyers. As Downer recalls it:

> There was a debate within the National Security Committee — it involved a lot of money — about whether the construction should happen in Melbourne or Adelaide.
>
> Costello wanted them in Melbourne. Hill, Minchin and I insisted they be built in Adelaide. We got our way. It would have been cheaper to build them in Spain. But, given they

were going to be built out here, there was no real financial difference between Melbourne and Adelaide. So we got them for Adelaide.

Downer also devoted considerable time and energy to securing two Chinese pandas for the Adelaide Zoo.

It was not only a diplomatic triumph (jointly announced by John Howard and Hu Jintao at the 2007 APEC summit in Sydney). The arrival of the pandas would become a tourism attraction for Downer's home town for years to come.

Displaying one of the pandas bound for Adelaide Zoo
(Anthony Reginato/Newspix)

In the competitive federalism that characterises Australia, the South Australians fought tooth-and-nail to ensure their state did not miss out.

This is not to say they always spoke with one voice. They hailed from different factions of the Liberal Party, with rivalries sometimes going back more than one generation. Downer, as an example, was never close to Robert Hill, a Senate leader and a Defence Minister in the Howard years. Hill's father, Murray, had been a Liberal powerbroker in South Australia, and had fought some factional battles with the Downers. In 1994, Robert Hill, a moderate, would blame Alexander Downer for the failure of his attempt to cross to the lower house.

Hill was seeking pre-selection for the seat of Boothby. He ran second to an impressive newcomer to politics, Dr Andrew Southcott. This was seen as a serious loss-of-face for a senior Liberal frontbencher.

Downer was Leader of the Opposition at the time of the ballot. "Rob Hill kept telling people that someone had seen my voting slip, and that I didn't vote for him," Downer recalls. "That's completely untrue. I couldn't block him. I just had the one vote. And I voted for him.

"I was the leader of the party. That's why I had a vote. He said he wanted to run for Boothby. I said, 'Well, I'd support him'. So the great day arrived, and I did vote for him. But he lost. And not by one vote. By quite a few. That was very humiliating for him, I suppose."

Downer explains that the vote against Hill was along strictly factional lines: "He had a big problem with the Conservatives. There was a guy called Stan Evans, and his wife — they were an important political family in conservative politics in South Australia. They were deeply against Robert Hill. It was a factional thing."

Supporters of Hill complained that Downer's support as leader had been lukewarm, at best. They had wanted him to pressure the Evans family to back off, and to give Hill a clear run at the preselection. Downer was unimpressed when Hill, during an ABC interview, implied the Opposition Leader had not given him sufficient backing … and voiced a degree of scepticism about whether Downer voted for him.

"That's what I was up against," says Downer. "I definitely voted for him. In the interests of the stability of the Liberal Party, it would have been better for him to have won the pre-selection. I didn't think he would flourish in the Lower House. But for him to lose the pre-selection, as Leader of the Opposition in the Upper House ... well, there would be fall-out from that.

"As leader of the party, that wouldn't be to my advantage. It was definitely in my interests, personally and politically, and in the interests of the stability of the party, for me to vote for him. So why wouldn't I? It would have been irrational — or an act of factional hysteria — not to have voted for him. But did I think he should run? No. I thought it was a stupid idea ..."

There would be not much of a thaw in this *froideur* between the two men in the months and years to come. Soon after Hill's setback in the Boothby pre-selection, there would be more salt added to the wound. As part of the Howard leadership deal, Hill was forced to hand over to Downer his role as foreign affairs spokesman.

Downer concedes this would have been a disappointment: "It's said he always wanted to be the Foreign Affairs Minister. And I got the job. Subliminally, if not consciously, he may have resented that."

In 2006, on Hill's retirement from the Senate, John Howard offered him the appointment as Australia's Ambassador to the United Nations. "It's a great job, and he was fine at the job," says Downer.

But there was a hitch. As ambassador, Hill would be reporting directly to his old rival, Downer, as Foreign Affairs Minister. He may have been disgruntled about that. "He seems to have briefed some journo that he wouldn't be going to the airport to greet me when I arrived in New York," Downer laughs.

The two met in Downer's office before Hill left to take up his appointment. Downer recalls saying, "Look, Robert, going on like this is not going to get us anywhere. That's just how the system works. You have to accept that. I won't be interfering with your work too often. I will be making decisions on how we vote on UN resolutions and so on. But otherwise... just get on with it'."

Across 20 years, Downer and Hill worked effectively as colleagues, if never really as close friends. But, given all politics is local, that did not stop them combining forces in government to extract the best results they could for their state.

Another senator for the state, Nick Minchin was a long-standing ally and friend of Downer — in politics, and as brothers-in-arms defending the interests of SA.

Minchin was state director of the Liberal Party during the late 1980s. When Minchin himself was elected to the Senate, he and Downer became housemates during parliamentary sessions in Canberra, sharing a rented home with another South Australian, Senator Alan Ferguson, in the iconic Canberra suburb, Swinger's Hill.

The former SA Liberal Premier, John Olsen, was another ally. So impressed was Downer by Olsen's energy, enthusiasm and networking skills, he appointed him Consul-General to Los Angeles — and backed Olsen's launch of one of the great 'soft power' initiatives of foreign policy at the time, the annual G'Day USA promotions of Australian business, food and hospitality and tourism in LA and, later, New York.

At these week-long events, Australian diplomacy would leverage off the star power of celebrities like Olivia Newton-John, Hugh Jackman and *The Wiggles* to generate positive media for Australia in one of its biggest international markets. The fizz surrounding these celebrations would attract all sorts of heavy-hitters from US industry and politics.

Christopher Pyne would become another member of the Adelaide Push in Canberra. He would go on to serve as a Cabinet minister, and Leader of the House, in the Abbott, Turnbull and Morrison Governments. It was no mean feat to straddle all three — but Pyne had proved himself from a young age to be a wily factional wrangler.

Pyne may have got under Downer's feet more than once as a brash, ambitious backbencher — and sworn factional opponent in the politics of the South Australian Liberals.

Yet Downer found it hard not to like Pyne's unbridled cheerfulness:

> He's very engaging. Very open. I always got on well with Chris Pyne really. He doesn't carry grudges. And nor do I.
>
> There's no point going into politics if you don't think someone is going to shaft you or try to shaft you. That's just the system. It's going to happen. And he shafted a lot of people... but not so much me. I've had a reasonable relationship with him. He was a sort of Captain of the Wets and I was more in the libertarian Dry camp.

Downer choosing to label himself a libertarian Dry — not as a Conservative — might come as a surprise to some of his colleagues.

But within the spectrum of Liberal Party belief-systems, the "broad church" as John Howard would routinely describe it, Downer finds himself in his later years adjusting his own sense of alignment as the world around him, and the Liberal Party as an organism, evolves.

This should in no way be interpreted as any sort of political epiphany for Downer. He is nothing if not a Liberal Party stalwart. It is more a gentle nudge of the axis on where he sits, factionally.

"Well, the Conservatives are a bit different now," Downer explains. "They are not libertarian and they are very religious. And although I believe in God, I wouldn't describe myself as very religious. I'm more libertarian. So, in that sense, I am estranged."

He laughs: "As I said to a Young Liberals gala dinner the other night, I find myself in a faction of one."

14

Neighbourhood Watch

In 1995, Alexander Downer climbed aboard a helicopter for a flight onto a troubled and divided island chain in the south-west Pacific. Civil war had been raging for six years on the islands of Bougainville.

More than 10,000 people had died, directly or indirectly, as a result of a violent guerrilla war between separatists on the islands and the police and defence forces of Papua New Guinea.

Much of the world would barely have been aware of the conflict. Yet the cost in lives was far greater than the death toll from three decades of sectarian violence in Northern Ireland. On arriving in office, Downer resolved that this humanitarian tragedy — and the violent instability — happening right on Australia's doorstep had to come to an end.

Back in 1995, Downer was visiting as a mere Opposition frontbencher. But almost everyone, including his hosts in PNG, were expecting him to be Australia's next Minister for Foreign Affairs. This was to be no junket. He had come on important business.

Joining him in the cramped helicopter cabin was an old friend, Bill Farmer, by then High Commissioner to PNG, and Downer's senior adviser, Greg Hunt. Their first stop had been the Ok Tedi mine in PNG's western highlands, where Farmer had introduced them to the PNG Prime Minister, Sir Julius Chan. They accompanied Chan to a meeting with local community leaders.

"The government of PNG took this visit very seriously," recalls Greg Hunt. "By this stage, it was clear there was going to be a change of government in Australia. Nothing is inevitable but it was obvious and overwhelmingly likely.

"So we went up to the Ok Tedi mine, and then visited the communities down river. Julius Chan said to us, 'This is a difficult country. We are just evolving in our history'."

Hunt believes that first exposure to the challenges of PNG gave Alexander Downer a "real feel for PNG, the people and the place."

Says Hunt: "He would later play a central role in the Bougainville Peace Agreement. But the foundation was laid on that first trip."

Indeed, the next leg in the journey was across the Star Mountains, and further east towards Bougainville. "So we're getting back into a helicopter, about to fly across to Bougainville," says Hunt. "It was still a hot area — you know, militarily. And I remember the pilot pulling out this flak jacket, and saying, 'Mr Downer, you will need to wear this'.

"And Alexander said, 'Well, what about Greg?' And the guy said, 'We only have one to spare'. Alexander turned to me and said, 'Sorry, buddy, you're expendable'. He was actually quite embarrassed and apologetic. So I said, 'No, that's how it has to be. Anyway, they will really be taking aim at you — not me'."

In an interview for this book, Bill Farmer explains that the security risks imposed strict limits on where they could go in Bougainville. At that time, the Australian Government was still viewed with some suspicion in Bougainville. The operations of the Australian-based Rio Tinto copper mine at Panguna had been a lightning rod for the Bougainville uprising, and there had been ongoing animosity towards Australia for providing military support to the PNG army.

"There was no active large-scale fighting going on at that time but we had to go in with an escort of PNG soldiers," says Farmer. "We couldn't go to the Panguna mine. But we could go to Arawa, the closest town. The Australian Government had built a hospital there but that had been trashed, burnt to the ground."

The chaos and violence in Bougainville was but a microcosm of the broader and deeper challenges facing Australia in its own Pacific neighbourhood. Indeed, the security crisis in Bougainville was only one of many problems facing PNG in its evolution as a developing nation. Among its other challenges were political upheaval, corruption, financial mismanagement, bureaucratic failures and violent street crime — in Port Moresby and the provinces.

"PNG is in many respects a beautiful country and on the whole its people are welcoming and warm," says Downer. "It is also a fragile country. Deeply Christian, relatively poor and politically volatile. It is very much in Australia's national interest to try to contribute to the stability and prosperity of our nearest neighbour."

During the Howard years, it became ever more apparent that PNG's political institutions were being compromised by corruption among some of its elected leaders. "We were really worried about the decline of governance, and the huge amount of corruption there," says Downer.

"And the level of lawlessness in PNG's cities was deeply troubling.

"So you had the political class playing all these games, and then you had the ordinary people who knew what was going on and felt totally disconnected from their political leaders. It was completely dysfunctional. We worried that Papua New Guinea could fragment ..."

The Howard Government's answer was a policy package to become known as the Enhanced Co-operation Program. "We sent in incorruptible Australian Federal Police, and put them in line positions," says Downer. "And we had our public servants in there to help advise on stabilising the political system, the bureaucracy, and the institutions of law and order. It was a mixed success.

"You can imagine why there were some politicians in Papua New Guinea opposed to all that. Although the PNG government reluctantly agreed to this program, nationalist politicians were able to shoot it down in the courts. Aspects of it were found to be unconstitutional by Papua New Guinea's Supreme Court so we had to withdraw some of it.

"But, for me, contributing to PNG's stability has always been a *sine qua non* (essential element) of Australian foreign policy."

PNG was only one of a wider set of challenges across the expanses of the south-west Pacific. The tropical beauty of the island nations of the Pacific, and the warmth and generosity of so many of its people, are well known to international travellers. Yet the region includes some weak and fragile states, prone to political upheaval.

The islands form part what is known among foreign policy analysts in Australia as 'the arc of instability'. This arc incorporates 4000 nautical miles of archipelagic island chains from the Cocos Islands in the Indian Ocean, across to New Zealand and the islands of the south Pacific. These are small nations — in some cases, micro-states — many with under-developed subsistence economies and poor infrastructure.

In his 1986 *Review of Australia's Defence Capabilities*, leading defence analyst Paul Dibb defined the inner arc of island chains from Indonesia to the west, PNG and the Solomon Islands to the north, and the Pacific islands to the east, "as the area from or through which a military threat to Australia could most easily be posed."

Through all his years as Foreign Minister, and in all the years beyond, Alexander Downer continued to press the case with his fellow Australians that the security and well-being of these island nations were of paramount importance to Australia. It was not only about their strategic significance. It was also about pressing humanitarian needs.

In 1997, Downer flew into Bougainville for a second time — this time, as Minister for Foreign Affairs. He recalls:

> We were flying in from Buka, down to Arawa. Buka is in the north, the administrative capital. Arawa is near Panguna, in the middle of the island. As we were flying down the coastline, there was an old shipwreck.
>
> Somebody in the helicopter said, 'What's that?' and the pilot said we could swoop down and have a closer look at it. But as we dropped to a few hundred feet above the water, we hit a frigate bird.
>
> This was to become one of my near-death experiences in an aircraft. It was a private, chartered helicopter. The front of it was a glass bubble. And the glass cracked. The pilot said, 'We need to land immediately because the glass is part of the structure of the aircraft, and, if it breaks, the aircraft will begin to disintegrate'. That was it.
>
> So we landed on this oval at a place called Wakanai.

Fortuitously, as the crippled helicopter came to a landing, Downer could see as many as 100 women gathering on the oval. "It was a meeting of the women of the district. They were there to talk about the peace process. So I went across and had a chat to them."

On this visit, and several to follow, Downer saw opportunities for a change of mindset towards the conflict, both in Bougainville and Port Moresby. He began to set in train plans not only to break the impasse in peace negotiations but to identify a formula for a lasting solution.

On a map of the south-west Pacific, the North Solomons Province of the PNG is located about 1000 kilometres north east of the capital, Port Moresby. It comprises two large islands, Buka and Bougainville, along with some smaller islands and atolls. At its southern end, Bougainville is barely 20 kilometres from the neighbouring Solomon Islands.

The secessionist campaign on Bougainville was driven partly by cultural and ethnic differences. Bougainville had sought independence in 1975, when Australia relinquished control of PNG. Some were arguing it should align with the neighbouring Solomon Islands. But this separatist push did not prevail. Instead, Bougainville would remain absorbed politically into the newly-independent nation of PNG.

While the Bougainville islands boast some mining riches (the independence campaign was in part driven by claims that local communities did not receive a fair share of revenue from the Panguna copper mine) the islands remained heavily dependent on PNG.

For the political leadership in PNG, the debate over the future of Bougainville was about preventing the disintegration of the nation.

From the start of the conflict in 1988, Canberra had backed PNG's sovereignty, providing military equipment and training. But the violence became ever more harrowing — and the death toll climbed.

Through the early 1990s, ongoing civil war was having a corrosive effect on the politics and security of both Bougainville and PNG.

A military blockade imposed by the PNG in its efforts to quell the armed rebellion had the effect of denying many Bougainvilleans access to critical supplies — only feeding the hostility towards PNG.

By the time Downer arrived in office, the worst of the violence and chaos of the early 1990s on Bougainville had eased. But there were still fears that, without a negotiated settlement of the issues at the heart of the conflict, a return to a desperate and destructive armed struggle would never be far away.

Repeated attempts by Prime Minister Julius Chan in the mid-1990s to pursue peace talks with the Bougainville Revolutionary Army had failed. As the years passed, and with no solution in sight, the sense of frustration in Port Moresby led to some desperate gambits.

In 1996, the head of the PNG defence forces, Jerry Singirok, acting on orders from Chan, was preparing to launch an all-out military offensive to wipe out the BRA. Australia and New Zealand refused PNG requests for logistical support. Operation High Speed II was called off after six days, with the PNG military forced to make a humiliating retreat.

In the first week of February, 1997, Downer learned of new plans by Sir Julius Chan to send mercenaries into Bougainville. This became known as the Sandline controversy. Chan met in early January with a former Lieutenant Colonel from the Scots Guards, Tim Spicer, who planned to assemble a team of former special forces personnel from the UK, South Africa and Australia to lead a renewed military campaign.

"We picked that up through intelligence, and I gave the story to Mary-Louise O'Callaghan on *The Weekend Australian,*" says Downer. "That caused a huge uproar in PNG. We were able to kill off the whole plan."

Bill Farmer, by then a Deputy Secretary at DFAT, had an officer follow up with O'Callaghan to reassure her that if he she broke the story, "there would be no egg on her face."

In other words, the story was right. "We were very determined to get this out. Mercenaries in the South Pacific — that would have been a very adverse development," says Farmer.

The fallout in Port Moresby was massive. Who was to wear the blame for this scandal?

Singirok insisted he had been kept out of the loop on the Sandline discussions. He threatened to lead a revolt by PNG forces, demanding Chan and his deputy resign on the grounds of corruption.

This was tantamount to the declaration of a military coup against a democratically-elected government. The alarm bells went off in Canberra. Farmer spoke immediately to Meg Taylor, a prominent mover-and-shaker in PNG who would go on in later years to head the Pacific Islands Forum. Farmer's message was blunt: "Meg, if Jerry Singirok moves against the elected government, you have no idea of the grave implications for relations with Australia." He told her Howard and Downer were very clear, very forthright, very forceful on this.

On March 17, Chan sacked Singirok. Howard phoned Chan to say the Australia Government welcomed his dismissal of the general. But the crisis still had some way to run.

Howard and Downer sent Philip Flood immediately to Port Moresby as a special envoy. When he landed, he went straight to PNG's Parliament for an urgent meeting with Chan. The discussion ran for four hours, during which Flood delivered some direct warnings. If Chan sought to persist with the plan to insert mercenaries into Bougainville, Australia would take drastic action that could involve Australia's entire aid contribution to PNG and all defence co-operation. Shaken, Chan accused the Australian Government of making threats to PNG.

That first meeting ended in a deadlock. But, the following morning, Chan invited Flood back to his office. This time, the outcome was swift. Chan advised that he would suspend the Sandline contract, and the mercenaries would be sent home that afternoon. He would order a judicial inquiry into the scandal. Sandline would never return.

The Howard Government had not been afraid to use its leverage to prevent PNG going down a path dangerous to democracy. "It was rough. But it worked," says Downer.

When the PNG Parliament resumed its sittings a week later, Singirok's successor, Major Walter Enuma, had to go into the chamber to assure MPs there would be no military coup. After a night of high tensions, with crowds milling around the Parliament, Chan himself resigned.

Over the coming months, Chan's replacement as PM, Bill Skate, sought to revive peace negotiations on Bougainville. A truce was agreed at peace talks held in Burnham in New Zealand.

Downer credits New Zealand and its then Foreign Minister, Don McKinnon, for playing a critical mediating role. "NZ had a degree of neutrality which we couldn't have," Downer says. "An Australian company owned the Panguna mine and, as far as the BRA was concerned, Australia was one of the guilty parties.

"We were not seen as being as impartial as NZ — even though we were. But New Zealand handled it really well."

The Burnham talks were an important move in the right direction. But they did not offer a solution. Australia was eager to pursue a more permanent formula for peace.

Downer recalls the difficult to-and-fro in negotiations between Port Moresby and the pro-independence Bougainville Islanders about the level of autonomy that might be agreed under any peace deal:

> I was always into the idea of PNG granting a greater degree of autonomy for Bougainville and that's what they got.
>
> But PNG was not going to grant independence. If PNG granted independence to Bougainville, what was going to happen in New Ireland or the Highlands and other parts

of Papua New Guinea? The country could atomise. That certainly worried me.

And Bougainville had about 180,000 people. I didn't think it was viable as a nation-state. It would have become just a mendicant state.

By 1999, however, Downer knew there was a pressing need for a breakthrough in the faltering dialogue. If the PNG Government and the BRA could not engage meaningfully with each other, Australia would seek to play a more direct, interventionist role in steering the peace process to a conclusion.

Towards the end of 1999, Australia sent in one of its most experienced diplomats and security specialists, Nick Warner.

Warner was appointed as Australia's High Commissioner to PNG after a career of tough assignments. In his early days with DFAT, he had worked on multilateral peace-building initiatives in Namibia and Cambodia. A former ambassador to Iran, he had also run the South-Asia and south-east Asia desk at DFAT, and was influential in the diplomatic build-up to Australia's intervention in East Timor.

Few if any Australian officials were better trained in dealing with 'hard bastards' who had to be persuaded to lay down their arms.

"I had a lot to do with Nick Warner," says Downer. "He was totally reliable. Knew the Pacific really well. He had my confidence, and John Howard's confidence. He was excellent." Howard confirms Downer's assessment of Warner's talents in demanding, high-stress environments: "I was always a great fan of Nick's."

From the moment he took on the job, Warner was acutely aware of the risks if the deadlock in peace negotiations continued. A resumption of open hostilities was everyone's nightmare. Devastation of the economy in Bougainville and the collapse of basic government administration had been among the consequences, along with the disease and malnutrition that resulted from many thousands of Bougainvilleans having to flee villages to live in makeshift refugee camps.

"As many as 16,000 people had died, if you believe some of the press reports " says Warner. "Not all were shot — but a lot of people had died through the effects of the conflict, including PNG defence forces. There had been a lot of atrocities."

Before Warner arrived, a peace monitoring group had been sent into Bougainville — as one of the initiatives arising from the Burnham talks in New Zealand. At its peak, this involved as many as 400 unarmed officials from NZ, Fiji, Vanuatu and Australia. But, according to Warner, it was under-achieving, with too much focus on logistics and too little investment at the "pointy end — where you had some very good DFAT officers and others out on patrol in the villages trying to build trust."

Meanwhile, the peace process itself continued to languish.

"The long-term solution to this dilemma — the Bougainvilleans wanting independence and PNG wanting them to stay — remained utterly unresolved," Warner says. "When I got there, there was pretty much no activity going on. It had stalled. it was a fragile peace."

The main priority of the PNG prime minister at the time, Mekere Morauta, was to undertake a sweeping program of economic reform and budget repair across his nation. He had given the founding prime minister of PNG, Sir Michael Somare, responsibility for Bougainville. But Somare made promises of progress he was unable to deliver.

Warner worried that, amid all the frustration on both sides, the appetite for a peace deal was waning. "These endless talks between the two sides were becoming increasingly acrimonious," he recalls.

"Increasingly, there were threats from the Bougainvillean side that 'we're out of this (peace process), we are going to throw you all out'. I had come to the conclusion that the threats from the Bougainvillean side that they would take up arms again were becoming real..."

Downer and Warner were in constant dialogue about how to prevent a collapse in peace negotiations, and to avert the risk of a return to armed conflict. There was a lot of cable traffic and extensive phone conversations. "He was intensely engaged in this," says Warner.

Downer and Warner agreed to confront both parties, directly and in blunt language, about the dangers in the failure to make progress. In December, 2000 — five days before a visit by Downer to Bougainville — Warner would engage in some intensive shuttle diplomacy.

"I went to see Mekere Morauta, and I said, 'I think your side and the Bougainvilleans are just talking past each other'," Warner explains. 'There's too much anger, there's too much history, you are just not listening to each other. So here are some thoughts of mine'.

"He listened carefully, then said, 'Why don't you come back after the weekend and have another chat with me, before I meet Alexander?'"

That weekend, Warner called to the High Commission residence a Bougainville specialist, Sarah Storey, a Melbourne law graduate who had already spent much of her first DFAT posting out in the remote villages, in places where the conflict had been at its rawest. "She knew the place and she knew the players better than I did," says Warner. They consulted close colleagues at the NZ High Commission.

Together, they typed up a succinct half-page document proposing the specifics of a plan for a final peace agreement. In essence, the proposal said there should be an offer by the PNG Government of a referendum for constitutional reform, not excluding the option of independence for Bougainville. However, it provided that any vote on independence should be deferred for 10 to 15 years, and should be non-binding. The PNG Parliament would have to ratify any final outcome.

In the meantime, PNG would allow much greater autonomy for Bougainville. The offer would be conditional on full and verifiable weapons disposal by the BRA. "All that sounds pretty straightforward," says Warner. "But what it did was to balance the competing demands of the two sides in a way they hadn't been able to do themselves. I took that to Mekere a couple of days later."

Morauta wanted Warner to run through the proposal with a trusted minister, Moi Avei, who asked Warner how the Bougainvillaeans would respond:

> I said, 'I dunno, I haven't showed it to them yet. But if you can live with this, I reckon they will be able to live with this'.
>
> So Sarah and I flew to Buka the next morning — with Alexander due to arrive later that day — and we sat in a little room with the key Bougainvillean leaders, Joe Kabui and James Tanis. We showed them the piece of paper and had a long discussion. There was a little questioning about the parliamentary ratification issue but, overall, they thought they could sell it to people.
>
> Good. So I have a tick from the government in Moresby, a big tick from those two — but not the whole Bougainvillean political pantheon.

Alexander then arrives in Buka. We show him the document, and explain that both sides have said, 'We can live with it if they can live with it'. There's a pause as he has a bit of a think about it and then he says, 'Yes. Let's do this'.

He tucks the piece of paper into his pocket. We go off and talk to Kabui and Tanis. He doesn't refer to the paper, but raises everything in the paper, and they respond positively. The next day we fly down to Arawa in a PNG military helicopter and we sit down with the more hardline elements of the Bougainvillean leadership, the BRA. Alexander runs through the points, doesn't show them the piece of paper, but gets the same very positive response.

We then fly to Moresby, and he sits down with Mekere, Moi Avei and others. He (Downer) says to them that he was very pleasantly surprised (by the progress). 'I think you have something here'.

They were really pleased to hear that. So the government in PNG has agreed. The Bougainvilleans have agreed informally and, by January, those propositions are formally agreed by the two sides. That forms the basis of the peace agreement signed in Arawa in August, 2001.

Downer was unable to attend the formal signing of the historic peace agreement. He was back in Australia dealing with the Tampa crisis.

On reflection, Warner thinks this was a pity.

"Way before my time, Alexander had a very significant role in brokering that peace," he says. "There was — and still is — this sense in Bougainville that Australia was not neutral. We had to work hard to show we were people who could be trusted."

Warner is also full of praise for the role of Morauta — "Papua New Guinea's best ever Prime Minister" — and the bearded former BRA fighter, Joseph Kabui — as pivotal to declaring an end to the civil war.

"Kabui was very influential," says Warner. "Patriotic, smart ... moderate." Kabui went on to become the first president of the Autonomous Republic of Bougainville. He died in 2008.

Despite the enmity towards Australia among many Bougainvilleans over many years, Kabui always went out of his way to credit the Australian contribution to the process of reconciliation.

Of Downer's activism, Kabui said: "He developed and negotiated a compromise on the referendum at a time when the peace process was floundering." Downer, likewise, admired Kabui's leadership: "He was the guy. He made it happen. He was the father of the whole thing."

Nearby, however, just as the Bougainville negotiations were concluding, another crisis would flare in the Pacific. This time, in Fiji.

In May, 2000, armed rebels from Fiji's military took hostage 36 members of the island nation's Parliament, and demanded the removal of Prime Minister Mahendra Chaudhry. The mutiny fuelled a rampage of looting and arson by young men in the capital, Suva.

At its core, this was part of a power struggle between ethnic Fijian nationalists (I-Taukei) and Fijians of Indian descent, whose families had been brought to the islands several generations earlier by the British colonial power to work on sugar plantations.

The armed insurgency was eventually suppressed by the Fijian military, without significant loss of life. Fiji's military chief, Commodore Frank Bainamarama, then chose to declare martial law, effectively suspending Fiji's Constitution. Fiji's President, Ratu Sir Kamesese Mara, resigned: "If the Constitution is going, I'm going too."

Initially, Australia threw its support behind Chaudhry, an elected leader who had been ousted in a coup d'état.

The Great Council of Chiefs in Fiji, in an effort to restore stability, appointed a career civil servant and banker, Laisenia Qarase, as interim Prime Minister, pending fresh elections.

Most observers assumed Bainamarama, the strong man, remained the power behind the throne.

But in 2001, Qarase led his party to victory in national general elections and asserted his mandate to rule as the elected leader.

In 2006, Bainamarama moved against him. When former Prime Minister Chaudhry came out strongly in support of the military chief's actions, opinion within the Howard Government turned very quickly. "That was shameless," says Downer. "We did our best to maintain democracy in Fiji, with mixed results," says Downer. "… then Bainamarama overthrew the Constitution …"

For as long as Bainamarama remained in charge — for 15 years to come — Australia's relations with Fiji would remain inherently uneasy. Ironically, in 2022, it would be the sweeping democratic victory of another former coup leader, Prime Minister Sitiveni Rabuka, that would create an opportunity to restore much closer ties.

Despite his role in a military insurrection in the 1980s, Rabuka was well known to a generation of Australian political leaders as an amicable and solid partner. Personal relationships play a critical role in the diplomacy of the Pacific — even when tensions are high.

In 2015, as Australia's High Commissioner to London, Downer ran into Bainamarama at a World Cup rugby match at Twickenham. It was a famous victory for Australia over England.

"Bainamarama turned up in an Aussie scarf," Downer recalls. "He treated me as if I was a long-lost cousin."

Among the most vexed of challenges to the rule of law in the south-west Pacific erupted in the Solomon Islands. In 1999, the island nation declared a four-month state of emergency after violent ethnic clashes between the Malaitan people and the Gwale people of Guadalcanal.

The Solomon Islands is a country of almost 1000 small islands and atolls, with a population at that time of less than 600,000 people. It is only three hours by air from Queensland.

Positioned directly in the north-eastern approaches to Australia, it was the site of the famous Battle of Guadalcanal between US-Australian and Japanese forces in World War 2. Over the years, many Australians may have forgotten the strategic significance of these islands. Australian Governments, and defence planners, don't have that luxury.

After the war, significant numbers of Malaitans resettled on the island of Guadalcanal, hoping greater opportunities might be available in the capital, Honiara. However, chronic unemployment and excess demand for meagre government services gave rise to tensions with the local Gwale people who claimed indigenous rights to Guadalcanal.

In the face of the civil unrest in 1999, the Prime Minister of the Solomons, Bart Ulufa'alu, issued a plea for assistance to Australia and New Zealand for assistance. But within Australia's defence and security establishment at the time, there was little enthusiasm for intervention.

The ADF and DFAT already had the East Timor deployment to manage, along with the risk of conflict on Bougainville.

Says Downer: "In the Solomon Islands, we resisted for a long time getting involved directly — on the advice of DFAT and Defence. When Bart Ulufa'alu begged me to send in peacekeepers, we refused.

"The departments didn't want us to do it at all. So I went along with that. Early on, I wrote an article for *The Australian* saying we shouldn't intervene and they should sort out their own problems themselves.

"But the situation in the Solomons kept getting worse and worse ..."

In late 1999, Australia, New Zealand and the UK agreed to finance a small security operation, involving 25 unarmed police officers from Fiji and Vanuatu. The so-called Commonwealth Multinational Police Peace Monitoring Group had a mandate to collect weapons and monitor and report on law and order in the Solomons. Briefly, this regional initiative helped ease the tensions. The state of emergency was lifted.

But very soon afterwards, in June, 2000, Ulufa'alu was taken hostage at his home by one of the biggest of the militia groups, the Malaitan Eagle Force. They were armed with semi-automatic assault rifles stolen from police headquarters. The Prime Minister was forced to step down.

He was replaced by Manasseh Sogavare, a former tax commissioner and Finance Minister seen as having close ties to the militia. The elected leader of the nation had been ousted in a coup. The Royal Australian Navy evacuated more than 1000 Australian expatriates.

Australia and New Zealand were able to negotiate a ceasefire but the political upheaval continued to escalate. Sogavare served only one year in office before suffering defeat at the 2001 election. He was replaced as Prime Minister by Sir Allen Kemakeza.

In 2003, the violence flared yet again. The island nation was on the verge of becoming a failed state. For the Howard Government, sidestepping direct involvement was no longer a credible option.

In April, 2003, Kemakeza wrote to John Howard asking Australia to send in a peacekeeping force. Downer was copied in on the letter.

This was a hectic year for the Howard Government, DFAT and the Defence Department. Australia had military commitments in Iraq and Afghanistan as well as the peace-keeping efforts in East Timor.

Australia and Indonesia were also still hunting down the extended circle of perpetrators and plotters of the Bali bombings.

"I got a submission from DFAT which said we should hold to our existing position. The position of Defence was that they were not in favour of sending any forces into Solomon Islands," says Downer.

Downer was becoming irritated by aspects of the opposition he was hearing from the top brass of the military. "Part of their argument was that if, we send them in, what is to be the exit strategy? Why do people become generals if that's their default position ... it seems completely feckless. First of all, you need to identify the problem and work out how you are going to address the problem if you are going to bother addressing it at all.

"Anyway, I read this letter and I read the department's submission and I thought to myself, 'I reckon this situation is only going to deteriorate. Maybe, this time, we should act'."

As Prime Minister, Howard's instincts were much the same. He phoned Downer in Adelaide. "I was at the Aldgate Pump Hotel, with the family," Downer recalls. "It was May, one of the children's birthdays.

"Anyway, he asked what I thought about this letter from the Solomons, and I said, 'Well, DFAT have given me this advice that we should do nothing' and he said, 'Yes, the Department of Prime Minister & Cabinet had given the same advice to him'.

"And I said, 'I've been thinking about this ... I don't think they're right. I think we should do something'. And he said, 'I've been having exactly the same thought'. So we agreed to have Sir Allen come over to Canberra so we could have a talk about it. Which we duly did. We had a lunch at The Lodge and we talked the issues through."

Howard and Downer agreed it was time to act. But sending in forces to quell the violence would be only one element of a long-term solution. To be effective, an intervention would require not just the disarming of militant groups. It would also require extensive reforms to the way the islands were governed and administered, including a clean-up of political corruption — in effect, a nation-building exercise.

"Kemakeza was a bit surprised when he was told he could not pick and choose," says one diplomat close to the process. "It had to be the whole kit and caboodle — top to bottom."

Ceremonial greeting in Solomon Islands (Department of Defence Images)

When Kemakeza returned to Honiara, he was warned by his political opponents not to proceed, and that his job was on the line. Kemakeza chose to defy them. He told Howard and Downer he would accept an offer of Australian support.

At Howard's insistence, Kemakeza had to seek the ratification of his Parliament for the proposal. He succeeded in achieving this. For its part, the Howard Government had its own balancing act to perform.

On the one hand, there was the expectation in Washington and elsewhere — probably heightened by the success of the East Timor intervention — that Australia had the capacity to step up to deal with challenges to security and stability in the south-west Pacific.

On the other hand, the Howard government had to weigh up the risks of Australia being seen as super-imposing itself on a Pacific neighbour. Says Downer: "There's a lot of sensitivity about 'bully boy' Australia, this half-witted idea of neo-colonialism. So I thought we should do this in collaboration with the Pacific nations."

Downer began testing the appetite across the region for a joint operation involving troops, police and civil servants from the other island-states. Initially, the biggest impediment he faced was a surprising level of resistance from New Zealand. "Phil Goff, the Foreign Minister, was in favour of NZ joining us," says Downer. "But Helen Clark as Prime Minister was against it. She had opposed the Iraq War and thought this was another example of Western powers invading developing countries. Phil Goff worked on her."

Later that year, Australia hosted a conference of Pacific leaders in Sydney to consider whether and how the region could respond to the continuing unrest in the Solomons. Traditionally, the Pacific Islands had adopted the stance that they would not interfere in each other's internal affairs. But the risk of violent upheaval, especially across Melanesia, was becoming a problem for the whole neighbourhood.

Under the Biketawa Declaration agreed in 2000 in Kiribati, the Pacific Islands had resolved to commit jointly to upholding "democratic processes" including the peaceful transfer of power, the rule of law, the independence of the judiciary, and "just and honest government".

Downer urged the island leaders to act under the auspices of the Biketawa Declaration. He was able to persuade them that the law-and-order crisis on the Solomon Islands was hurtling out of control, and traditional approaches of 'non-interference' would only mean greater pain and misery for its people, and a risk of greater instability in the neighbourhood.

"Everyone agreed we should do something — and so we put together what was to become RAMSI (the Regional Assistance Mission to Solomon Islands)," Downer recalls. The RAMSI deployment was called 'Operation Helpem Fren' — pidgin for Helping Friends.

Australia would provide the biggest contribution to the mission — both in financial support and manpower. Again, the Howard Government needed someone it could trust to head up the multi-national Pacific peacekeeping operation. Again, they turned to Nick Warner.

"I had come back from PNG, and I was Ambassador for Counter-Terrorism (after the Bali bombings)" he says. "Ashton Calvert rang me up and said, 'I have an even more important priority for you, and that's to run this peacekeeping operation in Honiara'. I had nothing to do with the planning or the decision to deploy... I came onboard about three weeks before it was operational."

Joining him in the RAMSI leadership, as commander of police

operations, was Ben McDevitt, who also came to the Solomons job with the experience of serving in Bougainville.

Pacific forces began arriving in Honiara in June, 2003. Downer came to visit in the first fortnight. By early September, Australia had a regional and military coalition force of around 2000 personnel supporting 200 RAMSI police and 50 Australian Federal Police.

The huge scale of the deployment — Australia's biggest in the Pacific since World War 2 — was critical to the success of a strategy proposed by defence chief, Peter Cosgrove. "The idea was to have an overwhelming military force deployed at the beginning," says Warner. "It included having warships, smaller patrol craft, military aircraft and helicopters. It was a serious deployment.

"That got the attention of everybody, as was intended.

"The militants knew there was no point having a potshot at us because we would go after them. We made clear that was exactly what we would do — and we meant it."

The first major step for RAMSI was to disarm the militants.

Under a nationwide gun amnesty, and the arrest of key militants, almost 4000 weapons and 300,000 rounds of ammunition were collected and destroyed. "We had to get the guns out of the community," Warner says.

"The militia were running wild and killing people and terrorising the country. We had to detain and charge those who had committed crimes. This included some of the local police — who were part of the problem, not part of the solution. And the leadership of the militia. That went amazingly well. We called it 'detention by invitation'."

Plan B would have been to send in special forces to round up the more belligerent militants. "We didn't have to do that," says Warner.

"The militias reached out to us, including a guy called Harold Keke down on the Weather Coast. He agreed to surrender to us, along with his key followers, and they agreed to disarm and hand over their weapons. We would chop up the weapons in front of crowds.

"We did the same on the island of Malaita, with this group called the Malaitan Eagle Force, a group of thugs dressed up as Rambos. They surrendered, they were disarmed. Then the police did their investigatory work. We focussed on those groups who were the greatest risk to the peace process. They were arrested, charged, convicted... and ended up in prison."

The second priority was to rebuild the derelict processes and structures of government and administration. Says Warner:

> Their budget had fallen apart, petty corruption was everywhere.
>
> Their primary institutions were not working. People were not being paid. People were not coming to work .... entwined with that was corruption and nepotism. Petty corruption at the bottom, big corruption at the top....the cops, everybody else.
>
> But because everyone was tainted, where did you start and where did you end? Where we collectively landed was that we had to go after the most serious crimes, the most serious corruption, and if they're guilty, nobody gets a free pass. But we needed to be careful and strategic in our targeting ...
>
> By the time I left, I think half a dozen government ministers had been arrested and charged. Eventually, Prime Minister Kemakeza, who had been extraordinarily brave in asking for RAMSI and was a key supporter while I was there, spent six months in jail.

But the troubles were far from over. In April, 2006, there were riots in Honiara, followed by three days of looting and shop break-ins the city's Chinatown and CBD. The anarchy was intertwined with political manoeuvrings by pro-Sogavare elements surrounding the election of a new prime minister, Snyder Rini.

Amid the political upheaval, Sogavare returned to power. Immediately, he began making demands that RAMSI withdraw.

"He wanted to get RAMSI out of the Solomons," says Downer. "That would be to his own advantage. But it would have been a disaster for the people of the Solomon Islands."

The issue of who ran the Solomons was becoming increasingly murky because of a bidding war between China and Taiwan, competing for the Solomon Islands allegiance in their global contest for diplomatic recognition. "Sogavare was receiving all sorts of support, if I can put it that way, from other countries. Other countries to our north," says Downer. "In that competition between Taipei and Beijing over recognition, a lot of money has changed hands. We knew money was changing hands and we had to try to stop it."

In response, Downer adopted an unconventional approach, by issuing a public statement as Australia's foreign minister to the people of the Solomon Islands. "I remember appealing to the ordinary people of the Solomon Islands, making the point that we were happy to continue with RAMSI and support the people of the Solomon Islands in the face of some other people who want us to leave. Sogavare duly lost."

This intervention prompted a firestorm of criticism from a range of academics and "Pacific experts", accusing Downer of exercising undue influence and compromising the sovereign rights of the Solomon Islanders. Yet Downer remained steadfast in his insistence that Australia must play the role of a constructive, stabilising force in the region.

Nick Warner believes Australia's intervention in the Solomons, ultimately, was highly successful. "RAMSI — and Australia — was immensely popular with Solomon Islanders, who welcomed us with open arms and enormous relief. When RAMSI left 14 years later, Australia's popularity and influence remained strong."

Downer remembers phoning Condi Rice to inform the US of developments: "We're sending in this peacekeeping force to the Solomon Islands to stop civil war breaking out there. And she said, 'That's remarkable. You must be the only ally which has initiated something like that and not asked us to help do it.'

"She continues to mention this — how we had quelled violence in the Pacific without begging the Americans to do it for us."

By 2021, however — less than five years after RAMSI's departure —Manneseh Sogavare was back as Prime Minister in the Solomons.

He would soon send ripples of alarm across the Pacific with his decision to sign a new security agreement with China would put him and his people "on the right side of history".

It was a provocative signal to Australia that the quest for strategic certainty in the Pacific was far from over. The two key questions: how had China been able to engineer this deal? And had the Morrison Government in Canberra been asleep at the wheel in not pre-empting this new and destabilising arrangement in its near-neighbourhood?

Downer is blunt in his assessment: "I would say that was a setback. I suppose it was a foreign policy failure, in the sense that they did know what was going on and they should have intervened. Early on. Not after the agreement had been signed.

"It's difficult to go to the Solomons and say, 'Now that you have signed this agreement, we want you to unsign it' That's probably not going to work. They should have made a significant public issue of it."

Downer says one clear focus should have been on the "money politics" — given a history of both China and Taiwan providing cash incentives to local politicians in the Solomons to achieve their strategic goals.

"They knew there was money involved and they should have made that public," says Downer. " I don't want to be critical of (the Morrison Government). I voted for them. But they were not perfect.

"I think they handled that quite poorly. The Foreign Minister should have been on the plane, going over there as soon as she saw trouble brewing... and not left it to a junior minister much later in the piece."

Here, Downer states a fundamental operating principle: "When things go really wrong in the Pacific, as they have in the Solomon Islands, it's important to call it out for what it is. If China is giving money to individuals in countries like the Solomons, I think it is incumbent on the Australian Government to make that public. Love the Pacific — but make sure you do expose things that are going wrong there."

Alexander Downer is not often heard commending the work of the Albanese Labor Government — or any Labor Government, for that matter. And he may not have been much of a fan of his fellow South Australian (and a successor as Foreign Affairs Minister) Penny Wong.

But, as he watched events in Australia's neighbourhood, he did offer praise to the new Labor Government in 2022 for its early initiatives to reach out to the island nations. In her first week in the job, Wong stopped off in Fiji on return from a Quad meeting in Tokyo.

A month later, she was in the Solomon Islands. She was there to remind Pacific partners of the importance of long-standing friendships.

The focus on Melanesia was both smart and strategic.

For at that very same time, Chinese foreign minister, Wang Yi, was making a whirlwind Pacific visit. China was seeking to extend its reach. He, too, would fly into the Solomons.

When Prime Minister Albanese visited London in September of that same year, for the funeral of Queen Elizabeth II, the Labor prime minister and Downer caught up at a dinner at Australia House.

"I was at King's College at the time, and he came up to me at this gathering to say g'day," Downer recalls. "I stood up from the table and we moved away for a private conversation.

"I told him I was impressed with what his government had been doing in the Pacific… the Morrison Government had dropped the ball (whereas) Penny Wong went immediately to visit these countries and spoke about the Australian Government's commitment to the region."

Downer wasn't alone in thinking Australia had dropped the ball.

In 2022, Warner wrote a searing article for *The Australian Financial Review*, lamenting Australia's failure to cement deeper, more enduring relationships with its neighbours in Oceania. "The people-to-people links that were once so strong with countries such as PNG and Fiji have fallen away," he wrote. "Successive governments in Canberra have been preoccupied with what were seen as more pressing and more important issues elsewhere in the world, rather than focusing enough attention on our closest friends and neighbours …

"… As a result, the Pacific became something of a backwater. It was quiet. It was remote. Few other countries took much notice."

Warner, who went on to head Australia's intelligence services, warned of the potential risks of this neglect: "Good things were done, but none of it was enough, and certainly not enough when China started to ramp up its presence and influence a decade ago. A rising China was always going to play a bigger role in the South Pacific … but China also came with strategic intent …"

Australia was caught off guard. "Oblivious until that point, we were sleepwalking into a new and dangerous strategic environment," Warner wrote. "A Chinese naval base or facility in the South Pacific would seriously complicate Australia's security."

In an interview for this book, Warner stands by his critique:

> That piece was critical of pretty much every Australian Government since the 1970s for not paying enough attention to the Pacific.

Downer did Bougainville and he did the Solomon Islands. Those were two big things in the Pacific. Those are standouts in Australian Pacific policy. Fair enough. Nobody else can point to that. Alexander did a lot.

And I think Penny Wong and Richard Marles have done extremely well in the Pacific. They've paid a lot of attention to it.

Downer insists maintaining strong and friendly ties with the Pacific islands must be a high priority for Australian foreign policy:

> It is bloody important for the Australian foreign minister to focus on the relationship with Pacific island nations.
>
> It is very important to them ... that we understand their challenges, embrace them. I was never in favour of having a junior minister look after Pacific affairs. I thought that was the role of the Foreign Minister.
>
> I would make ad hoc visits to the Pacific when things blew up— often in the context where something had gone wrong for them — and they were usually very appreciative. I would also make a point of visiting a Pacific Island country at the end of every year. That commitment matters. I got to know those countries and I got to know their leaders very well. That hasn't been happening so much in recent times.
>
> I think governments do need to invest very heavily in the Pacific. An Australian Government is going to have relatively little influence in a place like the Middle East, whereas we have a relatively more influential role in south-east Asia and Oceania.

At the time of writing, peace in Bougainville had endured for almost 25 years. But the PNG Parliament had still yet to ratify the vote by the people of Bougainville's at a 2019 referendum — by a 98 per cent majority — to fulfil their aspirations to be a fully independent nation.

On the Solomons, Warner is ever the diplomat in describing Sogavare as "a proud Solomon Islander, and a clever and mercurial politician who has been prime minister four times in a long career."

"A few years ago, I called on him in Honiara and, building on the work of the High Commission, talked to him about the risks of signing up Huawei to build an internet cable to connect Honiara and Sydney," Warner wrote in that same commentary piece for the AFR.

"He listened carefully. The deal didn't go forward and instead Australia funded the Coral Sea cable.

"Relationships – and alternatives and money – are important ... for better or worse, Pacific politics seldom provide certainty. It's not too late for Australia to shore up its place in the South Pacific and to protect its strategic interests."

So how to address China's 'charm offensive' in the Pacific?

One mechanism often raised by island leaders themselves is Australia's Pacific Labour Mobility Scheme. This program provides visas for Pacific Islanders to travel to and work in Australia, and to earn higher incomes to help support their families back at home. It also helps to fill labour gaps in Australia, as a source of skilled and reliable workers for farms and other businesses in regional and rural Australia.

"I think it could be expanded," says Downer. "No doubt about it. But you want to be careful not to hollow things out. You don't want to create a brain drain, where anyone who has skills just comes to Australia. Plenty have. They have gone to NZ as well.

"But when you think that issue through, as I did as the Foreign Minister, then you do have that risk. I am not sure that's the solution.

"By all means, come here and study and learn new skills. But then encourage people to take those skills back to their own countries, to try to strengthen the structures and economies of those countries."

Downer stresses the importance of developing strong people-to-people ties as one means of addressing Australia's potential strategic challenges across the Pacific islands. It helps explain his passion about Australia maintaining its profile as a reliable friend in times of need.

In July, 2007, a Royal Australian Air Force jet flew into Nuku'alofa, the capital of Tonga. Six months after an outbreak of wild rioting and ransacking on the Polynesian island nation, the scars were still visible. From the air, Alexander Downer could see the ruins of burned-out commercial offices and battered shopfronts.

This was the place Cook had called the Friendly Islands. Across its history, Tonga had accumulated significant economic and cultural influence in the South Pacific, as a respected elder of the Pacific family.

There were other island nations far more notorious as flashpoints of division and unrest. That Tonga had fallen prey to political instability and social discord was another wake-up call for the region — especially for Australia and NZ as the wealthiest, most advanced economically, and most politically stable nations in the neighbourhood.

At the height of the tensions in Tonga, Australia had sent in soldiers and police as part of a peacekeeping mission with New Zealand to help secure the capital. In July, Downer flew in for an on-the-ground update on Australia's assistance programs to help recovery and reconstruction from the upheaval of the previous November.

He had scheduled a meeting with Prime Minister Fred Sevele to discuss a joint Australia-New Zealand initiative to restructure and train the Tongan police force. And an audience with King George Tupou V.

Helping to equip Tonga to prevent another breakdown in law and order was only one element of plans to stabilise the country.

Downer would also discuss with Dr Sevele the progress of political dialogue in the country. One explanation behind the civil unrest in Nuku'alofa were demands by the pro-democracy movement for an end to Tonga's centuries-old absolute monarchy and the establishment of a genuine elected legislature.

Downer would return to Tonga only 12 weeks later, representing John Howard at the Pacific Island Forum's leaders summit. It would be one of his last overseas visits as Australia's foreign minister. Says Downer:

> Here's the secret. It's the personal relationships that matter in the Pacific. The people you know. The trust you can engender. You need to spend a lot of time there, talking to people about their problems.
>
> It's not just about spending cash. The Labor Party's solution to just about everything is to put their hand into the taxpayers' pocket and spray the money around. It's not always the answer. It's the people-to- people links that will be crucial.
>
> This is our region. Our allies like the United States have always expected us to be the metropolitan power responsible for making sure this region is stable. Nobody else is going to do it. Foreign Ministers need to get to PNG, Fiji, the Solomons and also Tonga, the Samoas, Kiribati, Tuvalu, Vanuatu. We need to go to all of these places.

15

THE NUCLEAR AGE

Alexander Downer had only just turned five when a mushroom cloud exploded above the desert scrublands in his home state of South Australia. The British Government was testing nuclear weapons at Maralinga, about 1000 km from his home in the Adelaide Hills.

The radiation effect across that distance would have been miniscule. But this massive blast in South Australia's backyard still carried a whiff of foreboding — just one chapter of a furious, fearful global arms race in the early postwar decades to develop weapons of mass destruction.

In November, 1956, Australia hosted the Melbourne Olympics, the 'Friendly Games'. Only a few weeks earlier, British defence scientists exploded a 26 kiloton nuclear blast at Maralinga — the biggest nuclear test on the Australian mainland. It was an eerie juxtaposition.

Downer has no memory of the blast — although he has clear recollections of the first Olympics staged in Australia as "an exciting time". He cannot remember much if any discussion of the British nuclear tests. "I mean, we didn't see the flashes of light. It was a long way away, and I was a small boy at the time. I would have had no consciousness of it."

Downer suggests there was very little controversy at the time about the British nuclear tests. "The fact people like my parents rarely if ever talked about it … I mean, I have sometimes said jokingly to the Brits that, at the time I was in kindergarten, they were bombing Australia with nuclear weapons. But I think, at the time, it was probably a fairly marginal issue. This was the Cold War. The British were a close ally. It was about mutual defence… why wouldn't we help them?"

Downer's approach to the challenges of nuclear weapons is nuanced.

He would spend all 12 years of his tenure as Foreign Affairs Minister working actively and arguing forcefully for more stringent arms control measures. Downer's focus was on practical action to help rein in nuclear weapons proliferation. The aim was to minimise the risk of accident, miscalculation — or the dangers of nuclear weapons technology falling into the wrong hands.

His three key policies were support for the Proliferation Security Initiative, to stop the flow of illicit WMD materials; support for US development of ballistic missile defences; and measures to strengthen global counter-proliferation architecture through the United Nations and its agencies. One of his personal career highlights was to steer the Comprehensive Test Ban Treaty through the UN General Assembly.

But it is important to understand that Downer was never about opposing the principle of nuclear deterrence. Nor was he opposed to the use of nuclear power for peaceful purposes.

In fact, he has been advocating for at least two decades the creation of a full-scale nuclear power generation industry in Australia — particularly in his home state of South Australia. "By the way, this never caused me any political grief," he says. "The ferals will always carry on whatever anyone in the Liberal Party says. But I think most mainstream people were interested in the idea. As they are now."

From those fateful days when atomic bombs dropped on Hiroshima and Nagasaki in 1945, the advent of nuclear weapons would become among the biggest strategic challenges in human history.

It took a thousand generations to develop the science. It took only 45 seconds for the first bomb to drop. "My God! What have we done?" said a crewman aboard the *Enola Gay* on that first bombing mission.

The event threw a shadow across the world, as the chase for new, and even more destructive, weapons fuelled the scenario of an all-out global war of annihilation.

Downer is avowedly a rationalist on this issue. He says it is all too easy to prey on people's fears about the destructive force of nuclear energy — he sees it as a debate too often overheated by emotion and panic.

"It's not something I think about every day of the week," he says. "When I was a child and the Cuban missile crisis came along, I didn't live in fear and hide under my desk in primary school because I thought the Soviets were going to send nuclear missiles into Australia. I have always thought that was complete bullshit."

On that first, fateful use of the atomic bomb, Downer brings to the debate the perspective of those who were the families of prisoners-of-war captured by the forces of Imperial Japan. In his view, the US decision to deploy its atomic weapons had brought a rapid end to the war in the Pacific, forcing a Japanese surrender, and arguably saving a million or more lives by preventing the need for a desperate, drawn-out Allied campaign to subdue Japan's home islands.

For him, this would become a debate in which he had a profound personal interest. As he sees it, it was far less likely his father would have survived Changi had Japan not been bombed.

So, from the very outset, this debate had real-world implications for his life, and that of his family.

That said, Downer is not blind to the power of political scare campaigns, especially when it comes to the nuclear debate. He pleads guilty to having exploited this politically himself.

When the French resumed nuclear testing in the South Pacific in 1995, he mounted a ferocious attack on the Keating Government — and his predecessor as Foreign Affairs Minister, Gareth Evans — for having stood back haplessly as the tests proceeded.

"That was one of my more shameful acts of expediency," he admits. "The French testing was not atmospheric testing. It was underground. It did no harm at all. Howard had his reservations about my campaign… until he saw how successful it was with the public.

"It really did Keating and Evans a lot of short-term political damage and it helped us win the election."

It was one among several public spats between Downer and Evans. Neither was afraid to let insults fly. Their uncharitable view of each other continued beyond their years in office. Even as recently as September, 2024, Evans had this to say of his successor as Foreign Affairs Minister: "I would normally ignore being offensively lectured to and misrepresented by a former foreign minister whose only memorable achievement in nearly 12 years in that office was longevity."

Downer, though, is prepared to acknowledge his attack on Evans over French nuclear testing was both cynical and opportunistic:

> I am not proud of it. I am not against the *force de frappe*. When I look back on my political career, I am really proud of a lot of the policy initiatives I took myself or I supported. But there are a couple of things that were acts

of successful but cynical expediency. And one of them was the campaign against French nuclear testing.

Was it my argument that France should not have nuclear weapons? No, it wasn't actually, given France was already a nuclear weapons state, a NATO ally, and it happens to be a country I quite like.

I remember initiating that campaign against Keating and Evans when we were in Cairns for a shadow Cabinet meeting. I was listening to the news in the morning. France had detonated an explosion.

Evans was being interviewed from Tokyo by the amiable (yet razor-sharp) ABC radio journalist, John Shovelan. The Press Gallery veteran put a loaded question to the minister: "Are you saying the French decision to go ahead, then, is not as bad it could have been?" Evan's response: "Exactly."

"I couldn't believe it," says Downer. "It was such a terrible political mistake to say that. I'm sure 'it could have been worse' but he was trying to minimise it. He wasn't always very adept politically, Gareth.

"So I held a doorstop, attacking the Labor Party, and it got a great run. Howard said, 'Are you sure this is the right thing to do?' And I said, 'I think it's very popular'."

As Evans himself would admit later: "All hell broke loose."

Yet Downer was never a critic of the principle of nuclear deterrence — or, indeed, of the policy of extended nuclear deterrence provided to Australia under the so-called "nuclear umbrella" of its ally, the American superpower. In the Cold War years, according to Downer, nuclear deterrence — and its ugly sister, the notion of "mutually assured destruction" — were critical to global stability.

"It worked a treat," he says. "I think slightly differently about this. I think the doctrine of 'mutually assured destruction' was a good idea. The Americans never really knew whether the Soviets would use these weapons or not, and the Soviets never really knew whether the allies — the Americans, the British and the French — would use these weapons or not. They never really knew. That was a good thing. But, in truth, none of them would have ever done it …."

Downer was satisfied of this in his own mind when, as a visiting fellow at the Hoover Institution at Stanford University, he discovered the library had bought a vast tranche of Soviet archives from the Cold War years. "They show Khrushchev and Brezhnev never had any intention of using nuclear weapons," he explains.

Not that there hadn't been instances where certain military or political leaders had called for nuclear strikes: Fidel Castro during the Cuban missile crisis had urged the Kremlin to unleash all its firepower against the US; likewise, during the Korean War, General Douglas MacArthur had advised President Truman to consider a nuclear attack on China.

"I'm with Truman on this. I think not," Downer smiles. "I think it might be far better to fire the General than to nuke the Chinese. I wouldn't want to nuke the Chinese. They seem nice enough people…"

But, in surveying the threat posed by nuclear weapons, what does he make of Vladimir Putin's threat — three times and counting, during the war in Ukraine — to consider deploying Russia's nuclear strike force?

Downer ponders the question carefully. But, ultimately, he holds to his view that, of all the nightmare scenarios in that war, a nuclear attack by Russia remained the least likely.

Recounting a conversation he had in Lugarno in December, 2024, with the Supreme Allied Commander in Europe, General Christopher Cavoli, Downer believes the US had made it clear to Russia's generals that if they used intermediate range nuclear weapons in Ukraine, the Americans would 'act decisively'. "Not use nuclear weapons — but act decisively," says Downer. "He wouldn't tell me exactly what they had told the Russians they would do. I asked him, 'Did you tell the Russians that the US would obliterate Russian forces in the Ukraine if they used nuclear weapons?' He just said, 'I would rather not talk about it'."

Downer seems confident the message from the Americans would have had the desired effect:

> That's what you need. That's how the Americans should behave.
>
> There's no way the Russians would use nuclear weapons. That would be my view. But I think it's worked quite well for the Russians because enough people in America really worry that they might use nuclear weapons. I wouldn't

worry about it — because they are not going to. That would be my view. I'm heretical on this in the sense that I won't necessarily go along with the mainstream view... I don't think any (nation-state) is going to use nuclear weapons.

Nonetheless, Downer remains an ardent supporter of strengthening workable, enforceable and meaningful international protocols to contain and discourage any spread of WMD technology. As Downer would state repeatedly as Minister for Foreign Affairs: "Australia does not and will not seek nuclear weapons. Australia has an enduring commitment to a world without weapons of mass destruction."

Under his stewardship, Australia, despite being a nuclear non-weapons state, pushed strenuously for more effective arms controls.

This had been a strong and consistent tradition for Australian Governments, throughout the Cold War years and beyond.

In 1967, the US and the Soviet Union put an agreed draft text to the UN aimed at stopping the further spread of nuclear weapons. It would become known as the Non-Proliferation Treaty (NPT). From July 1, 1968, member-states at the UN would be asked to sign up.

Australia's foreign minister at the time, Paul Hasluck, felt Australia risked antagonising both the US and Australia's Asian neighbours if it refused to comply. The practical realities had also to be acknowledged. The costs of developing nuclear weapons and a missile delivery system would be prohibitive. In any event, Australia could not expect to develop under its own steam an effective deterrent or first-strike capability against the likes of China.

Hasluck put the equation bluntly: "Our interests will continue to be best served by the retention and strengthening of the ANZUS Treaty, and the maintenance of a close United States interest and responsibility in South East Asia and the Pacific."

Prime Minister John Gorton did not agree. Under his leadership, the Australian Government set in train a series of projects to establish and build nuclear infrastructure, including plans for a nuclear reactor at Jervis Bay in southern New South Wales. Outwardly, it was about developing alternative sources of power generation. But, clearly, the government was keeping open the nuclear weapons option.

In the 1969 election campaign, Gorton promised he would not sign the NPT if returned to government. However, pressure was mounting.

Other 'near-nuclear' states like Japan and West Germany were among almost 100 nations that signed.

In February, 1970, Gorton agreed to sign — albeit reserving the right not to ratify. Australia was the second last country to do so before the NPT came into effect. Early the following year, Gorton was removed by his party as leader of the government.

His successor, William McMahon, mothballed the Jervis Bay plans. His government also got on the front foot on disarmament issues by signing and ratifying the Biological Weapons Convention (BWC).

The incoming Whitlam Labor Government ratified the NPT in January, 1973, within a month of coming to office. It sought to reassure Australians they had no need for nuclear weapons and that they lived in one of the world's most secure nations — "a difficult country to invade, conquer and occupy."

In 1977, the Fraser Coalition Government took up the baton. As a major exporter of uranium, Australia imposed the most rigorous export controls of any supplier country. The Fraser Government also helped to mobilise criticism at the UN of the laconic progress of the US and Soviet superpowers in negotiating nuclear arms reductions.

When Downer came into office, he determined that Australia should step up the momentum. One of his earliest diplomatic initiatives as foreign minister was on September 10, 1996, when he introduced to the UN General Assembly the Comprehensive Test Ban Treaty.

North Korea, Pakistan and India all refused to sign up. (Ironically, as far back as 1954, it was India's prime minister, Jawaharlal Nehru, who had issued the first international appeal for a "standstill agreement" on nuclear testing). All three nations were on the threshold of testing nuclear capabilities. It alerted the rest of the world to what was afoot, and led to a chorus of protests as well as diplomatic sanctions.

Downer rebuked all three publicly, as he did when the US Senate rejected ratification of the Treaty in 1999. "It's pretty hard to say on the one hand that we feel very strongly about Pakistani and Indian nuclear testing and on the other hand the US Senate won't ratify the treaty," Downer stated tersely. "The last thing the United States wants to see is a resumption of nuclear testing or the proliferation of nuclear weapons — and it is the last thing Australia wants to see. By refusing to ratify this treaty, the United States Senate has done a lot to undermine the arms control agenda that the international community, including Australia, has been working on."

After Australia's nuclear research experts trialled new safeguards methods at Lucas Heights, Downer was ready to lead by example. In December, 1997, Australia became the first signatory to bring the Additional Protocol to the NPT into force. In June, 1999, it invited the IAEA to inspect the Ranger uranium mine and concentration plant in the Northern Territory.

In April, 2000, Alexander Downer addressed the Sixth Review Conference of parties to the Nuclear Non-Proliferation Treaty confident that some progress was being made:

> The international community has already passed judgement on the NPT's worth in one highly significant manner.
>
> And that is in the growth of its membership. With 187 parties the NPT remains the single most important multilateral agreement underpinning global peace and security. Ten years ago some 60 states, including two of the five nuclear weapon states, were outside the Treaty. That number has now dropped to just four: India, Pakistan, Israel and Cuba.
>
> In achieving this near universal membership, we have seen a number of states — Belarus, Kazakhstan and Ukraine — turn away from possession of nuclear weapons and seek their removal back to Russia. All joined the NPT as non-nuclear weapon states.
>
> South Africa eliminated their nuclear weapons program in 1991, thereby demonstrating that the spread of nuclear weapons is not irreversible, and joined the NPT as a non-nuclear weapon state.

As Downer noted, even the leading nuclear weapons states were not oblivious to the international pressure: "They have reduced the total number of their warheads by nearly 50 percent from Cold War peaks (and) there is agreement between the US and Russia to ... to cut deployed Cold War arsenals by 80 percent from their peak."

Downer then spoke to Australia's role in the disarmament protocols, particularly through strict policing of uranium supplies. "Australia has long held to the principle that significant nuclear supply to non-nuclear weapon states should be based on their acceptance of full-scope IAEA safeguards."

After the September 11 attacks on the US, the non-proliferation agenda took on renewed urgency. The risks were both vertical and horizontal: 'rogue states' were seeking nuclear capability and global terrorist networks were known to be seeking black market access to cruder weapons technology such as radioactive 'dirty bombs'.

As George W. Bush declared in 2002, the US had little choice but to double down on the strategic imperative to stay ahead of the risks: "America has, and intends to keep, military strengths beyond challenge — thereby making the destabilising arms race of other eras pointless."

The Bush Doctrine shifted the focus from the major weapons states to non-state actors and the so-called 'axis of evil': namely, Iraq, Iran and North Korea. New national missile defence systems would become part of the armoury to guard against the gathering dangers.

Defiance of the global non-proliferation rules would not be tolerated. Frustrated by the conduct of the regime of Saddam Hussein in treating UN weapons inspectors with disdain, the Bush Administration set new parameters by invading Iraq and removing Saddam as leader.

The Howard Government got onto the front foot as well. Despite much domestic criticism, it joined the "Coalition of the Willing" in the US-led military operations in Iraq. It also pledged 'unequivocal' commitment to global non-proliferation efforts.

The UN Security Council was divided on the action in Iraq — but not on the need to contain the spread of WMD. Resolution 1540, adopted unanimously in April 2004, strengthened sanctions following NPT breaches by North Korea and Iran and the uncovering of an extensive nuclear black market operated by Pakistani engineer AQ Khan.

As Downer said at the time:

> We are working to avoid both horizontal nuclear proliferation ... and vertical nuclear proliferation. The NPT is crucial to these goals. It is the only global treaty dedicated to the containment of nuclear weapons and their eventual elimination ...
>
> For states which already have nuclear weapons the cessation of nuclear testing required when they join the

CTBT makes it more difficult for them to develop more sophisticated nuclear warheads. Negotiation of a treaty to ban the production of fissile material for nuclear weapons use ... is another priority.

In 2005, as another practical non-proliferation measure, Downer announced that Australia would make the Additional Protocol a condition for the supply of uranium: the first country to do so.

Through the 2000s, the main focus of the non-proliferation debate in Australia's neighbourhood was no longer French nuclear tests in the South Pacific. The greatest emerging threat was North Korea's ambitions to develop a nuclear bomb.

In October, 2002, the regime of Kim Jong-Il admitted to running a secret uranium enrichment program designed to make nuclear weapons — in blatant breach of an agreement North Korea had made with the US eight years earlier to abandon plans for a nuclear weapons capability in return for food and energy aid.

Fearing the prospect of US military action against North Korea, China, Russia, South Korea, and Japan (all members of the so-called Six Party Talks) urged the US to negotiate directly with North Korea. Pyongyang was signalling no intention to co-operate and would soon announce a boycott of the Six Party talks.

In response, Washington sought to extend the circle, insisting the UN Security Council must accept joint ownership of dealing with North Korea's delinquency. Through this process, Downer worked closely with George W.'s national security adviser, Condoleezza Rice, who would soon become Secretary of State. She proposed a new negotiating forum under UN auspices, dubbed the "five plus five".

This would include the five permanent members of the UN Security Council along with a handful of North Korea's neighbours from East Asia and the Pacific — Australia, Canada, Indonesia, Malaysia and New Zealand.

Undeterred, North Korea continued with its defiant approach. In September, 2006, to demonstrate its advanced military capabilities, it fired seven ballistic missiles into the Sea of Japan. Japan, the US and Australia all imposed sanctions on Pyongyang.

A month later, North Korea signalled it was beyond control and containment. It was about to step across a threshold where nobody wanted it to go, and conduct its first nuclear weapons test.

On Downer's instructions, the acting head of DFAT, David Spencer called in North Korea's Ambassador, Chon Jae hong, to register Australia's grave concerns. Spencer told Ambassador Chon a nuclear weapons test would make North Korea less secure, not more secure.

North Korea's weapons program was an egregious affront to the non-proliferation movement — and a travesty of the Kim regime's stated claim that it wanted a nuclear-free Korean Peninsula. Downer was uncompromising — publicly and privately. In meetings with his North Korean counterparts, he expressed outrage that a country relying on international aid to feed its people should devote scarce resources to missile and nuclear weapons programs.

He told ABC TV's *Lateline* program North Korea's actions would lead to a substantial escalation of tensions in North Asia. "The reaction from the Japanese and the South Koreans as well as obviously from the rest of the international community is going to be a very strong reaction," he said. "It seriously concerns me that North Korea thinks this would advance its security ... it would have exactly the reverse effect."

It was the same message he had delivered consistently at bilateral meetings with senior North Koreans — including on two visits to Pyongyang: "Why divert all these resources to weapons programs when you cannot feed your people? Some of them are eating grass."

In some respects, Downer was as worried about other aspects of North Korea's weapons manufacture — notably, its missile production: "I pursued them as much or more on ballistic missiles than I did on nuclear weapons. Those Scud missiles that Saddam Hussein used in the 1991 Gulf War, and the missiles our SAS neutralised in the 2003 Gulf War were, as I recall, based (in part) on North Korean technology ..."

After the Howard years, their successors in government in Australia had to adjust to rapidly-changing strategic circumstances. The announcement of the new AUKUS security agreement in September, 2021, reshaped the discussions around power politics in the Indo-Pacific. The AUKUS statement stressed the "enduring ideals and shared commitment to the international rules-based order" of three Anglo powers — the US, Britain and Australia. The centrepiece would be greater technology sharing in areas like cyberwarfare and AI — and, for Australia, the acquisition of nuclear-powered submarines.

Predictably, this met with unfavourable reactions in both China — and North Korea. It also created nervousness among those opposed to nuclear energy in Australia. For if you were to power a submarine based in Australia with nuclear energy, why wouldn't you use the same zero-carbon emissions energy to power industry and homes?

In 2025, Australia remained one of just a few countries in the world that banned nuclear power. It was one of only of three among the world's top 20 most advanced economies, along with Saudi Arabia and Italy, not to have nuclear power generation as part of its energy mix.

In more recent times, even the petro-chemical superpower, Saudi Arabia has foreshadowed plans for nuclear power generation, while Italy gets much of its imported electricity from France, where over 60 per cent of the electricity is nuclear-generated.

Nuclear energy is used to produce electricity in 31 countries, with 450 civil nuclear reactors in operation. Australia has ample stockfeed for a nuclear industry, given it has the largest reserves of uranium in the world. It is already home to one of the world's leading nuclear medical facilities, at Lucas Heights, just 30 kilometres from central Sydney.

The ban on nuclear power dates back to 1998, when the Howard Government was shoehorned into acceptance of a Greens amendment in the Senate. There was less than 10 minutes of debate on the matter. The Howard Government at the time was seeking legislative support to build a new nuclear research reactor at Lucas Heights. With no immediate prospect of a new civil nuclear power plant being built, the Government agreed so it could proceed with the new research reactor.

However, the emerging likelihood of Australia purchasing nuclear-propelled submarines under AUKUS pointed to a gap in logic in the ongoing debate: wouldn't a domestic nuclear energy industry be necessary to provide the skills and support industries to maintain an effective nuclear submarine project?

There was already a debate about whether the nuclear ban was compromising Australia's energy security. Might it also compromise longer-term national security?

Downer rejects the fear-mongering — in Australia as much as anywhere else — about the practical benefits of nuclear energy, when peacefully applied. Today, nuclear power provides around 10 per cent of global electricity, along with critical technologies for the treatment of cancer and other medical conditions.

"I've always found nuclear power, as in nuclear power stations, an incredibly clean and quiet way to produce energy," says Downer. He recalls a visit to a nuclear energy facility in Finland: "It's amazing how little space you need to store nuclear waste."

His advocacy for nuclear energy feeds into another controversial debate. Downer has little time for the more alarmist warnings about climate change. Not that he challenges the science — he accepts that global warming is a reality.

But what he finds harder to accept is that Australia should have to revolutionise its energy production — and carry the economic risk of denying relatively cheap baseload power to manufacturing industry and households — when Australia contributes so little as a country (about 1 per cent) to global carbon emissions.

Downer is especially critical of those who preach global catastrophe due to the effects of global warming while at the same time opposing vehemently the peaceful use of nuclear power.

How else, he argues, are emerging economic giants like India and China to reduce their carbon emissions while providing for the energy needs of their massive populations without the alternative offered by nuclear power? On this, he speaks to one of his most patient yet persistent diplomatic initiatives across his years in government.

Improved relations with a rapidly-evolving India would become a Downer priority. By opening up a nuclear energy dialogue with the south Asian giant, Downer pushed the pedal on a relationship that had been sleepy, if not shallow, for much of the postwar era.

In the mid-2000s, Alexander Downer set in train a political reversal that would begin to reinvent Australia's relations with India. It took almost another decade for the turnaround to reach fruition.

Entering the 21st century, as a large and rapidly-growing economy, India needed to generate far more electricity not only to meet the needs of its expanding industries but also to bring basic amenities such as refrigeration to many thousands of villages.

How was India to meet these needs while limiting a steep increase in its contribution to global carbon emissions? One answer was to provide its civil nuclear power reactors with the feedstock to bulk up the contribution of zero-emissions power to its energy mix.

In 1997, at the Commonwealth Heads of Government meeting in Edinburgh, India set a stake in the ground on the issue of energy security and carbon emissions. It refused to include a climate change reference in the communique without "differentiation" to allow for India's modernisation and industrialisation.

As it happens, the principle of "differentiation" was also critical to the Howard Government, which felt Australia would be disproportionately affected due to its reliance on energy and resources exports. It would have been left isolated and exposed without India's intervention.

Australia, as one of the world's largest uranium producers, was an obvious source of energy for India — except that it would have meant overturning a long-standing commitment not to supply uranium to countries that had not signed, ratified and honoured the NPT.

To achieve this turnaround was no easy matter. Downer himself had been part of a long, troubled history with India over its nuclear weapons programs.

In 1996, Alexander Downer told the Australian Parliament that the South Pacific Nuclear Free Zone Treaty banned Australian uranium exports to non-NPT states like India.

Under a strict interpretation of the South Pacific Nuclear Weapons Free Zone Treaty, uranium sales to India would be illegal unless India agreed to international inspections of all of its nuclear sites. As a matter of policy, India only allowed limited inspections over civilian nuclear plants. Its nuclear weapons research and production facilities remained off limits to inspectors.

In May, 1998, the standoff worsened. When India conducted the first in a series of nuclear weapons tests, Downer summoned the Indian High Commissioner to convey the Australian Government's 'condemnation of the tests in the strongest possible terms'. He also announced Australia would recall its High Commissioner from New Delhi.

When India conducted a second round of tests, Downer announced an end to all defence co-operation with India, cancelling ship and aircraft visits, suspending non-humanitarian aid, and suspending all ministerial and senior official visits. Says Downer:

> I remember calling in the Indian High Commissioner in

> Canberra. I think I might have over-reacted a bit because this was when we were starting to build our relationship with India.
>
> But because of my opportunistic behaviour over French nuclear testing, I was hoist on my own petard. I couldn't do nothing about it.
>
> Anyway, I called him in and I said to him, 'Well, High Commissioner, you've spent billions of dollars building this nuclear weapons capability but you'll never use it. You can't realistically use it on Pakistan or wherever else'. The Pakistanis were ahead of the Indians in terms of developing nuclear weapons ... but realistically they couldn't possibly use them either. What ... someone's going to drop a nuclear weapon on Ahmedabad and kill a million or more people?
>
> Realistically, they can't possibly use them. I told the North Koreans the same — 'a complete waste of money'.

When Pakistan retaliated with its own nuclear tests, Australia applied the same sanctions as it had to India. It had held to these non-proliferation principles for decades. Fastidiously.

But through its years in office, the Howard Government was having to confront the irreversible reality that these two large rival nations on the subcontinent had already crossed the threshold to become nuclear weapons states. What was Australia to do? Spurn them forever?

In the case of India, emerging as an increasingly significantly strategic player, both regionally and globally, this made little sense. Through the 2000s, in both the US and Australia, governments had been revisiting their assessments of India's role globally. Here was the world's largest democracy, steadily reforming and rejuvenating its industries and opening up its economy to the world.

As Downer explained in 2007:

> You've got to think about the history of modern India. I mean, here is a country which was colonised by the British for a couple hundred years or so. In 1947, it gained its independence.
>
> So the Indian perspective of the Western powers was seen through, if you like, that history of colonialism, which

is something they didn't particularly appreciate. And so as time went on, from the late '40s through the '50s — although India was one of the co-founders of the Non-Aligned Movement with Indonesia — it certainly had a tilt in its foreign policy towards the Soviet Union. It is a country that in many ways, at the time of the Cold War, defined itself in juxtaposition to the policies of the United States.

Since then, we have seen a quite dramatic transformation. The great changes that have taken place — you know, we'll call them the Reagan changes: the end of the Cold War, the massive paradigm shift that took place at that time, the victory for liberal democracy and for the market-based economic system.

India was already a democracy. But increasingly, since 1990, it had been embracing the market as well... so India has become, from our perspective in Australia, and we're an Indian Ocean country, a much better country to work with and a very good partner and that's strengthening all the time.

For its part, the US began, tentatively, to look at finding ways to end the treatment of India as a nuclear pariah. Downer had also begun reaching out to India, in the hope of a more productive relationship.

"I'm pleased to see the way the United States relations are warming with India," he would say at the time. "We look forward to seeing the United States successfully conclude its nuclear agreement with India sometime soon. That will be an important symbolic step forward, quite apart from the mechanics of it."

In 2006, the breakthrough came. The US would provide India with civil nuclear technology, even though it had not signed the NPT.

Under the deal, India promised to pursue a specific safeguards regime with the International Atomic Energy Agency. It would place 14 of 22 nuclear reactors under international safeguards in exchange for US guarantees that fuel supply to the reactors would not be interrupted.

This would be the centrepiece of a new strategic partnership with the US, effectively ending India's 30-year status as a nuclear outcast.

Downer was looking to engineer the same shift in Australia. As one of the world's largest uranium producers, Australia was an obvious source of the nuclear fuel to supply India's civil nuclear power industry — except that it meant overturning the long-standing commitment not to supply uranium to countries that had not signed, ratified and honoured the NPT.

Downer sought a new agreement on uranium sales from Australia. Under the proposal he floated, Australian nuclear inspectors would be allowed to check that the uranium was used only for peaceful purposes, and not diverted for India's nuclear weapons programs.

Any export of uranium to India would be closely monitored by the International Atomic Energy Agency, with the aim of folding India more tightly into the nuclear safety ambit, rather than pushing it away. Moreover, it would help India reduce its reliance on coal-fired energy. Australia had agreed to supply uranium to China on similar terms only a year earlier.

Downer's efforts to slowly and steadily reconstruct and revitalise Australia's relations with India would take some time to seed.

In 2015, nearly two decades after Alexander Downer had gone on the attack over India's nuclear weapons tests, Australian Prime Minister Malcolm Turnbull and Indian Prime Minister Narendra Modi would announce a turnaround on the sidelines of a G20 Leaders' Summit in Turkey. Finally, the Australia-India Nuclear Cooperation Agreement would make it possible for Australia to export uranium to India.

"As Prime Minister Modi noted, this is a milestone achievement," Australia's High Commissioner to India, Patrick Suckling, a former Downer staffer, said. "It marks a further maturing in the relationship between Australia and India and strengthens our bilateral strategic partnership with India …the supply of Australian uranium will help India to meet its rapidly growing electricity demand and improve the welfare of its people."

As Downer reflects, the relationship with India has undergone a significant structural and strategic shift.

After decades of under-performance, ties between the nations had probably never been stronger. "We have come through a lot, overcome a lot of that" he says. "The transformation in India actually has been quite dramatic."

However, India's postwar history as a leader of the Non-Aligned

Movement meant it would maintain a level of strategic ambiguity. As the US would discover in 2025, when the Trump Administration imposed 50 per cent tariffs on India for buying cheap oil from Vladimir Putin's Russia, the Modi Government would have no compunction about asserting its rights to operate to its own agenda.

Narendra Modi's conspicuous attendance at a Shanghai Summit with Xi Jinping and Putin in September of that year sent a sharp signal on the fluidity of his country's strategic positioning. While Modi responded positively to Trump's subsequent overtures to cut a new trade deal, India, a resurgent great power itself, was hedging.

16

THE FINAL STANZA

For all Prime Ministers, it is vital to have an aura of authority — challenged rarely, if ever. To get the job requires intellectual dexterity and sharp political instincts. To succeed in the job requires the courage of your convictions, and an element of cunning.

Advice can be accepted or rejected. Most prime ministers most of the time will back their own judgments. Yet no national leader in a democracy is likely to survive for long without some honest advice delivered crisply and candidly by people they respect and trust.

Among all of his ministers, Alexander Downer was always the one most likely to give John Howard the cut-through message — straight up, unadorned — when senior colleagues felt the PM was in danger of making a mistake.

The late Peter Reith, a senior Cabinet minister from 1996 to 2004, revealed in *The Howard Years* one such occasion. On his 61st birthday, Howard said on radio he would reconsider his future as Prime Minister if or when he had succeeded at the 2001 election. The "when I'm 64" comments took a lot of people by surprise, and fuelled an unexpected and unwelcome debate about Howard's plans for retirement.

"Alexander really got stuck into Johnno," Reith recalled. " 'That's the worst thing you have ever said. You should not have said it. You have to retract it by tomorrow'. Alexander was very unhappy about it. He was very good, Alexander, at giving John a complete bucket if he felt like it, and John was good enough to take it."

Howard chuckles at the memory: "Well, Reith did that, too. I liked Peter a lot. A good man. He was a big loss."

When Reith retired from Parliament at the 2004 election, it fell almost exclusively to Downer, among all of John Howard's parliamentary colleagues, to give the most powerful politician in the land frank and fearless advice.

In 2006, when Howard had reached his 64th birthday, the same subject matter, the same retirement speculation, would again dominate the headlines. Over the succeeding year, it would be Downer, amid rising tensions in the Liberal Party, who would front up to the Prime Minister to seek clarity on his plans for the future.

By mid-2006, the Coalition was performing sluggishly in the opinion polls. Howard's decision to push ahead with the Coalition's controversial *Workchoices* industrial relations reforms was proving highly unpopular, after being targeted effectively by a $30 million advertising blitz by the trade union movement.

Later, that year, the nation was hit by a searing drought and severe water shortages in some parts of the country. This only heightened heavy criticism of Howard by environmental groups over his refusal to ratify the Kyoto Protocol as part of a global response to the challenges of climate change. Politically, as Howard would acknowledge himself, it was building up into the perfect storm.

In private, in early 2006, Howard had told Downer he was contemplating retirement, and was planning to make his decision known before the end of the year. In fact, this had been one among several private conversations between them about the PM's plans for his future. "Howard and I were very close," says Downer. "We talked a lot about how we were going as a government."

But then came a news story that infuriated the PM. On July 9, 2006, the *Sunday Telegraph* published an article by Glenn Milne, under the headline "PM broke his Secret Deal".

It quoted the former Defence Minister Ian McLachlan, describing a meeting in December, 1994, where he claimed Howard had told both him and Peter Costello that, if elected as Prime Minister, he would serve only two terms in the role.

The implication — or at least the inference, according to McLachlan — was that Howard had given a commitment to Costello that he would hand over the reins after the 2001 election.

Howard insisted there had been no commitment. And he let it be known to Costello that the news of this purported deal had been counter-productive. It would make it harder for Howard to go. It would look like he was being pushed out — "and there was no way I was going to tolerate that, or that people around me were going to tolerate that."

"I think it changed his mind," Downer would say later.

Yet the political challenges facing Howard continued to mount.

"The polls started to turn really badly for us in late 2006, even before Kevin Rudd became Labor leader," says Downer. "With Kim Beazley still as leader, and about to be overthrown, the polls showed them having quite a big lead."

Downer was friendlier towards Beazley than he was to Rudd. But that didn't stop him from stepping up the political pressure on the Labor leader when it became evident a Rudd challenge was inevitable. Having been on the wrong end of Labor ridicule at the time of his own leadership struggles, he could not resist the temptation to offer some unhelpful commentary. He said Labor was in trouble because the Australian public still did not know what Beazley stood for, even after several years as opposition leader.

"Mr Beazley is somebody who is a bit ill-defined in the public mind," Downer told ABC television in November, 2006.

"Nobody quite knows what he stands for. He's a great champion of one issue one week and another issue the next."

Beazley had his office issue a sharp rejoinder: "Mr Beazley won't be taking any leadership advice from Alexander Downer, who was a failed leader born with a silver foot in his mouth."

On December 4, 2006, Rudd supplanted Beazley as Opposition Leader. The Howard Government's political challenges were about to escalate.

In the days after Australia Day in 2007, Howard went to South Australia for an announcement on the Murray River rehabilitation program. "My electorate included the mouth of the Murray so he came down there," says Downer. "After he did his media, he and I went for lunch at a cafe in Goolwa. Over this seafood lunch, we started talking about the polls.

"He asked what I thought we should do about it. And I said, 'We have to create a major debate with the Labor Party — a policy confrontation with the Labor Party'.

"He then said something that has stuck in my mind ever since. He said, 'The trouble is, we've done almost everything we set out to do'."

Downer reflects on this: "I probably thought that, too. Well, everything from deregulating the labour market, privatising Telstra, restoring a Budget surplus, paying off all government debt, fixing up East Timor, relations with Indonesia were swimming along — we had signed the Treaty of Lombok. I mean, some things may be unsolvable, like Indigenous disadvantage. There are always things to be done.

"But we had done the big policies and we didn't have anything — not that anyone has since — we didn't have any exciting reforms to come. We had to have something where Labor couldn't or wouldn't say they would do the same thing. Like tax cuts."

Peter Costello delivered his 11th federal Budget in May of that year. He announced a $10.8 billion surplus.

There was also a big education spend, concessions on superannuation tax for over 60s, and a $16-a-week tax cut for average income-earners. But it did not create the political dynamic Downer had been looking for. The opinion polls remained stubbornly stagnant. Says Downer:

> That Budget in 2007 was one of the most popular Budgets in history. Yet it didn't shift the dial. The public thought it was excellent. But they were so accustomed to excellent government, it was as though they thought — 'Oh well, we can put Rudd in charge, it will be fine'.
>
> Of course, Rudd is nothing like Howard — completely different in temperament. But the polling showed that, although the public thought we had done a pretty good job, they also thought it was time for someone else to have a turn.
>
> I mean, we had been there for so long.

Howard agrees the momentum surge in favour of his Labor opponents through 2007 seemed all but irreversible. "I think we made a mistake removing the 'no disadvantage' test from WorkChoices," he reflects. "But would that have made a difference? No. I think you get to the point where no matter what you do policy-wise, it is not going to make a difference. And we had been there a long time."

With an election fast approaching, the polls did not improve. Nothing, it seemed, could shift public sentiment.

In the meantime, Downer, his office and his Department had been working assiduously to end a long-running public controversy over the fate of an Australian captured by US forces in Afghanistan in 2001. An Adelaide man, David Hicks — with the *nom de guerre*, Mohammed Dawood — had been held in Guantanamo Bay for almost six years as an enemy combatant. He had attended Al-Qaeda's Afghanistan terror training camp in Al-Farouq, and had met Osama Bin Laden.

The political backlash over the treatment of Hicks had been an ongoing issue for the Howard Government. Not that anyone in the Labor camp or in the human rights movement sought to defend Hicks for entangling himself in an ultra-violent, fanatical sect. But the fact he was held for so long without trial in a grim and remote US-run high-security prison camp raised the temperature of the debate in Australia.

One night before Christmas in 2006, Downer's staff from his Adelaide electoral office were having an end of year dinner at a popular restaurant strip near the city. Alexander and Nicky joined them.

Nicky noticed angry stares from a group of men dining at an adjacent table. She suggested swapping seats with one of Downer's senior male advisers. The men, who had been drinking heavily, began making snide remarks about the war in Iraq and the treatment of Hicks.

Suddenly, one of the men leapt to his feet and lurched towards Alexander. One of Downer's advisers intervened and blocked his path. The restaurant waiters then rushed in to help. They held the man to the floor while waiting for police to arrive.

Downer was accustomed to occasional niggles from opponents of the war. Even verbal aggression. But rarely a display of open hostility. This appeared to have been fuelled by a mix of alcohol and the Hicks saga.

Whatever the arguments about his guilt or innocence, or the circumstances of his incarceration by the Americans, Hicks had become a political headache for the Howard Government.

"Howard and I agreed there needed to be some resolution of this," Downer recalls. "You couldn't just have him sitting in limbo. The Americans should either charge him, or release him. Not just leave him in prison without laying any charges. That was wrong."

While Downer faced criticisms among senior officials at the time for advocating a quick resolution of the issue — some intelligence officials held strongly to the view that Hicks should remain locked up — the controversy was hurting the government, and the Prime Minister wanted it dealt with more expeditiously. Downer faced internal pressures from some of his senior security and diplomatic officials for wavering on the issue. "But I think John Howard was probably right," says Downer. "And it was one of the barnacles he wanted off the ship before the election."

At the Munich Security Conference, in February, 2007, Downer set up a meeting with the US Defence Secretary, Robert Gates. Downer and US Ambassador Dennis Richardson had already sought support on Capitol Hill from the likes of Senator John McCain and Senator Lindsey Graham, two former military veterans and Republican heavyweights, in their search for ways resolve the impasse.

Gates offered Downer a compromise: the US could set up a special Military Commission to try Hicks over his activities in Afghanistan. "We will do that for you, if you like," Gates had said.

Downer rang Howard: "He was elated. This was fantastic news."

Downer's office had stressed repeatedly that the best hope for Hicks to find his way back to Australia would be to enter into a plea-bargaining deal with the US military authorities. If he continued to insist on a plea of not guilty, Hicks could be trapped interminably in a protracted quasi-judicial process.

Over the years, Downer's office was frequently in contact with Hicks' Adelaide-based lawyer, David McLeod.

In March, 2007, there was a breakthrough. McLeod had indicated he was prepared to put the option to his client. Says Downer: "I'm not sure whether it was my idea or his, but let's attribute it to him. One way or another, we agreed Hicks should offer a plea-bargain."

But this was unlikely unless McLeod could get direct, face-to-face access to Hicks himself, rather than Hicks relying solely on the advice of his American military lawyer, Colonel Michael Dante Mori.

It took some painstaking negotiations with the US military authorities over the next few weeks. But Downer and DFAT were able to persuade the Americans to allow McLeod to visit Guantanamo Bay.

"Mori wasn't very helpful," says Downer, curtly. "But eventually we got them to agree to this plea bargain."

Hicks pleaded guilty, and flew home in April. He was detained for several weeks in Australia to complete his negotiated sentence, and was then set free.

McLeod was pivotal to the outcome. But Downer made it happen. "I did get him out of Guantanamo Bay — whether I should have or not is another question," says Downer.

Some eight years later, Hicks was able to rescind the finding of guilt, amid a technical legal argument over whether the Military Commission set up to hear these cases was properly legislated.

Downer has never spoken to Hicks: "Why would I? He was consorting with terrorists. We only helped him for political reasons, really."

Downer quickly moved on to other pressing matters.

In September, the Howard Government hosted in Sydney the summit of the Asia Pacific Co-Operation grouping, including all of the heads of government of the major Pacific Rim economies. George W. Bush would be there, and China's Hu Jintao; so, too, the Japanese Prime Minister, Shinzo Abe, and the President of the Russian Federation, Vladimir Putin.

This was a high-water mark for Australian diplomacy. APEC had been created as an Australian initiative 20 years earlier. Now, John Howard and Alexander Downer would be hosting on their home soil many of the world's most influential leaders for just short of a week.

Problem was, behind the curtain, an epic of Shakespearean dimensions was playing out within the Howard Government.

There were rising pressures on the Prime Minister to consider his future, amid fears he would lead his party to almost certain defeat at the federal election due before the end of the year.

As another unfavourable opinion poll landed during the week of APEC, Howard decided it was time to seek out the thoughts of his Cabinet colleagues on whether a change at the top might bring about a shift in fortunes. "I over-reacted, really," says the former Prime Minister.

"I had the conversation with Alexander. He said he would test ministerial opinion."

Downer recalls Howard's approach to him to take on this unenviable role. "After one of our APEC meetings — I can't remember whether it was Hu Jintao or Putin — but we were in the Cabinet room ... and Howard asked me into his office.

"And this is when he said to me, 'Do you think I should retire?' So we sat down and had a talk about that.

"The trouble was, the polling showed they were happy enough with us but they wanted Rudd and Labor to be the government. They much preferred Howard to Costello, who wasn't popular with the punters. So this argument that we should change to Costello was a bit heroic ..."

Throughout that week, as Downer held meetings with a procession of world leaders, he was also engaged in tense discussions with senior colleagues about whether it was time for the PM to go.

Like others, Downer was having to weigh his loyalty to Howard against his loyalty to the party. These would be among the hardest conversations of Downer's career. By now, the government's very survival was at stake.

On the Wednesday night, Howard was hosting a dinner for George W. Bush and his wife, Laura. Condoleezza Rice was there, along with Alexander and Nicky Downer, the Costellos and Deputy Prime Minister Mark Vaile and his wife.

Downer recalls:

> Nicky, Condi and I were just there for drinks, before the dinner, and then we had to head off to this other function across the harbour. But Condi says to Nicky, 'You should come over here to meet the President'. And Nicky says, 'Look, I don't think so. What would I have to say to the President of the United States'?
>
> Condi says, 'No, I insist'. So she introduced Nicky to President Bush.
>
> And — I don't know what was going on — but then I heard Nicky suddenly say to him, 'What's it like being the most unpopular person in the world?' I thought, 'Aaargh!
>
> But Bush is such a charming guy. He just said, 'That's politics. That's how it is. You just have to do the right thing, and not worry about that'.
>
> Anyway, they got on like a house on fire. They chatted for ages.

The next morning, Downer arrived for a power breakfast at the Intercontinental Hotel. Joining Howard and Downer at the table were Bush and Condi Rice from the US, along with Prime Minister Shinzo Abe and Foreign Minister, Taro Aso, from Japan.

The breakfast among the leaders of the parties to the Trilateral Security Dialogue went well. Then, at the end of the meal, there was a moment of mild trepidation for Downer.

"As we were getting up to leave, President Bush said to me, 'Alexander, I would just like to have a word with you.'

And I thought, 'Why the hell does the President of the United States want to have a private word with me?' He took me over to one side of the room. And he said, 'I just want to say, "That wife of yours ..."'

Downer was not sure what was to come next. Bush smiled: "She's a wonderful woman. As we say in Texas, 'She's a real pistol'."

They both laughed. The President was paying tribute to Nicky Downer as a straight-shooter. "So for a while," Downer grins, "Nicky became known as Pistol Nic."

One of Downer's duties that week was to see the President off at the airport on the Thursday night that marked the end of the APEC formalities. He remembers a conversation they had standing at the bottom of the stairs of Air Force One. "He had been really supportive of Howard — 'Man Of Steel' and all that," says Downer.

"I said to him, 'You realise, Mr President, you probably won't see John Howard again as Prime Minister. We're heading for an election which — let's face it — we're going to lose'.

"And he said, well, he understood that. He said to me what a wonderful Prime Minister John Howard had been."

Downer has not seen George W. since: "But what a fantastic guy ..."

One of the biggest weeks in Downer's career was far from over.

On that Thursday night, Downer had summoned senior colleagues to a private room at the Quay Grand Hotel on Sydney's Circular Quay to take their pulse on whether Howard should continue in the leadership and what the implications would be of a decision either way for their prospects of winning the next election.

Downer knew many of his senior colleagues were anxious about whether the PM could ever make up the lost ground. While Costello might not be a fresh face, he could potentially create a sense of renewal for the Liberals. Were voters open to persuasion?

On Friday evening, Downer went for drinks with Indonesian President Susilo Bambang Yudhoyono, a mutual celebration. Both had birthdays the next day. Then, there was a dinner with the Thai delegation.

Finally, he went to see Howard at Kirribilli House, the official residence on Sydney's spectacular harbour front.

"It was about 930," Downer recalls. "I thought the Howards would give me a whiskey or something but it was just a cup of tea. I wasn't really feeling like a cup of tea at that moment ...."

Downer gave Howard his take on their colleagues' verdict: "I told him the majority of the Cabinet — not unanimous but the majority of the Cabinet — thought he should retire. And, although we probably wouldn't win, we should give Costello a go.

"We talked about it for ages. Howard's basic argument was, 'If the Cabinet want me to go, if that's what you're saying, they should collectively say so'.

"Well, sacking you would be political death for us all," Downer responded. "So we're not going to do that. Anyway, it's just their opinion that we might not win."

Did Downer agree with his senior colleagues? "I thought we would lose either way. I thought he may as well retire because we were going to lose anyway. His view was — and he said this to me — 'If I stood down, I would look like a coward....'

"Janette said the family would not want to see John humiliated. I understood all of that. I was accepting of this argument.

" But I had thought, all year, that he had run out of steam. You know, he had been the Prime Minister for more than 11 years. It's a huge length of time to do a job like that..."

Downer left the meeting knowing nothing would change.

By this time, Greg Hunt was Downer's parliamentary secretary. He remembers Downer being "terribly conflicted" by the choices facing Howard and the Liberal Party:

> I was an intermediary for Alexander. He really believed in Howard but the numbers were going down in the opinion polls. It didn't look good. So Alexander was doing this shuttle diplomacy between Howard and his senior Cabinet colleagues.
>
> It was like a 90 per cent chance we were going to lose and lose fairly convincingly. But if we switched, there was a one-third chance we could win, a one-third chance we would lose moderately, and a one-third chance it could have been catastrophic. Nobody knew. Had they taken him out, any of those three outcomes was possible ...

But if push came to shove? The fact was that any attempt to blast Howard out of the job would risk disaffection and desertion by the Liberal Party's conservative base. Everyone knew that much.

Hunt remembers a clever metaphor from the journalist, Annabel Crabb, at the time of the leadership crisis. "It was like a bunch of slightly scared kids poking a stick at an old brown snake. And the brown snake said, 'I'm going to strike you' ... and they all ran away."

Hunt recalls Downer explaining to him how Howard had bristled at the notion of bowing out ignominiously under pressure from colleagues:

> Alexander wasn't then going to blow it up himself.
>
> He tried to do it like he handled his own departure. He was not willing to sacrifice or knife Howard. It was very emblematic of his fundamental character at that most significant time.
>
> He was very conflicted... as conflicted as I've seen him ... between his loyalty to the party and his loyalty to the individual. And he wasn't prepared to trade on his loyalty to the individual.
>
> I happen to think that was the right decision because of the Howard legacy... it wasn't in Alexander's soul to do that. In the end, he said, 'Well, that's it then. I guess we are going to sail over the edge'.

Howard's recollection of the tense discussions does not vary hugely from Downer's. He acknowledges the government was lagging badly in opinion polls. "My recollection? Sure, everybody thought I was toast," Howard admits. "Did they think they might do better under an alternative, which could only be Costello? I think most of them thought they might. There were a few who said they couldn't work with Costello... and a number felt they wouldn't necessarily want me to go because it would not be popular with the Liberal-voting public.

"So there would be no regicide... in the end, it all sort of fizzled out."

Why did he ask Downer to undertake this stress-test of his leadership: "I trusted him both to be truthful and direct to me but also I trusted his instinctive affection for the Liberal Party. I didn't for a moment think he would do other than an authentic job. And that's what he did."

Did Howard find it a curious juxtaposition that the same conversation he had with Downer way back in 1995 — when it was Howard giving Downer the bad news that his leadership was terminal — would, in some ways, be played out in reverse more than a decade later?

In effect, these two conversations book-ended the Howard years. But the outcomes were very different. One leader stood aside, in the hope of delivering a better outcome for the party. The other stood defiant, in the belief the party owed him the right to depart with dignity.

Howard doesn't dwell on this. While he concedes his government was "in a weak position" by September, 2007, he does not see a direct parallel in the choices faced by Downer and himself in assessing the ongoing viability of their leadership of the party: "Well, I have never sought to compare them. It was a very different situation."

Through his decision to fight on, the Prime Minister had all but sealed his own and the government's destiny …. all that was left was for voters to make their decision.

"By then, I was resigned to our fate," says Downer. "I mean, there's always a faint hope a miracle will happen, as Scott Morrison showed

Final Countdown to the 2007 election — Howard, Downer, Costello and two senior National Party colleagues in the chamber during one of their last days in government (Ray Strange/Newspix)

(in 2019). Mind you, if you win an unexpected election, you always lose the one after, as both Keating and Morrison found out."

In the last week of the election campaign, Downer had to leave Australia on his last trip as Foreign Minister to represent Howard at the East Asia Summit in Singapore.

It was a gratifying symbolic moment for Downer. It had taken a determined campaign on his part two years earlier to ensure Australia was included as a member of this auspicious regional forum.

Howard had advised Downer not to pursue it, having been told by Singapore Prime Minister, Lee Hsien-Loong, that Australia was unlikely to get the support to succeed. But Downer persisted, despite the resistance of China, calling in favours from close friends in the region. "Japan and Indonesia went out of their way to help us," he recalls.

That last week of the election campaign was also a week of sadness at the Department of Foreign Affairs and Trade, with the death of its former and respected department head, Ashton Calvert.

Calvert had been a leading figure in engineering some of the crucial foreign policy shifts undertaken by Downer. In more than one way, an important era in Australian diplomacy was coming to an end.

Flying back into Australia from Singapore two days out from the poll, Downer had to head straight back into his electorate for the final days of the fight to survive the election. Nicky would attend Calvert's funeral service in Canberra on Alexander's behalf.

It was doubtless a heart-wrenching choice but the political imperative of fighting to the last in his electorate was basic to Downer's instincts. "I had to go and do some more door-knocking to try to save my seat," Downer says. "In the end, we won the seat easily …"

But not the election … nor John Howard's seat of Bennelong.

Under Rudd, Labor won a comprehensive victory, a 16-seat majority, including a swathe of seats in Rudd's home state of Queensland.

After almost 12 years, the Howard Era in Australia was over — and, with it, Alexander Downer's leading role in that government.

As for his involvement as a high-profile practitioner of global diplomacy, there were several chapters still to be written.

17

What Next?

In the aftermath of the Howard Government's 2007 election defeat, there was some speculation in the media — along with some in the Liberal Party — on whether Alexander Downer might yet return to the job of Opposition Leader. The truth was, he was never a candidate.

"People would put Alexander's name up. Of course they would," says Greg Hunt. "But he had no intentions on that front. He was not going to stay (in Parliament). He realised that was probably going to have to involve another decade of commitment.

"It was going to take at least another term to get back in and then you would probably have to do it for two terms beyond that. It was very clear after 2007 that he wasn't going to run again. He was going to leave. We talked a lot about that."

Like everyone else, most of the focus of senior Liberals at the time — including Downer — was whether Peter Costello would take on the job of rebuilding the party in Opposition.

"Costello could have had it if he wanted it," says Hunt. "He would have been unopposed if he wanted it after the 2007 election. He would not have been opposed by Malcolm after Brendan was falling over. And he would not have been opposed by Tony if he had wanted it when Malcolm was falling over. He could have had it. He could have had three shots at it at any of those times if he wanted it. He chose not to."

As the leadership of the federal parliamentary Liberal Party shifted to a new generation — with Brendan Nelson winning the Opposition Leader's job narrowly over Malcolm Turnbull — Downer began contemplating life after politics.

John Howard remembers conversations with his former Foreign Minister about the possibilities that might lie ahead for someone who had chalked up significant achievements in government.

"I thought he had been a great stabilising influence," says Howard. "He was quite conservative on a lot of things — but not as socially conservative as I was. I think that needs to be said. And he had a genuine immersion in the history of the Liberal Party. I thought he might have wanted to be federal President of the party. Then he told me about the aspiration he had for a UN job."

Downer had been approached to accept the role as special envoy to the UN Secretary-General with the aim of mediating a peace settlement on the divided island of Cyprus. The job offer came through Downer's Labor successor as Foreign Affairs Minister, Stephen Smith — but driving the recruitment was the UN Secretary-General himself, South Korea's former Foreign Minister, Ban Ki-moon.

"I had a good relationship with him as Foreign Minister," says Downer. He remembers Ban was particularly keen on golf, and they had played a round at a US air base near Seoul during one of Downer's visits.

Downer had no previous experience in Cyprus. He had never visited the island. But he did bring experience in conflict resolution in places like Bougainville and East Timor. Ban knew that history.

Ban had been elected to the leadership role at the UN in 2007. Downer remembers discussing the election of the new Secretary-General with Condi Rice during a visit to California. As Secretary of State for the US, a member of the Permanent Five on the Security Council, she had asked for Downer's thoughts on Ban, his main rival, the Thai Foreign Minister, Surakiart Sathirathai, and the third candidate, a senior Sri Lankan official at the UN.

Downer recalls the advice he gave: "I said I thought Surakiart was probably reasonably well-disposed towards the West and I had a good personal relationship with him (but) that Ban Ki-moon would be the most pro-American of the three and, in that sense, the most reliable."

Cyprus was just one among many intractable geo-political and security dilemmas Ban would inherit in the role of Secretary-General. Almost all of them carried an overlay of 'great power' competition — either from the Cold War years, or from the days of Empire.

Cyprus had elements of both.

At its essence, the conflict stemmed from a centuries-long contest between the Greek and Turkish traditions over sovereignty on the island. Yet, in the backdrop, there was never-ending jostling between

Russia, Turkey and the Western powers over whether Cyprus, a member-state of the EU, might one day become a member of NATO.

Greg Hunt welcomed the news that Downer had been approached for the mediator's role. "When he explained it to me, I said, 'That's it. That's your pathway out. If you want to do it. The (Rudd) Government will endorse it. You are not creating an issue for your own side'.

"He had thought a lot about his exit. When that opportunity came along, it was a natural extension. The opportunity arose. He took it.

"He lost the leadership and didn't look back. He left Parliament and he didn't look back. Personally, I think that's a really important model."

Howard and Downer might well have shared some scepticism about the bureaucracy, workings (and ideological bent) of many at the UN.

But Howard thought it a prestigious job for which Downer was amply qualified. He wanted to see a trusted colleague enjoy a new challenge after a long, distinguished career in political office: "I can honestly say that, of all my former colleagues, I've had the closest relationship — and friendship — with him. By a long way. We still talk regularly."

On July 4, 2008, Downer announced to the media that he was leaving the Parliament after 24 years as the member for Mayo. Before he flew off to New York to discuss in detail the role with Ban and officials at the UN, Downer sent a final message of thanks to his electorate in Mayo.

In his message, he provided some candid advice on what they should expect of his successors as political representatives in an electorate that, for almost a quarter of a century, had known only Downer as their MP. Almost mischievously, he described three varieties of aspiring politicians: "communitarians content to do local service; ruthless opportunists looking for cabinet rank and celebrity status; and conviction politicians with a clear vision for the future."

There is little doubt where Downer saw himself in that calculus but he was honest enough to acknowledge that his own career may have embraced at various times a mix of all three elements. "In truth, all politicians have a bit of each of these characteristics," he said.

Downer's departure happened during the Parliament's winter recess, so there would be no valedictories or farewell speeches.

And Downer was not all that fussed by some of the more fatuous retrospectives on his career as Foreign Affairs Minister — if he was aware of them at all. He was moving on, bringing his own distinctive approach to the challenge of mediating the divisions on Cyprus.

In an interview with *The Australian* newspaper, Downer pointed to his experience as a diplomat in dealing with the challenges of conflict in hotspots like Melanesia, Iraq and Afghanistan. Even so, he acknowledged the job of seeking to reunify Turkish and Greek Cypriots was likely to be nothing other than a steep, arduous, uphill climb.

The UN had been engaged on the Cyprus question since 1964. The challenges became greater still when Turkey invaded the north of the island in 1974, creating a new enclave, the Turkish Republic of Northern Cyprus. The physical division of the island reflected long-standing ethnic and religious differences. It was the British writer, Lawrence Durrell, who famously paraphrased the history of communal violence and religious hatreds on Cyprus as a "feast of unreason".

For all the beauty of Cyprus and its glorious Mediterranean coastlines — a magnet for tourists from Britain, Scandinavia, Germany and, increasingly, Russia — all attempts over the decades to bring about a workable political accommodation on the island had failed.

Downer approached the job with his usual gusto: "These things are always untidy. It's never easy to do (but) we ended the civil war in Bougainville... why not try to fix up Cyprus as well?"

As part of the protocols surrounding the appointment, Kevin Rudd, the new Australian prime minister, held a 25-minute phone conversation with Ban Ki-moon. In private moments, Rudd may have well taken some delight in the notion of his old antagonist venturing into the diplomatic equivalent of Mission Impossible.

Yet despite his past, sometimes poisonous, rivalry with Downer, Rudd gave the move his blessing. "I'm not sure whether Mr Downer is their final choice or one of a number of possible choices. I'll leave that to them and I will leave it to Mr Downer," he said.

"As you know, Mr Downer and I have had a difficult relationship over the years. But if the UN says they want Mr Downer to do a job on

Cyprus, I'm not going to stand in the road of that. He would have my complete support. This is an important role for the United Nations and we are completely behind Mr Downer's appointment."

The new Liberal leader, Brendan Nelson, was more fulsome in his praise. "Every Liberal Party member and supporter across Australia owes Mr Downer a great debt for the service he's given our party. But so too every Australian," he said. "Mr Downer did an enormous amount to elevate Australia's profile in the world in foreign policy."

The new Manager of Opposition Business in the House of Representatives, Joe Hockey, also weighed in: "I think Australians should be very proud of the fact that Alexander seems to have been offered a job by the United Nations."

But, whatever the support at home, the real challenge for Downer was to win the confidence of the parties to the conflict. In the realpolitik of the Cyprus peace process, both the Turkish Cypriots and the Greek Cypriots had an implicit power of veto over the appointment.

"I think the Greek Cypriots baulked at it for a while," says Downer.

"They knew I had been a supporter of the Annan Plan in 2004 (which the Greek Cypriots had rejected in a referendum vote)… anyway, in the end, after their initial reluctance, President (Demetris) Christofias and his people did agree to me."

Downer would spend the next six years commuting between Australia and Cyprus — along with Ankara, Athens, London, New York (and two summits in Geneva with Ban and the Cypriot leaders) — trying to broker a deal to end the conflict and bring the divided island together.

In June, 2010, the La Trobe University academic, Dr Michalis S. Michael, caught up with Downer over a dinner of steak and red wine at Nicosia's Hilton Hotel. Michael had written extensively on the challenges of reunifying Cyprus, notably in his major publication, *Resolving the Cyprus Conflict: Negotiating History.*

Only two years in, Downer was already being hounded by adverse commentary in the Greek Cypriot press. Yet Michael found Downer in good spirits. As he would report in a piece for *Neos Kosmos*, the pre-eminent Greek community news outlet in Australia: "He was utterly undeterred. He was not 'here to win a popularity contest'. He was not seeking public office nor was he a practising politician

Peace envoy — In Cyprus with President Nicolas Christofias, seated to his right (AFP/Getty Images)

seeking re-election. He was there to push ahead and in a very tenacious, robust, matter-of-fact Aussie way to get the two sides to agree to a settlement."

After six years, the mission failed. Ultimately, Downer believes it was a posture of rejection and resistance by the Greek Cypriot political leadership that prevented any breakthrough.

In February, 2012, the Greek Cypriot Parliament went as far as passing a censure motion against Downer. It was designed to scuttle one of Downer's key initiatives to bring negotiations to a conclusion.

The censure motion was intended as a preemptive strike, seven weeks ahead of Downer delivering a crucial report to the UN Security Council on the status of the peace process. His report was to recommend that Christofias, as leader of the Republic of Cyprus, meet the president of the TRNC, Dervis Eroglu, at an international conference for "end-game" negotiations.

In the censure motion, passed unanimously, Downer was upbraided for "undermining" the Cyprus Republic and making "lop-sided and damaging statements". MPs called on Ban Ki-moon to "restore" the special adviser's "objectivity and trustworthiness". During the debate, one MP told the Australian to "go home" while another accused him of operating as "an ambassador for the Turks".

Downer was far from the first UN Special Adviser to experience the wrath of the Greek Cypriots. As international commentator, Hubert Faustmann, noted at the time: "UN mediators are the most popular lightning rod for nationalist outbursts. Anybody who tries to solve the Cyprus problem is a target ... the politicians are posturing and trying to score points among the more hardline segments of the population."

At various times, former UN Secretaries-General, Perez de Cuellar, Boutros-Boutros Ghali and Kofi Annan had all suffered tongue-lashings from Greek Cypriot or Turkish Cypriot leaders. Often both.

Previous Special Advisers including Oscar Camillion and Alvaro de Soto had come in for much the same treatment. At the time of Downer's travails, De Soto, a respected Peruvian diplomat, noted wryly how the attacks on UN functionaries had become almost a ritual whenever a peace initiative neared a climax. "One of the things I was told when I started in late 1999 was that eventually this happened to pretty much everyone," he told the *Cyprus Mail*. "I was told first, the press will start behaving swinishly with any envoy, representative or adviser, and then, the rejectionist parties will start to undermine the UN chap. I was told this was standard practice ..."

De Soto told *The Cyprus Mail* he doubted Downer would be either surprised or intimidated by the rough and tumble: "Australia is famous for having one of the toughest parliaments on the face of the earth."

Downer knew from the start that he was always up against an entrenched stubbornness at the heart of the dispute:

> The most interesting thing about my experience in Cyprus is this — I don't think there was, or is, a Greek Cypriot politician who would ever have the courage to make a real agreement which would be remotely acceptable to the Turkish Cypriots or, for that matter, to Turkey. Not Christofias, nor his successor as president, Nicos Anastasiades — despite them always saying they were up for negotiations.

If this was the stark political reality on the ground, another factor in Downer's struggles to make progress as UN Special Adviser was more nefarious and underhanded. The email account of one of

Downer's UN officials in Cyprus, Sonja Bachmann, was hacked, and the contents leaked, in an attempt to discredit Downer.

"I was the victim of Russian intelligence," he reveals. "I subsequently found out that the Russians, collaborating with KYP (the Cyprus intelligence agency) were behind the campaign to destabilise my position. In the end, the Russians didn't want there to be an agreement because of the risk that Cyprus could join NATO."

In February, 2013, Downer had hopes and expectations that a new, more liberal leader elected as President in Cyprus, Nicos Anastasiades, might be more proactive in pursuing a peaceful resolution.

The two had been interlocutors for several years. Anastasiades was the leader of Democratic Rally, the main opposition party in the Greek Cypriot Parliament. "When Anastasiades became President, I thought it might be better. It actually turned out to be worse," says Downer.

Again, it would be agitprop from the Russians, fed into the political system through KYP — and ventilated publicly by Anastasiades — that would target Downer.

"I'm sorry to say this — but he (Anastasiades) sabotaged it all," says Downer. "To be fair to him, he had been given this fake intelligence — from the Russians through KYP — about different things I was said to have done (during the negotiations) which I had never done. Completely false. Not even remotely true. The fact is, the Russians wanted me out."

Today, Downer reflects on his time in Cyprus more generously than he might have at the time: "I found it fascinating. I learnt a lot more about conflict societies, and the challenges of conflict resolution. I realised that, ultimately, these questions are essentially about domestic politics, and that what diplomats and ambassadors can do is virtually nothing."

His conclusion on Cyprus is bleak: "There will never be a solution… I suspect it will probably be just more of the same. The stupidity of the Greek Cypriot position is that they are against a two-state solution. Yet, by never formalising an agreement, what they have is, in effect, a two-state solution."

That said, he values the strong relationships he fostered with those international partners he felt were genuinely invested in the search for a durable resolution of the Cyprus dispute:

The Americans were really good. The British were fantastic. I spent a lot of time in on-line meetings with David Milliband and then William Hague (British foreign secretaries, Labor and Conservative, under Prime Ministers Gordon Brown and David Cameron).

I think Erdogan (the President of Turkey), who I visited a couple of times, was pragmatic.

I had no problem with the European Commission. Athens? No problems. The problem was the Greek Cypriots.

As events transpired, a new Liberal Government was elected in Australia in 2014, and Prime Minister Tony Abbott was soon to offer Downer the job as High Commissioner to the United Kingdom.

"Obviously, I couldn't do both, so that was it," Downer says.

Ultimately, Downer left Cyprus much as he found it — an island divided by a contested history. But his contribution was certainly valued among those who worked alongside him at the UN mission.

One of the UN's international expert consultants in Cyprus was Professor John McGarry, a political scientist at Ontario's Queen's University — and a world-leading authority on the challenges of power-sharing in divided communities, including Northern Ireland, Bosnia-Herzegovina, Iraq and Ukraine. He has spent more than 16 years working on the Cyprus issue and understands better than most the all but intractable political and social divisions on the island.

"Cyprus is known as a 'diplomat's graveyard'," McGarry says. "Alexander, despite his name, did not cut its Gordian Knot, but he achieved more progress than all his multiple predecessors.

"He presided over agreement on the Joint Declaration (of February 11, 2014), which tackled the hitherto unsolvable dispute over 'sovereignty'. This was clearly the most important agreement made by Cyprus's leaders in some thirty years.

"This was not all. He built an extensive catalogue of convergences — known as the 'Downer document' — particularly on governance issues.

"These convergences (issues on which the two sides were beginning to align more closely) remain as a foundation for a settlement some eleven years after he left the island.

"Alexander was a leader in Cyprus, well respected by his staff, with a keen command for detail. 'Forensic' was one of his favourite words. If the 'Cyprob' is ever solved, he will be among the important architects of its settlement."

There was one other noteworthy experience from Downer's time on the island: in Cyprus in 2010, he spent a day with German Chancellor, Angela Merkel.

At a personal level, he found her articulate and engaging. Politically and strategically, however, he came to the view that she was at risk of being judged by history as "one of the great fools of the 21st century."

Important here is John Howard's reminder that Alexander Downer does not mince words when he delivers a character assessment. Nor is he too fussed about polite opinion.

"I spent the whole day with her — charming woman," Downer recalls. "As Cyprus is a member of the EU, she wanted to visit all the capitals. That meant sitting down with President Christofias in Nicosia."

Given the power of Germany as the leading economy and largest population within the EU, Downer's expectation was that Merkel would support efforts to nudge the Greek Cypriots towards an agreement with the Turkish Cypriots. He had sat down with Merkel's foreign policy adviser to work out how she could help persuade Christofias to pursue the best options for a negotiated settlement.

"She was hopeless," says Downer. "Her foreign affairs adviser and I agreed on the exact wording she would use. And when she got there, she didn't use it at all — she abandoned the agreement we had.

"Merkel and Christofias both spoke Russian.

"She just told him what he wanted to hear and gave the Greek Cypriots a 'get out of jail,' card rather than telling them how important it was for them to conclude the detail of negotiations.

"That's when I realised she was very friendly, very charming — very motherly. Mutti, they called her. She was absolutely delightful with the normal soldiers, the grunts. But weak. Just wanted to be liked."

Downer scowls: "Never trust a politician who just wants to be liked. We all want to be liked, of course. I like to be liked. It's one of the things I've missed out on. But it is not true leadership."

Some weeks later, I ask Downer to revisit his assessment of Merkel.

As he concedes:

> Well, there were many far greater fools in the 20th century, But she's one of these people who is very popular in the media because she is very charming, and outwardly very calm. Yet, as Chancellor of Germany, she made mistake after mistake.
>
> Germany has paid fearfully for her mistakes with energy policy. Closing down the nuclear plants for political purposes, not for any intellectual purpose. All of Europe has paid a price for that.
>
> Going ahead with Nordstream 1, leaving Germany very dependent on Russian gas pipelines — that was all her own work. As well as the decision not to spend what they should on Germany's defence.
>
> She also allowed in a million asylum-seekers from Syria in one year, completely destabilising Germany's political and social system. This triggered a huge public reaction which has empowered *Alternative fur Deutschland* (the anti-immigration populist party that, in more recent years, has outpolled the traditional parties in parts of Germany)....
>
> I think if she had truly understood the dilemma David Cameron was facing in Britain, she would have done a deal to allow him to put a handbrake on EU migration into the UK.
>
> And if she had agreed to an EU deal of substance with the British, then the Brexit referendum would not have passed ...

Downer cites another example of where he believes Merkel's exercise of her power and influence had a counter-productive impact.

"I had a conversation with Nicholas Sarkozy, the French president, just before the pandemic years.

"I said to him, 'Why didn't you appoint (former British PM) Tony Blair to head up the European Council. He said, 'I really wanted to. I tried to get other European leaders to agree to it. Many of them would have done it. But not Angela Merkel'.

"I said, 'Why wouldn't she? She's a centrist. She wouldn't have had any ideological objection to Tony Blair'.

"And he said, 'Well, the reason she didn't want him was because she thought he would be too powerful a personality'."

Distilling his judgement of Merkel, Downer says: "I actually think she was an incredibly damaging Chancellor.

"Unlike a lot of commentators, I have met her. I spent that day with her in Cyprus. I thought she was a lovely person. But she was only interested, as far as I could make out, in short-term popularity.

"She only wanted to please whoever she happened to be with at any given moment. Which is ok, I suppose… up to a point."

Downer's UN role in Cyprus was one among several appointments he would undertake in the decade following his departure from political life. As in his early days as a diplomat in Brussels, he would take a much closer interest in political machinations in Europe.

Even after Downer retired from Parliament, he would spend almost as much time overseas as he did in Australia.

After Cyprus, he served for five years in London, as Australia's chief emissary in Europe for three Liberal prime ministers: Tony Abbott, who appointed him; Malcolm Turnbull and Scott Morrison.

Then came several years travelling to and from the UK and the US, in his role as Chancellor at King's College in London, as chair of Policy Exchange, the British policy think-tank, and then joining Condoleezza Rice as a fellow at the Hoover Institution at Stanford University.

Across the journey of his life, almost a fifth of Downer's time had been spent beyond Australia's borders. Although an Australian patriot, he fits comfortably within the profile of a global citizen.

His post-parliamentary career provided the opportunity to take a long-range view of events not only in Australia, but also in the politics of the US, Europe…and the Middle East.

In 2009, as an example, Downer's UN role in Cyprus gave him fresh insights into the politics of the Middle East.

Sitting on the edge of the eastern Mediterranean, Cyprus is a 45-minute flight from Beirut, and an hour to Tel Aviv. From this vantage point, Downer could keep a watchful eye on turmoil in the Middle East during years, like today, of danger and volatility.

At that time, the extremists of ISIS were creating upheaval in Iraq. Israel and Hamas had engaged in a brutal three-week conflict in Gaza.

And, as ever, the unpredictability of events in the Islamic Republic of Iran commanded the spotlight.

The consequences of all of this would be profound, planting the seeds for the fateful confrontation the world would witness in 2025.

18

THE ONE THAT GOT AWAY

As Alexander Downer scans the broad sweep of recent history, he is still left pondering the momentous possibilities of events in the Middle East in 2009. For him, it remains a year — as much as any other in the early 21st century — of opportunities lost.

Back then, everyday Iranians were out on the streets protesting the re-election of the ultra-conservative president, Mahmoud Ahmadinejad. They suspected the election had been rigged by Iran's ruling theocracy to thwart a campaign to liberalise their society. In those last months of 2009, there seemed an elusive but exhilarating possibility of political change that could transform the Middle East forever.

At this moment, Iran was at the crossroads. It was 30 years after the Iranian Revolution, which led to the installation of a deeply conservative Islamic regime. It was 20 years after the end of a vicious eight-year war with neighbouring Iraq.

Iran under the ayatollahs had also engaged in a decades-long shadow war, an ideological confrontation, with the Americans, the Israelis and neighbouring Arab Gulf states.

There were many reasons for the hostile atmospherics. One was Iran's emerging role as one of the world's biggest state sponsors of terrorism. Another was its fanatical commitment to the destruction of the state of Israel. Another was the Islamic Republic's often denied — but barely disguised — ambitions to become a nuclear weapons power.

By the 2000s, however, even within the ruling order, there were reformers looking to engage constructively with the rest of the world.

As Foreign Minister, Downer had gone to Tehran both in 2000 and 2003 to meet perhaps the most prominent of Iran's advocates of political reform, the then President Mohammad Khatami.

Although by no means a moderate by Western standards, Khatami impressed Downer: "He was very serious, thoughtful… sophisticated."

During his presidency, Khatami had proposed a "dialogue among civilisations" aimed at improving Iran's vexed relations with Western and Asian powers. At home, he advocated greater freedom of expression, and economic policies to support more open markets and increased foreign investment.

In the 2009 election, Khatami did not run against Ahmadinejad. He supported a long-time friend and reformist ally, Mir Hussein Moussavi. In the days following the election, the public rose up in anger when it became clear that Moussavi was never going to be allowed to win. They called the protest movement the Green Wave.

For Alexander Downer, this was a pivotal moment. The ruling order in Iran appeared to be teetering.

All these years later — and knowing what we now know about Iran's incendiary trouble-making through its proxies across the Middle East, as well as the dangers the Islamic Republic posed to regional and stability through its nuclear weapons program — Downer cannot fathom why the Western world, and more particularly Washington, did not grasp that moment to come to the aid of Iran's true reformers.

"It's a bit of a disaster, really — isn't it?" he reflects. "To change how Iran behaves in the Middle East, you have to get rid of the theocracy. It's not Iran or the people of Iran — it is the ayatollah and the Islamic Revolutionary Guard who run Iran's strategies in the region."

The failure to back the 2009 uprising by the Iranian people is something that clearly gnaws at him. Downer is upfront about his disappointment with the Obama Administration's posture at that time.

He sees it as one of a series of decisions by White House administrations in the intervening years — or, in some cases, indecision — that served only to diminish and dilute American's prestige as the world's superpower:

> I think that could have been a great moment in history.
>
> The educated middle class in Iran, particularly women, rose up against the regime. And the Americans could and should have given them more support. Not military support. Intelligence support … and in a whole lot of other ways.
>
> Yet in came the Obama Administration. Instead of giving the insurgency moral and intelligence support and the like, the Obama Administration announced it wanted this

so-called nuclear deal with Iran. The Iranians essentially played them off a break ...

The history of Iran's nuclear ambitions was always controversial. In the 1950s, under the Atoms for Peace program, the US had supported the regime of Shah Mohammed Reza Pahlavi in pursuing scientific exploration of nuclear energy for peaceful purposes. In 1970, Iran signed the Nuclear Non-Proliferation Treaty, which mandated regular and independent inspections of its experimental nuclear facilities.

By the mid-1970s, however, the quest for nuclear power by two regional powers in the Middle East took a worrying turn. In 1975, German contractors began constructing for Iran the Bushehr nuclear power plant. The very next year, French engineers began work in Iraq, installing the Osirak nuclear reactor just south of Baghdad. All of this was a powderkeg in the making.

By 1980, Iraq and Iran were enmeshed in a gruesome war that would claim more than a million lives over the next eight years. At that time, neither nation was nearing the threshold of becoming nuclear weapons powers. Yet both were developing a nuclear fuel cycle that had the potential to create nightmarish possibilities.

By June, 1981, Israel could live with the risks no longer. It sent F-16 aircraft into Iraq to bomb the Osirak reactor, denying Saddam Hussein, at least for some years, his pathway to a nuclear weapons capability.

For his part, Saddam would not allow his enemy what he was denied himself. Over the course of the war with Iran, he would order three bombings of the Bushehr power plant.

The war between Saddam and the ayatollahs ended in a grim stalemate. And neither would abandon their WMD ambitions. Over the next 15 years, both would engage in subterfuge and obfuscation to sidestep the protocols of the Nuclear Non-Proliferation Treaty.

Under the ayatollahs, Iran would continue to pursue its nuclear ambitions in the shadows, with assistance from Pakistani scientists.

By the early 2000s, Opposition sources within Iran were reporting that the regime had ramped up its attempts to enrich uranium and develop weapons-grade nuclear material.

The US-led invasion of Iraq in 2003 — and the destruction of Saddam Hussein's regime — appeared to prompt a tactical shift within

Iran. The spectacle of one of Iran's most hated enemies losing control of his country over his failure to comply with international demands to disclose and dismantle Iraq's nuclear, biological and chemical weapons programs may have sent a shiver through Iran's power elites. At the very least, it appeared to represent a reality check for the regime.

Like it or not, it would have to come to the table to engage with international partners on the scale and nature of its nuclear programs.

A European initiative to persuade Iran to abandon its uranium enrichment programs collapsed in 2005. In 2006, the UN Security Council demanded Iran suspend all nuclear activities.

That demand was ignored. In early 2009, the incoming US President, Barack Obama, announced to the world the existence of the huge underground nuclear enrichment facility at Fordow, near the city of Qom. Israel, fully aware of the potential risks to its own security, threatened a military strike on the facility.

This was the subtext for Obama's efforts to cut a deal with the Iranians to end its nuclear programs — to reduce the risk of greater conflagration in the Middle East. So began the protracted haggling that led by 2013 to negotiations to have Iran commit to the Joint Comprehensive Plan of Action to suspend its nuclear programs.

Through all of this, Iran's regime used the cover of its engagement with the US and Europe to stomp on its enemies at home. As negotiations dragged on, the insurgency against Iran's theocratic regime was suppressed throughout 2009 and into 2010 by its police and paramilitaries. Brutally. There were beatings, rape, torture, imprisonment and executions.

Meanwhile, across the region, Iran's Revolutionary Guard Corps continued to arm and finance its so-called Axis of Resistance — deploying its proxies in Lebanon, Syria, Gaza and Yemen to wreak havoc on Israel.

"The Americans did nothing," Downer recalls. "They did nothing because the Administration wanted this nuclear deal with the Iranian regime and they didn't want to derail that.

"It cost them ... I don't know how many billions of dollars. To what effect? The theocracy in Iran went on supporting terrorism, and destabilising the region ..."

Downer checks himself: "There is no point in being emotional about it. You have to be forensic. They (the Obama Administration) would say the nuclear agreement was paramount. I would say that was the wrong analysis. I would say they missed a great moment."

Downer believes the US failure to support Iran's reformers in 2009 carried consequences that would reverberate down the years: "You would no longer have had Hamas ... or the war in Gaza. It could have completely changed the Middle East."

It would be six more years before Tehran would finally sign up to a nuclear deal — and only then when the US agreed to lift a range of economic sanctions against the regime. This would give the regime access to more than $US100 billion in assets frozen in foreign banks.

In return for that commitment, the regime in Iran pledged to curtail uranium enrichment programs that could lead to a weapons-grade nuclear capability. But the deal never demanded that Iran must abandon its nuclear ambitions. At best, it was only a freeze. And the mechanisms for enforcing compliance were limited.

Nowhere was the alarm greater than in Israel. Understandably.

Since the 1980s, the theocratic leaders of Iran had declared it their policy to wipe Israel from the face of the earth — or, as Ayatollah Ruhollah Khomeini, the spiritual leader of Iran's 1979 Islamic Revolution, put it, "to erase Israel from the page of time."

In December, 2000, his successor, Iran's Supreme Leader, Ayatollah Ali Khameini, doubled down on the threat: "Iran's position, which was first expressed by the Imam (Khomeini) ... is that the cancerous tumour called Israel must be uprooted from the region."

The slogan "Death to Israel" was ritually deployed at military parades in the Iranian capital, Tehran, on banners draped across ballistic missiles. The threat to annihilate Israel became official policy.

Across all those decades, Iran under the mullahs worked assiduously to assemble the means to achieve its strategic goals.

For Israelis, the reality of constantly living under the shadow of a regime sworn to the destruction of the Jewish state — and prepared to act on that threat, through its proxies — was bad enough. But the risk of such a state acquiring a weapon of mass destruction, along with the capacity to deliver a nuclear warhead by ballistic missile, presented a scenario that threatened Israeli's very existence.

Inevitably, Iran's trouble-making in the Middle East would eventually bring events to the brink of catastrophe.

"Let's think about this from the perspective of the Jewish people," says Downer. "Six million of them were killed during the Holocaust in the last century. They continue to be abused and persecuted, including in recent times in Western countries. They are endlessly condemned by resolutions in the UN. And they have a near neighbour who has a nuclear weapons program and a leader who has vowed to destroy Israel. As I often ask people, what would you do in this situation?"

19

ANCIENT HATREDS

> If you prick us, do we not bleed ...
> If you wrong us, shall we not revenge?
> — **Shakespeare,** *Merchant of Venice*

As a teenager, Alexander Downer was aware of the long and painful history of the persecution of Jews. He had read about the Holocaust and all that came before it. But the challenges facing the modern state of Israel — as a not-so-safe haven in the Middle East for an ancient culture — did not crystallise for him until his university days.

At the University of Newcastle, in northern England, he shared a house with four other students. One of them was a young Jewish woman, Judy Budd. It was in 1973, and Downer was 22. In October of that year, Egypt and Syria assembled a coalition of Arab states, with combined forces of 800,000 soldiers, to launch an invasion of Israel. They chose a Jewish religious holiday as the date for their surprise attack.

As Downer watched the impact on Judy and her Israeli cousin of the Yom Kippur War, he began to truly understand the darkening shadow over their lives — the sense of threat they experienced; the fears they held for their families, for the future of Israel and, as a consequence, for the security and survival of the Jewish people. As Downer admits:

> I can't say I had given it all that much thought until then. Judy's cousin had come to stay with her. Things were going very badly for Israel in the early days of that war. These young Jewish women were horrified. I will never forget them sitting hunched over the radio every morning, listening to the BBC reports from the war.
>
> Judy's cousin had a brother fighting for the Israeli Defence Forces, so she was particularly anxious. Until then, I had not thought much about the reality of being Jewish in

today's world. It only really struck me then about how incredibly embattled their history had been.

It was a miracle they survived at all. And I could never understand: why all this anger towards them — why the anti-Semitism?

I have never understood why. And there we were in 1973. Yet again, Israel was having to defend itself against invading armies. I felt incredibly sympathetic towards them.

That experience left a deep imprint on a young Alexander Downer. A year later, he was staying with a cousin in London who had an Australian friend of Lebanese heritage. They were driving in a car through the streets of London when talk turned to Israel. The friend had begun complaining how "the Jews had stolen the lands of the Arab people, the Muslim people". Downer could listen no longer: "I had to point out that the Jews had been there long before Islam even existed."

Downer says his impassioned aversion to anti-Semitism is rooted in fundamental liberal principles:

I have never liked to see people being discriminated against because of their ethnicity or their religion. For that reason, I became particularly sympathetic to the Jews of the Middle East. Not so long ago in history, they represented as much as 30 per cent of the population of Baghdad and there were prominent Jewish communities in other large cities such as Damascus. Today, they have only Israel — yet so many people want to see Israel destroyed.

Downer, as foreign minister, first set foot in the Old City of Jerusalem on an official visit to Israel in June, 1998. Downer's visit came at a time when the Oslo Accords had set out a roadmap for formal peace negotiations between the Israeli Government and the Palestine Liberation Organisation — one of those rare moments of hope and optimism where an end to the conflict between Israelis and Palestinians seemed almost within reach.

Later that same year, US President Bill Clinton would invite Israel's Prime Minister, Bibi Netanyahu, and PLO chairman, Yasser Arafat, to Chesapeake Bay for the so-called Wye River Summit.

Clinton's proposal was this: that if Israel would transfer more territory on the West Bank to Palestinian self-rule, the PLO would commit to curbing terrorist attacks on Israelis. Both would also agree a timetable to negotiate a resolution of the "final status" issues —the delineation of borders for a two-state solution, security guarantees for Israel and the vexed questions over the status of Jerusalem and the return of Palestinian refugees. These were always to be the last and most challenging obstacles to a sustainable peace.

As so often before, however, the peace deal collided with the brutal reality of politics in the Middle East. Within a year, Netanyahu's coalition government would collapse amid division and rancour over the potential handover of territory to the PLO.

In 2000, Clinton made another attempt in his final months in office to broker a new agreement. He invited Arafat and the new Israeli Prime Minister, Ehud Barak, to join him at his Camp David retreat. But this summit would also founder.

Within months, an uprising by Palestinian militants — the Second Intifada — would crush all talk of peace.

Downer was in frequent dialogue with US Secretary of State, Madeleine Albright, before and after the Camp David summit. He counted her as a good friend, and stayed in regular contact after her departure from public life in 2001 until her death some 20 years later.

He recalls sitting down with Albright after she left office to reflect on what went wrong with that last push by the Clinton Administration to end the conflict:

> They had laid out all these plans — how to draw the boundaries of two states, what to do about Jerusalem, the issue of right of return of the 1948 refugees — and their descendants. They were poring over all these maps of the streets of Jerusalem, and of a land corridor between the West Bank and Gaza.
>
> Clinton is taking Arafat through all the detail of how these issues might be resolved, and every time Arafat says, 'no'. Barak is putting up his own proposals yet, every time, Arafat says 'no'.
>
> So, wearying of this, Clinton turns to Arafat and says, 'You have rejected everything we have proposed and you have

rejected everything Prime Minister Barak has proposed. So why don't you put forward your proposal and we can have a look at that?'

Arafat looks directly at Clinton and Albright and says, 'No, I am not prepared to do that … if I did, I would be killed'.

According to Downer, the problem here was not necessarily the stubbornness, or the fears for his personal safety, of Yasser Arafat. Rather, as he sees it, Arafat's response spoke to a far deeper and broader reality: the absence of an appetite across the wider Palestinian populace for a negotiated peace — or, at least, a peace that would provide secure and defensible borders for Israel alongside a Palestinian state. "You can't negotiate a two-state solution with people who do not want a two-state solution," Downer says.

In April, 2001, Downer would eventually meet Arafat himself, on the sidelines of a summit in South Africa. He recalls urging Arafat to bring an end to the violence of the intifada and resume peace negotiations. Arafat's response? "I don't remember much of it," says Downer. "And the reason I don't is that there was nothing much to remember.

"He rambled and waffled. It was completely inconsequential. It was obvious to me you could never do a deal with him. That was the conclusion I reached."

Downer despairs about the hollowness in much of the talk, then and since, about implementing the 1947 partition plan for a two-state solution. "Almost immediately that plan was proposed, the neighbouring Arab states sought to obliterate Israel. And we've witnessed all the wars and violence that has followed.

"The problem is not, and has never been, the idea or the principle of there being a Palestinian state. There is no problem with that. The problem is that a lot of today's Palestinians, sponsored by the likes of Iran, are not interested in a two-state solution. It's as if they are not as concerned about Palestinian nationhood as they are about an overwhelming ambition that Israel should no longer exist … that Israel should be destroyed, eliminated, wiped off the map."

Downer had discussed this same quandary directly with Bibi Netanyahu when the Israeli Prime Minister was in Opposition. They had lunched at the Knesset in 2005. Even then, Netanyahu was casting

With Israeli Prime Minister, Bibi Netanyahu (Menahem Kahana/Getty Images)

in stark terms the reality, as he saw it, of the equation facing Israel. This was at the very time the Israeli Government led by Ariel Sharon was bringing a dramatic end to the occupation of Gaza — withdrawing Israeli forces and forcibly removing Israeli settlers from the territory. Immediately, Hamas moved in to seize control in Gaza.

When Downer had asked Netanyahu what he saw as the way forward for the two-state solution, the response was one of exasperation: "If we agree to a two-state solution, we would have Iran in East Jerusalem. That is not a proposition Israel could live with."

Nearly 15 years later, Downer was invited to join a delegation to Israel — alongside other prominent former politicians from Australia: John Howard, Wayne Swan, Brendan Nelson, Stephen Conroy.

They met with Netanyahu, who had returned as Prime Minister. His message was much the same: the greatest threat to Israel's security as a nation remained the Islamic Republic of Iran. "At the time, I felt quite confronted by that," says Downer. "As it turns out, it was true."

When the delegation visited the headquarters of the Palestinian Administration in Ramallah, Downer sought an explanation from then Palestinian Prime Minister, Mohammed Shtayyeh, about why the search for a negotiated peace seemed to be stalled.

"He gave us a long list of grievances about the occupation, the expansion of settlements," Downer recalls. "I sat there with John Howard and the others, listening to this litany of complaints. So I said, 'Prime Minister, you have stated many grievances. But what is your plan? What are you going to do about it?'

"He continued with criticism of the behaviour of the Israeli military, arrests and shootings. Again, I responded, 'What you say may be fully or partly justified — we have no way of knowing — but you are the Prime Minister. What are you doing about this? What is your plan?"

Shtayyeh paused. Then, perhaps in deference to Downer's former role as a UN peace envoy in Cyprus, he asked: "Well, what do you expect me to do about it? What do you think I should do about it?"

Downer offered Shtayyeh some practical advice: "I think you should sit down with Mr Netanyahu and talk about what you can reasonably agree upon. You need to come to some agreements with each other.

"You keep saying there are all these issues you have. Why don't you sit down and have a coffee with him — he is a human being — and have a discussion on what can be done? Because just complaining about the state of things is achieving nothing ..."

Shtayyeh's plaintive response: "Perhaps you could come work with us ... and help us." Downer had been hoping to hear of a strategy to achieve peace. Instead, he was left with an impression of hopelessness.

Five years after that meeting came the horrors of the October 7 massacre by Hamas of Israeli citizens. In turn, Israel would unleash a devastating military response in Gaza and southern Lebanon, and face mounting attacks on Israel's cities by missiles and drones being sent in swarms by Hezbollah, the Houthis — and Iran itself.

Downer found himself wondering aloud about whether and how an effective solution could ever be brokered. Approaching the first anniversary of the October 7 attacks, with the conflict continuing to escalate alarmingly, Downer, like everyone, was struggling for answers.

"There is no (solution) unless the Palestinian people want an agreement," he said. "But all the evidence suggests they do not want an agreement with Israel. Too many of them just want to destroy Israel. To kill Jews. It leaves me thinking there is no way through here. How can Israelis be expected to talk to people who want to extinguish their existence? The problem is not the Arab states. Or Israel. At its heart, the problem is the mindset of the Palestinians ..."

What saddened Downer as much as the renewed conflict in the Middle East was the reaction in Australia. Downer was appalled by the hostility shown towards Jewish people by hate-preaching elements within the Australian community.

There was also deep disappointment — in fact, barely disguised anger — at what he saw as the Albanese Government's failure to stand up unambiguously for the right of a democratic society such as Israel to defend itself against forces seeking its destruction.

In Downer's view, Australia has a proud and long-standing history of *bipartisan* support for Israel. This goes right back to Herbert Vere Evatt's frenetic activism under the postwar Chifley Labor Government in the diplomacy that led to Israel's admission to the United Nations. In 1949, Australia would become the first nation to vote in support of the historic UN resolution approving Israel's membership.

Under the Whitlam Labor Government from 1972, the bipartisanship in Australia on the issues of the Middle East frayed briefly. Amid the global oil shock, Prime Minister Gough Whitlam sought to strengthen ties to Arab nations, part of his wider push to build closer connections to the Non-Aligned Movement. Claiming "neutrality", his Government stepped up engagement with the Palestinian Liberation Organisation.

With growing numbers of Lebanese immigrants, domestic political calculations about securing the Arab or Muslim vote were becoming a factor. In 1973, when asked by a delegation of Jewish community leaders why he would not condemn the launch by Arab states of another war against Israel, Whitlam responded: "You people should realise that there is a large Christian Arab community in this country."

After Whitlam's landslide defeat in the 1975, election, the incoming Fraser Government moved quickly to restore the status quo ante. Australia again chose to refrain from voting for the ritualistic one-sided resolutions against Israel in the UN General Assembly.

The foreign minister, Andrew Peacock, made plain the Coalition Government's view that Israel could not be expected to negotiate with the PLO until it abandoned its call for Israel's destruction. He repeatedly stressed Israel's right to "secure and recognised boundaries."

Australia also committed in October, 1981, to send Australian troops to the Multinational Force and Observers (MFO) in Sinai, part of the monitoring mechanism for the 1979 Israeli-Egyptian peace treaty. Labor opposed the commitment.

After the Fraser Government's defeat at the 1983 election, Prime Minister Bob Hawke would restore Labor's more traditional pro-Israeli stance. Hawke's sympathies for Israel were well known. Hawke had attacked Whitlam for his policies during the Yom Kippur war, and had fought anti-Israeli segments of the ALP and union movement. He became an international champion of the campaign to free Soviet Jews.

As Prime Minister, Hawke was passionate in his advocacy to have the UN overturn its most notorious General Assembly Resolution — Resolution 3379 in 1975 — that declared "Zionism is the equivalent of racism."

In 1986, Hawke introduced a motion to the Australian parliament deploring the resolution and calling for its annulment. With bipartisan support, this passed almost unanimously. Through the 1980s, this campaign gathered strength. Australia would garner the support of many Pacific and Southeast Asian nations. The repeal of the resolution by the UN came in December, 1991.

During the 1990-91 war that followed Iraq's invasion of Kuwait, Hawke opposed strenuously the "linkage" arguments advanced by Saddam Hussein and some commentators that Israel should withdraw from the West Bank and Gaza as part of a deal for Iraqi withdrawal from Kuwait.

One of Australia's key contributions to the war effort was the capacity of communication bases in northern and central Australia, run jointly with the Americans, to provide real-time data on Iraqi Scud missile launches aimed at Israel.

Labor's Defence Minister at the time, Robert Ray, rejected criticism from the Left over this decision: "Essentially, they accuse me of allowing the Australian-American facilities at Nurrungar to be used to give early warning time to citizens of Israel that missiles are coming. If I am guilty of that ... that is my proudest moment in politics."

When the Howard Government won office in 1996, there was never any doubt it would uphold a position strongly in support of Israel.

The prime minister himself had visited Israel as a 25-year-old in

1964. "I went to Singapore, Malaysia, India — and then Israel," he recalls. "I stayed at the YMCA in Jerusalem ... just across the road from the King David Hotel..."

Why his interest in Israel as a young man? "I had formed some close Jewish friendships at university" he says, "and I had always admired the tenacity of the Israelis. I found when I was there a lot of similarities to Australia. There was a classlessness, and a 'we're all in this together' attitude which reminded me of Australia."

In 2000, as Prime Minister, Howard spoke of his ongoing admiration for Israel in its struggles: "The personal affection I have for the state of Israel, the personal regard I have for the Jewish people of the world, will never be diminished."

Howard and Downer were closely aligned on their views of Israel. "We agreed on most things," says Howard. "Some people suggested that I went even further than he did."

Through the late 1990s, the Howard Government sought to support peace negotiations between Israel and the Palestinian Liberation Organisation that began in Oslo in 1993. Howard was the first Australian Prime Minister to meet Yasser Arafat. At the UN, Australia voted against the extension of Israeli settlements on the West Bank. And it opened a representative office in Ramallah. All in support of the search for an effective two-state solution.

At the same time, Australia pushed back against the anti-Israel bias in international forums. Soon after taking office, Downer pledged to fight for Israel's admittance to the WEOG (Western European and Other) regional grouping at the UN to correct the situation where Israel was the only country in the world isolated from a formal grouping.

Then, in 2000, Australia played a significant role in the UN Durban Conference against Racism. After the Israeli and American delegations walked out in protest, Australia's UN ambassador John Dauth took the lead as the most vehement critic of the conference's anti-Semitic atmospherics and the ritualistic resolutions condemning Zionism.

However, the launch of the second Intifada by Palestinian militants later that same year would force a reappraisal of the Howard Government's stance on the conflict. Not only did the resumption of violence put the peace process in jeopardy, it raised doubts among otherwise neutral and dispassionate governments about the level of commitment of the Palestinian leadership to a negotiated solution.

In August, 2001, the wave of terrorism included a nail-bomb attack on a pizza restaurant during a children's birthday party in the commercial hub of West Jerusalem. Melbourne-born 15-year-old Malki Roth was among the 16 killed. This atrocity appalled all of Israel. Hearts hardened.

Then came the September 11 attacks on the US by al-Qaeda terrorists. By now, the Howard Government had zero tolerance for Islamist extremism in any form — whether Hamas, Hezbollah or Islamic Jihad.

In December, 2001, Australia would boycott a Geneva meeting of the contracting parties to the Fourth Geneva Convention, on the basis that the meeting had been convened solely to condemn Israel.

By 2003, Downer had also overturned the policy preference of his own department to abstain on UN votes where resolutions were one-sidedly critical of Israel. To this day, Downer remains proud of the fact that, under the Howard Government, Australia's voting record at the UN would be among the most pro-Israeli in the world.

At the 2004 election, under Downer's stewardship, the Coalition parties in Australia issued a formal, explicit statement on policy towards Israel:

> Under the Coalition Government, the relationship between Australia and Israel has never been stronger. As a staunch friend of Israel and as a country with strong interests in a peaceful and stable Middle East, Australia continues to provide high-level political support to facilitate a comprehensive, negotiated peace settlement. We have been active in using Australia's voice and vote in multilateral forums, especially the United Nations, to support initiatives that contribute to the peace process, and where necessary, oppose decisions and declarations that are unbalanced and unproductive.

In 2005, on his second visit to Israel, Downer spoke of his heartfelt support for Israel's never-ending fight for survival: "Australia and Israel may lie on opposite sides of the globe, but our relationship is far closer. We share your hopes and aspirations and your anguish at the loss of loved ones at the hands of terrorists. Above all, we admire the strength and courage of Israelis. These are traits Australians see in themselves."

Downer was at one with his Prime Minister on the perspective Australia would bring to the debate over the future of the Middle East.

During Israel's 2006 war with Hezbollah in Lebanon, Howard went on Australian television to defend Israel's response, saying: "Once you are attacked — and bear in mind the link between Iran and Hezbollah; bear in mind the exhortations from the Iranian President that Israel should be destroyed and wiped off the map — you can understand the tenacity with which the Israelis have responded."

Later that year, Howard stated: "There must be unconditional acceptance throughout the entire Arab world, without exception, of Israel's right to exist in peace and security behind recognised borders. The entire Arab world (and) Iran must give up forever the idea that the Israelis can be driven into the sea."

After he left office, Downer did not relent in his advocacy. In 2008, he delivered a speech to the American Jewish Committee in Washington. It was a speech that anticipated many of the same security conundrums that would confront Israel on October 7, 2023 — and the same impassioned and angry debates that would take place in Australia and other societies in the months that followed. As Downer observed:

> For those of us who live in Australia or America it is hard to conceive of life in a tiny country a fraction the size of our own, living cheek by jowl with people who want to destroy you.
>
> It is easy for Australians, Americans and Europeans in the relative security of our homes to lecture the Israeli government to be more accommodating with its enemies … to deplore Israeli attacks on rocket bases in Southern Lebanon and Gaza and Israeli attacks on Hamas terrorist leaders in Gaza and the West Bank.
>
> It's easy to lecture. But it is harder to understand. One of the lessons of history is to understand your adversary. Hamas and Hezbollah believe in the destruction of the Israeli State. That is bad enough. But behind them lies the power, the finance and the weapons of Iran.

When (Iran's) President Ahmadinejad says he wants to wipe Israel off the face of the earth, he means it. He believes there should be no Jewish State of Israel.

Demands that Israel negotiate with those who wish to destroy it are unreasonable and worse: those demands weaken Israel's diplomatic strength and help to undermine community support for Israel in Western countries. Indeed, I will go further: there has been a constant stream of criticism of Israel particularly from Europe and elements of the United Nations for each and every one of the defensive measures it takes. Building a security barrier is wrong, destroying terrorist bases is wrong, attacking terrorist leaders and planners is wrong, trying to stop missile attacks on villages in Northern and Southern Israel is wrong. It doesn't leave Israel with too many options!

These criticisms have been particularly vehement in much of the Western media. That has had an effect on public opinion which has become increasingly hostile to Israel. But Israel is a democracy. No Israeli leader can turn his or her back on the struggle against those who wish to destroy Israel. The world needs to respect that. We also need to send out again and again a simple, clear message to the international community that peace in the Middle East can never come until Israelis are allowed to sleep in peace.

This helps explain Downer's deep sense of frustration while watching the Albanese Government's shift from long-standing bipartisanship on the issue of UN General Assembly resolutions against Israel.

Back in 2012, Julia Gillard, as Prime Minister, held firm against internal Labor Party pressures for an about-turn in Australia's international stance on Israel and the Palestinian question — including the active lobbying of soon-to-be Foreign Affairs Minister, Bob Carr. Not only would she reject a proposal from Kevin Rudd to abstain from voting on an anti-Israel resolution at the UN, she decided her government should explicitly, as a matter of principle, vote against it.

Gillard was not acting on Downer's advice. She was upholding the historic position of almost all governments in Australia. "This (resolution) is not a path to peace," Gillard would tell her Caucus. "The only durable basis for peace in the Middle East is through direct negotiations between the two parties on complex final status issues such as borders, security and Jerusalem. A UN resolution will not change this reality."

The Albanese Government, through Foreign Affairs Minister, Penny Wong, chose a radically different path. On December 3, 2024, with wars still raging between Israel and its Iran-sponsored adversaries in Gaza, Lebanon and Yemen, Australia voted at the UN in support of demands for an end to Israel's "unlawful presence in the Occupied Palestinian Territory as rapidly as possible." The resolution also called for an immediate ceasefire — with no mention of Hamas or hostages.

This provoked an unprecedented response from Israel, with Netanyahu going out publicly to accuse the Albanese Government of adopting an "extreme anti-Israel position". Controversially, he also claimed the Australian Government's "anti-Israel sentiment" at the UN had played a part in encouraging anti-Semitic violence in Australia, including the fire-bombing of the Adass Israel synagogue in Melbourne.

On December 24, Israeli Foreign Minister, Gideon Sa'ar, followed up with a phone call to admonish Wong for comparing the Israel's defence against terror attacks by Hamas to Russia's aggression in Ukraine and China's breaches of international law in the South China Sea. Sa'ar described the feeling as one of betrayal by an old friend: "Australia chose to distance itself from Israel in its most difficult year, in which it fought against its bitterest enemies."

For the stalwarts of the Howard era, these political choices by the Albanese Government represented not only a gross geo-strategic miscalculation — but an irresponsible detour from a consistent Australian policy approach towards Israel and the Middle East.

Like all international observers, Downer was not impervious to the civilian suffering in Gaza that accompanied Israel's furious response to the October 7 massacre. He had discussed concerns about the Israeli Government's strategy in Gaza, including its management of humanitarian relief, with the likes of the former US defence deputy secretary, Paul Wolfowitz — whose father, a Polish Jew, suffered the loss of most of his family in the Holocaust.

Downer acknowledged that Israel was losing the propaganda war over its policies in Gaza. The pile-on by foreign governments and the international media had been unrelenting: "But it comes down to who you want to believe — the elected democratic government of Israel, or the terrorist leaders of Hamas and their sympathisers."

Downer sounded a warning about the implications of pre-emptive recognition of a Palestinian state:

> For a start, a state needs borders and there has been no agreement on where those borders should be.
>
> Second, statehood for Palestine will be followed by demands that the Israelis withdraw their defence assets from the West Bank. That sounds 'reasonable' except for two things. The Israeli settlements there would be without protection. That, you might think, is fair enough. The settlements shouldn't be on the West Bank. But this all makes assumptions about where the border should in fact be. Negotiations are supposed to sort that out.

Downer also argued that, without the presence of the Israeli defence force on the West Bank, there would be a high probability the Palestinian Authority would be subverted and supplanted by extremists, as happened in Gaza when Hamas seized political and military control after the Israelis withdrew from there in 2005.

"Indeed, the Israelis argue that every time they have withdrawn, from southern Lebanon and Gaza, militants have moved in, taken over — and fired rockets into Israel," he says. "These issues should be giving any peace-loving government pause for thought before they vote on this issue in the UN."

His warnings fell on deaf ears. In August, 2025, the Albanese Government confirmed Australia would support a vote for Palestinian statehood at the UN sessions in September.

"This is a huge change in Australia's historic position in foreign policy," Downer told *SKY News* on August 15. "We have gone from supporting a liberal democratic under siege from a terrorist organisation … to supporting that terrorist organisation and opposing the liberal democratic state. This is an extraordinary thing for Australia to have done. In a way, it is the worst foreign policy decision Australia has made since the Second World War."

His anger at the stance adopted by the Albanese Government was driven in part by his belief that it was motivated significantly by cynical domestic politics. Labor was engaged in a bitter competition with the Greens for some key constituencies in inner-city electorates — the "progressive Left", broadly defined; and the Arab-Muslim vote in traditional blue-collar Labor seats.

Downer was far from alone in suspecting that many in the Labor Party were calculating that a more pro-Palestinian stance would help shore up both voting blocs. Problem was, as Downer saw it, this meant a serious degradation of Australia's traditional support for Israel — and this, in turn, would embolden those who were subjecting Australia's Jewish communities to harassment, violence and vilification.

Here, too, the Iranian regime would be found lurking in the shadows. For decades, the Islamic Revolutionary Guard Corps had been exporting terror to other parts of the world. And so it would emerge that, at the very time the Albanese Government was distancing itself from Israel, the Australian Security Intelligence Organisation identified a missing link in a rash of attacks on Jewish communities. In August, 2025, ASIO went out publicly to accuse the IRGC of orchestrating an arson attack on a kosher deli in Sydney, as well as the firebombing of the Adass Israel synagogue in Melbourne. The Iranian regime was actively and insidiously fuelling anti-Semitic violence in Australia.

For all the heat and passion in this divisive debate, Downer was steadfast in refusing to relent on his long-established principles. Why would Australia abandon a long-standing security partner, a fellow democracy with which it had liaised closely for decades? For just as Australia had helped guard Israel against missile threats from Saddam Hussein's Iraq, so had intelligence tip-offs from Israel helped the authorities in Australia foil at least one major terrorist plot.

On August 19, after an elected Israeli MP was denied a visa to Australia, Netanyahu left no doubt about the deterioration in the bilateral relationship: "History will remember Albanese for what he is: a weak politician who betrayed Israel and abandoned Australia's Jews."

Again, Downer was asked by the Australian media to provide his take on the diplomatic brawl. Again, he responded forcefully. "I think it is tragic that the Australian Government, for domestic political reasons, has destroyed our relationship with Israel," he told the *Herald Sun*.

Since leaving federal Parliament, Josh Frydenberg had devoted much of his time after politics campaigning hard to prevent the trauma in the Middle East from stoking anti-Semitism in Australia. He knew intimately the fears and concerns of Jewish communities about the impact of race-hate on their security, their cultural identity ... and their children. He applauded his old boss in standing firm:

> In the wake of October 7, Alexander had been a consistent and courageous voice supporting Israel's right to defend itself and the Australian Jewish community's right to be defended from the rising tide of anti-Semitism.
>
> He just gets it. He knows where Australia's national interest lies and he is right. Not afraid to speak out even when he is in the minority, Alexander understands better than most what is at stake in this battle between good and evil. I know I speak for many when I say his heartfelt and powerful advocacy during these dark and difficult days will never be forgotten.

Like Downer, Howard was appalled by the policy shifts in Australia: "(We) are on the same page on this. We were both outraged at the abandonment and the betrayal of Israel by the Albanese Government. I mean every word of that. They have been absolutely disgraceful."

The former PM also deplored the failures by governments across Australia to act more resolutely to confront the plague of anti-Semitic attacks in Australia on synagogues, Jewish homes, Jewish schools — even a childcare centre: "As for this cop-out by Prime Minister Albanese, when he says — 'I've done everything I can, I have condemned all forms of discrimination'..."

Howard pauses. Like Downer, there is a steely conviction:

"Look, when you are dealing with the Jewish people, and the Holocaust, it's not 'any form of discrimination'. It is, historically, the most evil act of mankind."

20

BACK TO BRITAIN

Alexander Downer is, unapologetically, an Anglophile. Having lived in England for the best part of two decades, it is not surprising that he would have many British friends. Or that he might have come, like many other Australians abroad, to regard London as a second home.

Downer places high value on the shared cultural and legal traditions of Australia and Britain — the rule of law, the Westminster system of parliamentary democracy, the English language. "I know Britain very well," he says. "I lived there for a big part of my life. Not many countries are as alike, socially and culturally, as Australia and Britain."

That said, Downer is very much a proud and confident Australian, comfortable in the strength and vibrancy of his own culture, with its own history, its unique landscape and the character of its people. His mother, Mary, once spoke of the distinction between affection for Britain and love of your own country: "When you live in England, you feel very Australian. I'm glad I was born in Australia."

In his memoirs, former DFAT Secretary, Philip Flood, recalls Downer explaining his approach to dialogue with the British: "We should be assertively, robustly and distinctively Australian … but we should respect the (British legacy) of language, law, institutions and culture."

In the footsteps of his father, Alexander Downer would be appointed in 2014 as Australia's High Commissioner to the Court of St James in London — Australia's chief representative in the British Isles, and custodian of the nation's most enduring diplomatic relationship.

During his stint at Australia House in The Strand, Alexander Downer had a prime ringside seat as the British went through the anxiety and division of the Brexit debate — the referendum in 2016 to decide whether or not they would leave the European Union.

After 50 years as a member of the EU— the world's most ambitious attempt at pooled sovereignty, and the world's biggest and wealthiest trading bloc —the British voted, by a narrow margin, to go it alone.

For some Brexiteers, the vote represented a hankering for a return to Britain's past glories: for the days when this small island nation was *the* global power; the days when Britain ruled the seas.

There was in that Brexit vote an element of nostalgia for the two centuries when the British Empire governed as a colonial power across at least a third of the world — large slices of Asia and the Pacific, the Indian subcontinent, much of Africa and parts of the Caribbean. And, of course, its colonies in faraway Australia.

By the 1960s, that history was long gone. The draining effects of two World Wars taxed severely Britain's capacity to keep its Empire intact. Ultimately, it was unable to resist postwar decolonisation, which stripped Britain of sovereignty over most of its overseas dominions.

The "east of Suez" policy announced hastily by the Wilson Labour Government in Britain during the sterling crisis in 1968 declared an end to an era of Britain as a truly global power.

It would repatriate its troops and officials operating in India, Singapore and other dominions. It saw its future interests — economically and strategically — residing mostly in Europe. Other than Hong Kong (pending negotiations with China in the late 1990s) and the Falkland Islands in the south Atlantic, Britain had essentially packed up its belongings and gone home.

At the time, the British retreat to Europe did not go down well with Australia and New Zealand. Alick Downer, who was then Australia's High Commissioner in London, feared that, among other things, this would bind Britain into Europe's Common Market and reduce access to the UK economy for Australian primary producers.

Across the years, he sought to persuade the British Government that it should avoid confining itself to a sphere of interests extending barely beyond the eastern Mediterranean. But he failed to turn around opinion in London. The lure of the European Union was too great.

Fifty years later, however, Britain would think again.

In the early 21st century, Alexander Downer had more success than his father in encouraging the British to adopt a more global outlook. "They have had a tilt back towards the Indo-Pacific. That's a good thing."

Brexit was doubtless a key driver. Alexander Downer remembers acutely the moment Prime Minister David Cameron announced he would put to a vote of the British electorate the question of whether Britain remain in the EU — or depart.

"My immediate reaction was this would be a great opportunity to re-establish the relationship at government-to-government level," says Downer. "The people-to-people relationship had always been strong. But British governments by and large had shown relatively little interest in Australia over the previous few decades — despite (former PM) Tony Blair having lived in Adelaide as a child."

That said, the two countries had always remained close friends and allies — as people, and in defending the values of Western democracy. No matter what the political leanings of governments in either country, there were strong historical bonds. Notably in the security sphere.

The Howard Government's relationship with the Blair Labour Government in the UK was an example of this.

Tony Blair himself came to Australia in 2006 for the Commonwealth Games in Melbourne. Condi Rice, as US Secretary of State, happened to be in Australia at the same time. Downer was happy to escort them around: "We gave out medals at the swimming."

Downer remembers a dinner at Parliament House in Canberra, hosted by John Howard, where Blair met senior members of the Howard Cabinet. "Peter Costello was there. Brendan Nelson, I think. Mark Vaile, too. The discussion was mainly about education, as I recall. He was a very interesting guy, Tony Blair. Very knowledgable, obviously."

Downer says Blair and his Foreign Secretary, Jack Straw, proved solid allies to Australia — particularly during the wars in Afghanistan and Iraq. "I always liked Jack Straw. I still keep in touch with him."

Towards the end of that dinner in 2006, Downer made a play to engineer a step-up in Australia's relationship with Britain. "We have annual meetings with the Americans on security issues at ministerial level. We call it AUSMIN, " he told Blair. "I was wondering why we don't do the same with the UK?"

Downer thinks John Howard was a bit taken aback by his intervention. "That's not really been raised with me before," he said to Downer.

"No," said Downer. "I suppose I'm just thinking aloud here."

However, Blair appeared to react enthusiastically, while playing carefully the role of diplomat. "I think that's an excellent idea. Why don't we work on it?"

So began the process that led to AUKMIN, the first formal mechanism for Australia and Britain to talk defence and security since the dismantling of SEATO more than 30 years earlier. It would also represent the first embryonic move towards what would become another 15 years later the AUKUS joint defence arrangements between Australia, the US and Britain.

Downer had made this play because he thought Britain and Australia should build on the tradition of strong strategic ties, as they had during the shared experience of wars in Afghanistan and Iraq. He wanted to expand that further, and get more ballast into the relationship for the 21st century. Blair was attentive to the possibilities.

A visit by Blair's deputy, John Prescott, did not go quite so well.

Prescott had been to five nations across three continents in the space of 10 days. He was perhaps not as accustomed as foreign, defence or trade ministers to the rigours of official international travel, criss-crossing time zones and end-to end meetings, functions and dinners.

Howard hosted Prescott in a private dining room at Parliament House with senior Australian ministers. As Downers recalls it, silence fell across the room when it became clear that Prescott was fast asleep. "Something to do with my scintillating conversation," he grins.

Although the Howard Government would lose power in 2007, and Labour in Britain in 2009, the Conservatives under David Cameron would maintain the momentum in rekindling the relationship, sending Foreign Secretary William Hague to Australia in 2011 — the first formal visit by a Foreign Secretary in 17 years.

Leading into the 2016 Brexit vote, however, nobody was sure where Britain was headed. Downer, as High Commissioner, was phoned by Prime Minister Malcolm Turnbull, keen for his thoughts on the choice the British people would make. "I said, 'I could be very wrong about this, but I think at the end they will vote to remain in the EU. They would like to leave — and they may regret it — but it's just too risky."

When the vote came in on June 24, there was a narrow majority in favour of Britain exiting Europe. With its politics up-ended, and its government confronting the monumental challenge of unwinding four decades of being joined at the hip to the EU single trading bloc, Britain was now facing a future out on its its own. David Cameron, who had supported the campaign for Britain to remain within the EU, announced immediately that he would resign as Prime Minister, pending his Conservative Party finding a successor. Just over two weeks later, Theresa May would emerge as the new Prime Minister.

Turnbull was back on the phone to Downer: "Well, you were completely wrong on that (the Brexit result)," he told Downer, perhaps only half-jokingly. "What do you think we should do about it now?"

Turnbull knew Theresa May from their Oxford days. Downer saw this as an opportunity for Turnbull to call her directly and to launch negotiations on a Free Trade Agreement between Australia and the UK.

Turnbull had held exploratory discussions on this question with Cameron before he departed office. When he called the new Prime Minister, the offer to negotiate a free trade deal became the headline news. "She was thrilled," said Downer. "Number 10 Downing Street put out a public statement to that effect straight away."

Downer is proud of that achievement: "We ended up getting it done. In my view, it is second only to the CER agreement with New Zealand as the best Free Trade Agreement we have with any other country. We have almost completely free trade."

When Theresa May replaced Cameron as Prime Minister, Boris Johnson exploded onto the scene, first as Foreign Secretary and then as May's replacement as British Prime Minister. The efforts to build stronger bilateral ties between Britain and Australia went into overdrive.

Downer knew Johnson had a lot of affection for Australia — and, as High Commissioner, he sought to make the most of it. But not everybody in the Australia foreign policy and security establishment was ready to run at the same pace.

Downer recalls being told by an Australian general, "I don't think the military relationship with Britain is something of any significant focus for us, and it is never likely to be."

Downer smirks as he reflects on how far — and how fast — the relationship has since strengthened: "When Boris became Foreign Secretary, it became very easy to build up those strategic links.

"I remember a discussion about the South Pacific with the Brits, Julie Bishop and Marise Payne. I mentioned the British had withdrawn all of their ambassadors from the South Pacific and I was worried about that.

"I told them they still had a lot of 'soft power' in the Pacific island countries, not only Fiji, Tonga and Samoa but places like Vanuatu and Kiribati. I suggested they should think about putting some ambassadors back into the region.

"Boris warmed to the idea straight away, 'Why don't we do that?

"The Foreign Office officials didn't seem very keen. They thought it might be far too expensive. I said, 'it doesn't have to be all that expensive. At least put somebody in Tonga or Samoa'.

"'OK,' said Boris. 'Let's do it'."

Post-Brexit, Britain had to explore new ways of working with the world.

Downer, as High Commissioner, was relentless in advocating that — alongside the US, Australia and other like-minded democracies — Britain had significant trade and security interests tied to the future of the Indo-Pacific. Over the next five years, the seeds planted by Downer would lead to a step-up in strategic ties.

In September, 2021, Australia would sign its historic AUKUS defence pact with the US and Britain. This would include co-operation on cyberwarfare, advanced defence and surveillance technologies — and, for Australia, the promise of a fleet of nuclear-powered submarines.

Downer, of course, has another keen interest in the traditional links to Britain — he is a staunch supporter of Australia remaining a constitutional monarchy, with the king or queen of the UK also serving as the king or queen of Australia. That's how he voted at the 1999 republic referendum. He hasn't budged on the issue since.

If you raise with Downer whether it is time for Australia to sever its vestigial ties to the British monarchy, and become a wholly self-governing republic, he sits forward in his seat, pins back his ears, and gets feisty. It's not only that he rejects the core philosophical arguments for an Australian head-of-state, preferring the stability of the status quo. He is also mindful of the practical political hurdles confronting those arguing for a shift to a republican model.

"I don't see Australians ending the relationship with the monarchy in my lifetime — or yours," he argues, insistently. "William and Kate will come in. Everyone thinks they're great. So another Australian politician is going to come along and say, 'Let's get rid of the royals'? I think most people in this country will say, 'Come off it mate. There are more important things to worry about'."

That said, Downer has direct experience of how political leaders can get themselves into serious trouble with the symbolism of this issue.

As High Commissioner to Britain, he would be an eye-witness to the slow-motion train wreck of Tony Abbott's fateful decision in 2015 to award an Australian knighthood to the Queen's husband Prince Philip. Arguably, this decision, as much as any other, led to Abbott's demise as Prime Minister.

Downer only learned of the decision, unexpectedly and informally, in the week leading into the announcement. But he spent several weeks in the aftermath dealing with the consequences.

Downer had a foretaste of Abbott's disposition on these issues during a conversation at a party fund-raiser in Adelaide in March, 2013. Downer was president of the SA Liberal Party at the time. Abbott wandered over to him. "Mate, I'd like to have a word with you," he said.

Abbott told Downer he was thinking of reinstating knighthoods as the loftiest of honours available in Australia. Downer was not convinced: "I said, 'I think the time has passed for that. I don't think it's worth it anymore. What would you do with all the ACs? That's supposed to be the highest honour in Australia'."

Since 1986, the Companion of the Order of Australia (AC) had been the most elevated distinction under Australia's system of honours. Downer is himself an AC. A maximum of 35 are admitted each year.

Downer could see nothing to be gained by moving back to the old system of knights and dames. "Personally, I wouldn't take up a knighthood if it were offered to me. I didn't tell him that."

Perhaps he should have. Abbott pressed ahead with his plans, bestowing knighthoods in 2014 on Peter Cosgrove, Quentin Bryce (a serving and previous Governor General) former defence chief, Angus Houston, and retired NSW Governor, Marie Bashir.

Then came the decision that astounded many Australians.

"Peta Credlin, Tony Abbott's chief of staff, was in London at the start of 2015," Downer recalls. "It must have been three or four days before Australia Day. She had set up an appointment to see Andrew Parker (the chief of MI5 and later the Lord Chamberlain, the head of the royal household).

"I thought it might be a good idea, as High Commissioner, to go along to this meeting with Andrew Parker. I thought it could be a very interesting meeting. I got along well with Peta ... so no problem there.

"Anyway, as we were sitting in the waiting-room at MI5, Peta said to me, 'Look, keep this to yourself but, in the Australia Day honours, the Duke of Edinburgh is going to get an Australian knighthood'.

"I thought — 'well, that's interesting'. We then went into the meeting with MI5 and I didn't really think much more about it. We had the meeting with Andrew Parker and then we parted."

Given his source for the heads-up on the awarding of the knighthood, Downer assumed it was an initiative of the Prime Minister himself. Was he shocked? No. Did he keep it a closely-guarded secret? Not entirely.

"It was really only the next morning — I was in the car on the way to the office and I was giving a lift to my son, Edward — and I told him about it. He said, 'Dad, this is absolutely terrible. People will be outraged by this'. "I said, 'Really? That surprises me. I would not have thought he (Prince Philip) was an unpopular guy'."

Downer admits his own instincts would prove wrong. His son's political antennae were better attuned to the likely public reaction. "Edward was right. People were outraged. I hadn't really thought that at the time. I never understood why people cared so much ..."

Abbott spent much of Australia Day in 2015 fielding questions about Prince Philip's knighthood. He admitted it was a captain's pick.

Most of Abbott's Cabinet colleagues were ambushed by the announcement. Fronting the media at an Australia Day event in Canberra, Abbott said he was "really pleased" the Queen had accepted his recommendations. Abbott added that whilst the Duke had not called to say thank you for the honour, the Prime Minister did not "expect gratitude". Nor did he get it.

In the ensuing days, the Abbott Government's decision flared into a political uproar for the Prime Minister — and an awkward moment for Buckingham Palace. The Queen's long-serving private secretary, Christopher Geidt, phoned Downer to set up a meeting.

"The protocols meant that, at some point, the Queen would have to present this knighthood to her husband," Downer explains.

"Chris Geidt sought my advice on how they should handle this, given the controversy that had erupted around it.

"I said we shouldn't do it in secret. If it was to come out that this was done in secret, that would only become a scandal in itself. So I suggested a very modest ceremony where they could have a photograph taken and then simply put that out on the internet. Christopher Geidt takes up this idea, and makes the arrangements."

The ceremony would take place at Windsor Castle.

"I head down to Windsor Castle, and I'm taken into the yellow drawing-room," says Downer.

"The Queen is there, and the Duke of Edinburgh, and a photographer. That's all. Just the four of us. And sitting on the table is this insignia for the knighthood. The Queen picks up the insignia, and the photo is taken. Prince Philip didn't put it around his neck or anything. That's it. That's the ceremony..."

As soon as the photographer left the room, Prince Philip turned to Downer for a brief — but revealing — conversation.

"You know that I only heard through the media that I was to receive this award," he told Downer, barely disguising his agitation.

"Normally, the courtesy is that a person should be asked first whether they would be happy to accept the honour before it is announced. I had never been asked about it or told about it."

Downer could detect the Duke of Edinburgh's grumpiness. "He certainly wasn't happy about that. The Queen said nothing."

Downer is eager to put to rest what he considers unfair speculation that the idea of knighting Prince Philip arose because the Queen had somehow hinted through official channels that the Australian honour should be extended to her husband.

"I knew the Queen," says Downer. "That is not something she would ever do. Yet this story was put around ..."

Of Abbott's decision, he says: "I think it was his own idea."

Concern within the royal family about the lapse in protocols continued to percolate. This was reinforced a week or two later when Downer attended another function, this time with Prince Charles. "He said to me it was very strange that his father had not been asked…"

Downer is not sure whose responsibility it should have been to take these soundings with Prince Philip. But if Downer didn't know about the award until only days before, how many others were in the dark? The Queen must have known of the PM's recommendation. She had to approve it. Yet, constitutionally, she could hardly knock it back.

Downer is adamant the Queen had nothing to do with the decision at the heart of the controversy: "She would never have said her husband was a bit miffed that he hadn't received this award. That would not be remotely true. I am 100 per cent sure of that. I mean, the guy had more medals than anyone else on the planet."

So how did this happen? And why the lapse in protocols?

"I don't know why they didn't do this," says Downer. "It just seems that nobody in the Australian system approached the Duke of Edinburgh about whether he wanted to accept the knighthood or not. I am not saying he would not have accepted. If asked, he probably would have. But he wasn't asked.

"Look, I don't think (the royals) really minded that much. From their point of view, they thought it would all blow over …"

Ultimately, the controversy raged for far longer in Australia than it did in Britain. It was not so much about the royals.

It was more about the whole idea of restoring the tradition of Australian knighthoods and then awarding one to an ageing British aristocrat. It was what the debacle said about the political judgement of Tony Abbott as Prime Minister.

Andrew Bolt, a syndicated columnist from News Ltd, who had supported much of Abbott's agenda, could find no excuse for the fiasco, telling *2GB* radio: "This is just a very, very, very stupid decision, so damaging that it could be fatal."

And so it proved to be.

21

PERMAFROST

There was a time, briefly and not so long ago, when Russia's political leaders would deliver moral lectures to the Western powers on the futility of war. In February, 2007, at the Munich Security Conference, Alexander Downer sat near President Vladimir Putin and listened as he blamed the US for fanning conflicts across the world: "We're witnessing the untrammelled use of the military in international affairs... Why is it necessary to bomb and shoot at every opportunity?"

Putin's foreign minister, Sergei Lavrov, had made much the same plaintive cry in warning against any attempts to use force to pressure Iran to abandon its ambitions to become a nuclear weapons power: "No modern problem can have a military solution."

Today, that peacenik rhetoric sounds not only hollow — but haunting: an exercise in duplicity straight out of the old Soviet playbook. Putin's Munich speech would set the scene for a revival of Cold War tensions and a new era of Russian military adventurism in its neighbourhood and beyond. In the years that followed, Putin would set out brazenly to reinstate the outcomes demanded by Joe Stalin at Yalta in 1945 — control by Moscow over most of Eastern Europe.

Putin's address to the Munich Security Conference remains infamous not only for its audacity and hypocrisy — but also because it laid down clear and ominous markers for where Russia was now heading under his rule. After chastising the US for its power projection, Putin, virtually in his next breath, pledged himself to the task of correcting what he saw as a geo-strategic imbalance — he would seek to counter American power globally by restoring Russia's status in the world.

As Putin launched into a tirade of abuse over what he called NATO's expansionism in the East, the audience of European policy-makers seemed taken aback by the aggressive stance of the Russian President. They looked shocked. But more — much more — was to come.

Just over one year later, Putin would launch a killing spree that would continue for a decade or more to come: invading neighbours, poisoning political rivals at home and abroad, dispatching fighter jets to Bashar al-Assad's Syria to prop up a compliant regime, and threatening nuclear reprisals against any who stood in his path.

In August, 2008, Russian tanks rolled into Georgia. The war took only 16 days. By the time it had finished, Russia had effectively annexed South Ossetia and Abkhazia. In February, 2014, it was the Crimean Peninsula, with Russia claiming to be supporting the rights of pro-Russian separatists in south-east Ukraine. Then, in 2022, he launched Russia's brutal full-scale assault on Ukraine and its capital, Kyiv.

Alexander Downer would meet Vladimir Putin formally only the once, in September, 2007 — a year before the Russian President began declaring war on his neighbourhood.

Putin had come to the old Commonwealth offices in Phillip St, Sydney, during the Asia-Pacific Economic Co-Operation summit. The Russian president brought a large phalanx of advisers and security guards, and bustled through the doors for the meeting with the Australian Prime Minister and Foreign Affairs Minister. Alongside him was Lavrov.

Downer is a student of Russian history. He is also an admirer of Russia's rich cultural contribution through literature and music. In his role as Foreign Affairs Minister, he had pretty much enjoyed a decade of robust exchanges with Lavrov, with occasional humorous banter.

Downer first remembers running into Lavrov outside the office of the UN Secretary-General in New York in the late 1990s. Downer was heading to a meeting with Kofi Annan. Back then, Lavrov was Moscow's top man at the UN.

At the time, Annan had imposed a smoking ban in the environs of the executive suites at UN headquarters. When Downer walked by with the Australian Ambassador to the UN, John Dauth, Lavrov was sitting on a sofa, puffing away, apparently impervious to the new rules.

Dauth scolded him gently: "What about the ban on smoking, Sergei?"

With Russian foreign minister, Sergei Lavrov (Teh Eng Koon/Getty Images)

Lavrov laughed: "That doesn't apply to Ambassadors. The SG can't dictate to us."

Dauth chortled, "Well, what about the fact it is bad for you, Sergei?" Lavrov scoffed in reply: "John, Ambassadors don't live forever." Lavrov was too modest: he would spend the next 30 years as right-hand man to Putin, serving as Russia's foreign minister until well into his mid-70s

In contrast to Lavrov, Downer found Putin a different beast altogether when he met him during that APEC summit in Sydney: "He was cold. Very quiet. Didn't say very much. I looked into his eyes and thought, 'There is a cruel man'. And it turns out he was cruel. And very cold — as cold as a winter's day in Moscow."

Downer felt Putin revealed something of his character in his response to a gift Downer had personally arranged for the Russian President. Goodwill gifts are common at meetings with leaders of other nations.

"I had this magnum of Penfolds' *Grange Hermitage* that I gave him as he came into the room — just after John Howard had formally introduced us," Downer recalls. "It would have been worth a couple of thousand dollars. I said, 'Mr Putin, this is a bottle of Australia's finest wine. It comes from a part of Australia that I represent'. He took it and just handed it to one of his staff. He said absolutely nothing. I thought that was totally graceless."

As events would soon prove, poor manners was the least of the problems with Vladimir Putin. A year later, Putin began his predations against Russia's neighbours in the former Soviet republics.

Europe was caught napping, with NATO's military capacity in Europe much diminished by the 2000s. During this same period, Putin had invested heavily in modernising Russia's conventional forces in Europe. The military balance had shifted in favour of Moscow. Come the time of the attack on Ukraine in 2014, the Europeans seemed either powerless, or lacking the will, to provide any resistance.

Downer believes the Western powers should have taken a much stronger stand against Putin's aggression, there and then. As Australia's High Commissioner in London, he was in constant contact with senior British defence and security officials about how Europe — and the Americans — should respond.

His view — then and since — was that the NATO nations should have sent clear and direct signals to Moscow that its attempted land

"Cold as a winter's day in Moscow"— after their meeting, Downer watches on as John Howard introduces Russia's Vladimir Putin to other senior ministers (Office of the President of the Russian Federation/Wikipedia Commons)

grab in the Crimea would not be allowed to stand. He argued the Western allies should have told Putin that they would arm Ukraine with whatever was necessary to drive back the Russian occupying forces. "They should have said to Putin, 'Listen, mate. We all know what you're up to here — it's just not going to happen'."

Instead, the West threatened only economic sanctions. There was no appetite to arm and equip Ukraine to fight back against the Russian incursions. Downer suspects there were fears of escalation — that Putin might threaten nuclear reprisals if NATO was involved.

Almost exactly eight years later, stubbornly undeterred, the Russian military surged into the heart of Ukraine, bombing Kyiv and Kharkiv. This time, Ukraine fought back strongly against Putin's aggression, under its tenacious president, Volodymyr Zelensky. This time, the West offered Ukraine more support — not with troops but with weaponry.

Yet, entering 2025, the war had become a grinding slog. "Perhaps half a million people have been killed in that time," Downer noted bleakly, with Russia still holding almost a fifth of Ukraine's sovereign territory.

Along the way, Russia under Putin also re-inserted itself into the politics and conflict of the Middle East, providing military support to shore up the regime of Syrian dictator, Bashar al-Assad.

Putin's reign of terror reached across Europe. First came the assassination in London of the dissident, Alexander Litvinenko, with a pollonium-spiked cup of tea. Then, in 2018, Russian secret service agents planted the deadly nerve agent, Novichok, at the home of a former Russian spy, Sergei Skripol, in the cathedral city of Salisbury. Skripol and his daughter, Julia, both survived. But British citizen Diana Sturgess died when she found a discarded perfume bottle containing the remnants of Novichok while rummaging through a charity bin.

Back at home, Putin made a show of persecuting his one substantive political opponent, Alexei Navalny. First, by Russian agents contaminating Navalny's clothes with Novichok poisoning. And, next, by dispatching Navalny to the Polar Wolf, a bleak, bitterly cold prison camp in the Arctic circle, where he would die in February, 2024.

"He was a brave man. Very brave," says Downer of Navalny.

Downer was in Europe for much of the time as Putin embarked on these violent incursions and human rights abuses. He looked on with anger and despondency, believing Putin's spiral of atrocities was only possible partly because of a weak response by Western leaders.

Here, he concedes to Kissinger's analysis that Western governments misread badly the contours of post-Soviet Russia:

> After 1991, Russia didn't have a lot of influence. "From Australia's perspective they didn't have a lot of say in what happened in our part of the world.
>
> Russia was a bit player, really — not the global power it had been in the days of the Soviet Union, nor the great European power Russia had been for much of the past 1000 years. They seemed significantly weaker, and they seemed to be flailing away, in a sense.
>
> They would co-operate on some of our agenda. They were not in favour of North Korea having nuclear weapons. They were in synch with us on things like nuclear disarmament.
>
> We were not worried about them in 2007. At that time, you have to remember we were still in a unipolar world.
>
> Part of the problem for us — and not just for us — is that we didn't take them as seriously as we should. I would have to admit that ...

Was this failure by Western leaders, including in Australia, due to a tendency to treat Russia, and the Russians, almost as if they were the defeated power — the "vanquished" — at the end of the Cold War, following the ultimate collapse of the Soviet Union in 1991?

"I don't think of it that way," says Downer. "I thought there was a fundamental difference between Russia and the Soviet Union

"I always read Russian literature, loved the music. Russia, culturally and politically, was an important player in European history. I think the Russians, historically, have had a strong sense of the contribution they have made — whether this has always been in a positive or negative way is another question.

"My sense is that this languished a bit in the post Cold War period. They seemed just to become naysayers on almost everything. They adopted a defensive, not a constructive, diplomatic approach ...."

Then, from 2008, Putin began to announce his renewed ambitions to impose Russia's will on its neighbours. Downer admits the West's leaders were caught flat-footed — they should have seen it coming.

In 2008, Putin told the retiring US President, George W. Bush, that Ukraine was 'not a real country' but a part of greater Russia, a borderland protecting the Russian heartlands from the West.

The implication was blunt, the warning thinly disguised. Putin was letting the world know he would not tolerate Ukraine becoming some sort of pipeline for feeding either Western armies or Western cultural sensibilities, into Russia's borderlands. From that year on, Putin began dispatching armed forces into neighbouring countries. It was almost as if he dared the rest of the world to stand in his way.

According to Downer, a lack of resolve in the West helped open the door to this latest, more malevolent, version of Russia under Putin. "It was Obama who let them back into the Middle East," he notes, tersely.

Downer is at his most sombre, and surliest, in discussing the failures of the West — and failures of leadership in Washington in particular — that are contributing to uncertainty and upheaval in today's world.

"I am heavily critical of the Americans in recent years," he says. "Look, there will always be lots of explanations for all these things. But what concerned me most were the signs of withdrawal and disengagement.

"It started, I suppose, in the US reaction to the difficulty of wars in Iraq and Afghanistan but, in all honesty, there has been a lot more of it since. In 2009, just as Obama was coming into office, you had the Green Revolution in Iran ... and the US did nothing to support that. As for the Arab Spring, the Americans didn't seem to know whose side they were on... they didn't quite know who they should be supporting.

"At one stage, amid the chaos in Syria, they were on the side of the Sunni revolt against Assad. There were moderate reformers who were part of that revolt but it also included Al-Qaeda-inspired extremists, and America found itself on their side.

"Then, there was Mubarak in Egypt. For decades, he had been a mainstay of American influence in that part of the world. Egypt is an important country. Fifty per cent of the world's Arabs are Egyptian.

"Suddenly, Mubarak was gone. On top of that, you had the cave-in on chemical weapons. That was a terrible decision."

In this, Downer is referencing the Obama Administration's so-called "red line" in the Syrian civil war.

Obama had warned Damascus that if Bashar al-Assad was ever to deploy chemical weapons against his own people, which he did, the US would respond forcefully — which they didn't.

"It just corrodes your credibility," Downer says. "Do not threaten to do something you are not prepared to do. It's a bit like bringing up a child.

"You take them down to the beach. They might do something dangerous. You say to them, 'You must not do that again'. Yet when the child does it again, you let them straight back into the water."

Much the same principle applies, says Downer, in assessing the US response to Russia's serial delinquency under Putin: "The Russians march into Georgia and the Americans were tut-tutting but that's about all. That sent quite a message to Eastern Europe. Years later, the Russians march into Crimea and the Donbas. America does nothing."

Downer cites President Joe Biden's hasty withdrawal of US forces from Afghanistan in 2021 as feeding into the same narrative. He acknowledges Americans might well have grown weary of what Biden called "the forever wars". But Downer says the strategic and political consequences of another Saigon-style evacuation were also profound.

"It was an absolutely dreadful decision to do it the way they did," he says. "It was seen as weakness — American weakness. And, as the saying goes, weakness can be provocative. Is it really so surprising that the ayatollahs, or Xi, or Putin, might feel emboldened?"

22

THE AXIS OF UPHEAVAL

Alexander Downer has pondered deeply the lessons of the Cold War, and how they might apply to confronting today's multiple challenges to global security. How should the Western democracies respond effectively to the Axis of Upheaval — the territorial aggression and other provocations of Russia, China, Iran and North Korea?

The second Trump presidency in the US had cast doubt on some long-held assumptions about the workings of the Western alliance globally. For his part, Downer continued to hold true to the principles that secured peace and prosperity for much of the world for 70 years.

"We won the Cold War. How did we do that?" Downer reflects. "The liberal democracies created NATO and ANZUS. The US had security agreements with Japan, South Korea, Thailand, the Philippines.

"So you had this network of alliances. And they were too powerful for China under Mao Zedung, which at the time was economically quite weak. As for the Soviet Union — it was powerful militarily but still quite weak economically. They couldn't counter the US system of alliances."

Downer, though, is equally mindful of the lessons that followed victory in the Cold War:

> It completely changed the mindset of the liberal democracies. They thought, 'well, that rivalry is over, we don't have to worry about that anymore, we don't have to worry about defence anymore' — so you had this expression in the 1990s of spending the 'peace dividend'.
>
> But the end of the Cold War did not eliminate authoritarianism.
>
> China was changing. Certainly, economically, China was on a pathway to something very good. But many people also thought China was on a pathway, politically, to something very good. Personally, I did not think that. Many people did.

Now it's all gone wrong again. Xi Jinping has reverted to type. He's become more Maoist than Deng Xiaopingist. And Russia under the latter Putin — not the earlier Putin — has become more Stalinist.

Downer's answer to this destabilisation of the global order? "If they've gone back to what they were, we then have to go back to what we were. If you guys want to behave like that — we've shown you before what happens, through the 50s, the 60s, the 70s and into the 80s.

"So if that's what you want to do — we're very sad about that, we're very sorry about that, we think it's a huge mistake — but, nevertheless, we will not sit back and take it."

Downer says there is an underlying challenge for all the partners in the Western alliance. He hopes to see more commitment and resolve, including from Washington, based on the Reagan formula of "peace through strength". "The West has to show a new determination to stand up to its adversaries," Downer says. "Rather than the West and the Americans asking their allies (like Israel or Ukraine) to de-escalate, they should be demanding that their adversaries de-escalate."

With US Secretary of State, Condoleezza Rice, escorting former First Lady, Nancy Reagan, at the Reagan Library (Robyn Beck/Getty Images)

Following the Russian invasion of Ukraine in 2022, Downer saw the signs of the Western alliance slowly regaining its sense of common purpose and resolve:

> That was kind of happening. There were divisions in Europe over how to handle Ukraine and Russia. But, basically, the NATO countries came together pretty solidly in support of Ukraine and against Russia.
>
> Bad things happen .. but sometimes good things come out of bad things happening. What is good about the effect of the absolutely preposterous Russian invasion of Ukraine is that it recalibrated thinking. We've moved away from a dewy-eyed idealism that military forces aren't needed anymore and we can all live together and sing kumbayah — we've moved back to a world of realism.

As an example, Downer points to the shift in Germany, where a left-wing chancellor, Olaf Scholz, favoured a harder line on Russia than his centre-right predecessor, Angela Merkel. Dating back to his Cyprus days, Downer had never been a fan of Merkel.

"She seemed to think all this talk of confrontation and standing up to authoritarians was old language, the language of the Cold War … you know, we don't need to go down that path," Downer notes, slightly mockingly. "Well, people have learned the folly of that approach.

"Those types of regimes have not gone away. We have to stand up to them just as we did during the Cold War."

However, the problem exposed by war in Ukraine was that the Western alliance had a structural defect. For far too long, allies of the United States had operated on the assumption that, if Europe was to be seriously threatened, the US would unfailingly come to its rescue. "This was always going to catch up with them," Downer says.

The European Union's economy is 10 times that of Russia. Its population is five times larger than Russia's. Yet, for too long, says Downer, too many European Governments had diverted resources from their defence Budgets to other priorities — or, as he puts it, "spending money on welfare programs and windmills."

Thus, the shockwaves across Europe on witnessing the geopolitical negotiating style of Donald Trump in his second presidency.

Suddenly, unexpectedly, the American superpower would put the onus back on Europe to invest far more in defending itself.

Trump began to negotiate directly with Putin his plans for a ceasefire in the war in Ukraine. Zelensky was not in the room. Nor were the leaders of Europe.

The message from Trump could not have been more stark: not only was it likely Ukraine would have to cede some of its territory; but he also made clear that if Ukraine needed peacekeepers to protect against further Russian incursions, it would fall to Europe to provide them.

"There is a lesson in this for all of us," Downer wrote in *The Australian* on March 9, 2025.

In Downer's view, the Quad arrangements in the Indo-Pacific represented a robust example of how liberal democracies must be prepared to share the burden of security and defence. "The Quad is an illustration of a broader point," he says. "The liberal democracies of the Indo-Pacific, the European countries — and particularly the UK through AUKUS — are all sending a message that they are prepared to balance China's power: don't even think about trying to change the security status quo through use of force.

"Everything must be negotiated and everything must be done within the rules-based international system. If changes are to be made, that is how they must be made."

So how has Downer's thinking on China changed since its pivot under Xi Jinping towards a more rampant nationalism?

Downer recalls that, even in his time as Foreign Affairs Minister, there was always an underlying unease about what a richer, more powerful China might mean for regional stability.

Maybe this was always to be the trajectory accompanying China's rapid accumulation of wealth and power. What is not in doubt is that China's more bellicose approach in more recent years, including the biggest military build-up by any nation since World War 2, has brought an escalation in regional tensions — and rising fear and apprehension among many of the People's Republic's neighbours.

He remembers a jolting conversation even back when he was foreign minister with a counterpart in Tokyo who had raised very directly his concerns about China's threats to Taiwan. He confided in

Downer: "Japan will never say this publicly but if the Chinese attack Taiwan, Japan would go to war in defence of Taiwan."

Says Downer: "Today, that might not sound so surprising. But, at that time, it was very revealing about the heightening level of Japanese concerns about Taiwan."

As he has watched the ups and downs of relations between China and Australia, Downer tends towards the more pragmatic approach of the foreign policy "realist" on these questions. Like it or not, China is a leviathan of the 21st century global economy. That won't change.

Downer is a student of history and takes the lessons of history seriously. "I look in particular at the balance of power in Europe after 1815, the Congress of Vienna. If you leave aside the Crimea War, they maintained that balance of power across most of the 19th century, and it delivered relative peace and prosperity.

"They were able to collaborate with each other quite successfully. For similar reasons, it makes sense for us today to collaborate with China where we can."

Downer is wary when he hears some of the more hawkish commentators in the Western democracies proposing the economic isolation of China. He is not impressed to hear of radical policy shifts like "home-shoring" — relocating entire industries back to the West to reduce dependence on China's manufactured exports.

He cites, as an example, the push under the Albanese Government to expand the production of solar panels in Australia: "They want to build solar panels here in Australia that will compete on price and availability with what comes out of China? Good luck with that.

"It's all very well for politicians and geo-strategists to talk about taking supply chains away from China ... but China is incredibly competitive. It has economies of scale and technical skills and inbuilt cost advantages which make some of China's supply chains invaluable."

Downer also makes the point that Australia has been one of the biggest beneficiaries of China's economic growth: "The fact is, we as a country make a lot of money out of China. That's not meant to say it's our only priority in decisions we make. It's not everything — but it matters."

Downer readily accepts that the clash of Western political values with the ruling Communist Party orthodoxy in Beijing is all but impossible to reconcile. As an illustration, he recalls a conversation with former British Labour leader, Jeremy Corbyn. It happened in 2015, after a state dinner with Xi Jinping at Buckingham Palace when Downer was High Commissioner to London. Along with several Ministers of the Crown in Britain, and various other dignitaries, he had been invited to the official banquet for the Chinese President, hosted by the Queen.

On first impressions — and he has met Xi only the once — Downer felt China's leader had a charismatic presence: "He cut quite an impressive figure. When he walked into the room, everyone knew Xi was there."

As the evening went on, Downer found himself in a one-on-one conversation with Corbyn. He knew the then British Opposition Leader reasonably well. Corbyn had met with Xi earlier that day. "How did your meeting go?" Downer asked.

"I don't know," Corbyn replied, perhaps a little apprehensively. "I'm not sure I did the right thing... let me tell you what happened and you can tell me whether you think it was ok."

Corbyn said he had given Xi an envelope containing a letter setting out concerns in the British Labour Party about political prisoners and human rights campaigners being detained in China: "I said to Xi that the Labour Party was concerned about the rights of these people."

Downer was quick to reassure Corbyn: "It is entirely appropriate for you to do that. If you had these concerns, and you didn't raise them with him, that would have been a mistake."

Corbyn then revealed to Downer what Xi had said in reply — the words that may have unsettled him. "Xi Jinping said, 'We have a completely different view of society from you. You value individuals and their rights. We value society as a whole and the security of the State."

It was a blunt delineation by Xi of the stark differences in the value systems of the West and those of a one-party Communist state.

Downer says it would be naive to expect there to be a meeting of minds between the Chinese Communist Party and Western nations on these competing views of how societies best function.

The key is to prevent ideological differences degenerating into open hostility. Downer argues the safest route to that outcome is to maintain a powerful strategy of deterrence: "It demonstrates the importance of retaining a strong US presence in the region, and for like-minded nations to work together to ensure an increasingly well-armed China is not tempted to embark on any military excursions that could risk an escalation of conflict."

For all that, he understands better than most how the behaviour of China, and that of agents or apologists for the Communist State within Australia, have come to loom larger than ever in domestic politics in many Western countries, including Australia. The issues extend from allegations of improper interference in the political system to cyber attacks by state actors on Australian communications infrastructure. They include claims of land banking and bribery and of the intimidation of critics of the Chinese regime living in Australia.

Downer acknowledges these are thorny issues but says both countries should be careful not to exaggerate the impact. Over the last decade, he says he has seen too many over-reactions on both sides: "We didn't need to have these interminable disputes over security issues ..."

In the early 2010s, Downer found himself swept up in controversy over business dealings with China. His Adelaide-based consultancy, Bespoke Approach — which he partnered with former senior Liberal adviser, Ian Smith, and former Labor Cabinet minister, Nick Bolkus — had been commissioned by the Chinese tech giant, Huawei, to provide advice on how to manage its relationships with governments in Australia.

"They wanted to build their business in Australia — headphones, tablets, that kind of thing," Downer says. He accepted a role on the board of Huawei's Australian subsidiary, as well as serving on the company's international advisory board.

He would travel several times to Huawei's headquarters in Shenzhen. "I found it incredibly interesting ... to learn a great deal more about how things happen in business in China."

When the Gillard Labor Government announced its plans to build Australia's National Broadband Network, Huawei lodged a bid to involve itself in part of the rollout. Says Downer: "It would have been cheaper than the alternatives but there was a lot of discussion within government in Australia about whether this was a good idea."

Immediately, a signal flare went up from Australia's intelligence agencies. "It's not that they had any evidence of malfeasance by Huawei ... but they thought (the company) could be used by the Chinese Government to conduct various activities," says Downer. "They thought it wasn't worth the risk. So the (Gillard) Government banned (Huawei) from the core of the NBN."

Downer clearly felt the Huawei offer, at that time, was above-board and commercially competitive. He felt the then Opposition spokesman on communications, Malcolm Turnbull, thought so, too. "When he became Minister for Communications (in the Abbott Government) he became less sympathetic," Downer recalls. He says Turnbull's positioned hardened still more when he became Prime Minister.

This may well have been no more than a function of the reality that security around critical communications technology was becoming ever more challenging. The truth was that advances and innovation in the complexity and reach of communications technology could sometimes give rise to greater potential dangers of a system being compromised.

This was the strong view within Australia's intelligence community by the time the Turnbull Government had to make a decision on whether Huawei should be allowed to bid for involvement in the rollout of a new 5G wireless network in Australia. The expert advice to Turnbull as Prime Minister, which he accepted and acted on, was that there were far greater technical risks than with the 4G rollout and that a ban on Huawei's participation, announced in 2018, was the safest option.

While not related to the Huawei issues, the Dastyari Affair became another testing moment in relations with China.

In 2016, Turnbull had just attended a G20 summit in Hangzhou, including a head-to-head meeting with Xi Jinping, when news emerged of a major political scandal back in Canberra. Labor's Senator Sam Dastyari, an influential factional powerbroker from the NSW branch, had been revealed as receiving funds for travel from a Chinese donor suspected to have direct, high-level connections to the Communist Party elite back in Beijing.

The same Senator Dastyari had made public comments saying China was entitled to assert its rights in the South China Sea.

From the Laotian capital, Vientiane, the Prime Minister held a press conference where he denounced Opposition Leader Bill Shorten for not having sacked Dastyari immediately. Had Labor's foreign policy become a version of "cash for comment"?

"I'm not saying they (Turnbull and his advisers) did not have good reason to be concerned about China's behaviour," says Downer.

"But I think it's also true that he milked it politically. I have milked these things politically, too. If I was in Malcolm's position, I would probably have made a big political issue of it. Of course you would. But he did take it a very long way." For his part, Turnbull rejects any suggestion he went too far: "Dastyari was fair game on the basis of his comments on the South China Sea alone."

In latter years, Downer has conceded openly that the Chinese Government became more difficult to manage for the Howard Government's successors in Australia, as it has for others in the Western alliance.

He says the West cannot declare itself free of blame. Downer thinks the Obama Administration stood back too meekly as China muscled up.

"Xi Jinping gave Barack Obama a commitment not to militarise those reefs and islets in the South China Sea.

"Then they did it anyway. Xi just got away with it."

But wasn't it Xi, through his actions, who was primarily responsible for the escalating tensions?

Xi did not set up this ideological contest, this notion of strategic competition between political systems. Yet, through his words and actions, he elevated it to prime-time. In a speech to Communist Party apparatchiks in January, 2021, Xi boasted China's handling of the pandemic "made it evident which country's leadership and political system is superior." He added: "Time and momentum are on our side."

Downer says there is little point getting over-wrought about the challenges of a more muscular, assertive China under the more doctrinaire, domineering Xi Jinping:

> Often I found myself having to explain this to people. You may hate the Communist Party. You may hate what China represents — political values, human rights and so on.

But we have to co-exist with China. It is not going to disappear. You are not going to overthrow the Communist Party in China...

This is one reason I have always said — and Australia has said — we must have an effective balance of power in the Indo-Pacific: to prevent China exercising hegemony over others in the region and to deter any acts of dangerous aggression in the South China Sea or Taiwan Straits.

Yet we also need to work with China on other challenges where it's interests align with our own, co-operating where collaboration makes sense (climate change, pandemics, international terrorism) and pursuing mutually beneficial trade and investment.

The legitimate need to discourage and resist China's cyber attacks is not an argument for not doing business with China.

As Downer points out, Australia has become more dependent on trade with China than any other G20 country except South Korea.

A third of Australian exports go to China. China buys more than half of Australia's iron ore. And China has shown it is more than willing to use the leverage of its trading muscle as intimidation if it is displeased by the foreign policy choices of a trading partner.

"Through 2020-23, Australia had direct, and painful, experience of what can happen when China chooses to turn off the taps: beef, barley, wine and lobster exports from Australia were all shut down," he says.

"This is not unique to Australia. It has done the same to others, including Japan and the Philippines."

All the more reason, he says, for Australia and its regional partners to pull their weight on security and defence. This will be a critical commitment if the aim is to keep the superpower — under Donald Trump or any future US president — fully engaged in the region.

In a column for *The Australian* on February 25, 2025, Downer reminded Australians of what had happened in the preceding week just 600km off their eastern coastline.

Three Chinese naval vessels had disrupted and diverted civilian air traffic by conducting military exercises in the Tasman Sea.

The live-fire exercise happened in international waters. But it was intended clearly to intimidate both Australia and New Zealand.

Wrote Downer: "The arrogant Chinese live firing naval exercises in our immediate neighbourhood should remind us how critically important a strong, purposeful and energetic United States is to our security."

Downer argues that Australia should heed the lessons in Europe.

"Our country, too, is a rich country but the embarrassment we suffered over the circumnavigation of Australia by the Chinese warships demonstrates that we are not pulling our weight," he says. "AUKUS is years away and we need effective capacity now, not just depending on a call to the US President if things get tough for us."

Downer worries about complacency in Australia on these crucial issues of national security — and the apparent reluctance of many Australians to pay the price of defence self-reliance:

> I don't know why people have come to think the Americans are responsible for our security. The alliance is not about America just coming to our aid if Ruritania happens to invade Australia. If America was to support Australia militarily, they would only do so if it was in America's interests.
>
> It probably would be in their interests. But if we think we don't need to worry about our own security, and we can just rely on the Americans to sort it out for us, that would be a huge mistake.
>
> Australians love their country, and you would have thought they would be prepared to defend it to the last man. Why would they think America would be prepared to make the sacrifices to defend Australia while Australians spend all their money on welfare handouts?
>
> Look, the Americans are great friends and we get a great deal out of the ANZUS alliance. But, frankly, it is unreasonable to expect the Americans to pay for our defence.

Downer has direct experience of Washington's expectation that Australia can and should fend for itself in its own neighbourhood:

> We were able to intervene in East Timor to facilitate that

country's independence, we were able to sort out the Solomon Islands and we were able to do that with minimal support from the Americans.

That didn't weaken our alliance. The fact we could do things ourselves reinforced our value to the alliance. That's what the Europeans should be doing right now in Ukraine …

Downer is not as fearful as some more hawkish analysts about the threat of Chinese military adventurism in Australia's part of the world.

But he concedes military planners in Australia have to prepare for worst-case scenarios — as an example, in the event of a Chinese assault on Taiwan. If the US was to respond militarily, and sought the support of allies like Australia and Japan, what might be the risks for Australia? What might China do in those circumstances?

"I doubt they would be wanting to deploy too many resources to far-off Australia," he says. "But they might want to put a chokehold on. That is, by sending four or five warships and submarines into our waters, mining our major ports, and firing some ballistic missiles at military, communications and energy facilities. They would want to block our oil imports because energy drives the economy."

Downer says scenarios like this, albeit hypothetical, point to the urgent need for Australian governments to spend more on the defence capabilities that might deter or frustrate such a strategy — like, for example, minesweepers and missile defence systems.

He supports the AUKUS arrangements with the US and Britain, but worries that Australia's insistence on building most of the proposed nuclear-propelled submarines in Australia will add exponentially to the costs and likely delays in the project. "It's bloody-mindedness," he says. "We could save a lot of money by buying them off-the shelf, as we could also do with missile defences. That would save a lot of money in the Defence budget that is currently being diverted from investment in other important capabilities."

He says that Australians must come to accept that more defence spending is vital to future security. For one thing, it will be important in demonstrating to the US that Australians are lifters not leaners — critical if American taxpayers are to be convinced that the huge investment they make in military assets in the Indo-Pacific is worth it.

According to Downer:

> Economic dependence on trade with China, without the countervailing weight of the US strategic presence would leave Australia exposed.
>
> Australian security and foreign policy independence both depend on a balance of power in the Indo-Pacific that prevents China from coercing Canberra or the partners important to it. As a result, Canberra's aim should be to engage and hedge — reaping the benefits of extensive economic relations with China while enhancing its security relationships with the United States and like-minded regional partners.
>
> In this way, Australia's economic dependency on China enhances rather than diminishes the rationale for a closer security relationship with the United States and others.

Like all other close observers of China, Downer is keeping a weather eye on the economic challenges faced by the Communist Party into the 2020s. An industrial leviathan China may be, but it is also wrestling with some debilitating structural afflictions.

Essentially, China's relatively anaemic growth in more recent years is a product of over-investment by government in property construction. The effect has been to fuel a real estate asset bubble. And, in the mid-2020s, the moment of reckoning appeared to have arrived.

As many as 90 million houses and apartments stood empty across the country while local provincial governments drowned in debt. Described as the world's biggest Ponzi scheme, it left exposed and vulnerable the everyday Chinese families who had poured savings into real estate investment. Consumer spending began to dry up, profits slumped and youth unemployment spiralled. Banks became reluctant to lend. And, where once China was regarded as a relatively safe bet for global capital, foreign investors began to flee in droves.

Downer says the economic headwinds confronting China's political system are significant — but far from catastrophic: "China's economic growth is moderating. We may well be approaching that moment of

Peak China, when the decline of its working age population begins to stifle its capacity to grow.

> Yet it is and will remain a global power over the century to come.
>
> China must be taken seriously. Containment is not an option. We cannot contain China. We should not seek to contain China. We should aim for a policy of co-existence.
>
> But you don't do that in a weak way. Weakness is provocative.
>
> I think there's a strong way of doing that. And that's by having robust deterrence, and a robust power balance in the Indo-Pacific region. We can't allow the region to become a Chinese lake... that would be hugely destabilising. All sorts of catastrophic consequences would flow from that. So we have to stop that...
>
> Peace comes from strength. Australia has been really successful, in working not just with the Americans but with Japan, South Korea to some extent, and working with India as well — through the Quad, through AUKUS, and in just reinforcing the American network of alliances. I think all of this has done a great deal to underwrite that power balance the region needs.
>
> I think Australia won a lot of plaudits for the way it stood up to China despite the economic sanctions it imposed. I think it is one reason why China has — well, they haven't changed *strategy* but they have changed their *tactics*, in engaging with countries they see as allies of the Americans. They have gone softer on Australia.

So what would be Downer's advice to Australian governments today in their dialogue with China? He insists China must accept there are rules to be followed if the relationship is to flourish: no Chinese investment in key strategic assets like Australia's telecommunications; no cyber attacks on vital information networks; no attempts to limit or shut down the South China Sea as an international waterway for global trade; and no attempts by force or coercion to change the status of democratic Taiwan.

Says Downer:

> Look, if I were the Foreign Minister today, and the Chinese foreign minister was visiting Australia, I would say to him, 'It's like this. We're happy to trade with you and we're happy to have two-way investment.
>
> But you have to understand that there are sensitive parts of our economy where we will not allow you to invest just as there are sensitive parts of China's economy where you will not allow us to invest. I can't imagine you would be allowing us to invest in your telecommunications networks and so on. Well, we feel the same way. It makes us feel a bit insecure. So we will set these restrictions. Other than that, we're happy to have wholesale engagement.
>
> But we do expect you to abide by the rule of law, not the rule of the jungle. We expect you to adhere to international law. According to international law, the South China Sea is an open international waterway and there should be freedom of navigation. It's as simple as that. We expect you to acknowledge, and adhere to, the rule of law.
>
> So that's it. Just make simple, clear points to them, very politely.
>
> You have to be frank with them —politely, but tell it like it is. If we do that, we can get the relationship on the right footing. You won't get it right by fawning to them...
>
> The message we're sending to China is — don't cross the line. There is a power structure in the Indo-Pacific that you will not be able to defeat or overwhelm or subjugate and there are structures in place that demonstrate that. We're happy to engage with you — but operate within the rules-based system.
>
> The same goes for Russia. I signed a nuclear safeguards agreement which would have created a pathway for the supply of Australian uranium to Russian — for peaceful uses, of course.
>
> So we have been happy to engage with Russia. But, now, they have crossed the line, literally as well as figuratively.

A relaxed moment with UN Secretary-General Ban Ki Moon
(Chung Sun-Jung/Getty Images)

They have invaded a neighbouring country. I never thought I would see it …

So how is the "international community" to respond to naked aggression by powerful, well-armed nation-states with little apparent regard for a rules-based international system?

Downer says it is naive to expect the UN to be able to resolve questions of peace and security involving global powers. "We now have (in Russia) a member of the Permanent Five of the Security Council, a nuclear power, who has invaded a neighbouring country.

"Look, the UN is a huge organisation with many agencies, some of which do a lot of very good work. But when it comes to security issues, it is often deadlocked. That's always been thus, with the vetoes of the P5. So that's a weakness of the system. But the system itself, the organisation itself, would not have been created without those vetoes for the major powers. That was the price to be paid for setting it up."

Downer says the role of the UN Secretary-General can be influential. It carries an element of the bully pulpit: a power emanating through use of language, through persuasion, through moral standing. But it hinges almost entirely on the force of character of the individual in the job.

"To be brutally frank, Antonio Guterres (the current Secretary-General) doesn't do that. The guy was Prime Minister of Portugal. I dealt with him myself over East Timor through the 1990s.

"Nice man, and he was certainly very helpful on the East Timor issue. No problem there. But the fact is this is a job a couple of sizes too big for him. You need a really major global figure to be head of the United Nations. Someone who can inspire …"

Downer says this structural weakness is evident across the leadership of many multilateral institutions — partly because national leaders in many parts of the world are understandably wary about protecting their own sovereignty and therefore reluctant to bestow too much power on leaders of these organisations.

Over the years, Downer worked closely with Ban Ki-moon. As South Korean Foreign Minister. And at the UN. They go back a long way.

Yet Downer is not interested in gilding the lily about the challenges Ban faced in leading the UN: "Nice guy. Lovely guy. But when the Syrian civil war broke out, he went on TV and said, 'I call on all parties to lay down arms'. You could almost see them sitting around coffee shops in Damascus laughing. He was without authority."

So should Australia have supported Kevin Rudd's nomination for UN Secretary-General in 2016? Downer laughs: "I think he might have melted the whole system down, as he did the Australian Government."

23

THE LIGHTNING BOLT

At the time of writing, Alexander Downer had never met Donald Trump. Not was he expecting an invitation any time soon to the Trump private residence at Mar-a-Lago. The two men have a vexed history. "Some of the more hysterical Trump supporters actually wanted to have me locked up at Guantanamo Bay," says Downer.

In November, 2024, the morning after Trump's historic comeback victory, Downer offered some reassurance to Australians uncertain about what Trump's return to power might mean for the relationship with the superpower: "The only Australian I can think of who will be in bad odour with Donald Trump is me."

Alexander Downer's travails with the Trump Administration date back to 2016, when he found himself in the midst of a global political and media firestorm involving allegations relating to Trump's rumoured relationship with Russia. As Downer would later explain in a column for *The Australian*: "I don't think he will ever forgive me for passing on information his own aide gave me that the Russians had intelligence on Hillary Clinton that could be damaging."

In that year, it was almost impossible not to be aware of the headlines surrounding Downer's meeting with a young Trump adviser in May at a London wine bar. The outcome of that chat over gins-and-tonic helped fuel a controversy that raged for years to come, peaking with an FBI investigation into allegations of improper Russian interference in a US presidential election.

The central claim, never substantiated: that the Trump camp had inside information that Russian intelligence had a "dirt file" on the Democrat nominee Hillary Clinton and that this would be unleashed during the 2016 election campaign to destroy her chances and allow Trump a clear, unhindered run at the presidency.

Downer was Australia's High Commissioner to the United Kingdom at the time. As he explains it in an interview for this book, the saga began with him taking up an offer of a "get to know you" meeting with a member of the Trump team. One of his political counsellors at the High Commission, Erika Thompson, set up through a friend a conversation for her boss with Trump aide, George Papadopoulos.

Downer went into the meeting unconvinced that Papadopoulos could offer much in the way of piercing insights into the Trump election campaign or of the likely approach a Trump Administration would bring to US foreign policy. Nonetheless, he agreed to host drinks at the Kensington Wine Rooms, in London's inner west. The conversation lasted for only one hour. The drinks cost about $40.

Papadopoulos has since claimed he believed Downer was really only interested in the meeting because he wanted to scold Papadopoulos over a public attack he had launched on David Cameron, after the British PM made some negative comments about Trump.

As it turned out, Downer says he found the meeting useful enough. "Actually, he was very good," says Downer. "He seemed very young and inexperienced. But not wacky or anything. And what he had to say about Trump's foreign policy proved to be pretty right.

"He said Trump would not withdraw from NATO and that he would be tough on China. Would he impose sanctions on China? He said Trump would do that. So what he said was pretty much right.

"Towards the end of the conversation, I asked whether Trump would win the Republican nomination. He said he would.

"I then asked about the general election. Would he win the presidency over Hillary Clinton? He said he thought Trump would beat Hillary."

Here is where the conversation went off on a wild tangent.

As Downer remembers it: "He then said that while she was miles ahead at that time in the opinion polls, Russian intelligence had a whole lot of information about Hillary that they would release before the election. In his view, that information would do her a lot of damage.

"I didn't really place much value in what he had said. I didn't really believe it. But we sent two cables back to Canberra. Erika drafted them. I signed off on them."

Six weeks later, on July 22, after Trump had been endorsed as the Republic nominee, and three days before the Democratic National Convention voted to endorse Hillary Clinton as their nominee, Wikileaks unfurled a huge story. It dumped 20,000 documents claiming to be emails from the Democrats' archives. The source? Hackers said to be working for Russia's GRU intelligence agency.

"This was looking bad," says Downer. It is perhaps important to remember here that Downer himself, while the UN's special adviser in Cyprus, had been a victim of a 'black ops' campaign of disinformation orchestrated by Russian intelligence operatives. He knew their tricks.

Downer arranged to meet the US charges d'affaires in London, Elizabeth Dibble, to alert her to what Papadopoulos had told him. Things were about to heat up. Big time.

The FBI launched an investigation, then known by its codename Crossfire Hurricane. Within hours, it had sent two agents to London to question Downer. According to the New York Times, only a handful of officials were aware of the mission. The results, summarised and sent to Washington on August 2, reportedly laid the foundations for an investigation in the US by special counsel Robert Mueller.

Mueller would be exploring whether there was any evidence of collusion between Russian intelligence and the Trump campaign. Eventually, in December, 2017, the story broke publicly. "So this is all over the front page of the *New York Times*," says Downer. "And the Australian media went totally berserk."

In 2018, Papadopoulos would spend 12 days in a US federal penitentiary after pleading guilty to making false statements to the FBI when they interviewed him about alleged connections between the Russians and the Trump election campaign. He would later write a book about the controversy, claiming he had been set up as part of a conspiracy among Western intelligence networks to damage the Trump campaign. Describing Downer as pivotal to the plot, he denounced him as "the devil from Down Under."

Then and since, Downer has dismissed the Papadopoulos claims as a bizarre conspiracy theory. In an interview in 2019 with Chris Kenny on *Sky News*, he sought to clear the air, insisting he had reported back to Canberra only on what Papadopoulos had told him. He had felt dutybound to do so — even though the story seemed far-fetched.

"I have no idea why he was blabbering this," Downer said in the interview. "But if you say that sort of thing to somebody who is part of the Five Eyes intelligence community...(the shared intelligence network between the US, Canada, the UK, Australia and NZ) ... I mean, I would regard myself as a warrior for the Western alliance..."

Despite his attempts to dispel some of the hysteria around these events, Downer acknowledges he has paid a price: "Trump hates me for it. It's seen by his people to be the basis of the Mueller Report."

What did Trump know of Downer at that time? Probably only that he was a senior Australian diplomat and some sort of big wheel around Westminster and Whitehall. In inimitable Trump style, Downer would suddenly become "that Downing guy."

Downer would soon learn, second-hand, of a meeting at Mar-a-Lago where Trump used particularly florid language in denouncing Downer: "What the f**k is this guy up to? What is all this about?"

"I think he made a bit of a mistake, here," says Downer, curtly. "I was not a hostile force." Downer says that, whether or not Trump was someone to hold grudges, the issue had continued to bubble up via a lot of Trump's MAGA supporters: "I have had to put up with years of Trump's people claiming I was part of some sort of conspiracy with Hillary Clinton, the FBI, MI6, ASIS and who knows who else, to bring him down ... I didn't really bother about that stuff. I tried to ignore it."

In Australia, too, Downer came in for some stern criticism — from no less than his one-time colleague and former Liberal Prime Minister, Malcolm Turnbull. In a 2022 interview for a book by journalist Richard Kerbaj, The Secret History of the Five Eyes, Turnbull delivered a firm rebuke: "What he did would have got any other ambassador sacked. It was reckless, self-indulgent and put the Australian Government in a very awkward position... blurting out political gossip ... worst possible way to do it."

Turnbull's anger was not so much about the cable itself, with the information provided by Papadopoulos dismissed in Canberra as mostly wild innuendo. What infuriated the Prime Minister back in Australia was Downer's decision to go to the US Embassy in London and pass on through official circles the information he had been given.

For his part, Downer seems untroubled by the criticism from his friend and former colleague: "I don't think I ever spoke to Malcom about it. I don't think he ever spoke to me about it. Whatever he might have to say about it now, I doubt he would have tried to have me sacked."

Self-evidently, Downer does not speak as someone who belongs to a mutual admiration society with the US President. Far from it. This makes his analysis of Trump's foreign policy all the more fascinating.

It is hardly a revelation to make the point that Donald Trump's journey to the White House (twice) would prove quite unlike that of any other US President. As Trump stormed back into power in Washington in January, 2025, the world looked on anxiously as the most idiosyncratic 'leader of the free world' in history sent the planet into a spin, shaking and rattling the chessboard of global politics and the international trading system like almost never before.

In the first month alone of his second term as president, he embarked on a geo-political frenzy, proposing radical US policy shifts on Gaza, Ukraine, the Panama Canal, Greenland, and threatening trade wars with his closest neighbours, Canada and Mexico.

Temperamentally and tactically, Trump was a disrupter like no other ... the risks were high, the results unpredictable. Allies and adversaries of the US alike could never be entirely sure of Trump's aims or motivations. Like everyone else, Downer had been studying closely the strategic signals sent by Trump at the outset of his second term.

Downer has always sought to be forensic. There would be no snap judgments about Trump. He would look carefully behind the bluster and brinksmanship in search of what exactly Trump was intending: What were his top-end priorities? What were his over-arching goals?

The Australian experience of Trump's first presidency was that it proved more stable and benign than many feared. Broadly, across those first four years, the strategic dialogue with Trump and his Secretary of State, Mike Pompeo, was strong.

As soon as was he back in the White House in 2025, Trump provided a foretaste of his approach in his second term to global diplomacy. He began to unfurl some radically confronting visions for both Gaza and Ukraine. In both conflicts, he would seek to play the role of peacemaker. But this would be mostly through political and economic pressure and with one strict caveat — no US troops.

In Gaza, it seemed to be his expectation that Arab states would have to step up to forge a workable solution in the Middle East, particularly when it came to the fate — and permanent address — of the Palestinian people. Jordan, Egypt and Saudi Arabia all protested.

As for the Ukraine, he opened negotiations with Vladimir Putin with a proposal that sent shudders through Kyiv and most other capitals of Europe. At face value, it looked like the US expected Ukraine to surrender territory and deliver Putin permanent control over his ill-gotten gains.

Perhaps more significantly still, his approach also implied that the Europeans would have to do the heavy lifting to preserve the long-term security of Ukraine against any future threat of Russian encroachments. Without explicit NATO guarantees. Or US troops.

Trump was proposing all of this while at the same time threatening to punish allies and enemies alike with reciprocal tariffs — as well as unprovoked unilateral tariffs — to protect American industry from international competition. This departure by the leader of the world's biggest economy from the notion of an open, global trading system carried the risk of igniting global trade wars, fuelling higher inflation, and undermining the integrity of the free trade principles that had underpinned much of the world's economic growth and prosperity.

Questions were legitimately being asked: did Trump's policy of America First mean, in effect, the abandonment of the US model of global leadership? If so, where would this leave allies like Australia?

Downer, for his part, refused to be lured into panicked responses: "The first thing that needs to be said is that Trump has done exactly what he said he would do during his election campaign."

Downer opposes philosophically Trump's resort to tariffs — he sees it as a recipe for economic self-harm. He regarded Trump's tirade against Canada as especially harsh. Yet he could understand American frustration over the double standards of those condemning Trump's punitive tariffs policy: "I can see where Trump is coming from on this."

Downer finds it hard to stomach what he calls "the self-righteousness and moralising" of the EU, in particular:

> It is rank hypocrisy. The Europeans impose all sorts of

tariffs, including on American cars. They impose import quotas on steel, on agriculture ... you name it. It's not surprising that, one day, a US President would get cross about it.

We ourselves have complained over and over to the Europeans about the same thing. At one point, the (Albanese) Government abandoned the free trade talks with the EU on the basis they could not get anything done. But while they (the EU) don't care so much about us — when it's America, they do care — because it's such a behemoth of the global economy. That said, it's not good for America. Imposing tariffs is self harm. Unless it is used merely as a device by the Americans to leverage more and freer access to the markets of its trading partners.

On the strategic front, many saw Trump's posturing on Gaza and Ukraine as destructive and chaotic. Downer's initial diagnosis was less alarmist. He went in search of a coherent strategic framework behind Trump's series of announcements rather than simply writing it all off as a death-wish for the Western alliance.

Downer would withhold on hard-and-fast conclusions until there had been more opportunity to see how the Trump strategies unfolded.

As for the impact on Australia. "I don't think the ANZUS alliance is any more at risk than it was ever was, really," says Downer.

Through his newspaper columns, Downer took the opportunity, in the days before and after Trump's comeback election victory, to hose down some of the initial hysteria about Trump in his second iteration.

He issued some public guidance to the political class in Australia about the dangers of exaggerating the risk he represents. "Do we Australians have anything to fear from a Trump presidency? Generally speaking, I think Trump will continue to maintain a strong alliance and that AUKUS will be secure."

But Downer also warned that nothing was set in concrete. To ensure a strong alliance into the future, Australian Governments had to invest in the alliance ... financially, through a much-expanded Defence budget; and, strategically, by continuing to align unambiguously (and unapologetically) with the US as well as the broader Western alliance.

Ahead of the 2024 presidential election, Alexander Downer had made no secret of his disappointment in what he saw as the failed strategies of the Obama and Biden Administrations: leaving the Afghan people at the mercy of the Taliban; failure to more resolutely deter Putin's aggression in Europe; failure to stop Iran using its proxies to make mischief in the Middle East; failure to deter Chinese adventurism over Taiwan and the South China Sea.

Downer draws a parallel with Chamberlain's de-escalation approach in the 1930s. "It didn't work then and it isn't working now," he says.

He was hoping for a different brand of leadership from Washington to the style and approach of Obama and Biden:

> I think the Western alliance had become disoriented and less self-confident as a result of the troubles over Iraq and Afghanistan and the Global Financial Crisis. They have been unsure about what to do strategically.
>
> They needed more unity. They will never be completely united; as democracies, there will always be differences. But they need to be able demonstrate to their adversaries that they must not cross the red line.
>
> Since the end of the Cold War and the creation of a more united Europe, Europe should have made a much bigger contribution to regional defence, not just dependent on America.
>
> Instead, European nations have been spending their wealth on an ever-growing welfare system and, more recently, on eye-wateringly expensive climate change policies.

Just one month into his new term, President Trump's foreign policy initiatives alone were generating tens of billions of words of analysis and commentary around the world, in every known language. He was creating more headlines than any President in history.

Trump's approach to the conflicts in both Ukraine and Israel seemed to prompt more questions than answers. What was he up to? And what message did these early signals send to allies like Australia about Trump's preparedness to invest in and consolidate America's global alliances? What were his operating principles? What was his underlying philosophy about the exercise of America's global power?

For all of his chequered history with Trump, Downer spends a lot of time in the US and maintains regular contact with people who know the inside workings of the Trump Administration — people like Trump's former chief of staff, Mick Mulvaney. Downer was one of very few to argue in those frenzied early days that Trump might have had a bigger play in mind. He explained his line of thinking: "Over the past decade or so, America and its allies have been perceived as weak. As a result, China, Russia and Iran have shown no fear of the West, exploited its hesitancy and its weakness, and created havoc in Ukraine, the Middle East and the South China Sea. Turning around that failure of Western policy is going to be a huge challenge."

Downer says this might help explain why Trump saw the war in Ukraine from a perspective quite different to that of the Europeans:

> His perspective is that America is in an existential tussle with China, that Russia is a relatively small threat by comparison, and rich Europe should easily be able to take the lead in handling Russia — with back-up from the Americans. America should be fixing the Middle East and deterring Chinese aggression. Trump is right.

Downer said it was time for the Europeans in particular to take a look in the mirror when it came to their response to Russia's aggression: "We need to admit it: the West ceded Crimea to Russia in 2014."

Yes, the Western powers had imposed economic sanctions in 2014. But, for years after Russia's illegal annexation of Crimea, Germany had continued business-as-usual by importing vast quantities of gas from Russia via Nord Stream 1. It also pressed on with construction of Nord Stream 2. All while Russia still held 10 per cent of Ukraine.

Then, in February, 2022, Russia launched its all-out invasion of Ukraine. This time, the US, Europe and other Western allies supplied arms to Ukraine — but never enough weaponry to stop the invasion, or to provide Ukraine with the means to win back the Donbas and Crimea. They worried that if they did, it would "escalate" the conflict.

Three years later, Russia still controlled about 17-18 per cent of Ukraine. Enter Trump. "He wanted to end the slaughter," Downer wrote for *The Australian*:

> He had two choices. Either launch a huge attack on Russian

troops in Ukraine, driving them out of the country altogether, or negotiate a ceasefire with the Russians, and leave the Ukrainians and Europeans to negotiate a peace treaty.

America also has to deal with Iran and China. In the ceasefire talks in Saudi Arabia, I have heard — but cannot verify — that the Americans linked the ceasefire to Russian agreement not to supply Iran with S400 anti-aircraft missile systems.

What about the Europeans? Well, Trump was apparently shown a map recently that identified which countries made the most energetic contribution to the defence of the continent. Poland and the Baltic republics were identified and no one else.

Trump then asked about the GDP of Germany, Britain and France.

When told these countries were, in order, the fourth, fifth and sixth biggest economies in the world, Trump understandably wondered why the Europeans were so incapable of defending their own continent, and why were they so dependent on America. After all, Germany's GDP alone is more than double that of Russia.

It's little wonder Trump has started lashing out at the Europeans. They're happy for American taxpayers and servicemen and women to underwrite European security. For all their wealth, they are quick to condemn the Americans for Trump's rather outlandish language (while) their contribution to security is minimal.

Trump is giving priority to deterring China and will want to strengthen America's alliances with Japan, South Korea and the Philippines. He will also want to make sure ANZUS is in good shape.

So just because Trump's language drives the Europeans mad doesn't mean the end of the Western alliance. It's about reassessing priorities and re-allocating burden-sharing.

Trump is brutally telling the Europeans to lift their game and make a bigger contribution to their own security rather than being so dependent on American taxpayers' goodwill.

His language may be a little harsh but the messages make sense ….

Then, in June, 2025, Trump delivered a lightning strike. While several of his predecessors had mounted military action against adversaries in the Middle East, none of the previous seven US presidents had risked what Trump attempted — a direct hit on the nuclear weapons programs of the Islamic Republic of Iran.

In Downer's view, Trump's actions represented a marked shift in America's strategic posture, critical to re-establishing the principle of deterrence. By sending B2 stealth bombers to Iran to drop 14 massive bunker-buster bombs on Iran's key nuclear facilities at Fordow, Isfahan and Natanz, Trump sent an emphatic message to any adversaries of the Western democratic model intent on destabilisation through military brinkmanship — a message that the superpower was not afraid to act.

Contrary to all the conjecture about the American superpower pulling back from its global leadership role, Trump had demonstrated, at least in this instance, that the US would still be there for its allies in times of danger. But only on the proviso that those same allies had made a meaningful and proportionate commitment to mutual security. Says Downer:

> This is very powerful stuff. Trump succeeded in doing two things. He has got almost all of the NATO partners in Europe to increase their defence budgets — to take matters of defence more seriously rather that just leaving it to the Americans.
>
> Secondly, in effect, he authorised Netanyahu and Israel to take very strong action against Iran. Together, they have been outstanding in quelling Iran, if not neutering Iran. People in the media will never give Trump credit for anything. They hate Trump. They're happy to simply run the narrative that comes out of the Democratic Party playbook in the US. That narrative was that Trump was an isolationist who would withdraw from the world.
>
> So when he acted against Iran, proving it was not true to claim he was an isolationist, they said it wouldn't work. That it wouldn't stop Iran from rebuilding its nuclear technology.

Of course Iran could try to do that. You can't bomb out of existence the knowledge of how to build a nuclear weapon. But it would cost them billions of dollars they don't have. And they would be bombed again if they tried.

According to Downer, the US decision to intervene decisively in Israel's war with Iran was a big step in redefining dramatically many of the assumptions about American power projection under Trump.

For at least a decade, Trump had shared Israel's deep scepticism about whether Iran would ever step back from its nuclear weapons project. In his first presidency, Trump in 2018 had walked away from Barack Obama's Joint Comprehensive Plan of Action — a deal aimed at putting into a diplomatic deep freeze Iran's nuclear ambitions. Trump had demanded that the US Congress and America's international partners address what he saw as "the very serious flaws" in the deal.

Then, in January, 2020, only weeks before completing his first term in office, Trump sent another incendiary signal to Tehran of his frustration at the regime's role in destabilising the Middle East.

Arguing that Iran was still engaging in subterfuge over its nuclear program, building a formidable ballistic missile capability, and sponsoring terrorism and militancy across the region, Trump went on the offensive. Citing terror attacks on the US Embassy in Baghdad by Iran-backed militia, he ordered a pinpoint air strike on a military airport in Tehran that killed Iran's top general, Qassem Soleimani.

Over the intervening years of the Biden presidency, Iran, through its proxies, persisted relentlessly in its harassment of Israel. Then came the seismic moment on October 7, 2023, when Hamas militants launched their barbaric massacre of 1200 Jewish people in southern Israel. In response to the single biggest loss of Jewish lives since the Holocaust, the Netanyahu Government went on the hunt: first, for Hamas in Gaza; then, for Hezbollah operatives and military infrastructure in Lebanon and Syria, and the Houthis in Yemen.

Controversially, Downer admires the resolve of Israeli Prime Minister, Binyamin Netanyahu — in the face of a storm of global protest about the impact on the civilian population of Gaza, including from the Biden Administration in Washington.

"He is hugely brave that guy," says Downer. "Go back to the start of all this (in Gaza). What choices does he have? Does he have any choices? Of course he has. He could have just listened to the Americans: don't go into Rafah; negotiate a ceasefire with Hamas; don't cross the border into Lebanon and don't attack Hezbollah.

"'Thanks very much, guys, for that advice'. Remember, for Netanyahu, this is America, their great patron. They can't do without America. Yet he defied them. And he was proved to be completely right."

As events unfolded, the effectiveness of Israel's military response would stun the world. Over the next two years, it would decapitate the military and political leadership not only of Hamas but also Hezbollah and destroy much of the firepower of Iran's proxies in the region.

But Netanyahu wasn't finished. Sooner or later, there would come a day of reckoning for Iran. Come 2025, the return of Trump to the White House would bring that day closer.

In the first week of February, 2025, Netanyahu was among the first world leaders to visit Trump at the White House after his inauguration. Iran was high on the agenda. Both leaders were acutely aware of rising suspicions of a significant step-up in the Iranian regime's efforts to fast-track its acquisition of a nuclear weapon.

Confirming this, the International Atomic Energy Agency issued a report at the end of February stating that Iran was accelerating its production of weapons-grade uranium. The IAEA assessed that, as of February 8, Iran had 275 kilograms of uranium enriched to 60 per cent. This was half as much again as the IAEA had reported only three months earlier. And 60 per enrichment was, technically, only a small step from achieving the 90 per cent necessary for a nuclear bomb.

Yet, despite the offer of the Trump Administration in the US to broker a new deal, the hardliners in Tehran held stubbornly to their refusal to renounce their nuclear weapons program. As Downer observed bleakly in an article for *The Australian* on June 16, 2025, this had made the likelihood of direct confrontation all but inevitable: "The determination of the Iranian theocratic leadership to eliminate the Jewish state could only end in one of two ways. Either Ayatollah Ali Khameini, the Iranian Supreme Leader, and the hardliners in the Islamic Revolutionary Guard Corps would listen to the moderates in the regime or there would be war."

Downer says there had been a power struggle within the Islamic Republic regime from the beginning of 2025 over whether to resume a constructive dialogue. Pivotal to this would have been an agreement with the US to end once and for all Iran's nuclear weapons program.

One of the proponents of a deal was Mohammad Javad Zarif who was, until March, 2025, Iran's vice president. As a previous foreign minister, he had been at the table for negotiations over Iran's nuclear ambitions. The compromise he proposed to circumvent a direct confrontation with Trump was for a consortium of regional countries to enrich Iran's uranium — sufficient for civil power generation but far short of weapons-grade production. Later, Downer ran into Zarif at a think-tank conference in Beijing. It became apparent to Downer that Zarif had been forced aside by the hardliners.

On April 12, 2025, the US and Iran began a series of negotiations aimed at reaching a nuclear peace agreement and avoiding further escalation. Trump had written to Ayatollah Khameini setting a two-month (60 day) deadline for Iran to come to an agreement. On April 14, Trump outlined his terms for the negotiations: "Iran has to get rid of the concept of a nuclear weapon. They cannot have a nuclear weapon."

In all, over the subsequent two months, there were five rounds of talks. On June 9, the regime in Iran formally rejected the Trump administration's proposal for a new nuclear deal. The main points of disagreement included Iran's right to continue domestic uranium enrichment, the handling of its current stockpiles of highly enriched uranium, and the conditions for lifting economic and other sanctions. These had been much the same stumbling-blocks that had stymied negotiations since 2003.

On June 10, Trump stated in a Fox News interview that Iran was becoming "much more aggressive" in the negotiations. The following day, Iran's Defence Minister, Aziz Nasirzadeh, warned that if negotiations collapsed and conflict erupted, Iran would target American bases in the Middle East.

On June 12, the IAEA found Iran non-compliant with its nuclear non-proliferation obligations.

The IAEA raised concerns over Iran's uranium stockpile, and revealed it had uncovered plans to build a new enrichment site, with advanced centrifuges to speed up the process.

The following morning, at 3.30 am, the day after the expiry of Trump's offer to Iran of a 60-day window to negotiate a deal, Israel sent its Air Force into Iran, bombarding the vital organs of the Iranian regime — targeting its military leadership, its nuclear research scientists, its uranium enrichment facilities and its ballistic missile sites. Within hours, Israel controlled the skies above Iran.

In an opinion piece for *The Australian*, Downer argued Israel was left with no choice but to act: "Right now the Israelis have taken the opportunity to fix this once and for all. If they took the advice of feckless Western politicians such as those in our own government then the war with Iranian proxies would go on and on."

Downer remained convinced that it would be dangerously naive to declare a ceasefire and attempt to negotiate a peace for as long as Hamas still held power in Gaza: "In Jerusalem, I'm sure they've received the advice that they should conclude a two-state agreement with the Palestinians. They've heard that 10,000 times.

"They also know, however, there is no prospect of achieving a two-state solution when the Palestinian resistance is funded, armed and supported by an Iranian regime that wants to wipe Israel off the face of the Earth. Only a diplomatic child would think it was possible to reach an agreement with such people."

When Trump decided to send into Iran America's stealth bombers, accompanied by a barrage of Tomahawk missiles, the regime in Iran found itself more vulnerable and exposed than at any time since its war with Iraq. If it chose peace, it would have to surrender its nuclear ambitions. If it chose to resist, it would be inviting another crushing US response. Trump and Israel's actions left Iran and its proxies severely weakened, if not quite disintegrating as a strategic threat.

What did Downer assess as the medium-term consequences: "Let's ask ourselves what the Iranian people as distinct from the leaders of the theocracy think about all of this. I've asked several people who have lived in Iran in recent times what the reaction to the strikes would be. Their answers are surprising. First, they are frightened. Second, those who do not support the regime — and that is most people in Iran — hope that the attacks on the regime will be successful.

"As Australians, let's ask ourselves what we would want? We would want to see the end of Iran's nuclear program. We would want Israel to live in peace within recognised borders, rather than being subject to periodic and often very violent assaults from Palestinian extremists…"

And what of the implications for the global power balance more generally? In an interview for this book, Downer says the US-Israel action against Iran had sent a clear and dramatic signal: "The message to China is that you can get on with your lives, and we won't interfere with you. But don't mess with us. Don't invade Taiwan. In that sense, I think this will have been very effective."

Yet Trump remains unpredictable. His next foreign policy gambit was to invite Vladimir Putin to a summit in mid-August at an air base in Alaska to discuss proposals for a ceasefire in Ukraine. It presented a platform for Putin to return to the global stage, after being isolated as an international pariah after ordering the invasion of a neighbour.

Trump wanted to build an image as a peace-maker. But, when the Russians flew in, it was evident they had their own message to send, their own strategy to pursue. Foreign Minister Sergei Lavrov arrived early in Anchorage, walking into a hotel foyer in a jumper emblazoned with the initials CCCP — the acronym symbolic of the old Soviet Union.

Just a lame joke, by way of gentle provocation? Or more a branding exercise — implying, perhaps, that, under Putin, the USSR was on the comeback trail as a rival superpower to the US. In the meetings with Trump, true to the tradition of Stalin and Khrushchev, Putin would prove as intransigent as ever. There would be no immediate ceasefire. As both leaders flew home, peace for Ukraine seemed no closer.

Trump's next steps on the fate of Ukraine would be studied and debated by strategists the world over. More talks would follow, with Zelensky and European leaders. Could Trump broker a workable ceasefire? Said Downer: "Trump has to be given points for trying."

But would he succeed? "Well, the war will end one day," said Downer. "But what will that look like? The Ukrainians have said they will not cede any ground to Russia. I am not sure how that can be made to work without direct American (military) intervention… and you would have to think that is unlikely."

As for East Asia, the tensions in the South China Sea continued to percolate, with ongoing friction between Chinese ships and neighbouring navies seeking to sail through international waters contested by China.

Against this backdrop, Downer held fast to the view that the strategic nexus developed across the previous 70 years — co-operation among the likes of Australia, Japan, South Korea, the Philippines and the island nations of the Pacific, underwritten by the US itself — would continue to be critical to safeguarding regional stability.

Yet he warned there was no guarantee of the US coming to Australia's aid in the face of a serious security challenge in our part of the world without a commensurate commitment from Australian Governments, now and into the future, both to the values of the alliance and to sharing the costs and responsibilities of regional security.

As one prominent example, Downer cited the parting of ways with the US over support for Israel: "If we look at Australia's position on the Middle East, adopting these UN slogans about de-escalation — not to solve the problem, but to postpone the problem indefinitely — it's clear why (the Albanese Government) is getting offside with the Americans."

On August 20, 2025, Downer's instincts about serious concerns emanating from within the Trump Administration about Australia's strategic positioning on the war in Gaza were confirmed by Trump's former UN Ambassador, Kelly Craft. She set out the equation bluntly in an article for *The Australian*, in what she described as a "critical moment" for the alliance:

> In recognising a Palestinian state, Australia is rewarding Hamas's strategy, including its brutal October 7 terrorist attack, its ongoing theft of food aid and its refusal to release Israeli hostages. This is not just a moral outrage. It is also a political blunder. When so much hangs in the balance in the Australian-American relationship, this is no time to antagonise Israel's strongest ally by joining the disgraceful global pile-on.
>
> The Australian-American relationship is critically important to this region and the security of the world. Why on earth would the Prime Minister put President Trump in the position of having to choose between Israel and Australia?

Whether or not Australia's stance on the war in Gaza had come to be regarded in Washington or Canberra as a litmus test for the alliance, the Albanese Government was quick to fall in behind Trump's revised and super-charged peace plan for Gaza, announced in late September, 2025. Even so, it was likely Australia's future positioning on Taiwan and the South China Sea would prove a more critical calculation. Downer argues Australians should be considering very carefully the values at the core of the alliance: "The US is not going to step away from AUKUS. But whether they are going to sell Australia, as one component of AUKUS, the Virginia-class nuclear submarines is more of a question.

> My argument is that the more Australia looks like a weak ally, rather than a robust ally, the less likely it is that the Americans will want to give up that Virginia-class capability to Australia ... these are submarines they would otherwise have in the US Navy.
>
> There is an advantage to the Americans if we are a strong ally, with state-of-the-art military equipment. And that probably does mean having those submarines.
>
> But I think the Americans are having some doubts about Australia. Not that they think Australia is not an ally. There is no question of that.
>
> But is it becoming an ally like Belgium, for example, that takes for granted the US security umbrella?
>
> Alliances are a two-way street where both sides are expected to make a contribution. You are either in it or you're not. That's always been my view. That's why we were in Afghanistan and Iraq.
>
> If you think the Alliance only counts for something if we happen to need help — well, will we get that help? I am not sure.
>
> What Trump has taught the world is that the age of loading security responsibilities on the shoulders of American taxpayers without bothering with our own defence is over. The alliance remains strong. But it is reciprocal — not a relationship of total dependency.

Alexander Downer may never be Donald Trump's favourite Australian. But he is also likely to be the last Australian you could ever imagine going wobbly on the importance to Australia of the global and regional security networks anchored by the American alliance — or on the imperative to defend core Western values of democracy and freedom.

Whoever happens to be President.

24

THE ART OF STATESMANSHIP

There's a tendency to dismiss stalwarts from the Howard years as ghostly figures from the past. John Howard, Peter Costello and Alexander Downer, in particular, remain heroes in the Liberal Party pantheon. But today's teenagers would have no memory of their achievements — only perhaps a vague sense from older generations that there were days not so long ago when Australia was somehow governed differently from what they know today.

What was it that distinguished their leadership values from those of other governments in Australia? Together, Howard, Costello and Downer brought unity of purpose and consistency of principle to how they managed the nation.

Did they agree on everything? Hardly. Did they manage to contain and quell policy, political and personal differences — among themselves, and across the rest of the ministry and Coalition backbench? Not always — but far better than almost all other governments to have served in Canberra before or since. As a result, they got things done.

The Howard Government was far from flawless. It faced battalions of trenchant critics, given the many contentious and painful decisions it made: think new national gun control laws; think the intervention of Australia's armed forces in East Timor; think the decision to back the Bush Administration in wars in Afghanistan and Iraq; think the decision to turn back the *Tampa*, and to impose tough controls on illegal entry by boat of unauthorised asylum-seekers.

They very nearly lost office in 1998, at their first election since returning to power, when Howard took to the electorate a politically perilous proposal to rebalance the nation's tax mix through the introduction of a broad-based consumption tax.

Yet, by any comparative measure, those four consecutive terms in government were highly successful: economically, politically, strategically. The malaise of instability and infighting that would curse governments of both persuasions in the years that followed provides a stark contrast with the unflustered steadiness of the Howard Years.

As Alexander Downer remarked wryly in a 2023 speech in Melbourne: "Are you missing us yet?"

Downer, as an example, walked the halls of power across the world with an assuredness reflecting the Australian character of his times: confident, clear-eyed, outward-looking. He was driven by results — meaningful change for the better: how to safeguard the nation's security; how to create the conditions for increasing prosperity; how to enhance opportunities for more Australians to make more of their lives, at home and globally; how to build the nation.

It can seem like an era long ago. The Howard Government's extended stretch in office pre-dated the Global Financial Crisis. It was before any of Barack Obama, Donald Trump or Joe Biden had their feet beneath the desk in the Oval Office. The late Shinzo Abe was in his first iteration of power in Japan. Tony Blair's "New Labour" held sway in Britain.

It preceded the more hardline leadership of China's Xi Jinping. It preceded Vladimir Putin's military adventurism in Georgia, Syria and Ukraine. It preceded the US withdrawals from Iraq and Afghanistan. As for the global Digital Revolution, the i-Phone was still in nappies when the Howard Government departed office.

So what practical lessons are there to be drawn from the experiences of the Howard Government — from the way it functioned as a government, the values it adopted, the policies it pursued?

Can this offer any sort of template for how Australians seek to deal with the challenges they face in today's very different world?

In December, 2022, Alexander Downer gave a free-ranging speech in Melbourne entitled *The Art of Statesmanship*. The speech provided an expansive account of his thoughts on how and why the Howard Government achieved the successes it did. He went on to ponder lessons for the future. Delivered as the *10th annual John Howard Lecture* for the Menzies Research Centre, the speech also provided some insights into Downer's own philosophies on political leadership.

According to Downer, there were four key factors that helped to explain the success and longevity of the Howard Government. These were what he considered the essentials of enlightened political leadership for a centre-right government, in Australia or elsewhere.

The first of these was a strong commitment to underlying political values — which, in his view, meant the promotion of the liberal values of open markets, the rights and responsibilities of the individual, and the core principles of liberal democracy.

By interpreting wisely the trends of history, good leaders understood not only how these values could and would be tested, but how, with the right leadership, they could be strengthened and reinforced.

The second factor was the importance of acting on your convictions: demonstrating the political courage to do the right thing rather than what opinion polls may suggest is politically opportune or convenient. Winning public support for difficult policy choices can be an arduous process — but it can be done. The motto: do not despair; never give up.

The third was the critical importance of delivering clear and concise messages to the electorate. To win an argument, you had to be able to prosecute the case for your policy approach by communicating effectively to the public the need for a particular course of action.

Everyday people may not have time to drill down into macroeconomic trends, or to focus on great shifts in the tectonic plates of geopolitics. But, according to Downer, they would listen to leaders with the capacity to articulate cogently and forcefully what these trends might mean, and what policy responses would best serve the nation.

The fourth factor was unity of purpose within the governing parties. Political leaders could not expect to win the confidence of the nation unless they could manage their own party colleagues with skill and diplomacy. You needed your team to back you in.

According to Downer, both Robert Menzies and John Howard set a gold standard for leadership on all four elements:

> Menzies and Howard were guided by their values and their convictions. They operated within a very clearly defined framework. They were certain in their beliefs and they were confident that the policies they pursued which grew out of those beliefs would be successful ...
>
> Their success didn't just revolve around sensible, practical and effective economic policy, although that was an important part of it ... their success was broader than that. They understood the challenges of the nation and they defined its goals.

> Both Menzies and Howard were passionate believers in what Menzies called selfless individualism. That is, they rejected the popular postwar shibboleths of state control and the subjugation of the will of individuals to the will of the collective.
>
> This was a much bigger issue than economic management … it was about how society should be structured, how decisions should be made and who should make those decisions. They were leaders who put individual choice at the front and centre of their policies.
>
> … at the time, the values and policies of Menzies and Howard were ridiculed and attacked by their political opponents. Sometimes they were popular, often they were not, but these two men were leaders of conviction and courage and pressed on regardless.
>
> They both had a capacity to understand the Australian public and the country's moods without being slaves to opinion pollsters and political advisors with their cunning plans for electoral victory. And although both leaders were at times unpopular within their party and even spurned by the party in their early years, they learnt to manage their colleagues with supreme skill and diplomacy.
>
> These days, too much of politics is nothing more than managerial expediency. How often in private conversations do you hear politicians saying that this policy or that policy may not be popular — they've done the polling and the public don't like it?
>
> The challenge is to communicate with the public and explain to the public what policies are in the country's best interests.

Downer has his own heroes from the 20th century, with Churchill foremost among them for his epic role in the defeat of Fascism in Europe. He is also a devotee of the Centre-Right philosophies promoted by Ronald Reagan and Margaret Thatcher through the 1980s, which — economically and strategically — had the effect of overwhelming the former Soviet Union.

The values that underpinned the Reagan and Thatcher years — a

Meeting one of his political heroes, Margaret Thatcher (Private Collection)

vision of vibrant democracies, individual freedoms, and strict limits on the remit of the State to intervene in markets — were embraced and adapted wholeheartedly by the Howard Government in Australia.

In *The Art of Statesmanship*, however, Downer was forced to admit, grudgingly, that, in the years that followed, these same values had been steadily losing ground in the global battle of ideas:

> Over the last few years the values debate has been won by the progressive left, as they now like to call themselves – being ashamed of the term socialist! They have captured what journalists now would like to call the zeitgeist of the era.
>
> They are happy to see an ever growing proportion of GDP controlled by the state, thereby undermining the core value of freedom of the individual and limiting productivity growth.
>
> On social issues, they have become passionate advocates of identity politics (where) we are defined by characteristics over which we have no control such as our race, gender and our sex lives ...
>
> For most of my life, right-thinking people have regarded a society structured around race as anathema. We abhorred apartheid, we denounced discrimination on the basis of race in the United States, we celebrated the evolution of multi-racial societies. More than that, we abhorred discrimination against women ... and I never thought it was right to demonise homosexuality.
>
> But in recent years, the progressive left has shifted society to a new era of discrimination. Now we are to discriminate against men, against white people, against what is rudely described as *cisgender* people.
>
> If discrimination was wrong, well, it still is ...
>
> Pitting people against each other on the basis of their gender and their race is deeply divisive. We need to learn the lessons of history.
>
> Societies which have been divided into tribal groups, ethnicity and race are doomed to catastrophic failure. Ethnic identity was at the heart of the genocide in Rwanda

in 1994. Ethnic divides catapulted the Balkans into bloody conflict in the 1990s. A racial divide made South Africa a bitter and unsustainable society.

The societies which have worked best have been built on the foundations of tolerance not division. They are societies which respect and treasure each individual person regardless of their physical characteristics.

Downer went on to argue that the trend towards a progressive left orthodoxy had been accelerated by the climate change debate and the global COVID-19 pandemic. Both had presented an opportunity for the progressive left to exercise massive interventions in the economy

"… Just in case you're wondering, I don't think climate change is a myth. It is happening." he said.

"But it is best addressed by investing in research and development in new technologies including nuclear technology rather than imposing greater central control on every aspect of society by the state … to use this issue as a way of destroying aspects of a liberal society is going in the end to be counter-productive."

In that speech, and in many columns and commentaries he has published since, Downer has sought to offer his experience and insights in addressing the challenges facing Australians today.

It remains his view that the times demand more robust political leadership, to rouse Australians from a sense of complacency, and to generate a more earnest, open-minded debate about the choices for the future. As ever, some of these choices will be tough, involving sweat and sacrifice in exchange for greater certainty and security.

Intellectually, this will require a lot more people getting out of their comfort zone. Downer argues that a sometimes slavish adherence to popular or received wisdom — otherwise known as fashionable opinion — needs to be tested and challenged like seldom before. In the 2020s, he is looking for political leadership that breaks the mould.

In his view, only the very greatest leaders of democracies have been able to win the political struggle to persuade a nation to take actions — and to adopt policies — that defy conventional thinking. He puts Churchill at the top of the list in convincing the British people that war against Hitler's Germany was unavoidable to stop the evils of fascism:

> Imagine the pressure Churchill was under with Halifax and all those people saying 'let's make a deal with Hitler'.
>
> The older and more experienced I get, the more I appreciate the tiny number of people in public life like Churchill who have just defied all expectations. Imagine what it was like in Britain in the late 1930s — people in your village or in your suburb were killed 20 years earlier in wars. You knew of so many people who had been killed in the First World War ... 900,000 British soldiers, 1.4 million French.
>
> You can imagine the French and the British saying, 'We do NOT want another war'. You can understand that. And yet Churchill is out there saying to them, 'We have to fight these people'.
>
> Imagine what the average punter thought of that ... imagine the politics of that... well, it's the Overton Window, really.

Downer admits to being a student of the Overton Window, named in honour of the American engineer, lawyer, political scientist and free market libertarian, Joseph P. Overton, who championed the imperative within democracies of politicians being prepared to challenge the orthodoxy by promoting new approaches that might not, at face value, be politically acceptable to the mainstream.

As an example, Downer cites Konrad Adenauer for his capacity to rebuild postwar Germany as an active member of the Western alliance and a liberal market economy. "West Germany had choices and deep debate about whether to be neutral in the Cold War or to back the liberal democracies. Adenauer persuaded them to do the latter," he says. Likewise, he was impressed by the courage of Lech Walesa, the gruff Polish trade union leader, whose audacious campaign to stare down the might of the Soviet Union created a ripple effect across Eastern Europe that led to the dismantling of the Iron Curtain. "He's one of the most interesting people I have met," says Downer.

In 2003, Downer felt privileged to have a private audience at the Vatican with a frail and dying Pope John Paul II, another of the giants in the battle to reclaim the political freedom of hundreds of millions of Eastern Europeans who had lived for four decades under Soviet domination.

And Downer remains forever an admirer of Ronald Reagan and Margaret Thatcher.

"Their convictions turned out to be right," he says. "They took head-on the prevailing orthodoxy of a mixed economy and they promoted liberal market solutions which worked. Their convictions that the Soviet Union had to be confronted and ultimately defeated were ridiculed and decried at the time by supporters of detente and Ostpolitik but turned out to be heroically right."

Downer was a young Australian diplomat in Brussels at the time of the 1980 US presidential election: "The European *bien-pensant* were horrified by Reagan's ideas… but his approach prevailed."

As Downer explained it in a column for *The Australian* on November 18, 2024:

> Once, in America, the idea of detente between the Soviet Union and the West was in the Overton Window… there was no support for the idea that the Cold War with the Soviet Union could be won. Then along came Ronald Reagan and Margaret Thatcher.
>
> They thought detente would never bring lasting peace and was a demonstration of Western weakness. Reagan

A private audience with Pope John Paul II, one of the heroes in helping to liberate Eastern Europe (Private Collection)

deployed intermediate range missiles in Europe and began developing missile defence systems. The establishment was shocked. It was extreme, outside the Overton Window, unacceptable. Except it worked, leading to the end of the stalemate with the Soviet Union.

The Soviets could not compete with the overwhelming prosperity, military technology and determination of America.

How is any of this history of practical relevance in guiding the policy choices of Australians in the 2020s?

In *The Art of Statesmanship*, Downer spoke of the need for a greater sense of sturdiness and self-belief in Australia's political culture:

> In our country as elsewhere there is a great need for statesmanship, statesmanship based on the timeless values of a liberal democratic society and a capacity to make judgements — not all of which will be popular — about how to address the trends and the issues we all face.
>
> It doesn't take greatness to get opinion polls done and parrot back to the public what has been heard in those opinion polls.
>
> It's the job of political leaders to draw issues to the attention of the public and to persuade the public of the wise course to follow.
>
> Great leaders are able to do that …
>
> Such leaders do not come along very often. But they do come along.

Acknowledgments

Alexander Downer would never have written this book himself. Personally, I think that is a pity. He is a talented writer, bringing intellectual heft and a searing forthrightness to his observations and analysis. Yet, after leaving Parliament, he appears to have taken the view that political memoirs or autobiographies should be the preserve of a select few — perhaps only the most outstanding prime ministers and government leaders. The notion of him sitting down to chronicle his own life and career was never a starter.

Nor was he particularly welcoming of anyone else taking on the task. Indeed, after one of British Prime Minister Tony Blair's advisers crafted a biography of his old boss, Downer warned one of his own senior staffers (not the author) that he would look very unkindly on anyone who attempted the same with him.

There were always others who thought Downer's was a story that should be told in full. Former federal Treasurer and deputy Liberal leader, Josh Frydenberg, was prominent among them. Having witnessed at close quarters Downer's ambitions for Australia and Australians — and the resolve and conviction he brought to the task across more than a decade — Josh was adamant this contribution should be acknowledged and respected.

As those who know him can attest, when Josh Frydenberg gets an itch about something he thinks should be made to happen — something

Alexander Downer campaigning with Josh Frydenberg for
the Federal seat of Mayo

important and meaningful — he rarely if ever lets it rest. He was able to persuade a sceptical Alexander Downer to agree to the project; to persuade him there were enough people out there who thought this book mattered. I am thankful to those who supported this view — who backed in the idea that the Downer years in diplomacy provided lessons not just about the past but also for the present and future.

Certainly, Alexander Downer has been exceedingly generous in gifting many hours of interviews for this book — often early in the mornings or late at nights during his work in places like San Francisco or London. Without his co-operation, this book would never have been possible.

I am also grateful to friends and colleagues like Greg Hunt and Chris Kenny for sharing their insights. Likewise, I extend my thanks to Georgina Downer at the Robert Menzies Institute ... and to Nicky Downer for her hospitality in Adelaide, and for her forbearance when I routinely interfered in family time while conducting my research.

Detailed accounts of momentous events like the East Timor, Bougainville and Solomon Island interventions — and the renewal of relations with modern Indonesia — would have been much the poorer without the contributions of senior diplomats like Bill Farmer and Nick Warner. I thank Newspix and Getty Images (along with the Downer family) for the photos used in illustrating this book.

In particular, I thank former Prime Minister John Howard for agreeing to an extended interview — and for providing his foreword to the book. No study of Alexander's life and career would have been complete without John Howard's frank observations.

I am also indebted to Anthony Cappello at Connor Court Publishing for supporting this project. As the head of one of Australia's leading independent publishers, Anthony is a significant contributor to a genuine contest of ideas in this country. He is never afraid to publish those who might swim against the tide of fashionable opinion. I also express my appreciation to editor, Michael Gilchrist, for his patient and painstaking professionalism in bringing this book to life.

Finally, my gratitude to Kirsty and my own family for allowing me to indulge — near obsessively, some might say — in this project. It adds to the catalogue of the many times I have upended the normal rhythms of life to pursue my own interests or preoccupations. I thank them for their love and understanding.

Select Bibliography and References

For a broader, deeper understanding of Australia's foreign policy development in the postwar years — and more generally, the sweep of global politics and conflict in the years during and after the Cold War — I have found the following publications, among others, to be illuminating and instructive:

Australia and near-neighbourhood

Ball, Desmond & Cathy Downe, Editors, *Security and Defence: Pacific and Global Perspectives*, Allen & Unwin, 1990.

Edwards, Peter & David Goldsworthy, Editors, Department of Foreign Affairs and Trade, *Facing North*, Volume 2, Melbourne University Press, 2003.

Evans, Gareth & Bruce Grant, *Australia's Foreign Relations in the World of the 1990s*, Melbourne University Press, 1991.

Flood, Philip, *Dancing with Warriors: A Diplomatic Memoir*, Arcadia, 2011.

Goldsworthy, David, Editor, Department of Foreign Affairs and Trade, *Facing North*, Volume 1, Melbourne University Press, 2001.

Hawke, Bob, *The Hawke Memoirs*, William Heinemann Australia, 1994.

Holdich, Roger, Vivienne Johnson, Pamela Andre, Editors, *The ANZUS Treaty, 1951*, Department of Foreign Affairs and Trade, 2001.

Howard, John, *The Menzies Era*, Harper Collins, 2014.

Stockings, Craig, *Born of Fire and Ash: the official history of Australian peace keeping operations in East Timor*, UNSW Press, 2022.

Cold War and aftermath

Revel, Jean-Francois, *The Totalitarian Temptation*, Penguin, 1978.

Thatcher, Margaret, *The Downing St Years*, Harper Collins, 1993.

Cox, Michael, *US Foreign Policy after the Cold War*, Royal Institute of International Affairs, 1995.

Schlesinger, Stephen C., *Act of Creation: the founding of the United Nations*, Westview Press, 2003.

Sixsmith, Martin, *Russia*, BBC Books, 2011.

Middle East

Johnson, Paul, *A History of the Jews*, Harper Collins, 1988.

Laqueur, Walter & Barry Rubin, Editors, *The Israel-Arab Reader: a documentary history of the Middle East conflict*, Penguin, 1984 revised edition

Miller, Judith & Laurie Mylroie, *Saddam Hussein and the Crisis in the Gulf*, Times Books, 1990.

Counter-terrorism

Abuza, Dr Zachary, *Militant Islam in Southeast Asia: crucible of terror*, Lynne Reiner Publishers, 2003.

Gunaratna, Rohan, *Inside al-Qaeda*, Scribe, 2002.

East Asia

Beasley, W.G., *The Modern History of Japan*, Tuttle Publications, 1981.

Mackie, Jamie, *Konfrontasi: The Indonesia-Malaysia Dispute 1963–1966*, Oxford University Press, 1974.

Hinton, William, *Fanshen: Documentary of Revolution in a Chinese Village*, Pelican, 1972.

I have also valued insights shared by contemporaries of Alexander Downer in two news documentaries filmed by the Australian Broadcasting Corporation:

Australian Story: The More Things Change, producer Belinda Hawkins, two-part ABC documentary, 2007.

The Howard Years, executive producer Sue Spencer, four-part ABC documentary series, 2008.

For specific episodes of this book, I have sourced quotes from the following newspaper articles, speeches and podcasts. I have also referenced the following monographs, as well as a series of opinion pieces by Alexander Downer himself in *The Australian*, *The Australian Financial Review* and *The Adelaide Advertiser* and his regular interview slots with Chris Kenny on SKY News.

'Downer Makes A Difference', Christine Wallace, *Australian Financial Review*, December 9, 1993.

'The Day of the Dream Team', Mike Steketee, *The Australian*, May 23-24, 1994

'The Cruel Sea', Tony Parkinson & Gary Tippett, *The Age*, January 1, 2005.

'In Defence of More Freedom', Tony Parkinson, *Quarterly Essay*, Institute of Public Affairs, 2006

'Taking His Leave', Tony Wright, *Sydney Morning Herald*, July 2, 2008.

'Vale, Alexander the not so great', Peter Hartcher, *Sydney Morning Herald*, July 4, 2008.

'Liberty and Diplomacy', Tony Parkinson, *Institute of Public Affairs*, 2008.

'Indonesian leader was a man for all people', Bruce Grant, *The Age*, January 2, 2010.

'Malcolm Fraser: a Liberal at odds with his conservative peers', Geoffrey Barker, *Australian Financial Review*, March 20, 2015.

'A Sense of History', Georgina and Alexander Downer, *Afternoon Light podcast*, Robert Menzies Institute.

'The Art of Statesmanship', Alexander Downer, 10th Annual John Howard Lecture, Menzies Research Centre, December, 2022.

'Leading: General David Petraeus', Alistair Campbell & Rory Stewart, *The Rest is Politics*, November, 2024.

'Anthony Albanese's Palestine call comes at worst time for allies', Kelly Craft, *The Australian*, August 20, 2025.

Other historical background to the events covered in this book derives in part from my own experiences and personal observations, including several stints as a political correspondent based in Canberra, as a foreign correspondent in Europe, as a war correspondent in the Middle East and as International Editor of *The Age*.

Following a career in journalism, I was employed as a senior adviser to Alexander Downer as Foreign Affairs Minister, to Malcolm Turnbull as Prime Minister and, briefly, as an expert consultant to the United Nations — all of these opportunities offering access and insights into the workings of high-level diplomacy from an Australian perspective.

Any failings or shortcomings in the interpretation or analysis provided are mine exclusively.

INDEX

A
Abbott, Tony 112, 118, 207, 273, 276, 306-9, 324
Abe, Shinzo 259, 354
Abu Bakar Bashir 132, 135
Aceh 22, 45, 138-9
Adass Israel synagogue 296, 298
Additional Protocol, NPT Treaty 241, 243, 247, 239-40. 249-50
Adelaide Club 96-7, 175
Adelaide Hills 14, 55, 63, 72, 78, 128, 201-2, 234
Adelaide Zoo 204
Adenauer, Konrad 360
Adie, Kate 74
Ahmadinejad, Mahmoud 278-9, 295
AI (Artificial Intelligence) 244
Aiiku Hospital, Tokyo 180
Al-Aqsa air base, Iraq 143
Alatas, Ali 23-5, 32, 43, 192-3
Albanese, Anthony 229-30, 290, 295-9, 322, 340, 350
Albright, Madeleine 36, 41, 46, 146-7, 286-7
Aldgate Pump Hotel 201, 223
Al-Farouq, Afghanistan 256
agricultural subsidies, EU 188
al-Assad, Bashar 120, 311, 314, 316-7
Ali Ghufron (Mukhlas) 133
Ali Imron 133
Alkatiri, Mari 32, 195-7
Al-Muthanna Province, Iraq 174
Al-Qaeda 54, 56-7, 122, 133, 163, 256, 293, 316
Alternative fur Deutschland 275
Althorp, Johnnie (Earl Spencer) 78-9

American Jewish Committee, Washington 294
Amrozi bin Nurhasyim 133
Anastasiades, Nicos 272
Anderson, John 144
Annan, Kofi 38, 43, 115, 149, 164-5, 194, 269, 271, 311
anti-semitism 285, 299
ANZUS alliance 47-8, 52-5, 239, 318, 327, 341, 344
Arab Spring 169, 171, 316
Arab World 143, 169, 294
Arafat, Yasser 285-7, 292
Arawa, Bougainville 210, 212, 219
Arbury Park 78, 201
Arc of Instability 211
Armitage, Rich 178
arms control 234, 239, 241
ASEAN (Association of South-East Asian Nations) 38, 110, 147, 179
Asian Financial Crisis, 1997-98 22, 29-30, 50, 176
Asia Pacific Economic Co-Operation APEC) 140, 258, 260
— Auckland Summit 1999 43
— Sydney Summit 2007 204, 312
Aso, Taro 175, 179, 259
— Iraq deployments 175-6
— Trilateral Security Dialogue 7, 179, 260
Athenaeum Club 97
Atkinson, Rowan 74
atomic bombs
— Hiroshima, Nagasaki 235
Attorney-General's Department 112, 123, 154

AUKMIN 303
AUSMIN
— Sydney Declaration, 1996 48, 50, 106, 182, 302
Australia House, London 230, 300
Australian Army 61
Australian Broadcasting Corporation 17, 34, 85, 91, 205, 237, 254
— *Australian Story*, ABC documentary series 20
— French nuclear tests 243
— *Lateline* 55, 133, 244
— *The Howard Years*, ABC documentary series 19
Australian Chamber of Commerce and Industry 71
Australian Defence Forces (ADF) 45, 196, 199, 222
Australian Embassy, Jakarta 21-2, 58, 135, 158
Australian High Commission, London 79
Australian Federal Police 45, 128-9, 211, 226
Australian Labor Party (ALP) 6, 86, 291
Australian Secret Intelligence Service (ASIS) 129, 132, 165, 198, 338
Australian Security Intelligence Organisation (ASIO) 129, 132, 298
Australian Signals Directorate 198
Australian Wheat Board (AWB Ltd) 189-90
Australia's Place in the World
— foreign policy document, 1996 16
Avei, Moi 218-9
Axis of Resistance 281
Axis of Upheaval 8, 318
Azahari Husin 133

B

B2 stealth bombers 344, 349,
Bachmann, Sonja 272
Baghdad 40, 142-3, 148, 150, 153, 155-8, 162-3, 280, 285, 346
Bainamarama, Frank 220-1
Bali bombings
—accused perpetrators 56, 127, 132-5, 223, 225
Balkans 359
Ballistic missiles 146, 149, 243-4, 282, 329
Banda Aceh 138
Banham, Cynthia 21
Ban, Ki-moon 115, 266, 268, 270, 334
Barak, Ehud 286-7
Barker, Geoffrey 73
Barnard, Lance 74
Barroso, Jose Manuel 194
Barton, Edmund 78
Bashir, Marie 306
Bayu-Undan oil fields 192-4
Beazley, Kim 74, 148, 254
Belarus 241
Belgium 154, 352
Bennett, Christian 111
Bensouda, Fatou 119
Berger, Sandy 41
Bespoke Approach 324
Beveridge, Judith 74
Biden, Joe 52, 59-60, 171, 317, 342, 346, 354
Biketawa Declaration 225
Biological weapons — Anthrax, Botulinum toxin, ricin 142, 144, 146, 149-50, 165
Bird, Gillian 110

Bishop, Bronwyn 118
Bishop, Julie 305
Bjelke-Petersen, Joh 81
Blackhawk helicopter 164
Blair Government, UK 152, 164, 302
Blair, Tony 152, 276, 302-3, 354
Blix, Hans 150-2
BMD (German intelligence service) 165
Borchers, Susan 111
Bolkus, Nick 324
Bolt, Andrew 309
Bolton, John 164
Borneo
— 1963 confrontation 26
Bougainville 8, 36-7, 52, 209-10, 212-20, 222, 231, 266, 269
Bougainville Revolutionary Army 213-8
Boutros-Boutros Ghali 271
Bremer, L. Paul III (Jerry) 159, 162-3
Brereton, Laurie 107
Brexit 276, 300-3, 305
Brezhnev, Leonid 69, 238
British nuclear tests 234
Brown, Gordon 273
Brunei 13
Bryce, Quentin 306
budgets 255, 320, 345
Buka, Bougainville 212, 218-9
Burma 138
Burnham conference, New Zealand 215, 217
Bush, George H.W. 51, 184
Bush, George W.
—Afghanistan 177
—address to joint sitting of Parliament, 2003 184
—Bush Doctrine 242
—conversation with Nicky Downer 259
—first meeting in Texas 47
—Iraq War 142, 156, 177
—September 11 attacks 147
—APEC summit, 2007 204
Bushehr nuclear plant, Iran 280
Business Council of Australia 98
Butler, Richard 145-7, 164-5

C

Cable News Network (CNN) 6, 55
— East Timor and Clinton Administration 41
— Peter Fonda and Ted Turner 114
Cairns Group, free trade, Latin America 188
Calvert, Ashton 31, 33, 110, 225, 264
Cambodia 102, 216
Camdessus, Michel 29-30
Cameron, David 273, 275, 302-4, 335
Cameron, Eoin 97
Camillion, Oscar 271
Camp David 286
Canada 7, 189, 191, 243, 337-8, 340
Canadian Wheat Board 189
Card, Andy 142
Carr, Bob 295
Cartwright, Cheryl 84-6
Casey, Richard 69
Cavoli, Christopher 238
Chamberlain, Neville 8, 341
Changi prisoner-of-war camp 62, 180, 236
Chalabi, Ahmed 158
Chan, Julius 209, 213
Chaney, Fred 88

Chaudhry, Mahendra 220
chemical weapons
— VX, nerve agents, sarin, Novichok 142, 145, 150, 165, 281, 314, 316-7
Cheney, Dick 155
Chifley Labor Government 26, 290
Chile 151
China, People's Republic 19, 23, 50, 98, 102-6, 115, 118, 178-88, 199-200, 227-230, 232, 238-9, 243, 246, 250, 258, 264, 296, 301, 318, 320-6, 328-31, 335-44, 349, 354
— import assistance (DIFF) 105, 182
— nuclear tests 238-9, 245
— Taiwan elections 104, 182
— Tajikistan, Uzbekistan 186
Chipp, Don 202
Chirac, Jacques 153-4
Chon Jae hong 244
Christmas Island
— immigration 124
— people smuggling 125
— proximity to Indonesia 26
— *Tampa* episode 122-4
— Bali process 125
Christofias, Demetris 269, 271-2, 274
Churchill, Winston 47, 356, 360
Cipinang prison, Jakarta 32
Clark, Helen 225
climate change 2, 246-7, 253, 326, 342, 359
Clinton Administration 40, 54, 104, 146-7, 286
Clinton, Bill 4, 40-1, 43, 46, 107, 117, 147, 184, 194, 285-7
Clinton, Hillary 334-5, 338
Coalition of the Willing 54, 242

Coalition Provisional Authority, Iraq 159, 162
Cohen, Bill 43
Cold War 1, 13, 27, 41, 50, 53, 69, 102-3, 105-6, 121, 186, 234, 237-9, 241, 249, 267, 310, 315, 318, 320, 345, 360-1
Cole, Terence 190
colonialism 248
Commonwealth Heads of Government 247
Commonwealth Peace Monitoring Group 37, 217, 222
Communist Party, China 186, 322-3, 325-6, 329
Comprehensive Test Ban Treaty 235, 240
Congress of Vienna 102, 321
Conroy, Stephen 288
Cook, Robin 146
Coral Sea 52
Coral Sea Cable 232
Corbyn, Jeremy 322-3
Cosgrove, Peter 43, 226, 306
Costello, Michael 110
Costello, Peter 82, 86, 143, 253, 302, 353
— Asian Economic Crisis 30
— Boxing Day tsunami 138
— Indonesia relief packages 138-9, 141
— role as Treasurer 11, 255
— leadership 266
Court, Charles 95
Court, Richard 95
Crabb, Annabel 262
Craft, Kelly 351
Crean, Simon 74
Credlin, Peta 306

Crimea 311, 314, 317, 321, 343
Cuba 241
Cuban missile crisis 235, 238
Curtin, John 52
cyber warfare 244, 305, 323, 326, 330
Cyprus 115, 170, 266-74, 277, 289, 319, 336

D

Dalai Lama 182
Dastyari, Sam 324-5
Dauth, John 23, 110, 292, 311-2
Dawkins, John 85
Deakin, Alfred 50, 71
Dearlove, Richard 168
Deif, Mohammed 119
Defence Department, Australia 222
Department of Foreign Affairs and Trade (DFAT) 14, 17, 21, 23, 31-3, 67-9, 79, 103, 110-1, 127-9, 138, 154, 156, 158, 184, 191, 214, 216-8, 222-3, 244, 257, 264, 300
Department of Prime Minister & Cabinet 32, 223
De Soto, Alvarez 271
Dibb, Paul 211
Dibble, Elizabeth 336
Doha Round, trade negotiations 188
Donbas 317, 343
Douglas-Home, Alec 103
Downer, Alexander
— Adelaide Hills 14, 55, 63, 72, 78, 128, 201-2, 234,
— Afghanistan 1, 6, 58-9, 143, 169-71, 177, 222, 255, 268, 302-3, 316-7, 341, 352
— *Afternoon Light* podcast 63
— Annan, Kofi 38, 115, 164-5, 311
— ANZUS, US alliance 46-50, 103, 106, 114, 150, 154, 166, 169, 171-3, 178, 186, 318-20, 327-8, 337, 341
— Art of Statesmanship 354, 358, 362
— *Australia's Place in the World* 13, 16
— Australian Wheat Board 190
— Bali bombings 127, 132-5, 225
— ballistic missiles 146, 244, 329
— Ban Ki-moon 115, 266, 268, 270, 334
— Brussels posting 69-70, 276, 361
— Bush, George W. 47, 155, 177, 259-60
— car racing 10
— China, People's Republic (see China)
— East Timor 11, 25-6, 31-3, 36, 39-41, 45
— economic rationalist 66, 87
— *force de frappe* 236
— Geelong Grammar 73, 201
— High Commissioner, UK 221, 273, 300, 303-7, 314, 323, 335
— Howard, John 11, 20, 70, 74, 80, 82, 86, 95-6, 109-10, 164, 174, 199, 202, 206, 208, 216, 252, 256, 258, 260, 265, 274, 289, 355
— Hoover Institution 167, 237, 276
— immigration 14, 18, 65, 109, 125-6, 275
— India 16, 246-51
— Indian Ocean tsunami 22, 45, 137-8
— Indigenous Australians 89-91, 255
— Indonesia 21-3, 26, 29-46, 110, 125, 127-9, 131-41, 196, 199, 223, 254, 260

— International Criminal Court 115-7
— Iran 278-9, 281-3, 294, 342, 345-50
— Iraq 144-58, 162-72
— Israel 284-97
— Japan 174-80
— Keating, Paul 6, 11-13, 65, 72, 74, 82, 85, 87-96, 98, 102, 106, 181, 196, 236-7, 264
— King's College 230, 276
— Kirribilli House 75, 150, 260
— knighthoods 306, 309
— marriage 62
— Netanyahu, Bibi 116, 281-9, 296, 298, 345-7
— Newcastle University 67, 71, 73, 284
— nuclear weapons 105, 145, 234-50, 283, 310, 315, 345-8
— Opposition Leader 80, 86, 89-90, 92, 94-5, 100
— Overton Window 360-2
— parents 60-7, 78, 201, 234
— Pacific islands 225, 231-2
— Putin meeting 258, 310-2
— Radley College 73-4
— Reagan, Ronald 249, 319, 356, 361-2
— *Rocky Horror Show* 5, 107
— shadow Treasurer 84-7
— South China Sea 8-9, 326-7, 331-2, 342, 350
— speechwriter 87
— Taiwan 8, 104-5, 181-2, 321-2, 329, 331, 342, 350
— *Tampa* 122-6
— Timor Gap 45, 195
— Trilateral Security Dialogue 7, 179, 259
— Trump, Donald 318-21, 327, 335-46, 351-2
— UN special envoy, Cyprus 170, 266-71, 289, 337
— Xi Jinping 181, 319, 321, 323, 326

Downer, Alick
— Changi POW camp 62, 74, 177
— China 103
— christening of Charles Spencer 78-9
— immigration policy 78
— Menzies Government 178
— political beliefs 78, 301
— United Kingdom 103

Downer, Edward
— Prince Philip knighthood 307

Downer, Georgina 180
— *Afternoon Light* podcast 63
— interview with father 62-3
— Japan 180
— Menzies Institute, University of Melbourne 62-3

Downer, Henrietta (Hetty) 81
Downer, Henry 77
Downer, John 77-8
Downer, Mary 177
— dinner with John Howard 75
— marriage to Alick 62
— Mayo preselection 72
— World War 2 service 61-2

Downer, Nicky 55
— birth of Georgina 69
— birth of Henrietta 81-2
— George W. Bush 259-60
— marriage to Alexander 69

— Opposition leadership 87, 92, 256
— Things that Matter 92
Downer, Olivia 70
Dulmatin 133
Durrell, Lawrence 268

E
East Africa 138
East Asian hemisphere 13
East Asia Summit, Singapore 264
Eastern Europe 9, 122, 310, 317, 360-1
East Timor, Timor L'Este 2, 6, 11, 22-6, 28, 31-46, 53-4, 56, 112, 115, 132, 139-46, 163-4, 176, 192-200, 266, 328-9, 334, 353
— independence ballot 36, 38-9
— Indonesian invasion of Portuguese colony 28
— deaths of Australian journalists 28
— Kopassus and militia 37-8
— Liqica shootings 37
— Santa Cruz killings 28
— Timor Gap 192
economy, Australia
— deregulation, privatisation, investment 12, 185-8, 198, 332
— trade 187
education 19, 57, 73, 201, 255, 302
Egypt 170-1, 316
Ekeus, Rolf 145
Ellison, Chris 129
Enhanced Co-Operation Program, PNG 211
Enola Gay 235
'enmeshing in Asia' 13
Enuma, Walter 215
Erdogan, Recep Tayyip 273
Eroglu, Dervis 270

Europe 61, 69-70, 102, 171, 275-6, 295, 301, 313-4, 320-2, 342-3, 345, 362
European Union (EU) 69, 110, 188, 300-1, 320
Evans, Gareth
— comments on Downer 24
— East Asia 13
— French nuclear tests 236
Evans, Stan 205
Evatt, Herbert Vere (Doc) 290
export earnings, Australia 187

F
FA-18 Hornets 155
Falkland Islands 301
Farmer, Bill 14, 70, 184
— airport meeting, PNG 209
— Ambassador to Indonesia 21, 68, 139
— Bougainville crisis 210, 214
— Downer as DFAT trainee 110
— Garuda Airlines crash 21
— immigration 125
— unauthorised boat arrivals 125
Farmer, Elaine 70
Farrell, Terry 74
Faustmann, Hubert 271
Fightback! 82, 84, 87
Five Eyes intelligence community 338
five plus five 243
Flood, Philip 23, 110, 112
— DFAT Secretary 11, 17, 300
— inquiry into Iraq intelligence failures 166
— PNG and Sandline 214
Foley, Mike
— Labor Club 71

force de frappe 236
Fordow nuclear facility, Iran 281, 345
Ferguson, Alan 207
Fiji 217, 220-2, 228, 233
final status issues 286, 296
Finland 246
five plus five 243
Fox News 348
France 35, 151, 153-4, 167, 237, 245, 344
Fraser Government 70-1, 240, 290-1
Fraser, Malcolm 53, 71, 73, 87
Free market economics 106, 187, 380
Free Trade Agreement, China 185-6
Free Trade Agreement, UK 304
Free Trade Agreement, US 185, 188
Fretilin 32
Frydenberg, Josh 112
— Downer and Howard 112-3, 203
— International Criminal Court 118
— Iraq visit 156
— Israel and Jewish Australians 295
— Mayo campaigning
— staffer to Downer 53, 112, 118

G

Gaimu-sho (Japanese foreign ministry) 178
Galbraith, Peter 193-4
Gallant, Yoav 116
Garner, Jay 159
Garuda Airlines 21
Gates, Robert 257
Gaza 116, 119-20, 277, 281-2, 286, 288-9, 291, 294, 296-7, 339-41, 346, 349, 351
Geelong Grammar 73, 201
Geidt, Christopher 308

Georgia 311, 354
Germany 31, 167, 240, 268, 343-4
—Adenauer, Konrad 360
—*Alternative fur Deutschland* 275
—Merkel, Angela 274-6
—Nazi Germany 8, 360
—Nordstream 275
—Scholz, Olaf 320
Gillard, Julia 295, 324-5
global carbon emissions 246-7
Global Financial Crisis 342, 354
Goff, Phil 225
Goledzinowski, Andrew 111
Gorton, John 239-40
Gosse, William Christie 77
Graham, Lindsey 257
Grant, Bruce 45
Great Council of Chiefs, Fiji 220
Greater Sunrise oil and gas fields 195, 197-8
Greenland 339
Group of 20 (G20) 140, 250, 325, 327
Guadalcanal (Gwale people) 221
Guantanamo Bay 133, 255, 257, 335
Gulf states 278
Gulf Wars 114, 145, 156, 244
Gusmao, Jose Alexandre (Xanana) 32, 35-6, 194-9
Guterres, Antonio
— East Timor 334
— United Nations 334

H

Habibie, BJ
— Indonesia's democratic transition 30-1
— East Timor 33-5, 37-8, 43
Hague, William 273, 303

INDEX

Haines, Janine 202
Hamas 8, 116, 119, 144, 277, 282, 288-9, 293-4, 296-7, 346-7, 349, 351
Hambali (Riduan Isamuddin) 133-4
Hand, Louise 111
Hanson, Pauline 17-19, 202
Hard Rock Hotel, Bali 130
Harris, Rene 124
Hartcher, Peter 115
Harvey, Ron 87, 93
Hasluck, Paul 339
Hawke, Bob (Hawke Government) 11, 17, 54, 67, 72, 81-4, 95, 291
Hawkins, Amanda 111
Haynes, Brad 111
Hercules aircraft 128, 138, 157
Hewson, John 82, 84, 86-7, 90-2, 94
Hezbollah 8, 144, 289, 293-4, 346-7
Hicks, David (Mohammed Dawood) 255-8
Hill, Robert 203, 205-7
HMS *Glasgow* 43
Hockey, Joe 269
Holocaust 283-4, 296, 299, 346
Holt, Harold 51
Hong Kong 301
Honiara, Solomon Islands 221, 224-7, 231-2
Hoover Institution, Stanford University 167, 237, 276
Houston. Angus 306
Howard, Janette 261-2
Howard, John Winston 262-3, 265, 267, 274, 299, 302-3, 326, 355-8
— Afghanistan 353
— Appointment of Downer to Foreign Affairs 11, 264
— new DFAT Secretary, 1996 110
— Asian migration and Hansonism 17
— Bennelong 264
— East Timor 353
— economic policy 12
— first meeting in Brussels 70
— friendship with Alexander Downer 80, 267
— Indonesia 260
— Iran 294
— Iraq, decision to deploy 353
— Israel 288-9, 291-4, 296
— Kirribilli dinner with Mary Downer 73
— Liberal Party leadership contests 1993-1995 80-2, 84-8
— Liberal Party leadership 2004-2007
— 'Man of Steel' 260
— Papua New Guinea 211
— September 11 attacks 293
— *Tampa* 353
— 'When I'm 64' comments 252
— *Workchoices* 253
House of Representatives, Australia 81, 88, 105, 202, 269
Hu Jintao 183-4, 204, 258
Hua Junze 183
Huawei 232, 324-5
Hudson, Phillip 86
Human Rights Dialogue, China 183, 326
Hunt, Greg 7, 23, 28, 90, 94, 100, 105-12, 209, 261, 265
— Downer's handover of Liberal leadership 96-7, 99-100, 267
— East Timor 44

— 'enlightened realism' 7, 100
— Indonesia 44
— International Criminal Court 115-7
— Mind of the Minister 113
— Peter Fonda 114

I

immigration 17-18, 65, 77-8, 109, 122, 124-6, 202, 275
India 179, 246-7, 249-50
—Modi, Narensa 250-1
—Nehru, Jawaharlal 240
—Non-Aligned Movement 249
—nuclear tests 247, 250
—Operation Malabar 179
—Russian oil imports 251
—Shanghai Summit 251
—The Quad 7, 179, 331
Indian Ocean
— Indian Ocean tsunami 22, 45, 137-8, 179, 211, 249
Indian subcontinent 138, 248, 301
Indonesia
— Aceh 22, 45, 138-9
— Ali Alatas 23-5, 32, 192-3
— Asian Financial Crisis 22, 29-30
— Bali bombings 56, 127, 132-5, 223, 225
— Borneo 26
— East Timor 28-9, 31-44
— Gus Dur 30, 45
— Habibie, B.J. 31-5, 37-8, 43
— Jemaah Islamiyah 128, 132-3, 135-6
— Jokowi (Joko Widodo) 141
— Megawati Sukarnoputri 30, 129, 132, 194
— Suharto 22-4, 27-31, 43, 140

— Treaty of Lombok 139-40, 255
— West Papua 27-8, 36, 139
— Wirajuda, Hassan 140, 196
— Yudhoyono, Susilo Bambang 22, 131, 260
Indo-Pacific 7, 16, 48-50, 180, 244, 301, 305, 321, 327, 329-32
Intelligence Services Act 198
INTERFET
— UN peacekeeping force in East Timor 42-3, 192-3
International Atomic Energy Agency (IAEA) 149, 241-2, 249-50, 347-8
International Court of Justice 193-4
International Criminal Court 117
— Israel 116
— list of non-signatories 118
— Statute of Rome 115
— rule of complementarity 119
International Monetary Fund 29
International Stabilisation Force (East Timor) 196
Intifada 286-7, 292
Iran, Islamic Republic 31, 165, 278-83, 288-9, 294-6, 347-9
— Green Wave 279, 316
— Islamic Revolutionary Guard Corps 279, 298, 347
— nuclear ambitions 280, 282, 310, 346, 348-9
— sponsorship of terrorism 8, 144
— 2025 bombings 345-6
Iraq
—2003 ultimatum 145, 153
—Abu Ghirab 163
—Baghdad bombing, 1998 40
—Coalition Provisional Authority 159, 162
—Gulf War, Iran 280-1

—Gulf War, 1991 145, 156, 244
—Osirak nuclear plant 280
—Route Irish 157
—Saddam Hussein (see Saddam Hussein under 'S')
—Shock and Awe 142
—Water Palace 158
—weapons of mass destruction 16, 142, 145-6. 148, 164, 167-8, 234-5
—Western Desert 142
Iraq Governing Council 158
Irvine, David 112, 129
ISIS (Islamic State) 145, 277
Islam 285
Islamic Jihad 144, 277, 293
Israel 8, 102, 115-6, 118-21, 142-4, 153, 278, 280-99, 345-51
— second intifada 286-7, 292
— Yom Kippur War 284, 291
Italy 245
I-Taukei 220

J

Jackman, Hugh 207
Jakarta 21-4, 26-9, 32-7, 39-40, 42-3, 45, 56, 125, 128, 131, 134-7, 139-41
Jakarta Centre for Law Enforcement Co-operation 137
Japan 53, 61, 78, 174-80
—Abe, Shinzo 179, 258-9, 354
—Aso, Taro 175, 179, 259
—Changi 62, 180, 236
—Darwin bombing 61
—East Timor 44
—*Gaimu-sho* 178
—Imperial Japanese Army 52, 62, 177, 236
—Iraq, engineers 174, 176-7

—Trade Agreement 178
—Trilateral Security Dialogue 7, 179, 259
Jervis Bay 239-40
Jemaah Islamiyah 128, 132-3, 135-6
Jerusalem 285-6, 288, 292-3, 296, 349
Jews —people, religion, Middle East 284-5, 291, 298
Jiang Zemin 183
Johnson, Lyndon Baines 51
Joint Comprehensive Plan of Action 281, 346
Joint facilities
— Pine Gap, Nurrungur, Exmouth 53
Jokowi (Joko Widodo) 141
Jordan 142, 157, 190, 340

K

Kabui, Joseph 218-20
Kabul, Afghanistan 58-9, 111
Kangaroo Island 202
Karbala, Iraq 163
Karzai, Hamid 58
Kashmir 16, 41
Keating Government 24, 29, 72-4, 90-2, 106, 109, 140, 181, 236-7
— 1993 election victory 82, 84-9
— 1996 election defeat 11, 95-6, 98, 100-1
— *Fightback* 82, 84, 87
— gay rights, Tasmania 91
— *Native Title Act* 89-90
— the republic 93-4
Keating, Paul 6, 11-13, 18, 31, 43, 65, 72, 82, 86, 93, 101
Keating! The Musical 109
Keelty, Mick 129
Kelly, Fran 85

Kelly, Paul
Kemakeza, Allen 222-4, 227
Kemish, Ian 127
Kennedy, John F. 27, 51
Kennett, Jeff 70, 95
Kenny, Chris 112
— Bali Bombings 127, 130
— Downer chief of staff 127, 157
— tsunami relief
— *Sky News* interviews 111, 116, 132, 337
Khalid Sheikh Mohammed 133
Khan, AQ 242
Khameini, Ayatollah Ali 77, 282, 347-8
Khan, Karim Ahmad 119
Khatami, Mohammad 278-9
Khomeini, Ayatollah Ruhollah 282
Khrushchev, Nikita 238, 350
Kim Jong-Il 243
King George Tupou V, Tonga 233
King's College, London 230, 276
Kiribati 225, 233, 305
Kirribilli House 73, 150, 260
Kissinger, Henry 102-3, 162, 315
Kobbe's *History of Opera* 69
Koizumi, Junichiro 174-6
Kono, Yohei 178
Korean Peninsula 16, 244
Kosovo 41
Kroger, Michael 95
Kuwait 148, 153, 291
Kwasniewski, Aleksander 154
Kyoto Protocol 120, 253
KYP, Cyprus intelligence agency 272

L

Lavrov, Sergei 31-2, 350
Lawrence, Carmen 86
Lebanon 281, 289, 294, 296-7, 346-7
Lee Hsien-Loong 264
Lee Teng-hui 104
L'Estrange, Michael 7, 93, 110
Ley, Sussan 62
Liberal Party of Australia 5, 11, 62, 71, 81, 85-7, 89, 91-101, 109, 112, 120, 125, 205, 207-8, 235, 253, 261-3, 265-6, 269, 306, 349
Libya 169
Lindsey, Kiera 62
Litvinenko, Alexander 314
Lodge, The 63, 179, 223
Logan, Kate 111
London 61-2, 74, 78-9, 174, 177, 221, 230, 269, 276, 285, 300-1, 307, 313-4, 323, 335-8
Loughnane, Brian 93, 96
Lucas Heights nuclear research 241, 245

M

McBride, Kay 111
MacArthur, Douglas 185, 238
McCain, John 257
McCarthy, John 23, 110
McDevitt, Ben 226
MacDonald, Angela 111
McGarry, John 273
McKinnon, Don 215
McLachlan, Ian 81, 253
McLeay, John 71
McLeod, David 257
McMahon, William 240
McNarn, Maurie 158
Mahathir, Mohamed 18
Make America Great Again (MAGA)

338
Malaita 221-2, 226
Malaitan Eagle Force 222, 226
Malaysia 14, 18, 26, 53, 57, 68, 133-4, 138, 196, 243, 292
Mandela, Nelson 36
Manton, Lucienne 111
Mao Zedung 103, 318
Mara, Kamesese 220
Maralinga 234
Maria Aznar, José 154
Marriott Hotel, Jakarta 134
Mayer, Pam 111
Mayo, federal electorate 72, 81, 202-3, 267
Melanesia 27, 29, 225, 229, 268
Melbourne Olympics 234
Mellish, Morgan 21
Menzies, Robert 41, 62-3, 73, 178
— ANZUS 53
— leadership 65, 355-6
— Dame Patti 63
Menzies Institute, University of Melbourne 62-3
Menzies Research Centre 354
Merkel, Angela 274-6, 320
Mexico 339
MI6 (British intelligence service)
Michael, Michalis S. 269
Middle East 1-2, 9, 16, 44, 57, 116, 121, 151-2, 154, 170-2, 231, 276, 278-86, 290, 293-6, 299, 314, 316, 340, 342-3, 345-6, 348, 351
Milliband, David 273
Milne, Glenn 253
Minchin, Kerry 82
Minchin, Nick 82, 93-4, 96, 203,

206-7
Mitterrand, Francois 153
Modi, Narendra 250-1
Monash, John 51, 112
'money politics'
Morauta, Mekere 217-9
Mori, Michael 257
Morris, Grahame 98
Morrison, Scott 112, 207, 228-30, 264, 276
Morsi, Mohamed 170-1
Moscow 69, 310-4
Mosul, Iraq 162
Moussavi, Mir Hussein 279
Moylan, Judi 86
Mubarak, Hosni 170, 316
Mueller, Robert 337-8
Mules, Neil 157
Mulvaney, Mick 343
Munich Security Conference, 2007 257, 310
Murray River 78, 89, 254
Muslim Brotherhood 170-1

N

National Broadband Network (NBN) 324-5
National Farmers' Federation 81, 105
National Party of Australia 104, 118, 144, 187
National Security Committee 129, 143, 147, 150, 203
NATO (North Atlantic Treaty Organisation) 18, 41, 57, 72, 153, 167, 178-9, 206-7, 227, 237, 241, 267, 272, 310, 313-4, 318, 320, 336, 340, 345
Nauru 124
Navalny, Alexei 314
Nehru, Jawaharlal 240

Nelson, Brendan 265, 269, 288, 302
New Caledonia, Matignon Accords 33, 35
Newton-John, Olivia 207
New York 27, 44, 54-5, 102, 145-6, 164, 189, 206-7, 267, 269, 311, 337
New Zealand 19, 37, 53, 110, 196, 211, 213, 215, 217, 221-3, 225, 233, 243, 301, 304, 328
Netanyahu, Binyamin (Bibi) 116, 119-20, 285-9, 296, 298, 345-7
Newspapers —
Adelaide Advertiser 107
Australian Financial Review 21, 59, 85, 163, 230
Canberra Times 113
Cyprus Mail 271
Daily Telegraph 107
Herald Sun 86, 298
Neos Kosmos 269
New York Times 337
Sunday Telegraph 253
Sydney Morning Herald 21, 74, 115
The Age 45, 134, 167, 185, 201
The Australian 21, 85, 91, 163, 222, 321, 327, 335, 343, 347, 349, 351, 361
The Guardian 167
Nias 139
Nicobar Islands 138
Nixon, Richard 69, 102
Non-Aligned Movement 249-50, 290
Nordstream 275
North Africa 170
Northern Ireland 209, 273
North Korea 2, 16, 53, 118, 240, 242-5, 248, 315, 318
nuclear deterrence 235, 237

Nuclear Non-Proliferation Treaty 241, 280, 348
nuclear-powered submarines 245, 305, 329, 352
nuclear safeguards 241, 249, 332
nuclear tests 234, 243, 248
nuclear testing, South Pacific 236-7, 240, 242, 248
nuclear weapons 105, 145, 234-5, 237-44, 247-8, 250, 278-80, 283, 310, 315, 345-8
Nuku'alofa, Tonga 232-3

O

Oakes, Laurie 84-5, 128
Obama Administration 279, 282, 317, 326
Obama, Barack 316-7, 326, 342
O'Callaghan, Mary-Louise 214
October 7 massacre 116, 119, 289, 294, 296, 299, 346, 351
Office of National Assessments 110, 134, 166
Ok Tedi mine 209
Olsen, John 86, 207
O'Neill, Liz 21-2
Operation Helpem Fren 225
Operation Malabar 179
Oruzgan Province, Afghanistan 58
Osama bin Laden 56, 133, 255
Osirak nuclear plant, Iraq 280
Oslo peace process 121
Overton, Joseph P. 360
Overton Window 360-2

P

Pandemic (COVID) 275, 326-7, 359
Pacific Islands, Oceania 1-2, 23, 52, 211, 225
Pacific Islands Forum 214

Pacific Labour Mobility Scheme 232
Pacific Solution 124
Pacific War 60
Paddy's Bar, Bali 127
Pahlavi, Shah Mohammed Rezi 280
Pakistan 41, 60, 240-2, 248, 280
Palestinian National Authority 119
Palestinian people 289, 340
Palestine Liberation Organisation 285
Panama Canal 339
pandas 204
Panguna copper mine 210, 212-3, 215
Papadopoulos, George 336-8
Papua New Guinea 26, 209, 211
— Bougainville crisis 216
— Port Moresby 68
— Sandline controversy 214-5
Park, Andrew 111
Parker, Andrew 307
Pastika, I Made 130
Paterson, Bill 158
Pax Americana 8
Payne, Aubrey 62
Payne, Marise 305
Peacock, Andrew 42, 47, 72-3, 80, 82, 90, 95, 97, 290
People's Daily, China 182
People's Liberation Army 104
Pentagon 2, 38, 54, 152
Pescott, Roger 70
Petraeus, David 162
Philippines 133, 135, 318, 327, 344, 351
Phillipousos, Mark 112
Plimsoll, James 69-70

Poland 152, 154, 344
Policy Exchange, UK 276
Pope John Paul II 360
Port Arthur massacre 104
Portugal 37, 196, 334
Powell, Colin 149, 151-2, 162
Prescott, John 303
Putin, Vladimir 2, 312-3, 315-6, 342
—Alaska meeting 350
—APEC Sydney meeting 258
—Axis of Upheaval 8, 318
—Georgia 317, 354
—Munich Security Conference 310
—Novichok 314
—nuclear weapons 238
—Shanghai Summit 251
—South Abkhazia 311
—Stalin 310, 319
—Syria 311, 314, 354
—Ukraine 238, 313-4, 321, 340, 354
Pyne, Christopher 85, 207

Q

Qarase, Laisenia 220
Quad, The 7, 179-80, 229, 321, 331
Queen Adelaide Club 175
Queen Elizabeth II 230
— christening of Charles Spencer 79
— death of Diana 79
— knighting of Prince Philip 308
Queensland 51, 81, 221, 264

R

Rabuka, Sitiveni 221
Ragland, Thorbjorn 123
Ramos-Horta, José 32, 45, 194-6, 199
Ranger uranium mine 241
Ray, Robert 291

Rayner, Barbara 111
Reagan, Ronald 356, 361-2
— Cold War 249
— MX missiles 54
— Peace Through Strength 319
Regional Assistance Mission to Solomon Islands (RAMSI) 225-8
Reith, Peter 82, 98, 123, 252
Rice, Condoleezza 155, 171, 179, 243, 259, 276
Richardson, Dennis 110, 129, 257
Riding, Doug 38
Rini, Snyder 227
Rinnan, Arne 122
Ritchie, David 113
Ritchie, David 113
Republican Guard, Iraq 147
Robb, Andrew 87, 96
Rocky Horror Show
—fishnet stocking and stiletto heel 5, 107
Roh Moo-hyun 151
Roosevelt, Franklin D. 52
Roosevelt, Teddy 4, 50
Roth, Malki 293
Roth, Stanley 38
Route Irish, Baghdad 157
Royal Australian Air Force (RAAF) 27, 51, 128, 157, 174, 232
Royal Australian Navy (RAN) 124, 139, 222
Rudd, Kevin 133, 136, 254, 268, 295, 334
Rumsfeld, Donald 148, 159, 162, 167-8
Russia 1-2, 8, 16, 118, 121, 151, 186, 238, 241, 243, 251, 258, 267-8, 272, 274-5, 296, 310-21, 332-3, 335-7, 340, 343-4, 350

Rwanda 116, 358

S

Sa'ar, Gideon 296
Saddam Hussein 2, 6, 40, 142-9, 151, 154, 158, 162, 164, 166-7, 169, 171, 189, 242, 244, 280, 291, 298
'Saigon-style evacuation' 317
Samoas, The 233
Samudra, Imam 132
Sandline controversy 214-5
Sanglah Hospital 130
Sari Club, Bali 127
Sarkozy, Nicholas 275
SAS (Special Air Service Regiment) 57-8, 244
Saudi Arabia 245, 340
Scandinavia 268
Schacht, Chris 72
Schieffer, Tom 55-6, 175
Scholz, Olaf 320
Schumann, John 202
Scott, Mark 21
Scud missiles 142, 163, 244, 291
Seoul, South Korea 151, 266
Sevele, Fred 233
Shanghai Summit 2025 251
Sharif, Nawaz 41
Sharon, Ariel 288
Shia (Islam) 154, 159, 164, 173
Shock and Awe 142
Shorten, Bill 326
Shovelan, John 237
Shtayyeh, Mohammed 288-9
Sidoti, Chris 117
Singapore 53, 61-2, 78, 133-4, 171, 264, 292, 301
Singirok, Jerry 213-5

INDEX

Skate, Bill 215
Skripol, Sergei 314
Sky News 111, 116, 297
Slater, Mick 196
Smith, Ian 324
Smith, Mike 111
Smith, Ric 111, 128
Smith, Stephen 266
Sogavare, Manasseh 222, 227-8, 231
solar panels, China 322
Soleimeini, Qassem 346
Solomon Islands 6, 51-2, 211-3, 221-3, 225, 227-9, 231, 329
Somare, Michael 217
Somers, Larry 29-30
Southcott, Andrew 205
South Africa 36, 214, 241, 287, 359
South Australia 61-2, 67, 71-2, 76-8, 81, 85, 90, 93, 177, 202-3, 205, 207, 229, 234-5, 254
South China Sea 8-9, 179-80, 296, 325-7, 331-2, 342-3, 350-1
South Korea 7, 16, 30, 151, 243-4, 266, 318, 327, 331, 334, 344, 351
"South" hotel 62
South Pacific Nuclear Free Zone Treaty 247
Soviet Union 16, 103, 239, 249, 315, 318, 350, 356, 360-2
Spencer, Charles 79
Spencer, David 244
Spencer, Diana 79
Spicer, Tim 214
Staley, Tony 97
Stalin, Joseph 310, 319, 350
Steele, Brice 21
Steketee, Mike 85
Stockings, Craig 35

Storey, Sarah 218
Straw, Jack 162, 174, 302
Suckling, Patrick 111, 250
Sudrajat, Allison 21-2
Suharto 22-4, 28-31, 43, 140
— New Order regime 30
— West Papua 27
Sujarwo, Anton 135
Sukarnoputri, Megawati 30, 129, 132, 194
Sunni (Islam) 154, 159, 163-4, 173, 316
superannuation 255
Surakiart Sathirathai 266
Swan, Wayne 288
Syria 118, 120, 168-9, 275, 281, 284, 311, 314, 316-7, 334, 346, 354

T

Taiwan 8-9, 16, 104-5, 122, 181-2, 227-9, 321-2, 327, 329, 331, 342, 350-1
Taliban 56, 58-60, 143, 171, 342
Tampa episode 122-5, 219, 353
Tanis, James 218-9, 248
Taylor, Meg 214
tax cuts 255
Tentara Nasional Indonesia 37
Thailand 30, 53, 133-4, 138, 318
Thatcher, Margaret 356, 361
Thawley, Michael 110
The Howard Years
— ABC documentary series 19-20, 252
The Rest is Politics
— Alistair Campbell, Rory Stewart 162
The Wiggles 207
Thompson, Erika 336

Tibet 184
Timor Gap Treaty 45, 192, 195
Tokyo 31, 178, 180-1, 229, 237, 321
Tomahawk missiles 148, 349
Tonga 232-3, 305
trade 6, 14, 16-17, 20, 23, 57, 105, 114, 153, 178, 183, 185-9, 191, 251, 303-5, 327, 330-2, 339-41, 360
Treaty of Lombok 140, 255
Treaty of Perth 193
Trilateral Security Dialogue 7, 179, 259
Trinity College, Dublin 71
Truman, Harry S. 53, 238
Trump, Donald 7, 173, 179, 188, 251, 318, 320-1, 327, 335-52, 354
Tudge, Alan 112
Tunisia 169
Turkey 94, 118, 250, 267-8, 271, 273
Turkish Republic of Northern Cyprus 268
Turnbull, Malcolm 112, 183, 207, 250, 265, 276, 303-4, 325-6, 338
Tuvalu 233
Tweddell, Bill 111
two-state solution 272, 286-8, 292, 349

U

Uighurs, China 184
Ukraine 8, 154, 238, 241, 273, 296, 311, 313-4, 316, 319-21, 329, 339-44, 350, 354
Ulufa'alu, Bart 221-2
United Kingdom (Britain) 52, 63, 73, 126, 214
— AUKMIN 303
— AUKUS 7, 51, 244-5, 303, 305, 321, 328-9, 331, 341, 352
— Afghanistan 177, 302-3
— agriculture exports
— Alick Downer 61-2, 103, 301
— Cameron, David 273, 275, 302-4, 336
— Churchill, Winston 47, 356, 360
— Blair, Tony 164
— Brexit 275, 300-5
— east of Suez 301
— Empire 266, 301
— Foreign Office 79, 305
— Halifax, Lord 360
— Indonesia (Netherlands) 27
— Iraq 177, 302-3
— Johnson, Boris 304-5
— Kensington Wine Rooms 336
— knighthoods 306, 309
— May, Theresa 304
— monarchy 94, 305-6
— Nicky Downer, Chesterfield 69, 81-2
— Prince Charles 309
— Prince Philip 306-9
— Queen Elizabeth II 79, 230, 308
— shared language, culture 300
— Straw, Jack 162, 174, 302
— 10 Downing St 304
— University of Newcastle 67, 73, 284
United Nations 269, 290, 293
— Cyprus 115, 170, 266, 268, 270-3, 276, 289, 337
— Durban conference against racism 292
— East Timor 25, 36
— General Assembly
  — Resolution 3379 291
— Iraq (see Iraq under 'I')

— nuclear non-proliferation 235
— oil-for-food 189
— Permanent Five (P5) 266, 333
— Security Council 40, 42, 53, 146-55, 158-9, 169, 171, 242-3, 266, 270, 281, 333
— Security Council Resolutions
 —678 154
 —1441 148
 —1540 242
— West Papua 27
United States of America
— Afghanistan 56-7, 59, 121-2, 162, 171, 177, 255, 257, 316-7, 353-4
—ANZUS Alliance 47-8, 52-5, 239, 318, 328, 344
—AUKUS 7, 51, 244-5, 303, 305, 321, 328-9, 331, 342, 352
—Biden Administration 59-60, 171, 342, 346
—Bush Administration 146, 148-9, 152-3, 164, 185, 242, 353
—Bush Doctrine 242
—Central Intelligence Agency (CIA) 50, 133
—China 102, 104, 106, 182, 186, 238, 243, 318, 324, 326, 329-30, 336, 344
—Clinton Administration 40, 54, 104, 146-7, 286
—East Timor 2, 6, 38, 41-2, 46, 53-4, 56, 102, 193, 224, 353
—Federal Bureau of investigations (FBI) 335, 337-8
—Iran 2, 242, 279-82, 316, 344-50
—Iraq 40, 142-72, 176-7, 242, 280-1, 316, 349, 354
—Japan 7, 49, 52-3, 61, 177, 182, 329, 344, 351
—Kennedy Administration 27

—North Korea 2, 53, 242-3
—Nuclear deterrence 237
—Obama Administration 279, 282, 317, 326
—Pacific War, defence of Australia 60
—Reagan, Ronald 54, 249, 319, 356, 361-2
—Russia 151, 186, 238, 251, 310, 316-7, 335, 343-4, 350
—September 11 1, 54-5, 122, 128, 242, 293
—South China Sea 179, 326, 342-3
—Soviet Union 103, 235, 249, 318, 356, 361-2
—Taiwan 16, 351
— Trump Administration 251, 335-6, 343, 347-8, 351
United States Studies Centre, Sydney University 48
University of Newcastle, England 67, 73, 284
University of South Australia *61-2*
UNMOVIC 149, 151
UNSCOM 145-6
uranium 165, 240-1, 243, 245, 247, 250, 280-2, 332, 347-9
Uren, Tom 74
USS *Belleau Wood* 42
Utopia visit 89

V

Vaile, Mark 189, 259, 302
Vanstone, Amanda 97, 203
Vanuatu 217, 222, 233, 305
Vegting, Sandra 111
Victoria Cross 57
Vieira de Mello, Sergio 44, 115, 163
Vietnam 40-1, 43, 47, 53, 102, 202

Volcker, Kurt 167

W

Wahid, Abdurrahman (Gus Dur) 30
Wakanai, Bougainville 212
Walesa, Lech 360
Wallace, Christine 85
War on Terror 47, 56-7, 156, 185
Warner, Nick 111, 216
— Ambassador to Iran 31
— Bougainville 216-9
— counter-terrorism 225
— East Timor 31-3, 37, 39
— Pacific diplomacy 225-8, 230-2
— Regional Assistance Mission to the Solomon Islands 228
Washington Consensus 12
Water Palace, Baghdad 158
Waugh, Evelyn 6, 74
weapons of mass destruction (WMD) 16, 142, 145-6, 148-9, 151, 164-5, 167-9, 234-5, 239, 242, 280
Wei, Jiabao
Wensley, Penny 110
West Bank 119, 286, 291-2, 297
Western Alliance 67, 103, 153-4, 318-20, 326, 338, 341-2, 360
Western Desert, Iraq 142
West Papua, West Irian 27-8, 139
— *Act of Free Choice* 27, 36
— Australian deployment 222
— New York Agreement 27
— *Organisasi Papua Merdeka* 27
White Australia Policy 17, 78
White House, Washington D.C. 8, 46, 148, 155, 167, 179, 185, 279, 339, 347
White, Hugh 37

Whitlam, Gough 74
— East Timor 28
— Israel and PLO 290-1
— NPT 240
Willard Hotel, Washington 148
Williams, Daryl 112
Willox, Innes 111
Windsor Castle 308
Windsor, David 111
Wirajuda, Hassan 140, 196
Wiranto, General 38
Wolfowitz, Paul 167, 296
Wong, Penny 229-31, 296
Woodside Energy 197-9
Woolcott, Dick 33
Woolcott, Peter 111
World Economic Forum, Davos 174
World Trade Centre 54-5
Wright, Tony 74
Wye River Summit 285

X

Xi, Jinping 181, 251, 319, 321, 323, 325-6, 354

Y

Yalta, Agreement 310
Yemen 281, 296, 346
Yogyakarta 21
Yudhoyono, Susilo Bambang 21, 131, 136-7, 139-41, 260
Yuendemu visit 89-90
Yugoslavia 116-7

Z

Zarif, Mohammed Javid 348
Zelensky, Volodymyr 314, 321, 350

www.ingramcontent.com/pod-product-compliance
Lightning Source LLC
Chambersburg PA
CBHW052055300426
44117CB00013B/2134